To My

my

Jeanne

THE
MILLION-DOLLAR MAN
WHO HELPED KILL A PRESIDENT

George Washington Gayle
and the Assassination of Abraham Lincoln

THE
MILLION-DOLLAR MAN
WHO HELPED KILL A PRESIDENT

George Washington Gayle
and the Assassination of Abraham Lincoln

CHRIS MCILWAIN

SB

Savas Beatie
California

First Edition, first printing
ISBN-13: 978-1-61121-394-2

Library of Congress Cataloging-in-Publication Data

Names: McIlwain, Christopher Lyle, author.
Title: The Million-Dollar Man Who Helped Kill a President: George Washington Gayle and the Assassination of Abraham Lincoln / by Christopher Lyle McIlwain, Sr.
Other titles: George Washington Gayle and the assassination of Abraham Lincoln
Description: First edition. | El Dorado Hills, California: Savas Beatie, [2018]
Identifiers: LCCN 2018019665| ISBN 9781611213942 (hardcover) | ISBN 9781611213959 (ebk)
Subjects: LCSH: Gayle, George Washington, 1807-1875. | Lincoln, Abraham, 1809-1865—Assassination. | Lincoln Assassination Conspiracy Trial, Washington, D.C., 1865. | Advertising, Newspaper--United States—History—19th century—Miscellanea. | Lawyers—Alabama—Biography. | Legislators—Alabama—Biography. | Alabama—Politics and Government—19th century. | Southern States—Politics and Government—19th century. | Dallas County (Ala.)—Biography.
Classification: LCC E457.5 .M45 2018 | DDC 973.7092 [B] --dc23
LC record available at https://lccn.loc.gov/2018019665

SB

Published by
Savas Beatie LLC
989 Governor Drive, Suite 102
El Dorado Hills, CA 95762

Phone: 916-941-6896
(web) www.savasbeatie.com
(E-mail) sales@savasbeatie.com

Savas Beatie titles are available at special discounts for bulk purchases in the United States by corporations, institutions, and other organizations. For more details, please contact Savas Beatie, P.O. Box 4527, El Dorado Hills, CA 95762, or you may e-mail us at sales@savasbeatie.com, or visit our website at www.savasbeatie.com for additional information.

Proudly published, printed, and warehoused in the United States of America.

MIX
Paper from
responsible sources
FSC
www.fsc.org   FSC® C011935

But, thanks to a good Providence, Lincoln is not the incarnation of fate,
as some Tories and cowards have schooled their minds to believe.
He is but a man working with human instrumentalities,
and himself but a leaf floating on the endless stream of human destiny.

Selma (Alabama) *Reporter*
September 22, 1863

Table of Contents

Introduction

THE assassination of Abraham Lincoln by John Wilkes Booth on April 14, 1865, was a traumatic and pivotal event for the entire nation, both North and South. Public reaction in Washington, D.C. spread like a wild fire.

When Booth fled from the epicenter of that figurative fire at Ford's Theater, members of the audience reportedly "rose to their feet, rushing toward the stage, many exclaiming 'Hang him! Hang him!'"[1] Within hours a Washington correspondent wrote that the "entire city to-night presents a scene of wild excitement, accompanied by violent expressions of indignation, and the profoundest sorrow—many shed tears."[2] The next day, an Alabama soldier who was a prisoner-of-war near Washington noted that "[w]e were all right uneasy too, lest the Yankees might retaliate on us."[3] According to a northern correspondent in recently occupied Mobile, Alabama, "the news of the assassination of the great and good Lincoln came to this city like a clap of thunder. The feeling spread through the city in a moment that the soldiers and the negroes would instantly rise and murder the citizens."[4] There was a telegraphic report that an "Illinois Copperhead, for rejoicing at the death of the President, was shot immediately. He died instantly—fifteen balls entering his body. Everything is in deep mourning and sorrow."[5]

Not everyone was mourning Lincoln's death.[6] On the contrary, in Black Belt Dallas County, Alabama, the editor of a Selma newspaper was sure it was God's will that Lincoln answered for his war crimes.[7] In nearby Marengo County one reported the assassination under the headline "Glorious News."[8]

Others were more prudent in their comments. Recognizing the possibility that in its blind rage the North would not take the time to discern whether particular Southerners had been loyal or disloyal, one Alabama editor quickly offered an exculpatory theory of John Wilkes Booth's motivation. "[W]e believe [Lincoln's murder] to have been the deed of one who, however talented in his profession, has yet those gloomy and fantastic conceptions of his art which have culminated in a deed unequaled in tragic darkness since the days of romance."[9] In other words, Booth was simply a self-motivated, delusional actor. Some wanted to believe this. William Cooper, a North Alabama lawyer, wrote that he thought Booth "was evidently crazy and at least a monomaniac on the subject of killing A. Lincoln."[10] Prominent Southerners were bent on undermining the prevailing belief in the North that Booth and his team of assassins had acted with assistance from other Southerners in bringing about Lincoln's death.[11]

Like most presidential assassinations, the murder of Abraham Lincoln has spawned a multitude of conspiracy theorists who have offered many different ideas about who might have been behind Booth and his team of assassins. From the beginning, the primary theory relentlessly pursued by Secretary of War Edwin McMasters Stanton and federal prosecutors was that Confederate president Jefferson Davis had directed the taking of Lincoln's life, and had authorized a former Confederate senator from Alabama, Clement Claiborne Clay (known as C.C. Clay, Jr.), who was then serving as a Confederate agent in Canada, to recruit and finance a team to carry out the assassination.[12]

Some have theorized that Davis had, at least, expressly or implicitly, authorized Confederate efforts to have Lincoln kidnapped in 1863 or 1864 and brought south to use as bargaining leverage.[13] These theorists believe Davis may have been seeking to address a growing crisis of confidence in his leadership ability by bowing to intense public pressure from fanatical Confederates to take some such decisive, unconventional, action; that a failure to have done so might have led private parties to finance and attempt to bring about the scheme on their own;[14] and that Davis likely recognized that an unauthorized kidnap attempt by amateurs could be botched and that Lincoln might be killed.[15] Lincoln's death would galvanize the North in favor of the war effort and undermine months of Confederate efforts to encourage a peace movement there in preparation for the 1864 presidential election and a revolt after that election if Lincoln won. For this reason, Davis supposedly thought it wise to have close control over the kidnapping scheme.

Available evidence indicates that John Wilkes Booth had contact with Confederate agents in Canada in 1864, possibly regarding this kidnapping scheme. Some even surmise that Lincoln's kidnapping, not his assassination, was Booth's goal at that point.[16] But the sources of this information were all Booth's co-conspirators or their acquaintances who had every reason to mislead federal investigators and the public on this issue and claim that Booth never mentioned doing harm to Lincoln.

Recent scholarship has uncovered no evidence of official sanction of any of Booth's actions by the Confederate government or Jefferson Davis. And assuming someone did sanction Booth's kidnapping plot, why did Booth change the operation to the assassination of not only Lincoln but also Vice President Andrew Johnson and Secretary of State William Seward? Edwin Stanton and the federal prosecutors were certain Davis was behind this too, but they were never able to locate any convincing evidence supporting such a theory. This has not prevented Lincoln assassination buffs from digging in that direction, but so far, the evidence amassed is not convincing.

Another persistent theory supported by many prominent academic historians is that Booth suddenly and unilaterally changed the plan to murder because he became enraged when Lincoln advocated black suffrage in a speech on April 11, 1865, just three days before the assassination.[17] This is actually a cautionary tale about how the sausage of history is sometimes made. The seed for the theory was not one of Booth's writings or even of anyone who knew him. Instead, it was the pen of a newspaperman George Alfred Townsend, who published what he called a "romance upon the conspiracy of Booth"—a work of fiction—in 1886. In that book, titled *Katy of Catoctin*, Townsend wrote in a footnote that Frederick Stone, a Maryland lawyer for Booth gang member David Herold, had told him Booth transformed the plan from kidnapping to murder when Lincoln announced his support for black male suffrage. More specifically, Townsend wrote that:

President Lincoln addressed the people from his mansion in Washington on the night of April 11 saying:

"If universal amnesty is granted to the insurgents, I can not see how I can avoid exacting in return universal suffrage, or at least suffrage on the basis of intelligence and military service."

There were then hundreds of thousands of colored soldiery, and the insurgent President had demanded the right to arm the slaves.

Booth was standing before Mr. Lincoln on the outskirts of the large assemblage.

"That means nigger citizenship," he said to little Harold, by his side. "Now, by God! I'll put him through."[18]

Townsend planted this spurious seed, and it took root in the biography of Lincoln written by Lincoln's former law partner, William Herndon, which was published in 1888, two years after Townsend's book of fiction first appeared.[19] From this the anecdote became a treasured part of Lincoln lore because it portrayed Lincoln as a martyr for not only ending slavery but also for advocating political rights for the freedmen.[20]

Some have sought to corroborate Townsend's story by pointing to the testimony of former Assistant Secretary of War Thomas T. Eckert to Congress regarding his post-assassination interview of Lewis Powell, another member of Booth's team.[21] Eckert testified that Powell told him Booth and Powell had attended a public gathering outside the White House on "the night of the celebration after the fall of Richmond." "Lincoln," he continued, "made a speech that night from one of the windows of the White House, and he and Booth were in the grounds in front. Booth tried to persuade him to shoot the President while in the window, but Powell told Booth he would take no such risk; that he left then and walked around the square, and that Booth remarked: 'That is the last speech he will ever make.'"[22] Tellingly, Eckert's testimony does not indicate that Lincoln, Booth, or Powell made any reference to black suffrage on this occasion, or that David Herold [Little Harold] was present.

Neither of these anecdotes—Townsend's or Eckert's—support any of the heretofore dominant theories of Booth's motivation. Richmond had fallen to Union forces under General U.S. Grant on April 3 while Lincoln was in Virginia with Grant. Lincoln returned to Washington on Palm Sunday, April 9, while Robert E. Lee was surrendering his army to Grant. The following day, April 10, was a day of great celebration in Washington. Along with the roar of cannons, drinking, bonfires, bands playing, and happy people walking through the streets, a large crowd gathered outside the White House that night and repeatedly called on Lincoln to speak to them. Lincoln finally did, but his remarks, which were made from a window at the White House, were happy, celebratory, and totally free of substantive points. He made absolutely no mention of suffrage rights or amnesty at that time.[23] Lincoln's address that Eckert testified Powell had described may have actually occurred during this April 10 event. If so, Powell's statement to Eckert actually supports the proposition that Booth was already planning Lincoln's death before Lincoln ever mentioned black suffrage. So does the fact that, on the same night, Booth went to a pistol gallery for target practice and also alluded to an acquaintance his desire to produce and perform in a play called *Venice Preserved*, which involved a plot to assassinate government leaders in Venice.[24]

Some assassination scholars have either ignored the discrepancy or conflated Lincoln's April 10 remarks with his last public address at dusk on April 11, also from a window at the White House.[25] Lincoln then actually focused on *defending* the failure of Louisiana, which he was reconstructing under his "Ten Percent Plan," to include a provision in its recently adopted constitution guaranteeing suffrage rights to African-Americans. He did allow that "I would myself prefer that it were now conferred on the very intelligent and those who serve our cause as soldiers," but he made clear that this was, in his opinion, not essential. The "sole object to the [federal] government, civil and military," Lincoln declared, was to get Louisiana and the other southern states back into what he called the "proper practical relation with the Union." Lincoln did not mention, much less advocate, amnesty or universal suffrage.[26]

It should also be noted that if the states of the former Confederacy resumed their "practical" relationship to the Union—a return to their seats in Congress—and did so without guaranteeing suffrage rights to the freedmen, black suffrage would have been unlikely for decades, if not at least a century. The reason for this is that, under the federal constitution, the states had exclusive control over who could vote, and the states in the South were not going to voluntarily grant suffrage rights to the freedmen. And no amendment to the federal constitution could have been approved because of the requirement of two-thirds vote of each house of Congress.

As a lawyer, Lincoln would have known this, and there is no evidence that anyone misconstrued Lincoln's hollow words about voting rights. A correspondent in attendance wrote that Lincoln's speech "has caused a great disappointment and left a painful impression. It was mentioned in the crowd in explanation of a passage in his remarks, that Mr. Lincoln was opposed to the extension of the suffrage to colored men."[27]

Not only is Townsend's footnote account of what Lincoln actually said on April 11 inaccurate, but the idea that Booth was motivated by Lincoln's remarks to assassinate him does not explain why William Seward and Andrew Johnson were also targeted. Johnson in particular was adamantly and irrevocably opposed to compelling the South to grant suffrage rights to blacks.[28] Seward was not far behind Johnson in this regard.[29] On this score, Edwin Stanton would have been a much more likely target.

This book proposes a totally different theory about why Booth "changed" the goal from kidnapping Lincoln to assassinating him, Johnson, and Seward: money—a lot of money. One million dollars, which is equivalent to approximately twenty million today.[30] In the months leading to the assassination, Booth and the members of his team repeatedly talked of the large amount of money they would make.[31] The author submits that the assassination of Abraham Lincoln was brought about through the financial contributions of private individuals who hated Lincoln and the Union, who were increasingly concerned that the war would be lost due to growing war weariness and peace sentiment in the South in the fall of 1864 and the spring of 1865, and who were tired of Jefferson Davis's perceived failure to use more extreme measures to win the war. After all, they believed, if the murder of Lincoln, Johnson, and Seward galvanized the North, it might also reunite the South to fight to the death in order to avoid acts of revenge by the North.[32]

This book also maintains that the bounty money was amassed through a fundraising campaign initiated by the principal subject of this book, a South Carolina-born Alabama lawyer, George Washington Gayle. As the first half of the book will demonstrate, Gayle—like many other Alabamians—became increasingly radicalized during the latter part of the antebellum period. He grew to hate the North and was by far Alabama's most militant secessionist. As several assassination historians have noted, in December 1864 Gayle placed an advertisement in a Selma, Alabama, newspaper appealing for contributions to a fund of one million dollars to bring about the murder of only the three men Booth and his team eventually targeted.[33] For this Gayle became known throughout the country after Lincoln's death as the "Million Dollar Man." But unlike the northern public at the time, these historians have essentially dismissed Gayle as having any causative role in Lincoln's death. In essence, as did the federal prosecutors at the time, Gayle's advertisement is seen merely as expressive of southern animosity toward the federal government, and the desire to see that government's decapitation if necessary to achieve Confederate independence.

This book will also seek to answer several questions that federal prosecutors should have investigated more carefully. Who was George Washington Gayle? Was he sufficiently radicalized to bring about such heinous acts? If so, how and when did this occur? Had he done his duty to the Confederacy during the war, or was he in need of proving his dedication and support for the Cause? What was the significance of the timing of the advertisement? Was Booth made aware of the bounty?

In the process of answering these questions, we will examine the politico-economic influences that shaped society in antebellum Alabama. We will also address the impact of the course of the Civil War on diehard Confederates. Finally, we will analyze the execution of the assassination conspiracy and the investigation that followed, as well as Gayle's surprising fate.

The reader should not expect what lawyers call "smoking gun" evidence supporting every link in the chain of logic discussed in this book. Because

Booth was killed before he could be interrogated, no such direct evidence is available. While we have built the case on circumstantial evidence, so too are the other theories discussed above. The difference is that the theory proposed here is supported by George Gayle's previously unreported guilty plea to involvement in the conspiracy, and is substantially free of inconsistencies with the known, undisputed facts. It also provides a plausible explanation for the conspiracy including attacks on Lincoln, Johnson, and Seward. If the federal prosecutors had not been so focused on hanging Jefferson Davis, they might have concluded that Gayle was a critical key to the death of Abraham Lincoln—just as the northern public believed at the time.

John C. Calhoun, the pro-slavery South Carolinian and seventh vice president of the United States, was a leading inspiration for Southern secessionists.

Library of Congress

William Rufus Devane King, who helped draft the Compromise of 1850 and served for a brief time as the 13th vice president of the United States before his death in 1853, was George Gayle's political mentor.

New York Public Library

William Lowndes Yancey, one of the leading orators of his day and a sharp critic of the Compromise of 1850, competed with Gayle for the leadership of the secession movement in Alabama.

Alabama Dept. of Archives and History

Clement C. Clay, who served as a senator for both the United States and the Confederacy, was likely Gayle's link to John Wilkes Booth.

Library of Congress

John Wilkes Booth, the man in tactical command of the group that planned and executed the murder of President Lincoln and the attempted murders of Secretary William Seward and Vice President Andrew Johnson.

Library of Congress

Jefferson Davis, a moderate United States senator from Mississippi and the only man to serve as president of the Confederacy, was wrongly accused of authorizing the assassinations.

Library of Congress

Vice President Andrew Johnson, one
of the three targets of the assassination
plot.

Edwin M. Stanton (above), the
secretary of war who botched the
post-assassination investigation.

Richard Busteed (right), the Lincoln-
appointed federal district judge who
presided over Gayle's prosecution in
Alabama.

(Above) Fortress Monroe on the tip of the Virginia peninsula, Gayle's place of imprisonment in Washington DC. *Library of Congress*

(Below) The 48th NY Infantry inside Fort Pulaski, Georgia, in 1863. Pulaski was Gayle's final place of imprisonment. *Library of Congress*

Chapter 1

"A Faithful Disciple of the Old Pannel Jackson Democracy"

A reasonably competent federal investigator could have easily learned much about George Washington Gayle from public records, newspapers, and wartime Unionists who resided in his region. First and foremost, Gayle was a native of South Carolina during a period when the state of one's birth meant a great deal. Referring to the antebellum radicalization of South Carolina and its people, James Petigru, a nineteenth century South Carolina lawyer, famously quipped that the state was "too small to be a Republic, and too large to be an insane asylum."[1] The bedrock of that exaggeration was the destructive cocktail of state rights doctrine, anti-federalism, and sectionalism that characterized the political thought of many South Carolinians. This all grew from the fact that blacks outnumbered whites in the Palmetto State. Whites were determined not to allow any outside forces to upset the mechanism of control provided by the institution of slavery.[2]

The Palmetto State would exercise an increasingly significant influence over the politics of Alabama, and ultimately radicalize and lead Alabama and the rest of the South to ruin.[3] And the life trajectory of George Washington Gayle, born in Abbeville, South Carolina in January 1807, would provide further evidence in support of Petigru's observation.[4] This is odd because neither of his parents were born or raised in South Carolina, although they did live there from 1793 to 1811 before emigrating to the frontier in what would become Monroe County in the Alabama River region of the Mississippi Territory.[5] George Gayle—"Wat" as he was known—lived in South Carolina only four years, seemingly an insufficient period of time to internalize nineteenth-century South Carolina's world view.[6]

With the opening of the Federal Road from Georgia to Fort Stoddert in November 1811, the Gayles were joined by thousands of other South Carolina residents who moved from the lower-yield lands of their native state to the higher yield, relatively virgin lands of Alabama.[7] The year the Gayles relocated to Monroe County, the international price of cotton was 9¢ per pound and rising. In 1817, it would reach the antebellum high of 30¢ per pound, sparking what was known as "Alabama Fever" for Alabama land and the wealth it could produce. By 1850, 48,663 South Carolina natives would be living in Alabama, surpassed only by 58,997 Georgians.[8] Along with their predilection for slave-based plantation agriculture, many of these South Carolinians brought along with them their brand of political attitudes, as well as their strong loyalty to the interests and welfare of their home state, both of which would have a profound impact on the political dynamics in Alabama in the coming years.[9] As the editor of the *Charleston Mercury* later proudly declared, South Carolina's "sons are scattered over the South, and threads of sympathy that lead back to the parent heart, penetrate the circle of every Southern community, and make the remembrance and veneration of her, a part of the traditional sentiment of many States."[10]

Young George Gayle would have been made aware of the power and reach of the federal government during his formative years when President James Madison issued a proclamation forbidding the settlement of Monroe County until it was surveyed. When many disobeyed this edict, Madison incensed the settlers by sending troops to oust them. Congress defused this conflict, but it would not be the last between Alabamians and the federal government.[11] The following year Congress passed the first of several tariffs designed to protect domestic manufacturers from foreign competition by increasing duties on certain imports. Because most manufacturers were in the North, this was alleged to have a disparate impact on the South. Two years after its enactment, cotton prices, and therefore southern agricultural incomes, began a steady decline as the nation slipped into an economic depression that would devastate the South for more than a decade. Economic misery, in turn, produced sectional resentments that caused serious and lasting scar tissue on the body politic, particularly with regard to the commitment to nationalism.[12] Fault lines were exposed once again in 1819 during debates over the admission of the Missouri Territory to the Union as a slave state.[13] A bitter, bruising battle in Congress between Southerners favoring the extension of slavery into the western territories and Northerners opposed to its expansion was finally settled by the Missouri Compromise. Missouri was admitted as a slave state, but the compromise was costly to slavery perpetualists who acceded not only to the creation of another free state—Maine—but also a prohibition of slavery above 36°30' North latitude in the lands comprising the Louisiana Purchase.[14]

From this, Southerners in an economic squeeze knew that Congress could not only increase their overhead by taxation favorable to northern interests, but also indirectly decrease the value of their increasing but superfluous slave populations by eliminating potential demand for slave labor in those western territories north of the Missouri Compromise line. This, in turn, dramatically increased existing internal security concerns arising from mounting slave-to-white ratios in the South. By 1820, over 40,000 slaves lived in Alabama, and in 1822 the threat they presented was brought home by news of a failed slave insurrection in Charleston, South Carolina.[15] There, it was alleged, a former slave organized a group of slaves to murder all the whites, burn the town, and then escape by ship to seek exile in a foreign country.[16]

Although that revolt was unsuccessful, all Southerners knew that the next attempt might result in a repeat of the horrors of St. Domingo, a French Caribbean island that had been, like America, the most profitable and, therefore, most important colony of a foreign power.[17] Like America, Africans had been brought there, enslaved, and exploited to produce cash crops (sugar, coffee, cotton, and indigo) in a plantation system. Of a total population of more than one-half million, there were 40,000 whites compared to 452,000 slaves and 28,000 free blacks. As in America, men, both black and white, made great fortunes on the backs of their slaves.[18] Smoldering under the surface of the St. Domingo slave society were the resentments of not only free blacks denied political equality with the whites by French law, but also those of the enslaved blacks who were tired of being literally worked to death under terrible conditions. After the French Revolution began, free blacks aspiring to the same equality sought by French white peasants and encouraged by French abolitionists and revolutionaries, appealed to the new government in Paris for full citizenship rights. Raising the expectations of free blacks, a limited number of them were granted those rights in 1791. Raised expectations, if unmet, are often the mothers of revolution. When the whites in St. Domingo who opposed the French Revolution attempted to deny the newly granted rights to free blacks, a power struggle ensued. This agitation for rights and equality ultimately sparked a large-scale slave insurrection, following which the French government in Paris decreed the emancipation of all slaves on the island. Nonetheless, in the end, virtually every white man, woman, and child that did not flee the island was massacred.[19]

As a consequence of that ghastly event, southern slave owners were internally conflicted by paranoia and greed. Unable to sell for a fair price or simply release their increasingly redundant slaves in a stagnated economy, slave owners fearful of the fate of St. Domingo whites were forced to feed, clothe, and retain them and substantially increase control measures on the free black and slave populations, all at great expense.[20] As former president Thomas Jefferson described the South's predicament, "we have the wolf by the ears and we can neither hold him nor safely let him go."[21] The Alabama slave population, meanwhile, continued to skyrocket, reaching 117,549 by the end of the 1820s.[22]

The same thing was happening in Georgia, but citizens of the so-called Empire State of the South led by George Michael Troup, their fifty-five-year-old Alabama-born governor and Savannah lawyer-planter, were determined to expand available cotton lands and thereby disperse the slaves even if it meant a clash with the federal government and President John Quincy Adams. In 1825 Troup, who in the coming years would find an admirer in George Gayle, impatiently usurped the federal government's role to negotiate a treaty for Creek Indian lands in that state and did so with an unauthorized member of that understandably stubborn tribe. Troup then attempted to enforce that treaty over the violent opposition of the Creeks and the objections of the Adams administration, all to the dismay of many Georgians and other Americans.[23] Some called Troup a lunatic, but he was actually crazy like a fox.[24] After Troup brought the nation to the brink of civil war, Adams blinked and moved to extinguish the legal title of the Creeks to virtually all of their lands in Georgia—more than 10 million acres.[25] It was a valuable lesson for Southerners. They could defy the federal government to the brink of civil war and get what they wanted. And on top of all this, Troup's militancy in support of state rights was rewarded by his re-election in 1825.[26] Other southern politicians would take notice.

In 1828, the same year George Washington Gayle's father died, more disturbing news came from Washington.[27] What some Southerners called the "Tariff of Abominations" significantly increased duties on imports. The outraged editor of the *Mobile Commercial Register* cried that while "other states can resort to manufacturing, to the raising of Beef, Pork, Sheep, &c, &c and by an improved market in such products, gain an indemnity for advances on domestic consumption," Alabama could not. "From local causes"—which he described as a lack of capital—"Alabama never can become a manufacturing State." Instead, the "industry of our population must be confined, as it ever has been to Agriculture, and mainly to that leading branch of it [cotton], which must essentially depend upon a foreign market." As a result, "there is no state in the Union, which, in proportion to its wealth, will suffer so deeply from the increase of duties as Alabama." For the "enormous addition to their annual expenses of a hundred thousand dollars," the "cotton growers of Alabama" were "not offered even the semblance of an equivalent."[28] The tariff sparked protests throughout the South as well as calls by some for extreme measures.[29]

One of those extremists with whom George Gayle would ultimately establish a relationship was twenty-seven-year-old South Carolinian Robert Barnwell Rhett, who would later own the intensely pro-secession *Charleston Mercury*.[30] Rhett, who one wartime Montgomery, Alabama, newspaper credited with having "put the ball of revolution in motion" and given the "first impulse" to that revolution, was then a member of the South Carolina legislature. [31] He gained national attention when he called for armed resistance if necessary, albeit supposedly to "preserve the Union, and bring back the constitution to its original uncorrupted principles." Failing this, he warned, the institution of slavery would be the next southern interest to be jeopardized.[32]

This controversy came at a very inopportune time for South Carolina's leading political figure, United States Senator John Caldwell Calhoun of Abbeville, who was seeking the vice-presidency in the 1828 national election on a ticket with southern icon Andrew Jackson of Tennessee. Jackson, who recognized that several states with significant electoral votes supported the tariff, chose to finesse the issue by refraining from making anything but ambiguous public statements.[33] Not wishing to alienate Southerners by encouraging unmanly submission, Calhoun privately, and without Jackson's knowledge, suggested that the enforcement of this or any other allegedly unconstitutional law could be "nullified" by a specially convened state convention, which would be followed by a convention of all the states. If that national convention approved the law by at least a three-fourths vote, each state then had the choice of submission or secession.[34]

This anti-majoritarian doctrine caught on among many South Carolinians and sparked controversy nationwide. Some feared that it would result in civil war.[35] But South Carolinians were far from monolithic at this early point in the long road to secession and war. The Greenville, South Carolina, *Mountaineer* declared its opposition to the tariff and pledged that "[i]n a peaceable and constitutional resistance of those measures, we shall not be found wanting." It saw the nullification doctrine, however, as the catalyst for "the establishment of an aristocracy of the very worst kind" allowing "almost three-fourths of the people" to be "governed by one-fourth!" This, it was sure, "must end in anarchy." Rather than taking this "rash, fatal step" as a result of the "ebullition of passion," the editor hoped that South Carolina would be governed by "sober reason."[36]

The *Charleston Mercury*, as would be the case for the remainder of the antebellum period, was at the other end of the spectrum. Rather than leading to disunion and civil war, nullification, it maintained, would "preserve and perpetuate the Union." It was sure that with South Carolina in the lead, "every injured State will follow and support her" and thereby present "the sublime moral spectacle of united resistance to lawless outrage and arbitrary power." This, in turn, would force the "Tariff States" to "willingly compromise the matter," ultimately resulting in the repeal or reduction of the tariff.[37]

Most Alabamians publicly opposed the concept of nullification and encouraged opponents of the tariff to seek redress in Congress rather than utilize illegal means.[38] The *Cahawba Republican* reported on what was described as a "very large meeting of the citizens of Dallas County at Cahawba" who "reprobated the Tariff" but also "denounced Nullification, as being 'neither peaceful nor constitutional'; unwarranted by the opinions of the republicans of 1798, which have so often been quoted in its support;" and tending "inevitably in its operation to revolution and a disunion of our hitherto happy nation."[39]

A Tuscaloosa resident wrote a friend in South Carolina that "we have, say one out of a thousand, of our open-mouthed Nullifiers, such however, as would be Disunionists even in heaven."[40] But those few were very active. A Mobile editor reported that emigrants from South Carolina were everywhere "inculcating the heresy of nullification with the zeal of a fanatic and the perseverance of a missionary."[41] The physically largest of the breed of Calhoun nullifiers in Alabama was attorney Dixon Hall Lewis of Montgomery. Although not a South Carolina native, Lewis had attended South Carolina College where he had imbibed proslavery, free trade, and state rights doctrines from its new president, Dr. Thomas Cooper.[42] After graduating from that institution in 1820, Lewis emigrated to Alabama where he then read law at Cahawba, the new state's first capital. In 1823, Lewis was admitted to the practice of law, established a law practice in Montgomery, and married into the Autauga County family of John Archer Elmore, a former resident of South Carolina who was one of the most influential planters in the Alabama Black Belt. Lewis was elected to the Alabama legislature, and in 1829 to the U.S. House of Representatives for the first of several terms.[43] For the next twenty years, Lewis would be the leader of the growing and increasingly militant state rights movement in Alabama, channeling Calhoun's notions of southern nationalism and infecting the electorate with paranoia regarding northern intentions.[44]

Calhoun's nullification remedy, meanwhile, gained increasing traction in South Carolina, so much so that President Jackson boldly threatened to use military force to enforce the tariff there while also successfully working to have the tariff duties reduced.[45] South Carolina eventually won this battle of wills, establishing another important precedent for state defiance of federal power. A Hayneville, Alabama, editor, in responding to the charge by Jacksonian Democrats that Dixon Hall Lewis was the "high Priest of Calhounism in Alabama," compared the manner in which the dispute over the tariff had been resolved to the "story of a rude boy"—the federal government—"caught up a tree stealing an old man's apples." The old man—South Carolina—"made use of mild words and gentle means to induce him to come down," but was finally forced to resort to throwing stones at him. This worked, and the "young chap" came down and begged the old man's pardon. Likewise, wrote the editor, Carolina's efforts had brought on a result "favorable to the cause of State Rights, and to the confinement of the action of the General Government" within its constitutional sphere.[46]

Lewis agreed with those sentiments. He wrote that justice to the South could result only from resistance in a manner "perceived by our oppressors" that state rights "would be sustained at every hazard by the Southern people." "In this way alone," he concluded, "can the Union be preserved as an Union of liberty; on any other basis it was an Union of oppression, and will last no longer than it can be maintained by the tyrant's law of force."[47] Thus, as South Carolina Unionist James Petigru observed, "Nullification has done its work. It has prepared the minds of men for a separation of the States."[48]

But South Carolina extremists would not soon forget that they had been the only southern state willing to throw stones at the federal government regarding the tariff, much less secede and resist militarily.[49] Nor could they ignore the taunts of some southerners who saw them as aristocratic, selfish, arrogant, and reckless hotheads with the South's interests. Attendees at a rally in Jacksonian North Alabama had unanimously adopted resolutions affirming it to be "a duty we owe to ourselves, to that band of patriots who fought, bled and died, that we may be free, and to our posterity to whom we should transmit the liberty we enjoy as an inheritance above all price, to declare to the world" that if South Carolina "persist[s] in her mad career (which heaven forbid) ... we will never take the field unless the star spangled banner waves over us."[50] Henceforth, the efforts of southern extremists would include strategies for convincing other southern states to take the lead, while also portraying to reluctant South Carolinians that they would not be alone the next time sectional conflicts arose.[51] George Gayle would ultimately play a role in those efforts.

But at this point Gayle had more interests than just politics. He was a tall, handsome young man and considered a real catch by the opposite sex. His cousin-in-law wrote in her journal that as she and her husband arrived in Tuscaloosa, "we met George Gayle, with half a dozen girls hanging on his arm apparently in the very zenith of happiness."[52] Yet as Gayle reached manhood in the late 1820s and 1830s, he could hardly be unaware of increasing tensions with the North in general, and in Washington, D.C. in particular. When more challenges to southern interests occurred, it was seemingly inevitable that extremists like Rhett would multiply and spread outside South Carolina. It would not be long before an Alabama newspaper observed that nine out of ten Alabama disunionists were from South Carolina.[53] George Gayle would ultimately become one of those, but first he was diverted from that course by political opportunism as well as a politically beneficial marriage.

Gayle's ticket into Alabama politics was an older cousin, South Carolina-born John Gayle. John Gayle had migrated to the Alabama territory in 1813, where he read law and gradually climbed the political rungs through the legislature and the Alabama Supreme Court.[54] It was a classic pattern for the ambitious lawyer-planter-politicians who dominated the state during the antebellum period. John Gayle was an anti-tariff— but initially an anti-nullification—Jacksonian Democrat and was elected governor of Alabama in August 1831.[55] According to an editorial from the *Montgomery Planter's Gazette* reprinted throughout the nation, his election constituted a "triumph of the principles of our forefathers over the new-broached heresies of the Disunionists of the day."[56]

George Gayle followed his cousin's lead. After being elected assistant secretary of the state Senate in 1829, Gayle read law in Tuscaloosa, its designation as the state capital having been wrested from the town of Cahawba in Dallas County just a few years earlier.[57] While studying the law and performing his clerical duties in the Senate, he became embroiled in the first of many controversies sparked by his sometimes-prickly personality. Several powerful members of the Alabama Senate publicly censured him in 1830 for authoring a newspaper article that ridiculed a speech given by James Abercrombie, a prominent member of the growing anti-Jackson, state rights faction from Montgomery County. Rather than simply apologizing, Gayle defiantly submitted a long letter to the Senate declaring that his censure was an "unjust and unconstitutional" assault on his reputation.[58] He also wrote a letter to the editor of the *Tuscaloosa Enquirer* accusing one of the leading senators of political and moral dishonesty, and comparing him to a hyena.[59] He was very fortunate that he was not terminated from his clerical position, but it was an episode that would haunt Gayle for the rest of his political career, particularly when he made his decision on where to establish his law practice.[60]

Like John Gayle, George Gayle also attacked the South Carolina-inspired nullification doctrine with great gusto.[61] As a North Alabama

Democrat organ later recalled, "Gayle hated the South Carolina nullifiers and their kidney with a relish" and was "regarded as a faithful disciple of the old pannel Jackson democracy."[62] That would change.

The Alabama Supreme Court admitted George Gayle to practice law in 1832, a period in which that court included as one of its members a staunch Jacksonian Democrat from Dallas County, Reuben Saffold, Jr.[63] Born in Georgia in 1788, Saffold had migrated to Alabama in 1813 and later served with John Gayle in the constitutional convention that framed Alabama's first constitution in 1819. He was selected to serve simultaneously as a circuit judge and a member of the Supreme Court and had moved his growing family to Dallas County where he established a large cotton plantation southeast of present day Selma.[64]

George Gayle also decided to move to Dallas County, where he opened a law office in Cahawba, the county seat located adjacent to the Alabama and Cahaba rivers. Even though it was no longer the state capital, Cahawba remained an important commercial center until it was eclipsed many years later by Selma. There Gayle would remain for most of the rest of his turbulent life.[65] Among his first law partners was Reuben Saffold's eldest son, Joseph.[66] In addition to the normal challenges faced by all newly-minted young lawyers, Gayle and Saffold encountered the natural elements when the flood prone little town was inundated in 1833.[67]

George Gayle broke with John Gayle from a political standpoint over the next conflict with the federal government, which arose out of an uptick in the price of cotton and the resulting aggressiveness of settlers on Creek Indian lands in the new East Alabama counties of Talladega, Randolph, Coosa, Tallapoosa, Chambers, Russell, Macon, and Barbour. A correspondent to a Maine newspaper reported from the area that "it would seem as if North and South Carolina were pouring forth their population in swarms" in order to obtain more fertile land to grow cotton.[68] The Creeks had been allowed by federal treaty to retain rights in some of their ancestral lands, and the Jackson administration was required by that treaty to remove whites who were squatting on those lands. When those squatters disregarded the treaty and refused to move, federal troops were dispatched to forcibly oust them. In the process blood was spilled in present-day Russell County.[69] With chagrin, the *Montgomery Planter's Gazette* concluded its article on these incidents by declaring: "So much for the doctrine of Nullification when put into practice."[70]

When the Alabama legislature convened later that year, Governor Gayle reiterated his earlier stance on that doctrine. "As sure as it shall succeed," he declared, "its triumphs will be stained with fraternal blood, and the proudest of its trophies will be the destruction of constitutional liberty."[71] As a Tuscaloosa newspaper would soon announce, the governor intended to run for reelection, but he remained publicly silent on the dispute in East Alabama until after he was elected without opposition. Then he shocked the nation and delighted nullifiers everywhere when he finally denounced federal intrusion into Alabama's internal affairs and, in essence, sought to nullify the treaty with the Creeks.[72] A Baltimore editor blasted the governor, declaring that "if this be not nullification, it is something still worse. In fact, it is a more daunting and unscrupulous assault upon the rights and dignity of the General Government than the proceedings of the nullifiers of South Carolina." Rather than seeking a legislative determination as in South Carolina, the editor continued, "the Governor individually, without waiting for the meeting of the Legislature, or convoking it, assumes the responsibility of placing the State in such an attitude towards the General Government as would necessarily and immediately result in a civil war, unless the latter succumb to his menaces."[73] A North Alabama grand jury agreed, declaring that the governor's course was "eminently calculated to involve the people of Alabama in a bloody conflict with the General Government."[74] The Huntsville *Democrat* worried that if the nullifiers "shall ever prevail extensively in the Southern States, we are firmly of the opinion, that the Union will be dissolved."[75]

By this time George Gayle had made the acquaintance of a prominent and powerful supporter of Andrew Jackson's, North Carolina native William Rufus de Vane King.[76] Also a lawyer-planter-politician, King had been elected to the United States Senate by the Alabama legislature in 1819 and still served with distinction.[77] King, who also lived in Dallas County, interceded into the controversy and, after a personal conference with President Jackson, it was decided that settlers who had taken peaceable possession of the lands would not be removed. This was communicated to Governor Gayle during a personal visit to Alabama by the famous Francis Scott Key. As a result, the matter was defused, but the episode, as the *Huntsville Democrat* observed, had nonetheless given strength to the nullification movement in Alabama.[78]

George Gayle gravitated to King and improbably won election to the Alabama legislature as a Democrat at the age of 25, despite Dallas County being in a region of growing Whig strength.[79] Gayle returned the favor by orchestrating King's reelection to the United States Senate by the Alabama legislature, and in the process trouncing Dixon Hall Lewis' challenge.[80] Further solidifying his relationship with King, Gayle subsequently married Margaret Tabitha Kornegay, King's niece and ward.[81] This did not begin as strictly a marriage of convenience. During their courtship John Gayle's wife wrote in her journal that Margaret "appears entirely unaffected, affable, modest, and very pleasing—pretty too, in spite of her freckles. I do not wonder that George thinks her altogether irresistible."[82] But as with many marriages, the bloom eventually fell off the rose, although their union still had its advantages. As one contemporary observer later noted, by this marriage Gayle "added to his influence and prospects by the strong family connection."[83]

The following year when Dixon Hall Lewis sought reelection to Congress, Lewis caught a lucky break when abolitionists in the northeast motivated by religious convictions began a movement to convince Southerners to voluntarily emancipate their slaves. In 1833 they had begun *The Emancipator*, a newspaper initially advocating "immediate abolition gradually accomplished,"[84] and in 1835 New York members of the American Anti-Slavery Society (the "AAS") decided to focus their crusade of what was called "moral suasion" on whites in the South utilizing a direct mail campaign to appeal to the conscience of white southern ministers and community leaders regarding the immorality of slavery.[85] This sparked a firestorm of controversy among Alabamians and other Southerners concerned that talk of emancipation would cause a widespread slave insurrection. In addition, by this time the economics of slavery had changed once again; the market price of cotton had increased to 15¢ per pound,[86] ushering in what historians have called the "Flush Times" in Alabama.[87] Actually, the times were not as flush as in 1817, but similar good times appeared to be ahead as long as slavery existed. Evidencing that some Alabamians were in no mood for moral suasion, Dixon Hall Lewis was reelected to Congress without opposition.[88] Alabama's Attorney General then thrilled the public when he convinced a grand jury in Tuscaloosa to issue an indictment against Ransom G. Williams, a black minister in New York who was the publishing agent of the AAS. Williams was charged with mailing copies of the *Emancipator* newspaper containing anti-slavery appeals to Alabama citizens.[89] Alabama governor John Gayle dutifully sent a letter to New York governor William Marcy demanding that Williams be extradited to Alabama for trial, but Marcy ultimately chose not to comply.[90]

George Gayle did not seek reelection in 1835, and party politics preceding the 1836 presidential election blocked his effort to move up another political rung.[91] When Gayle sought to have himself elected by the legislature to the circuit court bench in late 1835, Whigs led by a nephew of John Calhoun, James Martin Calhoun, who was also a legislator from Dallas County, engineered the election of his South Carolina-born law partner, Ezekiel Pickens, by a vote of 74 to 42.[92] Disappointed, George Gayle accepted an appointment by Alabama governor Clement

Comer Clay, a Huntsville Jacksonian Democrat who had succeeded John Gayle in 1835, to serve as an aid-de-camp with the rank of lieutenant colonel in the Alabama militia in connection with what became known as the Second Creek War.[93] Establishing a pattern that would serve him well in the coming decades, Gayle's decision to serve in this capacity meant others would have to fight and shed their blood. The war ended in 1837, but it was during this period that Gayle became acquainted with Governor Clay's then nineteen-year-old son, Clement Claiborne Clay, who was also known as C.C. Clay, Jr. Young Clay had graduated from the University of Alabama in Tuscaloosa in 1834 and was then serving as his father's private secretary. But he was destined to achieve much higher office and, like Gayle, have a major role in bringing about Alabama's almost irretrievable economic destruction.[94]

It was also during this period that another key figure in Alabama's political history—and one whose reluctance for personal involvement in conventional warfare mirrored George Gayle's—moved to Dallas County. Twenty-two-year-old William Lowndes Yancey purchased a plantation near Cahawba in 1836 adjacent to one of his uncles, Jesse Beene, another lawyer and Jacksonian Democrat who would greatly influence the first few years of Yancey's political career. Like Gayle, Yancey had connections with South Carolina but then opposed nullification. Yancey also possessed a poor temperament, having run afoul of the law back in South Carolina after shooting and killing one of his wife's uncles during an argument. As a result, he would soon be forced to spend time in a South Carolina jail before returning to Alabama.[95] Gayle had not embarrassed himself to this degree yet, but the two were so much alike that it is not surprising they never had a warm relationship with each other. Yet their unilateral but parallel efforts would have a crucial impact on the future of Alabama.

Although John Gayle served as an elector for Whig Hugh Lawson White of Tennessee in the 1836 presidential election,[96] George stuck with Andrew Jackson's hand-picked successor, New Yorker Martin Van Buren, who won Alabama and the nation. George's decision to support Van Buren was not an easy choice. In the Black Belt where abolitionists were considered devils incarnate, Van Buren was repeatedly denounced as an abolition sympathizer.[97] But Gayle's loyalty to the National Democratic Party paid off. In early 1837, George Gayle and Joseph Saffold established a satellite law office in Alabama's largest and most prosperous city, Mobile, and Gayle moved there to man that office. Not long thereafter, the Mobile office added John Gayle and William J. Van de Graff as partners.[98] Mobile had become a boomtown in the 1830s as cotton prices had risen during Alabama's "Flush Times," but the bubble burst with the Panic of 1837. This began another long, very serious depression in the South as well as in the nation at large.[99] George Gayle was one of the fortunate ones, however, as Van Buren offered him an appointment to the office of United States District Attorney for the Southern District of Alabama. Rather than sticking it out in private practice with Joseph Saffold, John Gayle, and Van de Graff, George elected to jump ship and accept the appointment.[100] There is no evidence Gayle distinguished himself in that position.

While George Gayle was in Mobile, another man with South Carolina connections assumed an arguably more important position. The Reverend Dr. Basil Manly, a graduate of South Carolina College, was appointed president of the University of Alabama in Tuscaloosa, replacing its northern-born president, Reverend Alva Woods.[101] Manly's hate for Yankees was only surpassed by his love of slavery.[102] He became the foremost spokesman in Alabama for the bible-based defense of the institution of slavery, and successfully agitated for a split between northern and southern Baptists in the 1840s. For those students or others who might have questioned the morality of enslaving others, Reverend Manly gave comforting assurance that it was God's will.[103] It was said by an Alabama editor that "over the students, Dr. Manly exercises an authority, at once firm and gracious. The students submit to it, from the pride they take in obeying and obtaining the favor of so good a man, rather than from fear."[104]

South Carolina continued to spread its wings across the Deep South in other ways. George Gayle would have had ready access to news regarding the efforts of South Carolina business interests to construct railroads to expand their market areas to Alabama at the expense of Mobile, and to encourage southern nationalism. Mobile lawyer John Forsyth, Jr., who had recently purchased a half interest in the *Mobile Commercial Register*, sounded the alarm.[105] Charleston, he wrote, "must not be permitted without opposition, to complete her gigantic chain of internal improvement and foreign intercourse, or to divert any part of the trade of the West from its natural outlet, the Gulf of Mexico, to the Atlantic."[106] But South Carolinians would not be denied. John Calhoun, who was obsessed with creating a political party composed of Southerners dedicated to southern interests, declared in a letter to budding radical North Alabama lawyer-politician David Hubbard that this road would "do more to unite & Conciliate the slave holding States, than can be effected by anything else; and will change not only the commerce, but the politicks of the Union."[107]

The gradual erosion of Jacksonianism in Alabama politics was evidenced during the 1840 presidential election cycle, which pitted President Van Buren against Whig challenger William Henry Harrison of

Indiana. With the national economy still in the tank, Van Buren and the Democrats were in trouble. In desperation Alabama Democrats reached out to John Calhoun and the State Rights faction for support.[108] That support came with a heavy price. To the followers of Calhoun's creed, the federal government was potentially a clear and present danger to the South's peculiar institution—slavery.[109] For their support against the Whigs, southern Democrats would have to join in pushing that exquisitely divisive sectional issue.[110]

The Jacksonian Democrat faction in Alabama, led by William Rufus King, was undoubtedly influenced by King to join hands with the Calhoun faction, led by King's rival, Dixon Hall Lewis, in support of Van Buren's reelection. King was motivated by his desire to become Vice President of the United States—a quest that would consume him for the next twenty years.[111] Like a good soldier, George Gayle readily adapted to King's opportunistic change in direction.[112] In April 1840, he participated in what a pro-Van Buren Mobile newspaper described as a "meeting of the Democratic and State Rights citizens" in Selma "for the purpose of forming a 'State Rights Club'" for the "better defense of the Democratic cause, against the attacks of the combination which is planning its downfall."[113] At a subsequent meeting of the club, Gayle introduced resolutions reiterating the claim that Harrison was an abolitionist, and declaring it to be the duty of every southerner to vote against "any and every Whig, of any and every non-slaveholding State."[114] Gayle, Joseph Saffold, and others engaged in a public debate in Selma with the local pro-Harrison "Tippecanoe Club" of Dallas County in May.[115] Later that month, however, news reached Alabama that King's bid for a place on the national ticket had been unsuccessful.[116] But like King, Gayle stuck with Van Buren and even stumped for him outside Dallas County. At a rally in Tuscaloosa, Gayle made a speech that the pro-Van Buren Tuscaloosa *Flag of the Union* described as "peculiarly happy, appropriate and eloquent."[117]

George Gayle's cousin, John Gayle, was meanwhile working just as hard for Harrison. After being elected to Congress from Mobile earlier in the year, John Gayle helped orchestrate the first statewide convention of Whigs in Alabama, and then was selected one of its presidential electors.[118] In the end, Harrison lost Alabama, but the Democrats' focus on the slavery issue was not enough to divert the South's attention from the continuing economic depression that had begun on Van Buren's watch. Certainly to the chagrin of George Gayle, Van Buren even lost Dallas County along with the national election.[119]

The prayers of Democrats were presumably answered when President Harrison died a short time after his inauguration,[120] the first United States president to die in office. The saddened editor of the pro-Whig *Tuscaloosa Independent Monitor* wrote that "it may not be that during our lives or those of the next generation, such a national calamity as the death of the President of the United States, will take place; and as this is the first, and we pray to Heaven that it may be the last, we should be pleased to see a general manifestation of respect by all classes and pursuits."[121]

George Gayle also suffered loss during this period. In 1841 his wife, Margaret, died leaving him two small children, including one who was nursing. According to King family lore, Margaret expressed fears to William Rufus King on her deathbed that if she died the baby would "starve to death," certainly not a good reflection on her husband.[122] The following year, Gayle's term of office as U.S. District Attorney expired and President Tyler did not reappoint him.[123]

Gayle returned to Cahawba and began a solo law practice. According to a moonlight-and-magnolias style history of the town written by one of Gayle's relations, Gayle's law office as well as his residence were situated on the grounds where the Alabama capitol once stood. His house, she wrote, was "a pretty frame cottage, with a long gallery in front standing far back in the yard at the end of a broad avenue, shaded by wide-spreading mulberry trees, said to be the same that ornamented the capitol grounds." There, she continued, "were enjoyed many social pleasures in the old days in the genial society of Colonel Gayle and his family, who loved to gather their friends around them."[124]

Gayle devoted most of his time to his profession.[125] He had a number of different law partners over the years, not unusual during this tumultuous economic period.[126] There is evidence that Gayle was a highly successful lawyer—a litigator who not surprisingly was extraordinarily competitive, relentless, and resourceful. An observer once described him as "argumentative and pathetic before the Court and Jury, and as a comedian is hard to excel, even in the narrative of Mrs. O'Flanegan."[127] His colleagues in the Dallas County bar later recalled him as an "advocate of great power" whose "eloquent voice" was "fearlessly raised to vindicate the right and denounce the wrong." As a criminal defense lawyer, they maintained, Gayle had few equals. "Endowed with a bold spirit and a quick and strong mind, and ardent and impulsive by nature," Gayle "devoted his energies and labors with no reservation to the defense of his client, and never lost hope of success as long as there was a forum to which he could appeal."[128]

Gayle also hated losing. He would occasionally take the unusual step of protesting his losses in the newspapers. On one such occasion he complained in a letter-to-the-editor of a Selma newspaper that a special court established by state law to try slaves without a jury who were charged with serious crimes was unconstitutional as a violation of the Alabama Bill of Rights affording all "persons" a trial by jury. Slaves, Gayle argued, were not merely property. They were, as a matter of law, also "persons" within the meaning of the Alabama constitution. He called on the next legislature to repeal the law establishing the special court—to "wipe it from our statute book"—and thereby stop what he called "judicial murders."[129] One should not interpret the fact that Gayle took this position as an indication that he was in any way personally dedicated to equal rights for slaves. Slaves were valuable property, and their owners were more than willing to hire good, aggressive lawyers like Gayle to zealously defend their slaves who were charged with capital crimes. The alternative would be the loss of that property if the slave were convicted and executed. And with fellow slave owners on the jury, an acquittal was at least possible.[130]

Gayle also frequently appealed his losses to the Alabama Supreme Court. In fact, beginning with a murder case in 1840—which he lost at trial but won a reversal on appeal—Gayle was counsel of record in over 100 appeals, a very large number for this period.[131] An examination of those cases indicates that, like most lawyers of the era, Gayle handled a mixture of criminal and civil cases.

Among his criminal cases federal investigators might have found very interesting was *Jones v. State*, which involved a charge of petty larceny against Gayle's client. Gayle sought to establish that the defendant was insane at the time of the commission of the crime and therefore incapable of forming the *mens rea* or criminal intent required for conviction. For this purpose, Gayle called as a witness a physician who examined the defendant and testified that the defendant had been "laboring under a progressive insanity" before and after the theft and was "greatly" insane at the time of trial. The jury did not believe it and Gayle's client was convicted.[132] On appeal the Alabama Supreme Court affirmed the conviction but made an interesting comment that likely stuck with Gayle. "The evidence strongly indicated, perhaps was conclusive, of the prisoner's insanity *at the time of the trial*. Under such circumstances, it was not proper that he would have been put upon trial." And under the common law, the Court further remarked, those deemed insane could not be arraigned or, if convicted of a capital offense, executed "while he remained thus demented." Yet the court did not reverse on this basis, although it did suggest another remedy. "If, amid the mystery and veil which shrouds the phenomena of mental aberration, so difficult to penetrate, the judge should be mistaken, and try an insane man (as we incline to think has been done in the case before us), it will present a case in which there may be a strong appeal to executive clemency."

Given Gayle's experience with this traditional insanity defense, he likely took great interest in the controversial trial in which an American court first recognized the defense of "temporary" insanity. As was reported in the Alabama press, the case involved a murder charge against a New York congressman, Daniel Sickles, who was accused of shooting his wife's paramour, the son of Francis Scott Key. A large defense team that included former Mobile, Alabama, attorney Philip Phillips, James Topham Brady of New York, and Abraham Lincoln's future Secretary of War, Edwin McMasters Stanton, used that defense to convince a Washington, D.C., jury to acquit Sickles.[133] The superiority of this new defense to criminal charges was immediately apparent to every lawyer. Not only had Sickles—in layman's terms—"gotten away with murder," but he had not been committed to an insane asylum as was the fate of other defendants who had claimed they were insane to avoid execution.[134]

A case in point involved the first man who had ever attempted to assassinate an American president. While William Rufus King served in the Senate, Richard Lawrence, a young man residing in Washington, D.C., who was described as a journeyman painter, had attempted to shoot President Andrew Jackson in front of hundreds of witnesses following a funeral service at the nation's capital. Both of Lawrence's pistols misfired, however, and he was quickly arrested. One of Jackson's many political enemies, United States Senator George Poindexter of Mississippi, was suspected by Jackson and his supporters of hiring Lawrence to commit the deed, but no solid proof of this sensational charge was ever found during a subsequent congressional investigation. The evidence against Lawrence was irrefutable, but it appears that, on advice of counsel, he gave his accusers the impression that he was insane and thereby unduly influenced by the political rhetoric of the day, which charged that Jackson was a tyrant who had ruined the country. It worked. Lawrence was tried (the prosecuting attorney was Francis Scott Key) but a jury acquitted him based on his insanity defense after deliberating for only five minutes. Unlike Dan Sickles, however, Lawrence was jailed and ultimately placed in an insane asylum where he remained for the rest of his life.[135]

The temporary insanity defense was obviously preferable and seemingly a blueprint any lawyer could use to get his client totally off on even a high-profile murder charge. In fact, the more outrageous or horrific the crime, the easier it would be to establish that the client was insane. After all, why else would he commit such a terrible offense? And given the "mystery and veil" that shrouded mental illness during this period, as well as the absence of modern diagnostic techniques, how could the prosecution ever overcome a clever defendant's acting job and the cooked-to-order testimony of the defendant's (or his lawyer's) respected family doctor?

George Gayle nearly placed himself in a position that might require him to assert an insanity defense. In a series of extraordinary articles published in the *Dallas Gazette* and other Black Belt newspapers, Gayle presumed to critically evaluate members of the lower court judiciary in his biting style. Among Gayle's targets was James Blair Clarke, the equally volatile Chancellor of the Middle Division of Alabama, who was charged by Gayle with "tyranny" and "unfitness for the office he holds."[136] According to Gayle, Clarke was not only "an ungrateful man, necessarily wanting the element of a good heart so indispensable in a Chancellor," but a "tyrant to the officers of his court ... the members of the bar ... litigants in court" and "prisoners in jail." Gayle also accused Clark of playing "favorites among the members of the bar," a pet peeve of lawyers of every era. Gayle, who wrote these articles under the pseudonym "MARSHALL," but whose identity as their author was apparently well known, impudently averred that his "anxious desire" in so publicly venting his spleen was that his "*quondam* friend" might "learn to improve himself!"[137]

The unnamed "favorites" of the targeted judge were bound to come to his defense. Sure enough, anonymous letters attacking Gayle written under the pseudonym "Joseph" began appearing in other newspapers.[138] For some reason Gayle mistakenly assumed that "Joseph" was actually George Washington Stone, then a forty-two-year-old lawyer who had previously served as a Circuit Judge before resigning and establishing a law practice in neighboring Lowndes County.[139] Gayle published a counterattack charging "Joseph" with improprieties but not expressly referring to Stone by name. Nonetheless, Stone took offense and demanded that Gayle admit he was "Marshall" and that he intended the article to refer to Stone. When Gayle admitted both requests conditioned on Stone admitting he was "Joseph," Stone challenged Gayle to a duel by using the typical euphemism of suggesting in a note that they resume "our correspondence out of the State of Alabama." Backing down from challenges was not in the feisty Gayle's personality, and his acceptance was delivered to Stone's representative.[140] But as would be reported across the South, after the parties finally agreed on Stone's proposal that their "correspondence" would take place in Pascagoula, Mississippi, where yellow fever was then rampant, cooler heads finally prevailed on them to submit their dispute to a "Board of Honor," akin to an arbitration panel. After what appears to have been a very brief period of examination, the Board, which included John Forsyth and three others selected by the parties, rendered a widely publicized decision concluding that because

Stone was not "Joseph," there was "no foundation whatever for any controversy" between Gayle and Stone. The Board did fault both for having "acted hastily and without due reflection." Gayle, it held, should not have assumed Stone was "Joseph," and Stone should have immediately informed Gayle that he was not.[141] George Gayle thereby avoided his own death, or alternatively a murder charge. He would ultimately face both. Meanwhile, he would continue with his extensive law practice, as well as his political activism, and soon complete the radicalization process.

The growing Calhoun State Rights faction was, meanwhile, handed another opportunity to consolidate its power using the slavery angle. Heretofore obsessed with protecting the institution where it was, the efforts of the Republic of Texas to be annexed to the United States offered them the possibility of expanding slavery and the nation.[142] Annexation of Texas was immediately popular in Alabama as evidenced by what were described as "demonstrations in favor of Texas" in Tuscaloosa and elsewhere.[143] In Jacksonian North Alabama, some adopted a resolution shockingly declaring that the "possession of Texas is infinitely more important to us of this section of the Union, than a longer connection and friendship with the northeastern states, and if we have to yield either it cannot and shall not be Texas."[144]

But at the time, the odds-on favorite to receive the Democratic nomination for the presidency, Martin Van Buren, had not revealed his current stance on Texas. George Gayle, nonetheless, offered resolutions at the 1843 Democratic State Convention nominating Van Buren for the presidency and William Rufus King as his running mate, and offering a platform making no mention of Texas whatever. Despite some disagreement on this from supporters of John Calhoun, Gayle's resolutions were finally unanimously adopted.[145] But this certainly did not mean that the lid could be kept on the Texas issue and that Van Buren and King would receive the nominations when the Democrats met in their national convention six months later. A lot happened in the interim.

President John Tyler, who was seeking the nomination of either party that would take him, had begun negotiations with the Republic of Texas for a treaty of annexation. As part of this effort, Tyler also sought the support of John Calhoun's followers by selecting Calhoun as his Secretary of State to complete the negotiations.[146] Tyler then appointed William Rufus King to serve as minister to France,[147] a position King may have accepted because he knew the Texas issue would ultimately overwhelm Van Buren. It did after both Clay and Van Buren issued public letters opposing immediate annexation. Democrats then turned to James Knox Polk, not Tyler, as their presidential nominee after Polk announced his unconditional support for annexation. He would go on to win Alabama and the election.[148]

Tyler's appointment of King to a foreign post allowed Alabama governor Benjamin Fitzpatrick to appoint Dixon Hall Lewis to King's seat in the Senate.[149] This, in turn, opened Lewis' seat in the House.[150] Demonstrating that George Gayle had not yet sold his soul to the Calhoun faction, he challenged Dixon Hall Lewis protégé, William Lowndes Yancey, for the Democratic nomination to the House. But according to Selma editor John Hardy, who knew Yancey quite well, Yancey "smuggle[d] into the District Convention at Centreville, a lot of bogus delegates from Coosa and Autauga counties to secure his nomination over Col. George W. Gayle, who was the favorite among the Democracy of the district for Congress. Yancey secured the admission of his bogus delegates into the Convention," Hardy alleged, "and he was nominated for Congress, and the Democrats rather than raise a disturbance, and for the sake of their party, permitted the election of Yancey."[151] Demonstrating the impact of Henry Clay's unpopularity within the Whig party in Alabama, Yancey defeated his Whig opponent by 718 votes in a district that had given a 655 vote majority for Harrison in the 1840 presidential election.[152] Even more telling, when the pro-Democrat *Florence Gazette* endorsed George Gayle for the next governor's race, the pro-Whig *Selma Free Press* seconded that idea.[153] But the incumbent, Benjamin Fitzpatrick, eventually received the nomination and was elected without opposition.[154]

When the legislature met in December, Gayle sought to have William Rufus King returned to his Senate seat. Both apparently assumed that— as Gayle put it—this could be done "by the spontaneous action of the legislature." But Gayle quickly concluded that since King's departure for France, Lewis and the Calhoun element had become even stronger, so much so that Gayle withdrew King's name from nomination in the Democratic caucus that preceded the vote in the legislature.[155] One of Calhoun's supporters reported to Calhoun the happy news of the result of the caucus vote: "your friend D.H. Lewis is to retain his seat" and Alabama Calhounists "hail this result, as a demonstration in favor of your peculiar views."[156] But in the process, Lewis suffered an embarrassing setback. According to John Forsyth's newspaper, "during the progress of the elections," the gargantuan Lewis sat on one of the benches in the lobby and "crushed the frail seat and received a mighty fall upon the floor."[157]

George Gayle favored the acquisition of Texas. With the support of Alabama's entire congressional delegation, Congress adopted a joint resolution consenting to the admission of Texas to the Union, but William Yancey's antics marred the process.[158] In his maiden speech, Yancey insulted a Whig member from North Carolina and ended up in a duel in

Maryland where the bullet of neither found its mark.[159] A few months later, George Gayle announced that he would run against Yancey in the August congressional election. For some unknown reason, however, Gayle abruptly withdrew from that race and announced he would seek a seat in the Alabama legislature.[160] As a result, Yancey was reelected without opposition, but Gayle's breach of party etiquette protecting incumbents was taken personally by Yancey and contributed to a gradually widening rift between the two principal factions within the Alabama Democratic Party, the relatively moderate King faction to which Gayle was still attached, and the more extreme, pro-Calhoun faction of which Yancey and Dixon Hall Lewis were members.[161]

Gayle, however, won his subsequent bid for a seat in the legislature. The primary issue at that time was whether the state capital should be moved from Tuscaloosa, and if so, where. According to one political observer, Gayle's election in August of 1845 was "mainly with the view of having his influence in the Legislature on the removal question, as Selma put forth claims for the new Seat of Government."[162] Selma was among several towns vying for this prize.[163] Local Whigs likely recognized that the key for Selma would be the votes of primarily Democratic North Alabama legislators who were usually loyal to the King faction, and so Gayle was a logical choice to lead the charge for this potent economic engine in a time of continuing economic depression.[164]

Gayle was such an outspoken and determined leader of the removal forces that he became the primary target of fierce rhetorical barbs by those who preferred that Tuscaloosa remain the home of the capital. After Gayle made a speech in the House gloating over the increasing number of "new recruits" in the legislature for the "Ship Removal" resulting from a questionable procedural trick, a North Alabama Union Whig, Thomas Peters, blasted Gayle as an "arch deceiver" and the "Great Mokanna," a reference to the villain in a well-known Irish poem, *The Veiled Prophet of Khorassan.* In that poem, the Mokanna is a veiled, charismatic, messiah figure who is practiced in the arts of deception and manipulation. He dupes his followers into believing he is a god who will, through revolution, lead them to freedom and equality, but who actually leads them to destruction in the end.[165] Gayle would eventually help lead Alabama to destruction, but he was unsuccessful in bringing home the state capital to his constituents. That prize, instead, went to Montgomery County, which had promised to build a new capitol building at no expense to the state.[166]

Even though George Gayle probably owed his election to the legislature to the Whigs of Dallas County, he could not resist bringing party politics into this session. He gained national attention and a rebuke from the pro-Whig *Mobile Advertiser* when he introduced resolutions condemning the federal tariff and the Whig policy of enacting protective tariffs.[167] Another issue that arose during Gayle's service in this legislature involved efforts by William Yancey to remove his legal disqualification for political office arising from the duel in which he was involved in Maryland. Alabama's Democrat governor, Joshua Lanier Martin, refused to issue a pardon to Yancey, and so the Calhoun faction pushed a bill of very questionable constitutionality through the legislature to attempt to accomplish that result. Martin vetoed that bill, but the legislature overrode his veto, a pyrrhic victory for Yancey given the high likelihood that the bill could be struck down by the courts as a violation of the separation-of-powers doctrine.[168] This was the last time George Gayle would hold political office. But he would remain politically active, and events would soon drive the Great Mokanna toward a level of extremism that would ultimately lead to secession, civil war, and the destruction of Alabama's economy.

CHAPTER 2

"Leave This Accursed Union"

IN May 1846, a war erupted with Mexico that John Calhoun had opposed but in which some young Alabamians were anxious to participate.[1] The New Orleans *Picayune* reported that a "very large meeting was held at the town of Cahawba on the 15th inst. for the purpose of raising volunteers, and a company of 53 was formed who tendered their services to the Governor." In addition, "the Selma Rangers also tendered their services."[2] No evidence appears to exist that George Gayle was one of these volunteers. To be fair, by this time Gayle had remarried and had another child on the way. His new wife, Massachusetts native Joanna Gleason of Tuscaloosa, would bear him two more children in the coming years.[3] How this marriage affected Gayle's relationship with William Rufus King is unknown.

William Yancey did not volunteer to fight either. He did not even remain in Congress, choosing instead to shock all political observers by abruptly resigning that summer and moving to Montgomery to practice law. There he entered a partnership with the brothers-in-law of Dixon Hall Lewis, John Archer Elmore, and Elmore's brother, Rush Elmore.[4] By contrast, Rush Elmore left that law practice and patriotically led a 105-man company called the Montgomery Blues from Montgomery to the front even before any requisition was made by the federal government for Alabama troops.[5]

George Gayle was spoken of as a likely candidate to replace William Yancey in Congress, but he did not receive the nomination.[6] If Gayle had been elected, he would have witnessed the most shocking—at least to him—display by a northern Democrat since the birth of the Republic. A Pennsylvania congressman, Democrat David Wilmot, proposed that slavery be prohibited in any lands acquired from Mexico in peace negotiations. When Wilmot successfully rode this idea to reelection, Northern politicians in both political parties took note. So did those in the South.[7] Wilmot's radical proposal never passed both houses in Congress, but its popularity in the North raised anxieties in Alabama, particularly in counties like Dallas where there were large slave populations.

To those who were fully radicalized, this was a golden opportunity to now sever the South's connection with its strongest remaining political tie to the Union, the National Democratic Party. William Yancey bellowed that the South ought to have nothing more to do with Democrats of the north or west. In "such a party organization, the South, which is the only portion of the party sound on all [the key] questions, is used merely to foot the bill, and to aid in giving a power which shall give to our Northern brethren the spoils!" Yancey declared that the South should "never again meet in a common Democratic Convention" these men "who have vigorously opposed us on principle.[8] Less than two months later, Mobile attorney John Archibald Campbell, a frequent correspondent of John Calhoun's, declared that "party distinctions and differences which have so long disturbed the peace of the country should find their termination," and the convention system for nominating presidential candidates "ought to be destroyed."[9]

Others, however, were still unwilling to renounce these traditions, although their pledge to support their respective party's nominees was fatefully made conditional. On May 3, 1847, a bipartisan meeting attended by George Gayle and James M. Calhoun took place in Cahawba where resolutions were adopted declaring that Congress had no power to adopt any law affecting slavery, and that no candidate for the office of President and Vice President would be supported who did not pledge to oppose and veto any anti-slavery legislation by Congress, or who did not favor the extension of slavery south of the Missouri Compromise line in lands acquired from Mexico.[10] The Montgomery *Flag and Advertiser* likewise allowed that on the question of the exclusion of slaves from any new territories, "we know no distinction of party—we are Southern men; and we shall hold all Wilmot proviso men—we care not whether they choose to call themselves whigs or democrats—as enemies to the South and traitors to the constitution."[11]

But as demonstrated by the efforts of Dixon Hall Lewis to be reelected to the United States Senate, and thereby further position himself as a possible nominee for Vice President on the Democratic Party's ticket in the 1848 national election, personal ambition and the tug of party loyalty created headwinds to the creation of John Calhoun's Southern

Party. Thus, while William Yancey denounced the Democratic Party, Lewis sought to strengthen his connections with northern Democrats.[12]

George Gayle subsequently attempted to ride the Wilmot Proviso protest into Congress, but again did not receive the nomination.[13] Lewis's quest for the vice presidency, in turn, compelled William Rufus King to challenge Lewis for his Senate seat. King's ensuing campaign, which was managed by George Gayle,[14] forced Lewis even further from Calhoun's position in order to assure support from North Alabama Democrats in the Alabama legislature. The conquest of Mexico was very popular in North Alabama and John Calhoun's opposition to it was used by King's supporters to paint Lewis as anti-war. It was also alleged that Lewis had secretly pledged his support to the probable Whig presidential nominee, Mexican War hero and slave owner General Zachary Taylor.[15]

Lewis nonetheless defeated King, but only after giving written assurances to North Alabama legislators that he would support the Polk administration's war policies, *and* a Northerner as the next Democratic presidential nominee.[16] John Calhoun's friends in Alabama were aghast. John Archibald Campbell reported to Calhoun that "Mr. Lewis I fear, has made pledges which will greatly embarrass him and estrange his friends in this section."[17]

The effect of Lewis' defection from Calhoun's third-party movement was to force William Yancey to change his tactics. Rather than remaining aloof from the process of nominating a Democratic party candidate to replace Polk—who was not seeking reelection—Yancey attended the Alabama Democratic Party's convention in Montgomery in January 1848 and sought to prescribe conditions for the nominees to receive Alabama's support.[18] These conditions required the nominee to oppose the Wilmot Proviso, a position with which most Alabama Democrats agreed.[19] Resolutions ratifying this proslavery extension presidential litmus test were adopted by party leaders.[20] If the Democrats could select a candidate who was not cut by its double edge, they could seemingly retain the White House for the next four years and protect the progress made on tariff reduction and other issues important to the South and the West.

As the voting of the Alabama delegation at the upcoming national convention would demonstrate, however, Alabama Democrats were deeply divided on the question of who should be the Democrats' nominee for president. The faction of the party led by William Rufus King supported King's friend (and some believe homosexual partner), James Buchanan of Pennsylvania. Then Secretary of State, Buchanan was planning to reciprocate by supporting King's bid for the vice-presidential nomination.[21] But William Yancey was supporting United States Supreme

Court Associate Justice Levi Woodbury, a New Hampshire Democrat and political associate of John Calhoun, for the presidential nomination. For the vice presidency, Yancey was backing quixotic John Quitman of Mississippi, a nullifier, Mexican War veteran, and militant southern expansionist. Quitman had visited Montgomery in December of 1847 where he had been honored during a celebration orchestrated by Yancey.[22]

Alabama Democrats did not formally endorse either Buchanan or Woodbury at the State Democratic Convention. They initially adopted a platform simply pledging to support whichever candidate received the nomination. In an effort to improve Woodbury's chances by tying the hands of the Alabama delegates at the national convention, however, Yancey offered six additional platform planks opposing any efforts to exclude slavery in the ceded Mexican lands unless by way of the extension of Missouri Compromise line or a state constitution by individual new states at the time of their admission as a state. In particular, a congressional prohibition on slavery in any new territories, recognition and continuance by Congress of existing Mexican law prohibiting slavery, and even the prohibition of slavery by territorial governments, was forbidden. Yancey also proposed that delegates selected to attend the national convention be instructed not to vote "for men for President or Vice President, who will not *unequivocally* avow themselves to be opposed to either of the forms of restricting slavery," and "who shall not *openly and avowedly* be opposed" to them.[23] Yancey's resolutions were adopted by the delegates, who included George Gayle, but as Yancey would discover, his wording actually allowed more leeway than he intended.

At the Democratic Party's national convention in Baltimore, Maryland, United States Senator Lewis Cass of Michigan received the presidential nomination despite his failure to oppose bans on slavery by territorial legislatures.[24] Obviously miffed, Yancey (who had been elected as a delegate) and another Alabama delegate voted for Quitman—and therefore against William Rufus King—for the vice presidential nomination after the first ballot, an embarrassing personal slight the King faction would never forget.[25] When the platform committee reported a platform simply declaring that Congress had no power to ban slavery in "the several states" and denouncing "all efforts of the abolitionists," but which was silent on the issue of slavery in the lands Mexico had, by then, ceded to the United States by treaty, Yancey, who had been placed on the platform committee, offered a minority report and an amending resolution stating that "the doctrine of non-interference" also applied in the territories. To his chagrin, not only was this amendment overwhelmingly rejected 216 to 36, but a large number of the votes against it came from southern delegates, including bell cow states like Virginia, Tennessee, and even

Mississippi. Consistent with their charge by the Alabama convention, the Alabama delegates voted in favor of Yancey's amendment, but it quickly became obvious that this was done as a matter of duty rather than conviction.[26]

Yancey found this out when he attempted to lead the southern delegates out of the convention in protest, and to his embarrassment only one other delegate, a young man from Montgomery, followed him.[27] Yancey continued his childish behavior in public appearances after the convention, beginning with a very controversial speech made in Charleston, South Carolina, during his trip back to Alabama. In that speech he portrayed himself as a martyr and patriot, while angrily accusing the pro-Buchanan members of the Alabama delegation of having "abandoned their principles" and disregarded their instructions in an effort to secure the vice presidential nomination for William Rufus King.[28] Yancey reiterated this theme in a speech in Montgomery, specifically charging that Addison Saffold, another of Reuben Saffold's sons and an Alabama delegate who was a member of the King faction, had announced at the national convention that he "would not vote for any candidate for the presidency whose friends were not favorable to making [King] Vice President."[29] Then Yancey made another effort to create a third political party to advocate "Southern rights," reaching out to disaffected Democrats as well as Whigs.[30] Cass, Yancey charged, was actually a supporter of the Wilmot Proviso and therefore not to be trusted.[31]

While Alabama Whigs watched with delight, King's faction attacked Yancey with great ferocity. Addison Saffold publicly ridiculed him for "supposing that he can assume the ridiculous attitude of planting himself upon some towering elevation, and in a tone and spirit of superiority dictate action to others."[32] George Gayle supported Cass, and in an editorial that he may have authored, the Cahawba *Dallas Gazette* blasted Yancey as akin to "the viper, ready to strike the hand that had warmed and nourished them." The editorial also characterized Yancey's positions as being "as wild and useless as the dream of a visionary, or the speculations of a mad man."[33] Similarly, a Mobile editor who was an acquaintance of Gayle accused Yancey of being motivated not by principle, but by "his ruling appetite—a thirst for notoriety" and "that disease of excessive ambition and egotism."[34] These attacks greatly undermined Yancey in what was probably his quest for a seat in the United States Senate. Both Alabama seats came open in the months leading up to the 1848 presidential election when Dixon Hall Lewis died, and Arthur Bagby was appointed Minister to Russia. Alabama's governor filled them with Cass supporters, however, William Rufus King and Benjamin Fitzpatrick.[35]

Telegraph wires finally reached Cahawba in the summer of 1848, and the very first message transmitted to the town announced that Zachary Taylor had received the Whig nomination over Henry Clay.[36] For Democrats, this product of new technology was an evil omen. It meant that the Whig party would likely survive in the South.

On many levels, the forthcoming announcement that gold had been discovered in California was also an omen. Initial reports greatly exaggerated the extent of the find and the ease by which anyone could instantly become rich. According to a report that appeared in a Huntsville newspaper in September 1848, "the gold is obtained on the surface of the earth to three feet deep—the workmen needing only a pickaxe and a shovel to dig up the dirt, and a tin pan to wash it in."[37] With the price of cotton still in the doldrums and most Alabamians insolvent and unable to pay their debts, the news from California was seen by many as a godsend.[38] And as a Mobile newspaper observed, "a wild fever is pervading many parts of our country in reference to these regions. 'Ho! For California!' is the cry."[39] The California Gold Rush was on.

Many southern slave owners envisioned selling or taking their redundant slave populations to this new Eldorado, there putting them to work mining for gold.[40] But the South was not the only interested party. Fear of losing California gold to slave owners made sectional conflict over the extension of slavery even more acute.[41] A proposition in Congress to abolish slavery in the District of Columbia was, moreover, seen in Alabama and elsewhere as a signal that nonextension of slavery would be followed by its ultimate abolition.[42]

At least initially, cooler heads prevailed in Alabama. The editor of the Tuscaloosa *Independent Monitor* maintained that most of the South recognized that disunion was no remedy for these threats. "Of South Carolina we say nothing; for South Carolina is a moral and political anomaly, of which nothing is too wild or mad or absurd to be expected."[43] Jefferson Buford, a south Alabama Whig who was among a number of South Carolina émigrés who resided in Black Belt Barbour County, warned that the public discussion of disunion to avoid abolition where "slaves are auditors" and could hear this talk was making the slave population there "restless, unhappy, vicious and dangerous."[44]

Cass narrowly won Alabama, but Taylor prevailed in Dallas County and nationally.[45] Shortly after his inauguration, Taylor appointed John Gayle, one of his key Alabama supporters, Alabama's lone federal district judge.[46] Taylor, though a southern slave owner, proved to be a disappointment to the South with regard to the extension of slavery. In President Polk's final address to Congress, he recommended that the Missouri Compromise line be extended to the Pacific Ocean, thereby guaranteeing slavery at least to Southern California.[47] But Taylor did not endorse that idea in his inaugural address or push for its adoption in Congress.[48] Then it was revealed that New York Senator William Henry Seward, an ardent free-soiler, was one of Taylor's principal advisers.

This, in turn, caused mainstream Alabama Democrats to again move toward the Calhoun Southern Rights wing of the party.[49] Fearing defections from their own ranks, Alabama Whigs fought back, charging that this latest wave of propaganda was being manufactured by the "politicians of South Carolina." "It has been their constant aim," wrote the editor of the *Mobile Advertiser*, "to depreciate the value of the Union and exaggerate the benefits of disunion."[50] Senators William Rufus King and Benjamin Fitzpatrick nonetheless supported the efforts of John Calhoun to produce southern unity. Both signed his famous Southern Address charging the North with a long list of aggressions against the South in general, and slavery in particular. Calhoun warned that there would soon be enough free states to adopt a constitutional amendment abolishing slavery, and he used a classic parade-of-horribles argument to encourage southerners to unite against the doom he prophesied.[51]

Support for the extension of the Missouri Compromise line to the Pacific Ocean was, meanwhile, growing in Alabama.[52] At a rally in Cahawba, the crowd pledged resistance unless that policy was adopted.[53] At the same time, Taylor's approval rating in Alabama was sinking while previously disaffected Democrats—including William Yancey—were returning and being welcomed back to the Democratic fold.[54]

But there was no sign of unanimity in Congress. On January 15, 1850, William Rufus King wrote George Gayle from the nation's capital that the "slavery question is the all absorbing subject here, and how it is to terminate God only knows." King vaguely assured Gayle that all of his efforts were aimed at reaching a compromise, if possible, of "this dangerous question" that would "maintain the honor and constitutional rights of the slave holding states" and "prostrate this fanatical spirit and preserve the Union as found by our fathers." But King also vaguely represented that if the "aggressions upon our rights continue," he intended to "resist at every hazard," and at "every sacrifice"—commonly understood to mean secession—if necessary.[55]

No compromise was immediately forthcoming, and in the midst of this acrimonious session of Congress, John Calhoun died of tuberculosis on March 30, 1850. South Carolina's governor appointed Calhoun supporter Franklin Elmore, the brother of Montgomery lawyer John Archer Elmore, to Calhoun's seat in the Senate. But he too became ill and died, leaving the door open for Robert Barnwell Rhett to be selected when the South Carolina legislature met late that year.[56] Patient negotiation was not

Rhett's style. He was determined to fulfill his and Calhoun's dream of a southern political convention organized to present an intimidating, united front to the North on the issue of slavery.[57]

There was division in Dallas County over whether such a convention would do any good. A majority of those who attended a meeting in Selma opposed it, but the result was different in Cahawba.[58] At least publicly, for some of those who favored a convention, the goal now was to attempt to scare the North with threats of secession should slavery be banned from California.[59] A convention of delegates from southern states was ultimately held in Nashville, Tennessee, in June 1850.[60] As part of Whig strategy in the upcoming congressional elections in Alabama, the *Mobile Advertiser* charged that the convention was orchestrated by the "politicians of South Carolina" to encourage disunion.[61] As the Alabama press reported, Rhett and other South Carolina radicals were, indeed, very active behind the scenes at the convention, and Rhett authored the threatening public address adopted by the delegates.[62] He also took to the stump in South Carolina and Georgia favoring secession if the Missouri Compromise line were not extended.[63]

Rhett's open agitation for secession fell flat in North Alabama. It was ridiculed as "Rhettism" by the pro-Whig Huntsville *Southern Advocate*, and the pro-Democrat *Florence Gazette* assured that "the word Rhett, will soon become synonymous with treason." The *Gazette* also erroneously predicted that Alabama would never "be induced on any consideration to follow the madcaps of South Carolina."[64] And in terms of assuring slavery in some part of California those madcaps' efforts were an abject failure. After President Taylor died of cholera in July,[65] a compromise was reached in Congress under which slavery was effectively banned throughout California. Alabama's entire congressional delegation voted against it, but that was to no avail.[66]

William Rufus King had voted against the admission of California as a free state, but afterwards began to encourage Alabamians to stand down, cease agitation over slavery, and support what became known as the Compromise of 1850.[67] King's entire rationale for this about-face is beyond the scope of this particular book.[68] But as King would discover, putting the genie of radicalism back in the bottle in Alabama would prove more difficult than he anticipated, thanks in part to George Gayle.

Eufaula lawyer John Cochran observed that "there is amongst us here a leaven of disunion, which by a more or less rapid, but perceptibly certain process, will leaven the whole lump."[69] Like many, if not most, of the constituent elements of that leaven, George Gayle was a native of South Carolina, and that state's then intense opposition to the Compromise, and its very public preparations for secession, had led to talk of its subjection by federal military force. That, in turn, triggered strong anti-government, pro-secession feelings among its natives in Alabama,[70] leading a clearly frustrated Senator William Rufus King to write an Alabama constituent that "nothing short of divine interposition can prevent a dissolution of the Union."[71]

Part of his frustration arose from the complete radicalization and public defection of George Gayle. On September 19, 1850, ten days after the adoption of the bill admitting California in its entirety into the Union as a free state,[72] Gayle sent a letter prepared and signed by him and endorsed by forty-two other residents of the Cahawba area addressed to Alabama governor Henry Watkins Collier. It requested that Collier issue a call to convene the Alabama legislature in special session "for the purpose of having a convention of the people called to determine upon a proper mode of redress."[73] Federal investigators should have noted that Gayle cited the March 11, 1850, speech by United States Senator William Henry Seward in which Seward sought to undermine the constitutional protections afforded to the institution of slavery by boldly declaring to the outrage of Southerners that there was "a higher law than the Constitution," and that this law of God dictated that slavery should not expand and, instead, should be eliminated.[74] From this, Gayle argued that the bill admitting California as a free state was a prelude to an attack on slavery in the South that justified, "in our opinion, the strongest measure of redress; and, in view of our safety for the future, a withdrawal of Alabama from the Union is a matter worthy [of] the immediate consideration of a State Convention."[75]

As the Union Democrat editor of the Greensboro *Alabama Beacon* charged, Gayle and his followers actually wanted more than just *consideration* of secession.[76] At a subsequent rally at Cahawba, the speakers were reportedly "frequently interrupted by bursts of applause, especially those who took the extreme ground—all avowed themselves in favor of secession and gave their reasons." In addition, badges were worn by those in attendance with the inscription "If this be Treason, make the most of it."[77] And while upon returning to Alabama, William Rufus King was issuing letters and making public appearances around the state encouraging citizens to accept the compromise and cease agitation over the issue of slavery,[78] George Gayle was busy making speeches in the Black Belt counties denouncing the compromise.[79] King's longtime Cahawba organ, the *Dallas Gazette*, was meanwhile criticizing King as a "Trimmer".[80]

Gayle was subjected to a steady torrent of criticism and ridicule for his efforts, particularly from the Whig press. A correspondent of the *Mobile Advertiser* dubbed him "Windy Gale" and a member of the *genus* of "ravenus, blood thirsty, fire-eating, cannibal calibre heroes."[81] A correspondent to the Tuscaloosa *Independent Monitor* described Cahawba, Gayle's hometown, as "a kind of hospital for decayed politicians," and Gayle's pro-secession faction there as being afflicted by the "disunion epidemic."[82] Noting that a "Deaf and Dumb Asylum" was being constructed in Tennessee, the editor of the Huntsville *Southern Advocate* expressed regret that Alabama could not have a similar institution. Alabama, wrote its editor, "cannot attend to such trifling matters" because "her fire-eaters" wish to secede and destroy," and for this reason he thought the state "needs a large Lunatic Asylum."[83] That wish would later be fulfilled.

Democrat organs—particularly those in North Alabama—were similarly merciless. "Speaking of a called session of the legislature," wrote the editor of George Smith Houston's hometown newspaper, the *Athens Herald*, with his tongue firmly planted in his cheek, "we *would* like to see a squad of those South Alabama 'fire-eaters' assembled together. The way they would cavort, and snort, and rave, and rant, and pant and blow and swell, and drink and smoke, and pass funny resolutions, and kick the government into pieces with their high-heeled boots, and froth and foam—would be some[thing], it would. We expect they would even fight some, if they could get any body to 'come to the rescue.' You must pay your own expenses, though, boys, understand that before you start."[84]

Undaunted, Gayle went so far as to lead a group of approximately two hundred men into a pro-Compromise meeting in Cahawba on October 14, 1850, to warn of the probable repeal of the fugitive slave law and to propose the adoption of resolutions advocating "non-acquiescence." When the leaders of the pro-Compromise group ruled that these resolutions were out of order, Gayle's group reportedly "withdrew to the street, and amid shouts of 'Southern rights,' organized another meeting." Anti-Compromise resolutions were "unanimously adopted" after which Gayle and others "made speeches, in which 'they viewed secession as the only probable ultimate remedy.'"[85] Gayle certainly recognized that secession meant war, but he dismissed that risk. "If secession brings on a conflict of arms," he wrote, "let it come!"[86]

Senator King never openly denounced Gayle for his activities, but he was clearly unhappy. In one of King's public letters during this period, he criticized those "who are laboring to inflame still more the public mind, and to induce our people to believe that their only safety is to be found in a dissolution of the Union. With such men I have no sympathy—I am no disunionist." In the same letter King further declared that "as to the charges with which I have been assailed, of having proved faithless to the South—of being a craven Submissionist—they pass by me as the idle wind. I fully understand the motives by which those who make them are actuated, and I view their puny efforts to impair the confidence reposed in me by my honored constituents, with the contempt they deserve."[87]

Recognizing that Gayle was jeopardizing his own career by crossing King, United States District Judge John Gayle issued a public letter in which he encouraged a "kind and conciliatory course" toward those critical of the Compromise and claimed that their true object and purpose was not to dissolve the Union, but to "guard against future aggression, which they have, or think they have, every reason to anticipate." Judge Gayle also urged that the proper strategy was to "convince our Northern friends, that henceforth the hand of aggression must be stayed—that the South has been driven to the utmost verge of endurance—that the great legacy of the Constitution and the Union is in their own hands, to be disposed of as they may determine, and that it is for them to say whether they will hazard it on a game invented by the madness of fanaticism, and played and practiced by political Demagogues, or preserve it as the means of conducting this great and glorious republic to the high and exalted destiny that awaits it."[88]

But George Gayle was quite seriously advocating secession, and in this regard was supported by William Lowndes Yancey, who wrote a supportive public letter to Gayle and Gayle's followers. "I am for action, gentlemen, and not talking,"[89] Yancey claimed. Yet as they would soon discover, due in large part to economic relief through rising cotton prices, average Alabamians were becoming opposed to secession, leading Alabama Whigs to attempt to curry favor with the electorate prior to the 1851 state and congressional elections with a massive propaganda campaign intended to encourage acquiescence in the Compromise and, more importantly, to paint *all* of those who were critical of it as dangerous traitors to the nation who would selfishly risk civil war and the destruction of the South's way of life in order to achieve political dominance. As the Whig organ in Montgomery told its readers in its September 26, 1850, edition:

The issue now made is secession and disrupture of our glorious Union, under which we have enjoyed and are now enjoying prosperity and happiness as a people, such as the world and all history have never before exhibited. In exchange for this prosperity, we have the specter of Disunion appearing through the misty future, a fearful phantom, surrounded by all 'horrid shapes and crimes,' feuds implacable and merciless, hideous and blood stained—murder, incendiarism, and misery, in all the forms and grades with which it has visited man since the first Cain. Aside from those disastrous but inevitable effects, too terrible for contemplation, who will be benefitted? Certainly, not the property and slaveholder. Taxation, instead of being diminished, must be vastly increased. Slave property, so far from being safer, would be imminently periled, and its value greatly depreciated in the market. Who can be benefitted then? If any, only those who, having nothing to hazard, and every thing to gain, may survive, and succeed in riding the whirlwind and directing the storm to their own purposes.[90]

Wrapping themselves in the flag of Union, Whigs orchestrated a huge non-partisan rally in Mobile in early October,[91] and in an effort to attract moderate Democrats, arranged public dinners for Senator King in Tuscaloosa and Selma.[92] Recognizing that it was a Whig ploy, King graciously declined. But it was also apparent that some Democrats were recoiling from the prominence of pro-secession extremists in their party and were gravitating toward a Democrat-Whig coalition being promoted by moderate Democrats and Whigs.[93]

In October 1850, Governor Collier announced his decision refusing to convene the legislature into special session, thereby eliminating the possibility that any state convention would happen any time soon given that the legislature was not scheduled to meet for another year.[94] As a result, some of those who had signed Gayle's letter to Collier abandoned their demand for immediate secession.[95] But George Gayle did not. Responding to accusations that he was committing treason, Gayle wrote a widely published public letter declaring that it remained his intention to "openly advocate the secession of Alabama alone, from the Union, as soon as it can be done by a State Convention." In support, Gayle invoked the fate of whites in St. Domingo. The Union now was "not the Union of our fathers, but a Union hostile to the institution of slavery in the South—growing in its strength, and desperately set upon its destruction. Its longer continuance perils not only the right to private property, but the safety of our wives and children. In the language of a revolutionary patriot [Patrick Henry]," Gayle declared, "if this be treason, make the most of it."[96]

In the same letter Gayle also acknowledged his complete break with William Rufus King. By that prior allegiance, Gayle wrote, "I have sinned against South Carolina and her people, to my present shame; and, without any scruple, confess the gross injustice I have done them. She is the intrepid vanguard of the South, and our triumph or defeat in the pending slavery warfare, will be found in her high sense of our equality, her valor, and her determination. She is ready to maintain her rights, and pauses only, with 'her lance couched, and not a feather trembling in her cap.'"[97]

The editor of the pro-King *Florence Gazette* lambasted the "bold, dashing, chivalric, impetuous, Gayle." He had "at last, unceremoniously 'submitted,' soul and body to the nullifiers and disunionists of South Carolina." Referring to his mea culpa regarding the Palmetto State, the editor exclaimed:

"Whew! Jerusalem! Such a change is indeed sickening—as nauseating as coffee and castor oil! Uph! George is a good hater and used to hate the South Carolina nullifiers and all their kidney with a relish—a perfect hatred. He used to be regarded as a faithful disciple of the old pannel Jackson democracy... But alas! alack-a-day!! For poor frail human nature. George has been beguiled—surrendered horse, foot and dragoon. He has stultified himself—deserted his friends and gone over and joined his ancient enemies. The nullifiers and George W. Gayle have united!! Who would have thought it? They have laid down their arms and run into each other's embraces, smacked lips together and sworn eternal friendship. Verily, the millennium is not far off."[98]

As support for secession continued to diminish around the South, and some secessionists advocated against public declarations of support for separate state secession in order to avoid alienating moderates before upcoming elections, Gayle remained openly resolute in his advocacy of Alabama's secession even if no other state followed. He wrote a letter published in the *Dallas Gazette* in which he again declared that "I advise, mediate and openly advocate the secession of Alabama alone, from the Union, as soon as it can be done by a State Convention."[99] This was also Robert Barnwell Rhett's position for South Carolina.[100]

The Mobile organs of both political parties made short shrift of Gayle and Gayle's stance. Wrote the pro-national Democrat *Mobile Register*, "We apprehend that Col. Gayle, himself, stands well nigh *alone*, in the advocacy [of] this course."[101] The pro-Whig *Mobile Advertiser* observed that "He who had been the Ajax Telamon in the past trials of this tried and faithful statesman [King]—the very Murat of his battles—the Hotspur ever impassioned in the vindication of his political character and the assertion of his claims to distinguished honors—who had pursued the little South Carolina colony with virulent hate and an unwearied energy—who looked upon Palmetto as a political Upas tree—whose truculent wit, with the direst curse in the alphabet, had 'damned to fame' a portion of his opponents as 'C.P.'s' (for an explanation of which we must consult the mystic lore of the Cabala)—yes, even Giles deserted him and mustered in the ranks of his bitterest enemies." Never was "victory more complete than that of the chivalry. Verily the lion and the lamb shall lie down together, and a little child shall lead them."[102]

But Gayle remained determined, and for this he was given positive reinforcement by South Carolina secessionists. "Mr. Gayle," wrote one admiring Palmetto State editor, "does not beat about the bush, like a good many who hold the same opinions he does of the compromise, and intend the same course, but they talk of it gingerly, as if they were afraid to say all they think in plain unvarnished language."[103] Gayle cooperated with his and William Rufus King's old political adversary,

William Yancey, responding positively to Yancey's January 1851 call for a Southern Rights convention in Montgomery in February by engineering the selection of thirty delegates from Cahaba.[104] Among Gayle's goals was to give assurance to reluctant voters in South Carolina who, on February 10, 1851, were scheduled to elect delegates to a convention that would consider whether that state would secede in protest of the Compromise.[105] The intended message was that, unlike the 1830s when no other southern state supported South Carolina's effort to nullify the federal tariff or secede, this time South Carolinians would not be alone. As the approving *Charleston Mercury* put it on January 7, the Southern Rights Association movement in Alabama was "the first step to the exertion of a steady and active influence upon the whole community around them, *and upon the Southern mind at a distance.*"[106] If South Carolina could be convinced to secede, it was believed—and feared—other southern states would follow.[107] "Let South Carolina go out of the Union by herself, and if the federal government dares to raise her hand against her, the slave states will secede in a body, and fly to her rescue," wrote a secessionist in Montgomery.[108]

With such a large delegation from Dallas County, it was possible that Gayle could heavily influence, if not control, the convention's actions. Because of an outbreak of smallpox in the Montgomery area, however, turnout for that convention, which met at Montgomery's Estelle Hall on February 10, 1851, was lower than expected. Of the thirty delegates from Cahaba, only seven—including George Gayle—showed up. Only eleven of fifty-two counties had delegates present, and of these only twenty-two delegates were from counties other than Montgomery, Lowndes, and Dallas. The only North Alabama county represented was Talladega, whose four-man delegation was led by Talladega lawyer and South Carolina native Samuel Farrow Rice. [109]

Judging from newspaper reports throughout the nation, George Gayle and William Yancey appear to have dominated the event. But careful choreographing could no longer conceal differences between them on the process of secession. Consistent with his prior course, Gayle offered a set of resolutions that, when boiled down, proposed that Alabama secede alone if necessary, but only *after* both the adjournment of a Southern Congress which was tentatively scheduled for 1852, and a subsequent state convention to consider that congress's proposals. As Gayle correctly recognized, secession would require widespread public approval, or it would not take. This was the same plan being followed by Robert Barnwell Rhett and other secessionists in South Carolina.[110] Yancey, however, proposed an amendment advocating that Alabama secede only if another southern state seceded first. Given that South

Carolina was then expected to secede later that year, Yancey's resolutions predicted that the question of the secession of Alabama "is reduced to that of time and policy only."[111] Yancey's more conservative position was ultimately adopted.[112]

The *Charleston Mercury* nonetheless gave the resolutions its seal of approval. The proceedings in Montgomery "have been marked by a fine spirit, and show that there are wise as well as brave men in it."[113] The resolutions were published by the *Mercury* in their entirety,[114] but they were immediately denounced in Alabama by the mainstream Democrat press. The conventioneers were labeled "fire-eaters" and the *Mobile Register* deemed their proposed policy "a wild, Quixotic, injudicious and impracticable scheme, affording no remedy for past evils, and calculated only to plunge the country into irretrievable ruin. It is the worst form of political and social suicide; and would kill the patient instead of relieving his sufferings."[115] Even the generally pro-Yancey Montgomery *Advertiser and State Gazette* attempted damage control, denying that the resolutions should be considered as a platform for Southern Rights candidates across the state in the 1851 elections, instead of merely "an individual expression of opinion by the delegates assembled here representing their respective clubs."[116] The Whig press was also critical. "If they wish to destroy every hope for well-regulated liberty; if they desire to bring about the destruction of the institution of slavery, secession is the very best agent they can possibly recommend," wrote the editor of the *Mobile Advertiser*.[117]

With state and congressional elections in Alabama less than six months away, the proDemocrat press continued to minimize the significance of the convention as a reflection of Democrat candidates in Alabama. "We doubt," wrote the editor of the Greensboro *Alabama Beacon*, "if the majority of the voters of any one county in the State, could be polled to-day in favor of this proposition to secede."[118] Similarly, the Huntsville Southern Rights Association, whose president was former Governor Clay, avoided direct criticism of the secessionists but instead proposed as an alternative the establishment of a "general system of commercial non-intercourse with the North" as the proper response to northern aggression.[119] The Southern Rights Associations in some other counties expressly rejected the platform adopted in Montgomery.[120]

One object of Alabama Unionists was to convince South Carolinians that if they supported secession, they would go out of the Union alone. The February election of delegates in South Carolina had resulted in the selection of a pro-secession majority, but the *Mobile Advertiser* jeered that the turnout was light and that, in any event, "with all her talk and bluster, we have never supposed that South Carolina would be so silly as to make the attempt to leave the Union by herself. When she gets to the jumping off place she always finds some good reason for not making the final leap."[121] The editor of the Tuscaloosa *Independent Monitor* agreed. "Let Alabama, and other Southern states, in the approaching elections" set "the seal of condemnation upon all who advocate disunion or secession for causes that now exist." This would "open the eyes of the South Carolina disunionists to the fact that they need to expect no sympathy or cooperation in their headstrong, unreasonable course."[122] The editor of the Lafayette *Chambers Tribune* agreed. "We are willing to concede to South Carolina a spirit as much akin to madness as ever possessed any community of civilized people, but we do not think that the wildest headed of her pure blooded Huguenot sons would ever dream of secession but for the help which they expect from states which have shown no disposition to secede."[123] The *Selma Reporter*, a Whig organ, concurred.[124]

Alabama secessionists like George Gayle believed the reverse was also true; that a victory for Southern Rights candidates in Alabama would embolden South Carolinians. To this end, the Cahawba Southern Rights Club assembled on March 10, 1851, and adopted a series of resolutions reportedly "approving in its length and breadth the Montgomery Platform."[125] This dovetailed with the efforts of Robert Barnwell Rhett in South Carolina. If South Carolina seceded, Rhett assured, the other southern states would follow and there would be no war.[126] In this regard, he could cite George Gayle who, according to the pro-Whig Montgomery *Alabama Journal*, "advocates secession *per se*. There is no crawfishing, no throwing of grass, in his political composition."[127]

Gayle was certainly committed to disunion, but it is interesting that he again refrained from seeking elective office despite the fact that several of the members of the Southern Rights Association in Dallas County had declined to run for the legislature or Congress in the August elections. The editor of the pro-Union Whig *Mobile Advertiser* poked at Gayle on this topic. "Why don't Col. Gayle run for Congress? He would be considered, we suppose, as he understands the term, a true Southern Rights man. The Cahawba Club," he concluded, "is looking the way the crawfish went."[128] But in all likelihood, Gayle and the others saw which way the political winds were blowing in Alabama and realized that his degree of extremism was losing traction even in south Alabama.[129] William Yancey was apparently of the same mind, as he declined newspaper nominations for the governorship and Congress.[130]

For those that did enter the various races, the question with which they were met on the campaign trail was whether they favored Alabama providing support to South Carolina if it seceded and possibly went to war.[131] This was not only a litmus test for Unionists; secessionists like

George Gayle also applied it. When Governor Collier refused to commit one way or the other, but expressed concern that armed conflict with the federal government might "involve the members of the Union in the most bloody civil war known to modern times, if not to all history," Gayle urged that the States Rights Association that convened in Montgomery in June 1851 nominate a candidate to run against him. This idea was rejected, and Collier remained unopposed by any pro-secession candidate.[132]

Fearful of lukewarm support from other southerners, Unionists in South Carolina were, according to the Union element of the Alabama press, rallying support there in opposition to its unilateral—or "separate state"—secession.[133] The *Charleston Mercury* noted the response and attempted to rally support for its cause. It predicted that "if Southern States stand by and allow South Carolina to be warred against and crushed by the Free States in the great controversy in which she is engaged for the maintenance of the institution of slavery, they abolish slavery in the south" by sending a message "to the whole world, that the institution of slavery is at an end."[134]

Before South Carolinians went to their polls to select delegates to the Southern Congress in October, Alabamians went to the polls in August, and the result was likely bitterly received by both Gayle and Rhett. In the race for the congressional seat that included Dallas County, the incumbent Democrat only barely defeated a Unionist Whig.[135] All of the other congressional races were won by Unionists.[136] The Tuscumbia *North Alabamian* was ecstatic and joined in the chorus of anti-South Carolina rhetoric. "Well, the election is passed, and Rhettism in this region has received a drubbing at the hands of the sovereign people, which should serve as a caution in all time to come to political tinkers. Thanks to the stern patriotism of the yeomanry of the country, the South Carolina madcaps have received no 'aid and comfort' in their mediated treason from North Alabama."[137]

Nonetheless, political observers in Alabama worried over the fact that all Southern Rights candidates made a strong showing as a whole even though Union Whigs and Union Democrats had successfully forged majorities to oppose secession for now.[138] But the result in Alabama allowed Unionists in South Carolina to undermine the secession movement there, at least for the time being. The strategy of South Carolina Unionists was to convince South Carolinians that secession would inevitably lead to war and, therefore, should occur only when *each* of the slave states agreed that it was necessary and left the Union simultaneously. This was a seemingly insurmountable bar. As they, their opponents, and apparently everyone else well knew, this "cooperative state secession" doctrine was tantamount to foreclosing any possibility of secession, given the absence of that degree of cooperation among the Upper and Lower South slave states on most issues.[139]

But George Gayle still did not give up and instead continued to try to stir the pot in South Carolina. Although he declined an invitation to address a rally in Charleston in September, Gayle wrote a letter to be read to the crowd that the *New York Times* described as having been "written in the emphatic style, half italics and the other half exclamation points." In that letter, which was also published in Alabama newspapers, Gayle urged immediate secession and warned that if this did not occur the federal government would achieve emancipation of the slaves "through the levy of a direct tax, perhaps of three hundred dollars upon a slave." Gayle also ridiculed the idea of "submitting to federal aggression until we can get the co-operation of the South." "When a Southern Convention of only six or seven States could be assembled at Nashville while the Compromise bills were upon their passage and the Union trembling under an excitement upon the slavery question which it never before experienced, it is vain to talk of *co-operation for what the government may hereafter do.*" "When a subsequent Southern Congress has been appointed to be held in Montgomery, Alabama, in December next, and no other State but South Carolina has appointed Delegates to the same, is it not idle to talk of co-operation? We cannot, then, preserve slavery by *waiting for co-operation* .... Turn a deaf ear to the unwise counsels of co-operation before secession," he pleaded, and "wait no longer, but when your convention meets, invoke God's blessings and leave this accursed Union!!"[140]

The *Mobile Advertiser* unmercifully ridiculed Gayle for his dogged support of secession and, no doubt for consumption in South Carolina, portrayed him as unrepresentative of public opinion in Alabama. "George is a firm and consistent member of the Southern Rights party, and the only real *honest* man politically that we know of in that party. Indeed, all there is left of that party is, *George Gayle.*" Gayle, it continued, "now stands, 'solitary and alone'—but still grand and majestic in his —the sole embodiment of all the patriotism, all the courage, all the honest, and all the true southern feeling of the recently powerful but now defunct, Southern Rights party of this State." Gayle had, it concluded, been "cruelly deserted by those who professed to be with him and promised to stand by him; [and had] no press at his command through which to promulgate those burning sentiments of patriotism which are well nigh consuming his noble soul." But out of what the editor called "humanity" and "sincerest friendship," he elected to publish "this last and most elegant epistle of the 'chivalric George'," which was "doubtless *doomed to immortality.*"[141]

South Carolinians, like most Alabamians, had a different plan. The majority shocked most political pundits by repudiating Gayle, Yancey, and Rhett's pleas for immediate secession. They, however, left that door open in case further northern aggressions regarding slavery occurred.[142] Many believed that with South Carolina's capitulation, those aggressions were sure to come, and so Gayle, *et al.*, knew secession was still only a matter of time.[143]

The secession movement in Alabama did not die in 1851 in pursuit of its quarry,[144] unlike the relentless but doomed Captain Ahab in Herman Melville's nautical yarn, *Moby Dick*, first published at about this time.[145] It was, however, definitely at low ebb. The pressures applied by the existing party structure in preparation for the 1852 presidential election threatened the movement even further, despite warnings to its members to avoid involvement with either of the traditional national political parties.[146] George Gayle and his followers did not succumb to these pressures even though William Rufus King received the National Democratic Party's nomination for the vice presidency on a ticket with Franklin Pierce. When one Democrat organ in Alabama urged the *Dallas Gazette* to endorse the Pierce and King ticket on its masthead, the *Gazette's* editor coldly replied that "when the love of power and spoils becomes with us a stronger motive to action than the love of the South, we will." Until then, the *Gazette* would have "nothing to do with whiggery or democracy."[147] Gayle's failure to support King reportedly caused him to incur the "lasting resentment of his own kin-people."[148]

Gayle and many other South Alabama secessionists also refused to support the Virginia-born Whig nominee, General Winfield Scott, and instead nominated aging secessionist George Michael Troup of Georgia as the Southern Rights party candidate.[149] Troup obviously had no chance to win and even issued a letter stating that he intended to vote for Pierce and King.[150] But according to Gayle—who was selected as a Troup elector—and several other secessionists, it was necessary to back a third party candidate in order to prevent the total disintegration of the Southern Rights party organization through defections by Democrats and Whigs returning to their respective parties during the election campaign.[151] In this regard, Gayle was in lockstep with South Carolina secessionists. As one wrote, "we consider it as far more desirable for the South, that its enemies should triumph at the next election, than that it should be led to place a delusive reliance on what they will find when it is perhaps too late." Backing Troup "will yet be a commencement, a nucleus, around which our friends can gather to co-operate—and as we earnestly believe will prove the glimmery dawn of a glorious day for Southern rights and Southern Institutions."[152]

Yet, even William Yancey defected, announcing his support for Pierce and opposing any nomination by the Southern Rights Party apparatus in Alabama.[153] The editor of the formerly pro-Southern Rights, but now firmly pro-Pierce and King, Montgomery *Advertiser and State Gazette,* teased Gayle and others in response to a jab by the *Dallas Gazette.* He asserted that a few newspapers, including the *Dallas Gazette,* and "a few politicians who hang around them were the getters of [the Troup nomination]—the *life, soul* and *all* of it."[154] Given this, it was foreseeable that the only thing that would be accomplished by Troup's third party candidacy would be to prove precisely how weak that third party actually was in a period when scientific polling techniques were not yet dreamed of, and party support before an election was often assumed to equate with the decibel level of its supporters. But Gayle remained committed to Troup and opposed to both traditional political parties.[155] Troup received only 2,148 votes in Alabama, while Pierce and King—who was dying from tuberculosis—won by a landslide, including the state of Alabama, by a margin slightly greater than James Knox Polk in 1844. And for the first time since the creation of the Whig Party, the Democratic presidential ticket won Dallas County, ironically thanks to the fact that the Troup ticket siphoned off 244 votes presumably from the Whigs.[156]

The efforts of George Gayle and others had, nonetheless, endangered the nation by encouraging all Southerners to increasingly think in terms of sectional rather than national interests, and to seriously question whether the Union furthered or jeopardized those interests. They had already been successful in convincing a large minority of the Alabama electorate to vote for State Rights candidates in the 1851 congressional elections,[157] and were now just waiting for the next controversies to come along that would allow for an opportunity to agitate to increase that percentage.[158] On inauguration day the *Dallas Gazette* optimistically assured that the enmities engendered by a recent domestic sectional conflict, the fiercest witnessed since we became a nation, are liable to be rekindled at any moment by the slightest indication of hostility on either side. The party which so triumphantly elevated [Pierce] to power, and which is today exulting in its strength, possesses no adhesiveness, and may, ere the close of another year, become more feeble than its conquered foe. Blending in its ranks every antagonism known to the country, its continued harmony for four years would be more a miracle than its dissolution in one."[159]

As fate would have it, William Rufus King would not live to see the final bloody consequences of Gayle's actions, or even be able to attend a gathering called in his honor at Selma following the election. In his letter giving his regrets, King revealed that "the infirm state of my health, and the very limited time in which I must arrange my private affairs before setting out for Washington, will compel me to deprive myself of that pleasure."[160] While awaiting his inauguration, he nonetheless proceeded to Washington and took his seat in the Senate as President *pro tempore*, but abruptly resigned a few weeks later and was replaced by Benjamin Fitzpatrick. King did not immediately return home. Instead, he boarded a United States naval vessel that took him and an entourage to Cuba. The purpose of this trip was supposedly to recruit his health, but it may possibly have also been an effort to lay the groundwork for the purchase of that island, a key goal of the incoming Pierce administration. Perhaps symbolically, King took his oath of office there on March 24, 1853, pursuant to a special act of Congress before returning to Dallas County where he died on April 18 at age sixty-six.[161]

Presumably George Gayle attended the funeral of his long-time mentor, which was performed by an Episcopal priest at the gravesite near King's Dallas County mansion on his plantation, Pine Hill, six miles east of Cahawba.[162] The pro-Whig Montgomery *Alabama Journal* eulogized King as "though not, perhaps, brilliant, he was better-sensible, honest, never running into ultraism, but in the contests between the State and federal government, maintaining the true conservative medium, so necessary to the preservation of the constitution, the rights of the States and the Republic."[163]

Perhaps to George Gayle's surprise, President Pierce proceeded to make several appointments that seemingly gave credibility to those in the South who had participated in the Southern Rights movement. From Alabama he selected Mobile attorney John Archibald Campbell to a seat on the United States Supreme Court. Pierce also appointed future Confederate President Jefferson Davis of Mississippi to serve as his Secretary of War. It was a message that Southern Unionists took hard.[164] According to the *Dallas Gazette*, it was now established that the "isolated doctrine of State Rights, so long battled for, is at length yielded, and to day there is no more prominent principle in the democratic creed than that of State Rights."[165] That doctrine was something that no Alabama politician could ignore without consequences.

Another Southern Rights advocate, John Anthony Winston of Sumter County, received the Democratic nomination for governor of Alabama.[166] Winston had opposed the Compromise of 1850, but he had also supported Pierce and King.[167] Whether this made him suspect in George Gayle's mind is unclear, but it did cause pause to some. The *Dallas Gazette* quickly endorsed Winston,[168] but at a meeting of the Southern Rights Club of Dallas County, Gayle offered a resolution— which was adopted—declaring that the members of the club "will vote in the next State election in August, for the man or men, who entertain principles nearest those advocated by the Southern Rights Troup and Quitman party in the late Presidential election, and recommend the same course to be pursued by every friend of the South."[169] Gayle ultimately supported Winston but this likely had less to do with the slavery issue and more to do with the now burning local issue of state financial aid to railroads. Like Winston, Gayle opposed state loans and expenditures on behalf of private railroad construction, but advocated federal land grants for that purpose.[170] This was not the dominant view among Dallas County Whigs, but Winston narrowly won that county and garnered a landslide victory statewide.[171]

As George Gayle knew, however, this did not necessarily mean a uniform victory for southern rights statewide. Staunch Jackson County Union Democrat Williamson R.W. Cobb soundly defeated C.C. Clay, Jr. in the race for the Huntsville congressional district. Indeed, Clay did not win his home county of Madison or any other county in the district.[172] Later that year, however, Clay got the last laugh when he parlayed his Southern Rights credentials into a seat in the United States Senate.[173] Only thirty-six at the time, Clay would soon be thrust into a major political firestorm when two bills were adopted by Congress in 1854 that would be of little benefit to Alabamians, but outrage many in the North.

Designed by Illinois Senator Stephen Douglas to facilitate the construction of a railroad to the Pacific Ocean from the Upper Midwest instead of the South, these bills established the Kansas and Nebraska territories, while also expressly repealing the Missouri Compromise. This created the illusion that one or both of the future states, as well as any of the others above the old line, might become slave states.[174] Douglas had reluctantly agreed to the demands of South Carolina-born Alabama congressman Phillip Phillips of Mobile, then on the House Committee on Territories, and a contingent of southern senators, to include the repealer provision—which they may have assumed would serve as a poison pill to kill the bills. Douglas famously remarked that the repeal would "raise a hell of a storm,"[175] and a Mobile, Alabama, newspaper agreed. In an article titled "Signs of War," its editor observed that "it is generally apprehended that the bill of Mr. Douglas ... will restore the sectional difficulties which were buried by the public acquiescence in the compromise measures. Unless the South be ready for asserting an independent sovereignty," he opined, "all discussions of this sort are to be feared."[176] Striking while the iron was hot, the *Dallas Gazette* called for a movement of armed Southerners to the Kansas Territory to counter similar movements there by anti-slavery Northerners intent on assuring that the territorial legislature to be elected would ban slavery.[177]

Chapter 3

"The Slaveholder"

GEORGE Gayle and the Dallas *Gazette* would soon have another outside threat to target. The Republican party was being formed for the express purpose of opposing the spread of slavery.[1] The *Gazette's* remedy for this opposition to the rights of slave owners was simple. "They have thrown down the gauntlet of defiance, and shall we not accept it? It sometimes becomes necessary to fight instead of to sue for peace," its editor maintained, "and the time has now arrived when we must retaliate some of the gross injustice and wrong we have received at the hands of our Northern brethren. Let us give a few of the sleek and puritanical money seekers from beyond Mason's and Dixon's line, when they come among us, a coat of tar and feathers," he advised, "and if that will not do, let us see how they can 'dance on nothing.'"[2]

Among those George Gayle and other Southerners would later wish to see make that fatal dance was a little-known Illinois lawyer, Abraham Lincoln. A former Illinois Whig congressman, Lincoln came out of political retirement in 1854 in response to the repeal of the Missouri Compromise line. In a series of debates with Stephen Douglas, he boldly opposed the further spread of slavery. Although Lincoln also paradoxically maintained that he did not favor the forced abolition of slavery in the South, he made clear that, in his opinion, the institution was immoral. It was, Lincoln declared, a "monstrous injustice" that was "founded in the selfishness of man's nature."[3] Such sentiments were heresy to men like George Gayle.

Reports of the potential for more widespread armed conflict in the Kansas Territory were, meanwhile, teaming in the Alabama press.

According to those reports, pro-slavery settlers from Missouri formed armed units in the fall of 1854 to oust anti-slavery settlers from New England from lands the Missourians had claimed, prompting the New Englanders to militarize and tension to escalate. "Everything betokens war," wrote a correspondent. "God grant it may not come! but the passions of desperate men are the most unreasonable things in the world."[4] Shortly thereafter, the first election held in the Kansas Territory, which resulted in the selection of a pro-slavery delegate to Congress, generated apparently well-grounded charges by anti-slavery forces of election fraud on a massive scale, and calls by both sides for an even larger influx of settlers in order to influence the coming state elections in the spring of 1855 for seats in the territorial legislature.[5]

With sometimes exaggerated claims of the productiveness of Kansas lands being broadcast by land speculators, such appeals were probably unnecessary. According to a Philadelphia newspaper article published in early 1855, "the rush of emigrants to Kansas and Nebraska is astonishing." "At this rate," it predicted, "it will take but a single season to prepare the Territory of Kansas for admission as a State."[6] But what kind of state, in the geo-political sense, was the critical issue. When the pro-slavery faction succeeded—again allegedly with the aid of fraud—in winning a majority of the seats in the territorial legislature in April 1855,[7] and that legislature, sitting at Lecompton, began taking steps toward seeking admission as a slave state and calling for a constitutional convention to frame a pro-slavery constitution,[8] the approximately 8,500 beleaguered residents of the territory were brought considerably closer to civil war than to statehood.[9] Slowly but surely, so was the nation.

In Ohio, the pro-Republican *Cleveland Herald* asserted in a call for a state convention in the spring of 1855 that "if the outrage upon the rights of the Free States by the repeal of the Missouri restriction made it the duty last year to bury all minor differences in a united effort to arrest the progress of the slave power, how much stronger has that duty become by the more recent exhibition of fraud and violence at the Kansas elections, and the denial of the rights of citizenship and the possession of property to free citizens of Missouri and Kansas? The day of 'compromises' has gone by. We, therefore, appeal to our fellow citizens to be active and vigilant."[10] At about the same time, the *Montgomery Advertiser and State Gazette*, while condemning "one-idea men and one-idea parties as utterly unfit to accomplish any permanent good," was attempting to rally support for the Democratic party in the upcoming state elections in Alabama by hypocritically reminding its readers not to forget "the slavery question" arising from northern opposition to the extension of slavery to Kansas.[11]

For George Gayle, the issue of slavery in Kansas was not the only one that implicated his quest for secession. Of critical importance was retaining in office an Alabama governor who was dedicated to the Southern Rights agenda and who, unlike former Governor Collier, might accede to a request for a secession convention when the time came. In this regard, Southern Rights advocates assumed they had their man in Governor Winston. For this reason the *Dallas Gazette* editorialized in favor of his reelection.[12]

But Winston was increasingly vulnerable in some circles over his opposition to financial incentives by the state to railroad corporations for the construction of new railroads. John Hardy, the Unionist editor of the Selma-based *Alabama State Sentinel*, had savaged Winston when no aid was provided to the Alabama and Tennessee Rivers Railroad, whose southern terminus was in Selma. Hardy went so far as to call for a convention of the Democratic party to select a gubernatorial nominee other than Winston to lead the ticket in the 1855 state elections.[13] This was not standard procedure when an incumbent desired re-election.

Referring to the opposition of Hardy and others, the editor of the *Dallas Gazette* declared that "those who have any attachment to principle should no more regard the garrulous effusions of the papers mentioned than they would the sighing of a pig, or the moaning of a dog."[14] Thus began a cold war between Hardy and the fanatical Southern Rights faction in Dallas County that would continue unabated for the next decade.[15] George Gayle certainly shared the *Gazette's* sentiments,[16] and Hardy appears to have concluded that Gayle was behind the *Gazette's* criticism of him. Following a pro-Winston, anti-state aid meeting at the county courthouse in Cahawba on May 14, 1855, Hardy belittled and ridiculed not only Gayle but others at the gathering in his inimitable style:

> Col. Gayle, we learn, was fully in his glory, but would have been much better pleased if there had been more persons taking part in the meeting, as there were not more than five or six persons voting in the meeting on any one question. Take it altogether, we must confess that it was rather a slim affair—slimmer in fact, than the other immense meeting held at the same place on a *very cold day* when there were but few persons in town. As Col. Gayle has ruled us out of the democratic church, over which he presides as Chief Priest in Dallas, we, of course, can only occupy the position of an independent looker on, and therefore, have the privilege of speaking out. But speaking seriously, there are a few men about Cahaba who want to rule the democratic party of Dallas, and unless they can rule they have always been ready to ruin. If they ruled, the party was ruined, and in that way the democracy of Dallas has always been kept in the minority and always will be until a few of the present ambitious, would-be rulers, either emigrate or pass off of the stage of action."[17]

As it turned out, Hardy's attacks on Winston and Gayle were for naught, as Winston won his bid for reelection despite losing Dallas County.[18]

While George Gayle continued his role as ultra-extremist-supreme in Alabama politics, he hoped that the increasingly violent controversy over the western territories would finally radicalize a majority of the Alabama electorate. However, headwinds could already be felt as a result of another moderating presidential election cycle. It would be the last of that Union-saving type.

The presidential election year of 1856 was chock full of evidence that, as James Gordon Bennett's *New York Herald* predicted, the conflict over slavery—which he blamed on "two hundred thousand hungry lawyers"— would "rapidly carry us downward headlong into the condition of universal ruffianism and anarchy, from which there will be no escape but in the strong hand of some self-appointed military masters."[19] George Gayle continued to do his part to raise sectional tensions to the boiling point. He orchestrated his own election as a delegate from Dallas County to the Alabama State Democratic Convention in January 1856. There he offered a series of resolutions seeking to move Alabama toward secession. One called for all Alabamians to support no one for the presidency or for vice president who resided in a free state. Another recommended that Alabama Democrats boycott the national convention and support two southerners, Henry A. Wise of Virginia and Jefferson Davis. Yet another directed that "if the free states make another aggression upon the institution of slavery" within the next twelve months, the South ought to "dissolve this union of the American States" and "form a Southern Confederacy."[20]

Gayle likely realized that his resolutions had little chance of being adopted, and he may have had another goal in mind. There is some evidence that William Yancey, who was the chairman of the convention's resolutions committee, and who was named one of two at-large electors of the state, had succumbed to personal ambition and was angling for a cabinet appointment if the Democrats won the presidency again.[21] Yancey had just reported several more conservative resolutions when Gayle offered his, and it is possible that Gayle was attempting to embarrass Yancey for Yancey's dedication to the party.[22] According to the report in the *Montgomery Advertiser and State Gazette,* the reading of Gayle's resolutions "caused considerable merriment."[23] Another delegate sought to embarrass Gayle by suggesting an even more extreme resolution, calling for Alabama to take Northerners in the state hostage if any Alabama slaves were abducted. This too reportedly "gave rise to considerable merriment," and in reply Gayle announced that he would support the measure "if the penalty for the second offense should be hanging."[24]

But Gayle was not kidding about the dissolution of the Union, or a zero-tolerance for further anti-slavery activities. At the same time, he was quite willing to continue to promote sectional controversy during this very frightening period in the nation's history. Reports reached Alabama that on May 21, pro-slavery forces in the Kansas Territory sacked the free-soil town of Lawrence, and three days later abolition terrorist John Brown led a squad that massacred pro-slavery settlers near Pottawatomie.[25] Like adding fuel to the already raging fire there, George Gayle organized a meeting in Cahawba in support of efforts to send more money and pro-slavery settlers to that growing war zone.[26] A few months earlier, Jefferson Burford and other South Carolina natives living in Barbour County, Alabama, had organized efforts to send emigrants from the South to the Kansas Territory in hopes of controlling its future politics on the issue of slavery.[27] Despite every encouragement, however, the response from slave owners had been minimal.[28] According to one report, by mid-1856 there were "not a hundred slaves in the territory." Alabamians knew that anti-slavery emigrants from the North were becoming increasingly militant and that emigrants sent there through the efforts of Gayle and others could only broaden and intensify the conflict.[29]

Later in the year Gayle's bitter opposition to the Democratic party's 1856 presidential nominee, James Buchanan of Pennsylvania, made national news. "However much I have esteemed Mr. Buchanan as a Democratic statesman, of the patriarchal order," he wrote, "I hold the preservation of slavery, assailed as it now is, as of highest importance, and I will not vote for him because he believes that 'Congress has exclusive jurisdiction over slavery in the Territories'—a policy of indirect abolition."[30] In the end, Gayle did not vote for any of the three candidates in the election.[31]

Hopeful that the Republican party's nominee, John Fremont, would win the election, the *Charleston Mercury* assured its readers that the resulting "speedy dissolution of the Union" was a "fixed fact." So sure of this, its editor was already writing editorials regarding "the terms on which the Southern States should unite in a confederate government."[32] Buchanan nonetheless won Dallas County and Alabama and he also beat Fremont.[33] But according to the *New York Herald*, it was not merely because of Buchanan's southern supporters. Instead, it was ironically the result of the extreme stance taken by men like George Gayle, which scared many. "No doubt, to us, the threats of disunion, the talk of civil war and forced marches on Washington, appear very poor and sorry stuff; but no matter how sorry and absurd they were, they indicated a diseased state of the public mind in the South; and that diseased state of mind was enough to alarm commercial classes in the central States, where nearly all commercial interests of the country are concentrated."[34]

Whether this was accurate or not is, of course, unknown, but the upshot was that, absent some compelling event, secessionists would have to wait until the 1860 presidential election to try again. William Yancey blissfully declared that "there is hope for us in the Union" because the South has the "power to control that great Democratic Party," and that party has the "controlling power in the Union."[35] But in South Carolina, Robert Barnwell Rhett did not see it that way at all. The North still controlled Congress and was free to continue to pursue northern interests antagonistic to those of the South. "Tyranny is ever sateless," he declared, "and usually goes on plundering, torturing, or crushing its victims to the last."[36]

For George Gayle and others who examined the vote totals for the three presidential candidates, the results of the 1856 election were harbingers of opportunity. Buchanan had won only three northern states and but a plurality of the popular vote.[37] The Republicans were growing in strength, Gayle later wrote, and "in 1856 they ran Fremont, the abolitionist for the Presidency, against Buchanan and [Millard] Fillmore, and came very near electing him."[38] Gayle and other secessionists recognized that if Buchanan's two opponents had not split the vote against him, the Democrats might have lost the election.[39] The chance the opposition to the Democrats would unify in the 1860 presidential election was substantially increased by the United States Supreme Court's very controversial split decision in the famous *Dred Scott* case in 1857 holding that persons of African descent were not citizens of the United States and had no right to sue in federal courts regarding their enslavement, but also gratuitously announcing in *dictum* that Congress had no authority to ban slavery from any western territory.[40]

Coincidentally, George Gayle was in Washington at the Supreme Court going through the process of being admitted to practice before that Court on the very day Chief Justice John Taney read the Court's blockbuster opinion.[41] He, therefore, had an opportunity to witness the very negative northern reaction to the decision first-hand. The editor of the *New York Tribune* expressed public outrage, declaring that the upshot of the decision was "that *Slavery is National;* and that, until that remote period when different Judges, sitting in this same Court, shall reverse this wicked and false judgment, the Constitution of the United States is nothing better than the bulwark of inhumanity and oppression." Until then, the editor continued, one would consider slaves as property from a constitutional standpoint, and "no local or State law can either prevent property being carried through an individual State or Territory, or forbid its being held as such wherever its owner may choose to hold it."[42] This misrepresented the Court's holding, but the perception that pro-slavery interests had once again succeeded in projecting slavery where it did not belong encouraged northern Whigs, who had supported the relatively moderate Millard Fillmore in the presidential election, to strongly consider joining forces with the Republicans in the next election cycle. Just as significantly, some northern Democrats were also defecting.[43] If that trend continued, civil war was a distinct possibility following the 1860 election.

Fear of war influenced the Alabama gubernatorial election in August 1857. For the first time in many years, a South Carolina native, Perry County attorney Andrew Barry Moore, was nominated and then elected without opposition.[44] When the legislature convened, James M. Calhoun was unanimously elected president of the Alabama Senate.[45] Concerns about civil war also materially assisted C.C. Clay, Jr., in his effort to overcome serious opposition from former Governor John Winston and North Alabama Unionists to Clay's reelection to the United States Senate during the 1857-1858 legislative session. His opposition could not unite on a single candidate, so they decided to oppose the resolution offered by Clay's supporters calling for the election to take place during this session, hoping to fight this battle after Clay's term expired in 1859. But thanks in part to the lobbying efforts of newly elected congressman J.L.M. Curry of Talladega, eleven North Alabama Senators and a majority of the North Alabama House members voted for the resolution, joining a large majority of the legislators from south Alabama.[46] The election was anti-climactic as no one was nominated but Clay, and he was reelected for a term that would not end until March 4, 1861.[47]

This legislature, which honored the late John Calhoun by renaming Benton County in his honor, also unanimously adopted a joint resolution requiring Governor Moore to call for the election of delegates to a state convention if Congress refused to admit Kansas with the pro-slavery "Lecompton" constitution. Such a convention, according to the resolution, was to determine a "course of action" for Alabama's citizens. Whether the convention's determination was then to be submitted to the people for their ratification was unstated.[48] The editor of the pro-Union Tuscaloosa *Independent Monitor* saw the resolution for what it was. "We regard those resolutions as the most conspicuous overt act that has yet been made in the beginning of the new War in Alabama for dissolving the Union." The editor also feared that the trip wire established by the resolution would be sprung, just as the secessionists had planned all along. "We believe the Lecompton constitution *will be refused* by Congress. Every evidence before us tends to confirm this conviction."[49]

Increasing the chances that this convention mechanism would be utilized, Illinois Senator Stephen Douglas alienated many in the South when he attacked the Lecompton constitution on the basis that it had not been ratified by the residents of the Kansas Territory. In this, Douglas was acting contrary to the position of President Buchanan.[50] Supported by a fiery, threatening speech by C.C. Clay, Jr., a bill admitting Kansas in accordance with Buchanan's recommendation passed the United States Senate, but it ran into opposition in the House.[51] This, in turn, led to calls in Alabama for Governor Moore to follow the legislature's instruction and call for the election of delegates to a convention.[52] But technically, Congress had not yet *refused* to admit Kansas and so Moore took no action.

It was during this period that another Southern Commercial Convention met, this time in Montgomery. Predictably, the Convention selected a South Carolinian, Andrew Pickens Calhoun of Marengo County, Alabama, to serve as president of the convention. Like his famous late father, Calhoun warned of the threat from the North to the institution of slavery and urged the South to be united.[53] The Montgomery *Confederation,* the local organ of relatively moderate Senator Benjamin Fitzpatrick, read between these lines and charged that "every form and shape of political malcontent" was there, and "ready to assist in any project having for its end a dissolution of the Union, immediate, unconditional, final."[54] George Gayle certainly fit that description. Given the presence of many influential South Carolinians such as Robert Barnwell Rhett, Gayle was likely there to meet with them informally and discuss future strategy. William Lowndes Yancey was an official delegate to the convention, and afterwards he wrote a soon-to-be famous letter to a Georgia supporter, James S. Slaughter, explaining a portion of that strategy. Southerners must be organized into committees or "leagues" of safety to "fire the Southern heart—instruct the Southern mind—give courage to each other" so that when the "next aggression" comes, "we can precipitate the Cotton States into a revolution."[55]

By this time the issue over Kansas had seemingly been finessed with the passage of a compromise measure—the so-called English Bill—admitting that territory to statehood but on the condition that the residents there adopt an ordinance agreeing to accept less land within its borders than its application for admission had requested.[56] This compromise bill, which C.C. Clay, Jr., and each of the other members of Alabama's congressional delegation supported, avoided the trigger of the Alabama legislature's resolution and, as a result, Governor Moore did not call for a convention to meet.[57] But as was broadcast across North Alabama and beyond utilizing the Memphis and Charleston Railroad, the pro-Southern Rights *Memphis Avalanche* correctly predicted that this would not put an end to northern agitation over slavery. "There is no appeasing of fanaticism, and the Kansas agitation looks to the [1860]

Presidential election, to the future of abolitionism." Indeed, "before the present session of Congress closes, new questions will have been spawned up like mushrooms from a rotten tree trunk."[58]

George Gayle and other secessionists were counting on this, but they were not waiting on that natural process. When noted filibuster William Walker visited Cahawba in 1858 to raise money and men for the invasion and subjugation of Nicaragua, he was overwhelmed with support. According to a Selma newspaper's report, "quite a number of our most substantial and largest planters came forward and made proper appreciation of their earnestness, by putting down large sums of money. Gen. Walker to-day could raise a million of dollars in Dallas County to Americanize Central America" and thereby extend slavery.[59] And once the South was outside the Union, the federal neutrality laws that had hamstrung Walker and others who had sought to open Central America to southern slaves would no longer be in the way of the South's version of manifest destiny.[60]

George Gayle was among those who were adamantly opposed to the English Bill and incensed that the members of the Alabama delegation had voted for it.[61] Like the *Charleston Mercury*, which saw the "triumph of Abolition in seizing the Government" as inevitable, and compared further compromise to "the man pursued by wolves [who temporarily] arrested their attacks by throwing one child after another out of his carriage— [before they] over took and devoured him at last."[62] Gayle believed it was time to secede and prepare for war. To place that issue before the people, Gayle announced his candidacy for the position of Major General of his area's division of the state militia, consisting of Dallas, Wilcox, Autauga, and Montgomery counties. With support from the *Montgomery Advertiser*, Gayle chose to make the election, in essence, a referendum on Kansas as well as on secession.[63] One of Gayle's supporters wrote that "Gayle's friends, in supporting him, make the issue between a *soap-tail* and a Southern Rights man. He wishes to be supported by those who do not *hesitate.* He wishes, in this election, a clear and distinct issue made of pure *Southern Rights doctrine*, against the doubting, hesitating and I believe I should add, *traitorous course*, of those who favor a *National party*. He puts his election on his love for the South—and takes the ground that he *cares more for her than he does for the Union*—that by the interest of the South he is willing to stand or fall."[64]

One of Gayle's two opponents, Samuel G. Hardaway, a Mexican War veteran who was supported by the moderate Montgomery *Confederation*, opted not to center his candidacy on the issues raised by Gayle, or even to reveal his personal position on them.[65] But Gayle's brand of loyalty politics eventually forced Hardaway to declare that he would be "as true to my section as any of those who desire to make *Secession* or *Disunion*, an issue in the election of a Major-General" if "in the future it should become necessary to resort to means outside the Constitution, to protect Southern Rights and Southern Institutions."[66] By the time the vote was taken on August 28, however, passions had apparently cooled and Gayle won only Dallas County and lost handily to Hardaway in Montgomery and the other counties within the militia division.[67] According to the positively gleeful Union Democrat editor of the Greensboro *Alabama Beacon*, "Col. Gayle was announced, in the columns of the Advertiser, as a *disunionist—supported as a disunionist*—and, badly beaten as a disunionist. Had he been content to run on his qualifications for the office, and his personal popularity, the probability is, that if beaten at all, it would have been by a much smaller majority."[68] "We are glad," he concluded, "that the *Disunion* Colonel has been beaten, as it may teach him and the 'Leaguers' *that the masses are not with them in their disunion schemes.*"[69]

Gayle's defeat did not slow the proliferation of extremist groups in South Alabama. It was probably no coincidence that not long after the election, the Montgomery *Confederation* reported that some in Dallas and Lowndes counties had formed themselves into a "Vigilance Committee, for the purpose of keeping a 'vigilant eye on the illegal acts of citizens in their midst, as well as strangers'."[70] Some of this was directed at keeping slaves in their place, and lynching those suspected of serious crimes.[71] But monitoring—and punishing—pro-northern sentiment was also part of their mission. The efforts of several Alabama newspapers during this period dovetailed with those of the vigilantes to keep the people in a state of high alert and fear. Abraham Lincoln was then seeking to unseat Senator Stephen Douglas, and was denounced by the press as a "coarse, uneducated, vulgar man; a vile and black-hearted Republican," and an "uncompromising enemy" of the South and her institutions.[72] William Henry Seward was also subjected to editorial abuse after giving a fateful speech on October 25, 1858, in Rochester, New York, in which he maintained that the South was the aggressor and was threatening the rights of the North. There was, Seward declared, an "irrepressible conflict" between free-labor and pro-slavery forces that would determine whether the country became "entirely a slave-holding nation or entirely a free-labor nation."[73] One Alabama editor maintained that both Seward and Lincoln enunciated what he called the "abolition creed"—"the equality of the negro with the white, socially and politically; the subversion of the Supreme Court and the Constitution; and the incompatibility of free and slave States existing together under the same government."[74]

That Douglas was reelected to the Senate over Lincoln convinced many Alabama Unionists that he was the only hope for winning a sufficient number of electoral votes in the North to beat the Republican candidate in the 1860 presidential election.[75] For that same reason, Douglas would soon become the target of Alabama secessionists like George Gayle intent on making sure that he would not receive the Democratic party's nomination.

In 1859, as the 1860 presidential election began coming into focus, Douglas supporter John Forsyth of the *Mobile Register* warned that unless southern Democrats united behind the nominee of the National Democratic party to be selected at the party convention in Charleston, South Carolina, the Republican nominee—whomever that might ultimately be—would be elected. If that occurred, he wrote, a "revolution would result" and disunion would occur.[76] That was music to George Gayle's ears. When he turned his attention to the election, Gayle, like Robert Barnwell Rhett in South Carolina, attempted to focus southerners on the issue of slavery as of singular, paramount importance, and to blame the compromising nature of the national political parties for the gradual loss of the rights of southern slaveowners.[77]

But even Dallas County Democrats were not yet fully radicalized. At a meeting of party members in Cahawba on April 16, 1859, a South Carolina native and attorney, Nathaniel Henry Rhodes Dawson, introduced a resolution that "under no circumstances will we support Stephen A. Douglas for the Presidency, if nominated by the Charleston Convention." According to an account of the meeting, this resolution was adopted but only "after a spirited discussion."[78] Surprisingly, the *Dallas Gazette* was critical of even this small degree of anti-partyism. Its editor, Charles Haynes, called the resolution "impolitic and premature" because a "far more objectionable and dangerous man than Judge Douglas might be—and we believe *will be*—nominated by the [Republican] party, and if Judge D. should be the nominee of the Charleston Convention, the advocates of this resolution, to be consistent, would be forced into a mischievous neutrality."[79] The following month Haynes went even further when he minimized the threat to slavery. Southerners still had their slaves and their land, he pointed out, and should not be so militant over "anticipated evils, or in favor of a string of abstractions so contradictory and impractical that it would puzzle the shrewdest metaphysician of the age to expound them."[80] Translation: men should not focus on the issue of slavery in the western territories in deciding whether they would support the eventual Democratic presidential nominee. Even William Lowndes Yancey was still blowing the trumpet of partyism. At a large Democratic party meeting in Montgomery on April 23, Yancey—who had his eye on the seat of Alabama United States Senator Benjamin Fitzpatrick—offered a resolution that "the only general party organization which professes to respect the rights of the South in negro property is the Democratic party," that "the overthrow of that time-honored party will insure the triumph of the Black Republicans under whose rule it is impossible for the Southern people to live;" and that it was the "imperative duty of every patriot to labor zealously for the success of Democratic nominees."[81]

By contrast, at a rally of the Whiggish American party in Cahawba on May 16, 1859, George Gayle, who the approving *Charleston Mercury* described as "the great fire-eating chieftain," was reportedly "fully at himself, and thundered forth his denunciations of all national parties." To the further dismay of local American party leaders attempting to strengthen support for their own national party, Gayle influenced the group's resolutions committee to report a resolution proclaiming that those in attendance "do now organize ourselves into a Southern rights party exclusively—repudiating our old party and party names, until the paramount question of slavery is permanently settled in the United States, or a division of the Union occurs."[82] Gayle was not discriminating against the American or "Know Nothing" party as it was known by Democrats. In a public letter, he decried that the Southern people were then "divided and distracted by the Democratic party." In his opinion, the only remedy was to "break down that party by all lawful means, and remove it from our great pathway, as a loathsome nuisance, until the slavery question is settled." Therefore, he continued, "I shall pray for the speedy overthrow of that party."[83]

The respective leaders of the Democratic party and the American party in Alabama were clearly worried that Gayle's rhetoric would damage their respective parties' prospects in the 1860 presidential election. John Forsyth ridiculed Gayle and those who agreed with him as a hopeless minority in the South whose only effect would be to divide and weaken Southern resolve. "Abolitionism will only stand by to witness and enjoy the rash movement," Forsyth declared.[84] The pro-American Party Tuscaloosa *Independent Monitor* was also critical, declaring Gayle's faction was "nothing more nor less than a disunion party on the ruins of the abortive [Southern] 'League'." "Verily we have fallen on strange political times," it opined. After noting Gayle's presence and influence at the Cahawba meeting, it stated that "we caution conservative Whigs to be careful how they affiliate with those eccentric 'opposition' elements."[85]

Gayle's efforts, nonetheless, appear to have forced Dallas County Democrats to redouble their efforts to at least sound more loyal to the South and slavery than the "Opposition." Another worried Douglas supporter in Dallas County, John Hardy, attended a county nominating convention on May 23 and reported that, "instead of hearing the good and glorious old democratic principles expounded and advocated, it were *disunion!* DISUNION!! DISUNION!!! No true lover of this great, glorious and free country," he continued, "could have listened to the disunion harangues delivered in the Court House at Cahaba, on last Monday, under the cloak of Democracy, without coming to the conclusion that the time has arrived when the lovers of our present free and happy institutions, arouse in their might, and put down all such destructive elements as were shown in the Democratic meeting at Cahaba."[86] This meeting also adopted several extreme Southern Rights resolutions that not only advocated the repeal of another portion of the Compromise of 1850 prohibiting the sale of slaves in the District of Columbia, but declared that "the failure of the federal government to give [positive] protection [to slave property in the territories] will justify the Southern States in throwing off such government."[87] Clearly, this was not a platform on which Douglas could stand, and Hardy knew that it was a formula for disunion and disaster.

In response to an invitation to address a Southern Rights organization in Mobile, Gayle further illuminated his intentions in a letter to the *Mobile Mercury* that was widely republished. "The object of uniting the people of the South on the slavery question alone," he explained, "is to prevent further aggression, by presenting a united front to the aggressors, and holding up our strength in terror over them." According to Gayle, "if this uniting will stop aggression upon our rights, then 'stay in the Union and enjoy them.'" But, he declared, "if otherwise, 'we will be united' to leave the Union together, and set up for ourselves as a slave confederacy."[88]

The approving *Charleston Mercury*, now owned and edited by the family of South Carolina secessionist Robert Barnwell Rhett, published Gayle's letter on its front page and assured its readers that his rhetoric "shows the progress of things in Alabama."[89] Later that month, the *Mercury* again reported on Gayle's activities in Alabama, this time with regard to a newspaper Gayle began publishing from Cahawba in competition with the *Dallas Gazette*. Gayle provocatively named it *The Slaveholder*. For Gayle, the final straw fell when the *Gazette's editor,* Charles Haynes, breached the faith by shockingly announcing that he was not opposed to popular sovereignty to decide the slavery issues in the western territories, and implying that he might support Stephen Douglas if Douglas received the Democratic party's nomination for the presidency. Haynes explained he would do this to "save us from the horrors of a civil war, or a dissolution of the Union."[90] George Gayle was not pleased. According to his prospectus, *The Slaveholder* was intended to promote his idea of putting down "all the old parties" and uniting the South "upon the question of slavery alone."[91] In other words, disunion and civil war did not worry him.

The reaction of the mainstream press in Alabama to Gayle's latest genre of extremist activism reflects the various views prevailing in this pre-Harper's

Ferry period. The sympathetic *Montgomery Mail*, for example, playfully warned "ye wishy-washy, peddling, tricky, South-selling politicians! If George Gayle doesn't make the 'fur fly,' we'll consent to be cropped. He has talent, integrity, nerve, and ambition; and loving the South as a true son, he will so flagellate the time-serving and venal, that all the people shall hear their yells, the country over. And so the paper will be well worth reading, even to those who do not go its full length in politics. If you would have something racy, piquant—something, as old Owen used to say, 'that will stir your haslet'—subscribe for the *Slaveholder*."[92]

Still moderate John Forsyth of the *Mobile Register* wrote that it was "quite evident that the 'Slaveholder' must be classed as an anti-Democratic paper. In fact it is started for purposes of antagonism to the Democracy. As such, while we wish all manner of good and happiness to our old friend Col. Gayle, we shall have to fight him politically under the old and honored State Rights banner of Democracy."[93] The pro-Douglas Montgomery *Confederation* jeered that it hoped Gayle would convince other secessionists to stay away from the 1860 National Democratic Convention in Charleston, where Douglas needed to shed as much southern opposition as possible to receive the nomination. "We call upon our friend Col. George W. Gayle" to convince them, through the *Slaveholder*, to prevent pro-secession editors from contaminating their "spotless garments by bringing them in contact with those villainous bipeds at Charleston, Yelept *National* Democrats."[94] Alabama moderates like the veteran Union Democrat editor of the Greensboro *Alabama Beacon*, John Harvey, saw Gayle's new venture for what it really was. "The design of the paper, as gathered from its Prospectus, and editorials in the number before us, is—*to advance the cause of disunion.*"[95] Similarly, John Hardy charged that Gayle's motive was to "do all that in him lies to effect disunion, confusion and anarchy in this great, glorious and happy government."[96] There is no evidence indicating that Gayle disputed these accusations in the least.

The editor of the pro-Yancey *Montgomery Advertiser and State Gazette* noted that the desire for dissolution was "now by no means general" in the South, but it warned the North that more anti-slavery agitation might cause "the spirit of disunion, which is evidently spreading and strengthening daily" to overrule the "conservative element which at present exists in the South." If that occurred, he continued, "the smoldering fires of resistance shall burst forth with a fury which cannot be controlled."[97] That was precisely George Gayle's goal, and militant northern abolitionist John Brown and his financiers would soon provide Gayle with an abundance of editorial fodder as well as some other ideas that would influence his later actions and ultimately save his life.

CHAPTER 4

"Great God What a Country"

And now comes the eventful year of '59
Political differences culminate and combine;
John Brown, on his raid, into Virginia rode
To arm our negroes with fire and sword
To set them free and ruin our land,
And to destroy the Southrons to a man.

Anna Maria Gayle Fry
Memories of Old Cahaba, '87

JOHN Brown's famous and shocking raid on Harper's Ferry, Virginia, which occurred on October 16, 1859, was a game changer for George Gayle.[1] Not only had what the Tuscaloosa *Independent Monitor* described as a "handful of fanatics—whites and negroes—instigated by northern abolitionists [taken] possession of the government arsenal" there, but Brown's failed plan to incite slave insurrections across the South terrified southerners. Newspapers in Alabama reported that maps discovered during the ensuing investigation revealed that Brown's planned invasion route was through the plantation regions in the South, and that the Alabama Black Belt, including Dallas County with its extremely high slave-to-white ratios, had been targeted.[2]

A bloody sequel to St. Domingo was seemingly averted, but for how long? Paranoid Alabamians now saw Brown's agents behind every bush. A Cahawba book peddler was reportedly one of several arrested for suspicion of being "an emissary of Old Brown." It was also said that a search of his trunk revealed "documents showing him to be one of the

original men to be stationed on the line of the published Brown Map."
The nearby Marion *American* hoped the Lord would have mercy on the
peddler's soul, "for we know the people of Cahaba well enough to feel
confident that they will give him full justice, terrible as it may be."[3]

It may not have escaped George Gayle's notice that some Southerners
were favoring such direct, lethal action against abolitionists in the North.
An advertisement published in a Richmond, Virginia, newspaper pledged
$25 toward a $100,000 reward "for the heads of the following Traitors"—a
list that included a number of Republican senators and congressmen. The
advertiser also promised to be "one of one hundred to pay five hundred
dollars each ($50,000) for the head of William H. Seward."[4]

Gayle likely concurred with the *Montgomery Mail* that "Providence
sent us John Brown."[5] It gave men like Gayle credibility among those
who had heretofore been reluctant to give up their life-long allegiance
to the traditional political parties, as well as the Union. Gayle initially
used his new-found *gravitas* to promote a presidential ticket that would
have heretofore been the subject of general ridicule. He placed the names
of South Carolina extremist Robert Barnwell Rhett and C.C. Clay, Jr.,
on the masthead of the *Slaveholder* signifying his support of them for
president and vice president respectively, but not as the nominees of any
traditional political party.[6] The Whig party was already defunct, and Gayle
had earlier advocated the destruction of the National Democratic party,
which he called a "loathsome nuisance" controlled by its Northern wing
and willing to "sacrifice the best interests of the South." The Democracy
was, wrote Gayle, a Union party and, therefore, "an incubus upon the
rights of the South, deserving to be crushed."[7]

Gayle's endorsement of Rhett and Clay to carry the banner of a
southern party is interesting. Gayle described Rhett as having "no equal,
as a man devoted to the South."[8] Judging from Clay's controversial
public pronouncements, he was also now in lock step with Rhett and
Gayle.[9] Earlier in the fall, the southern press had published a lengthy
account of a speech the increasingly militant Clay had given in Huntsville
denouncing Stephen Douglas's position that the settlers in the western
territories should be allowed to determine for themselves whether slavery
ought to be allowed there, and that Congress had no right to dictate on
that issue. More importantly to Gayle, Clay reportedly "utterly adjured"
nationalism, and declared that he "never was, am not now, and never will
be a national democrat," but instead had always been a "States Rights
democrat." As such, said Clay, he would "not support Mr. Douglas or
any one occupying his platform, although nominated by the unanimous
vote of the Charleston Convention, of the democratic party, or any other
party whatever."[10]

The *Charleston Mercury*, which had taken this editorial position several weeks earlier, published a detailed report of Clay's speech on its front page, and praised him as an "honest and fearless statesman." Its editor was certain that "if the South had many more such men to guide their councils, she would not only be safe, but safe with honor and peace."[11] Forgetting that Clay had voted for the English Bill, George Gayle called him "the noble, bold, and honest Senator of the United States, from Alabama." Clay, he continued, was "raised in the Calhoun school of politics, is a southern star, rising in the morning of a new era, with 'might and majesty,' to fix, for the South, an honorable destiny for weal or woe. The State of his birth loves him for his political honesty; and when he takes the political flag of his section in his hands, she will follow him across the bridge of Lodi, and spike the enemy's cannon."[12]

This favorable publicity evidently went to Clay's head. When Congress convened after the suppression of Brown's raid, Clay viciously attacked the Republican party for causing the deaths at Harper's Ferry. On December 13 and 14 he continued this tirade in a fiery speech entitled "Invasion of Harper's Ferry—Dangers and Duties of the South" in which he warned that secession would occur if a Republican were elected to the presidency.[13] Clay subsequently engaged in a fistfight on the Senate floor with a pro-Douglas Senator from North Carolina.[14] But the Alabama Democratic Convention, which convened in January of 1860 to select delegates to the Democratic National Convention, did not officially endorse Clay and Rhett.

At least publicly, Gayle's position on the Democratic party and the 1860 election was then in advance of that of even the *Charleston Mercury*. Three days before Brown's raid, the *Mercury* had at least left the door open for Southerners to support the Democratic nominee if the party and the candidate "plainly and distinctly" affirmed and supported the "rights of the South, as plainly deducible from the *Dred Scott* case," meaning that Congress would enact no laws barring slavery in the western territories. Failing that, wrote its editor, "let the southern States nominate and support candidates of their own, plainly and faithfully reflecting and supporting their rights." If those southern candidates lost, and the Republican candidate won, the southern legislatures should recall their members from Congress and "invite the cooperation of their sister southern States to devise means for their common safety."[15]

This, of course, was ultimately a formula for disunion. Northern Democrats would never agree as a body to this type of southern "rights," and without southern support the Democrats' nominee would likely lose, particularly if southern candidates like Rhett and Clay were run to split the Democratic vote. In that case, the Republicans would win, making secession very likely. Gayle's preemptive endorsement of southern candidates was, thus, intended to bring on secession regardless of the outcome of the Democrats' national convention in 1860. He predicted that the convention would "either break up in a row, or the southern delegates [will] repudiate any nomination which is not of southern men, and nominate a southern ticket—in another Convention." Gayle emphatically declared that "we 'draw the sword, and throw away the scabbard,' and will have victory for the southern people, or be martyrs in their cause!"[16]

After Brown's raid, the *Charleston Mercury* adopted Gayle's position. It openly discussed the benefits of forming a separate nation, and recommended that no delegates be appointed to the Democratic National Convention. It also called on the South Carolina legislature to "arm the State."[17] The pro-Douglas Montgomery *Confederation* ironically attacked the *Mercury*, not Gayle, alleging that it "has taken charge of the factionists and disorganizers of our State, and is urging them on in the work of destruction. The disintegration and demolition of the Democratic party is now the only obstacle to the darting scheme of its ambition, viz: the disruption of the Union and the formation of a Southern Confederacy."[18] But the reality was that the *Mercury* was taking care to follow the lead of extremists like Gayle in other states, lest the movement toward secession be derailed by public reaction to the stigma of South Carolina radicals.

This made Gayle even bolder. Earlier, the *Charleston Mercury* had reported on a meeting in South Carolina where those in attendance unanimously adopted resolutions calling for the African slave trade, which had been prohibited by federal law for over fifty years, to be reopened. According to the resolutions, "our safety in the Union makes it necessary to increase our supply of slave labor." Otherwise, the "constant drain" on the Upper South slave states to furnish laborers for the Deep South, and the "high prices of that species of property," would continue to serve as "active agencies in promoting the designs of the abolitionists."[19] But it was obvious that even if Southerners wanted the importation of Africans to be resumed, that would not be possible within the Union. Therefore, Gayle, of course, supported the idea. "*The Slaveholder*," wrote the editor of the Huntsville *Southern Advocate*, "a rabid Disunion paper in Dallas County, Ala., by G.W. Gayle & Co., is in favor of the re-opening of the African Slave Trade! And it would, we suppose, dissolve the Union on that or any other issue, for it is for Disunion *per se*. Like all the politicians of its class it is full of denunciations of Douglas, the Administration, the National Democracy and the Union, as well as the great mass of the Southern people who do not agree with its insane ravings."[20]

Consistent with Gayle's previous pattern of having nothing to do with the Democrats' party apparatus, he did not seek to become a delegate to either the state or the national convention.[21] But Cahawba lawyer John Tyler Morgan, who the *Montgomery Advertiser* described as the "Ajax of the true Calhoun Democracy," was a delegate from Dallas County to the state convention and may have been acting as Gayle's surrogate.[22] Gayle's *Slaveholder* had listed Morgan as one of several leading Democrats who were opposed to Douglas, and who had pledged not to support Douglas if nominated by the Charleston Convention.[23]

Unlike Gayle, the *Charleston Mercury* faced the reality that many prominent southern Democrats—especially Douglas Democrats—could not bring themselves to forego attending the national convention. If secessionists refused to attend, Douglas would likely receive the nomination and the Union might be prolonged if he were elected. And so the *Mercury* reverted back to its prior recommendations. "If Alabama and other Southern States think proper to enter [the convention], a double obligation for a redoubled vigilance and firmness lies upon them." Alabama, it declared, should "go into the Charleston Convention [and] instruct her delegates to demand an explicit recognition of the rights of the South on all the great matters at issue with the North, particularly that which involves our expansion; and if this recognition is refused, that they shall withdraw from the Convention."[24] Through the efforts of William Lowndes Yancey and others, this is exactly what the majority of the delegates at the Alabama Democratic Convention required the Alabama delegates to the Charleston convention to do.[25] The *Mercury* approvingly proclaimed that Alabama "now leads the van of the Southern hosts."[26]

Gayle's approval of the Alabama convention's adoption of resolutions requiring affirmative protection by Congress for slavery in the western territories, and its selection of John Tyler Morgan as one of two presidential electors at large (the other was David Hubbard), drew fire from John Hardy's *Alabama State Sentinel*, which was still supporting Douglas. "George Gayle, it is well known, is for disunion at once. He is the only man in the State who has had the manliness to declare that to be his object. Col. Gayle warmly endorses the action of the Montgomery Convention, and declares that body has planted themselves on his (disunion) platform, and that the Southern Rights wing of the party, have all come into his fold. Col. Gayle boldly defends John T. Morgan, and holds him up as a perfect personification of disunionism."[27] Hardy also asserted that "there are a large number of men and democrats too, in Alabama, who desire to take several more meals within the union, and therefore, cannot endorse the wild and suicidal schemes and designs of George W. Gayle" and others.[28]

That was probably true, but the question now was whether a majority of Alabamians and other southerners, and just enough northerners, would unite to vote for a single candidate against the Republican nominee. This question was even more important given the action of the Alabama legislature. James Martin Calhoun of Dallas County successfully pushed a joint resolution in the Alabama Senate requiring Governor Andrew Barry Moore to issue a call for the election of delegates to a convention if the Republican nominee won the presidency. Those delegates were authorized to "do whatever in the opinion of said Convention the rights, interests and honor of the State of Alabama require to be done for their protection."[29] That, many assumed, meant secession.

George Gayle knew it was at least possible that a compromise could be reached at the National Democratic Convention that would prevent the southern vote from being split. Before waiting until April to see who the Democrats might select, however, southern pro-Union Whigs unwittingly improved the prospects of the Republicans by launching a new third party called the Constitutional Union Party. Its stated purpose was, wrote the supportive but pessimistic editor of the Tuscaloosa *Independent Monitor*, to "put down the agitators and ultraists of both sections, and restore peace and concord to our distracted land, lofty goals as hopeless as the new party itself."[30] A state convention of this fledgling party was scheduled to take place on May 23 in Selma, and former Whigs busied themselves in selecting delegates to attend.[31]

The National Democratic party did not adopt what became known as the "Alabama Platform," and, as George Gayle had hoped and predicted, the party finally did split, resulting in the nomination of two separate tickets—one headed by Stephen Douglas and the other by Vice President John Breckinridge of Kentucky—further fragmenting the anti-Republican vote.[32] The *Charleston Mercury* endorsed Breckinridge,[33] and so did George Gayle. But Gayle did not stump for him.[34] He instead kept his focus on secession, not electing the next president of the Union.[35] Gayle was quoted throughout the nation as appealing to Southerners to "break up this rotten, stinking, and oppressive Government."[36] The Tuscaloosa *Independent Monitor* had men like Gayle in mind when it charged that Breckinridge's role was not to win, but "to carry a large number of slave States" and elect Lincoln, and thereby "afford [secessionists] a pretext for attaching all the Southern States to the coattail of South Carolina, and let her drag them out of the Union."[37] And so he was.

Given the split of the anti-Republicans, all Gayle really had to do was to sit back and watch the Democratic Party he had grown to hate finally implode, confident that secession was, therefore, finally just a matter of time. When Charles Hayne and the *Dallas Gazette* finally defected from the Douglas faction, Gayle could even sell and cease publication of the *Slaveholder*.[38] When requested at a Bar dinner in Montgomery in the summer of 1860 to make the traditional toast to "Our Country," Gayle looked to the future and responded with a toast to "Our Native Land—It is bounded on the east by the Atlantic, on the west by the Pacific, on the south by South America, and on the north by Mason's and Dixon's Line. Great God! What a country!"[39]

CHAPTER 5

"Lincoln Will Have His Assassin"

And when in '60 Abe Lincoln's elected,
Our hearts the bitterest resentment reflected.
Alabama seceded – bitter passion is rife
The North and the South are ready for strife.

And now, in place of party and ball,
Political banquets are given by all,
At one of these banquets, a brilliant ovation,
In speeches the North was condemned as a nation,
And George W. Gayle joined his glass in toast
With "death and damnation to the whole Yankee host."

At the tap of the drum, with the blue cockade,
Are gathered the flower of our land
To don the gray and march away
To meet an invading band.

Anna Maria Gayle Fry
Memories of Old Cahaba, '87-'88

THE Republican nominee, fifty-one-year-old Abraham Lincoln, had actually charted a relatively moderate course.[1] Although unreported in Alabama, Lincoln denounced John Brown's raid and the use of violence to end slavery, and even approved of Brown's execution.[2] To the Republican Association at New York City's Cooper Institute, Lincoln essentially repeated his Peoria speech: he denied that the federal government possessed the power of emancipation, and admitted that only the states had that authority. He still maintained that "we can yet afford to let [slavery] alone where it is, because that much is due to the necessity arising from its actual presence in the nation."[3] But what if Lincoln was lying and, as many Alabama secessionists breathlessly predicted, executed a policy of involuntary abolition following his election? According to the *Montgomery Mail*, abolitionist raids and fiery destruction constituted "practical Lincoln-ism! This is what we must 'acquiesce in,' if we 'acquiesce in Black Republican government!'"[4] The *Charleston Mercury* relentlessly demonized Lincoln, declaring that he was a "horrid-looking wretch"—"sooty and scoundrelly in aspect; a cross between the nutmeg dealer, the horse-swapper, and the night man,—a creature, 'fit evidently, for petty treason, small stratagems, and all sorts of spoils." Lincoln was also a "lank-sided Yankee, of the uncomeliest visage, and one of the dirtiest complexion, and the most indecent comparisons. Faugh! After him, what decent white man would be President!"[5]

The implications of Lincoln's prior speeches were the primary fodder for the *Mercury's* propaganda. It reminded its readers across the South that Lincoln had declared that "I believe this government cannot endure permanently half slave and half free." One alternative, according to Lincoln, was that "it will become all one thing or all the other." The *Mercury* alleged that the "opponents of slavery will arrest the further spread of it, and place it where the public mind shall rest in the belief that it is on the course of ultimate extinction." Many Southerners were convinced that this was Lincoln's goal.[6] And of the many consequences of that outcome, the financial loss would be devastating. "Slave property," said the *Mercury*, "is the foundation of all the property in the South." The stability of the institution would be so shaken that many slave owners would put their slaves on the market, causing the value of slaves generally to drop and costing slave owners millions. Real estate would also devalue, as would stocks, bonds, and debts secured by slave property.[7]

But what if the South seceded? Could this fate be thereby peaceably avoided? The *Charleston Mercury* and other pro-secession newspapers certainly said so. Yet the *Mercury* also published an abstract of one of Lincoln's speeches in which he assured that "if constitutionally, we elect a President, and, therefore, you undertake to destroy the Union, it will be our duty to deal with you, as Old John Brown has been dealt with. We can only do our duty."[8] As election day approached the *Mercury* dubbed Lincoln the "*beau ideal* of a relentless, dogged, free soil border-ruffian—a Southerner by birth, and a Northerner in feeling and association—a fanatic in philanthropy, and a vulgar mobocrat and a Southern hater in political opinions—he is the very man for the occasion. If ever in possession of the executive powers of the Government, he will neither turn back from his work, nor do it by halves—fit chieftain of those who selected him—the author who first gave expression to the doctrine of the 'irrepressible conflict,' now chosen to be the finisher of that faith."[9]

The goal of demonizing Lincoln in this way was to assure that states like Alabama would, in fact, secede with South Carolina. Alabamians were still divided on this issue,[10] and so secessionists in Charleston were, according to the *Montgomery Mail*, flooding Alabama with pro-secession pamphlets.[11] And when the time came, the *Mail* assured, "glorious South Carolina will lead the way, and Alabama, Florida, Georgia, and Mississippi will follow and stand by her side!"[12]

The day finally came when one announced Lincoln's election.[13] Governor Moore subsequently issued a public address announcing that on December 6, the day after the votes of the electoral college would be formally submitted (but not formally counted), he would issue his call for an election of delegates to take place on Christmas Eve, December 24, for a convention to meet in Montgomery on January 7, 1861.[14] South Carolina, by contrast, had already scheduled its election for December 6 and its convention was to meet on December 17.[15] Alabama secessionists like C.C. Clay, Jr. called openly for South Carolina to secede first rather than waiting on Alabama to take the lead. "Let South Carolina act alone and at once—the sooner the better," wrote Clay. He, among others, assured that Georgia, Alabama, and Mississippi "will soon join her."[16] Based on these assurances, delegates to the convention in South Carolina voted unanimously (169-0) on December 20, 1860, in favor of an ordinance purporting to dissolve the connection between that state and the Union.[17]

The news of this fateful event reportedly caused "tremendous excitement" in several parts of Alabama, including Dallas County where cannons were fired in celebration, and "every hill and dale reecho[ed] with sounds of joy."[18] In the ensuing weeks, convention delegates in Alabama (the president of its convention was a South Carolina native, Perry County attorney William McLin Brooks), Mississippi, Florida, Georgia, Louisiana, and Texas quickly voted to follow the Palmetto State's lead.[19]

A very perceptive Pennsylvania editor charged that this was all a consequence of decades of what he called "education in the hatred of the federal Government." The "present generation" in South Carolina had "imbibed their treasonable sentiments from the maternal front and have only waited a favorable occasion to make good the threats of rebellion which have heretofore proved impotent, or have been restrained by motives of policy." This same feeling, he continued, "extends to portions of Georgia, Alabama, Mississippi and Florida, whereunto South Carolinians have emigrated, and where the theories of their great head [John Calhoun] were favorably received and carefully nurtured."[20]

George Gayle could now enjoy the fruits of over a decade of labor, or so he thought. But compromise efforts were nevertheless still ongoing in Congress, and Virginia, Kentucky, Missouri, Arkansas, North Carolina, and Tennessee were hesitating.[21] There were also those in Alabama who were actively encouraging a reconstruction of the Union.[22] One of that ilk was a Coosa County lawyer and former associate of William Lowndes Yancey, South Carolina-born Robert Tharin. He attempted to unite those who did not own slaves into a grassroots movement to take over the state in the 1861 state election scheduled for August. Part of his plan was to launch a newspaper called *The Non-Slaveholder*— evidently a parody of George Gayle's *The Slaveholder.* Tharin made a mistake by taking his campaign to the Black Belt, where, according to the *Dallas Gazette*, a vigilante group in Lowndes County arrested and punished him.[23]

Some Alabama secessionists believed that the only way to stop this back-sliding was to start a war.[24] According to news accounts, President Buchanan concluded that "South Carolina wishes to enter into a conflict with me, and upon the shedding of the first drop of blood, to drag the other States into the movement of dissolution." There was much truth in this assertion, despite denials by the *Charleston Mercury*.[25] But initial efforts to provoke a northern military response that might unite the South were unsuccessful. Under orders from Governor Andrew Barry Moore, for example, Alabama troops seized the federal military installations in South Alabama in January 1861, but President Buchanan refrained from taking any retaliatory action.[26] Something more provocative was needed, and some Alabamians were determined to be a part of it.[27] Indeed, some in the Black Belt had already publicly pledged to resist Lincoln's inauguration "BY FORCE if necessary."[28]

Even before Alabama seceded, the Montgomery *Mail* reported talk on the street in Montgomery that president-elect Abraham Lincoln and vice president-elect Hannibal Hamlin ought to be hung "on the same gallows on which John Brown was hanged."[29] This sentiment was not only in Alabama. A correspondent to a New Orleans newspaper advised the South to "take the motto of the Old Dominion—'sic Semper Tyrannis!'—and crush out forever the tyranny of free niggerdom!"[30]

But how would one pull off what would certainly be the crime of the millennium? John Brown's raid and its aftermath were actually instructive in this regard. The raid had ultimately failed, but it demonstrated that a well-financed team could plan and implement a surprise attack, and could likely be successful if the objective were narrower. The fate of one of the masterminds and wealthy northern financiers of the raid, New York businessman Gerritt Smith, also demonstrated that with good lawyers armed with the temporary insanity defense, those who solicited or conspired to bring about such an attack could escape justice.[31]

If George Gayle or anyone else wanted to start a southern-solidifying war by having Lincoln eliminated, it would take money but also someone with the audacity to execute the plan. Both were available in the 1860s, as had been demonstrated two years earlier when William Walker had come to Cahawba during his fundraising tour of the South seeking financing for the invasion and conquest of Nicaragua.[32] If Alabama slave owners would contribute for that purpose, what wouldn't they offer to get rid of Lincoln? But by the time of Lincoln's election, Walker's services were no longer available. According to the New Orleans *Picayune*, by September 1860, Walker's plan had broadened to involve "nothing less than the regeneration and consolidation of the five Central American States, as in days gone by, in one Federal Republic." Walker and his men had invaded Honduras on August 6, 1860, but with the assistance of a British man-of-war, Hondurans had captured them, and Walker was executed and his second in command was imprisoned.[33]

There was another strike force available, however, the "K.G.C." or Knights of the Golden Circle.[34] Members of this paramilitary organization led by another Upper South manifest-destiny-dreamer, Dr. George William Lamb Bickley, had visited North and South Alabama on at least two occasions in 1860 to enlist men and solicit financial contributions to support an invasion, occupation, and later annexation of civil war-torn Mexico in order to allow for the expansion of slavery. Bickley's organization was publicly endorsed by George Gayle,[35] and a number of Alabamians joined the K.G.C., whose headquarters would soon be established in Montgomery.[36] But filibustering was not the K.G.C.'s only mission. According to the September 12, 1860, edition of the Huntsville *Southern Advocate*, "Messrs. Spanlger, Bickley and Clarke spoke [in Huntsville] in advocacy of the Knights of the Golden Circle in their efforts to Americanize and to Southernize Mexico."[37] One would later accuse some knights of being involved in the successful plot to assassinate Lincoln, and one of those who would be convicted for a role in that conspiracy was a man named Edman Spangler, possibly that "Spanlger" referred to in the Huntsville newspaper.[38]

At the time of the national election in November 1860, another knight and Lincoln assassin, actor John Wilkes Booth, was in Montgomery, Alabama, in connection with his appearance in plays at the theater there.[39] Whether he met George Gayle during this period is unknown. If so it would have happened in either the theater or a local brothel, where Booth spent most of his time. If they had met before the election, Gayle and Booth would have clashed politically. Like Stephen Douglas,

Booth despised abolitionists and secessionist alike. After the election, however, Booth and Gayle were of the same mind regarding Abraham Lincoln.[40] They both attended the St. Andrews' Society Celebration in Montgomery on November 30, where anti-Lincoln militancy was on full display.[41]

Ironically, one of the men who would labor to prevent Lincoln's assassination, former Chicago policeman Allan Pinkerton, was also focused on Alabama in 1860. He successfully directed the investigation of an embezzlement from the Adams Express Company in Montgomery.[42] After Abraham Lincoln's election, Pinkerton was involved in the provision of security to the president-elect in his journey by train from Illinois to Washington, D.C., for his inauguration on March 4, 1861.[43]

A few days before Alabama seceded, Lincoln had begun receiving anonymous letters threatening violent opposition to his inauguration.[44] Rumors were rife throughout the nation that he would be assassinated before he could take the oath of office.[45] One southern secessionist publicly warned that "Caesar had his Brutus—Charles the Second his Cromwell, and Abraham Lincoln will have his assassin whenever he attempts to stain with his foul touch the consecrated Chair."[46] As Allan Pinkerton would discover, there were multiple plots afoot in Maryland to ambush Lincoln there while he made his way from Illinois to the nation's capital. One of these plots was led by a K.G.C. officer.[47]

Alabamians may have been involved in these schemes. According to one widely reported account:

> It was arranged in case Mr. Lincoln should pass safely over the rail road to Baltimore, that the conspirators should mingle with the crowd which might surround his carriage, and by pretending to be his friends, be enabled to approach his person, when, upon a signal from their leader, some of them would shoot at Mr. Lincoln with their pistols, and others would throw into his carriage hand grenades filled with detonating powder, similar to those used in the attempted assassination of the Emperor, Louis Napoleon. It was intended that in the confusion which should result from this attack, *the assailants should escape to a vessel which was waiting in the harbor to receive them, and be carried to Mobile, in the seceding State of Alabama.*[48]

John Wilkes Booth was a native of Maryland but may or may not have been a member of this particular plot. He was, however, acting in a play in Albany, New York, in February 1861 where Lincoln would make one of his stops on the way to Washington.[49] But while at the theater there on February 12, Booth supposedly accidentally fell on his own dagger, "inflicting a muscular wound under his right arm between one and two inches in depth."[50] The press reported that the injury was actually inflicted by an actress motivated by "disappointed affection" but there is no further evidence of this.[51] In any event, he was, therefore, in no condition to stop Lincoln.

In the end, no one would be forced to plead the defense of temporary insanity to a charge of murdering the president-elect in 1861. Lincoln was made aware of the plots by Pinkerton and others, and allowed himself to be clandestinely smuggled in to the nation's capital where he arrived safely on the morning of February 23, 1861.[52] But as fate would have it, other opportunities to serve as Lincoln's Brutus would present themselves in the future, and George Gayle would ultimately do his worst to take advantage.

Most of the South was, meanwhile, united in secession following a provocative act of a different kind—South Carolina's attack on Fort Sumter in April 1861. Alabamians fearful of an active reconstruction movement in their state and elsewhere in the South had previously requested South Carolina to take this fateful step.[53] An anonymous correspondent from Cahawba wrote the *Charleston Mercury* that "I pray to God that [each of the forts in Charleston Harbor] are all in possession of the State. The taking of the forts has been delayed too long, in my judgment. It should have been done the day after secession. Don't flinch an inch from the d___d rotten villainous government of ABE LINCOLN, and his abolition *millions*. Let them come and we will 'welcome them with bloody hands and hospitable graves.'"[54] But Confederate President Jefferson Davis and Secretary of War Leroy Pope Walker had deferred taking that step until a South Carolina native and South Carolina College graduate, Lowndes County, Alabama, attorney James Graham Gilchrist, burst into Walker's Montgomery office and warned that reconstruction would occur "unless the breach was made wider by an act of war." The solution, Gilchrist declared, was to "sprinkle blood in the face of the people."[55]

On April 12, 1861, George Gayle received a telegram from Montgomery containing the welcome news. "[Confederate General P.G.T.] Beauregard opened his batteries on [Fort Sumter] at twenty minutes past four o'clock this morning. The greatest excitement prevails here." Gayle rushed the telegram to Charles E. Haynes, who quickly produced an extra of the *Cahaba Gazette* publishing the contents of the telegram under the headlines "The War has Commenced!," "Batteries Opened on Fort Sumter!!" and "Gen. Beauregard has Opened the Ball!!!"[56]

As hoped, the attack on Fort Sumter, coupled with President Lincoln's bold response, had the desired effect on most Alabamians. When Lincoln issued a call for troops to suppress the rebellion, four additional states, Tennessee, Virginia, North Carolina and Arkansas seceded. But the North was now also fully aroused, and a bloody war of wills would soon ensue.[57] The threat of reconstruction had only been lessened, however, not eliminated. And the threat of war was now very real. How long would the South fight? As far as George Gayle was concerned, other southerners—besides him—should fight forever if necessary.

The *Selma Reporter* had sounded the tocsin of war even before the attack on Fort Sumter had begun. "The voice of War to-day is ringing through the land and calls the brave, the virtuous, and the noble to the field. Let the clashing bayonets of Selma's gallant soldiery echo a response to the sacred call. Let all who wear the 'cloth of honor'—aye, all who would vindicate their country's liberties and the honor of those they love—let them meet to night in council, and prepare for driving back the vandal minion of our Pharisaic foe."[58]

The pressure of such rhetoric had been augmented by the strong influence of what the *New York Times* dubbed "Southern Petticoat Rule,"[59] which in Selma, ironically and quite sensationally included two of Abraham Lincoln's sisters-in-law, Martha Todd White, the wife of Selma physician Clement Billingslea White, and Elodie Todd, now the fiancée of secessionist lawyer N.H.R. Dawson.[60] Dawson had earlier summoned the "Magnolia Cadets," who on April 10 answered the call of Alabama Governor Andrew Barry Moore for 3,000 volunteers by reportedly voting unanimously to join and be transferred to the Confederate Army. This prompted the *Selma Reporter* to call on the other men in the community to follow suit. "Let them assemble and act at once," the editor implored. "They have borne themselves nobly heretofore—let them not be tardy now."[61]

Cahawba residents were not to be outdone. A relative of George Gayle's who was nine years old at the time later recalled that "as in every other place in the county, the people were intensely loyal to the Confederate cause. Political meetings were a nightly occurrence. Blue cockades were on every breast; the greatest excitement and the wildest enthusiasm prevailed. The Cahaba Rifles were mustered into service and went at once to the front."[62] The commander of the company, which became a part of the Fifth Alabama Infantry, was South Carolina native and Cahawba lawyer Christopher Claudius Pegues. He would be one of many who would ultimately give his life for the Cause.[63] John Tyler Morgan, who joined the unit before it boarded the aptly named steamship *Southern Republic*, would survive.[64]

Before travelling to Dallas County to be with her sick mother, famed South Carolina diarist Mary Boykin Chesnut had expressed concerns about the effect of the war on the slaves. "Not by one word or look can we detect any change in the demeanor of those Negro servants." They seemed to her "as respectful and as profoundly indifferent" as before, but she thought they "carry it too far." She wondered whether they were "stolidly stupid, or wiser than we are, silent and strong, biding their time."[65] When Chesnut arrived in the Alabama River community of Portland, she "saw for the first time the demoralization produced [among the slaves] by hopes of freedom."[66] Many of the departing Dallas County men had been part of the county's internal security network that protected white residents from the potential of slave violence and revolts during the antebellum period. Efforts were made to form Home Guard units to take their place, but the romantic magnetism of military service was too great.[67]

The response to calls for troops was so overwhelming in George Gayle's region that he wrote Jefferson Davis on May 22 pleading that the Confederate War Department be instructed not to receive any additional volunteers from Dallas County. Because it was the "largest slaveholding county in the Southern Confederacy," Gayle reasoned, the county needed a "*home* support" to "save ourselves from the horrors of insurrection." Of the 1,600 voters, Gayle estimated that over 500 were already "now in the field." The remainder was needed "to keep the slaves down." Gayle was certain that unless the government acted, "our whole white population will volunteer (men, women & children, I believe) and *anarchy* will prevail and the slaves become our masters, if they can." Thus, he emphatically concluded, "for Heaven's sake, bring this popular madness, if you can, into discipline, or we will ruin ourselves by the recklessness of our patriotism."[68]

Gayle's patriotism in support of slavery was certainly of the reckless variety, but the evidence conflicts regarding whether the appeals for troops led him to volunteer to fight for the Confederacy he had advocated for years. The inscription on his gravestone in Selma's Live Oak Cemetery suggests that he served as a private in "Lee's Battery of Alabama Light Artillery."[69] But after the war ended he made an affidavit stating that he had merely "encourag[ed] enlistments in the Confederate army, and to the extent of his means, by contributions and by aiding and assisting Confederate soldiers and their families" had supported the Cause. He swore under oath that he was "old and feeble, and did not go into the army for that reason."[70]

Gayle was fifty-four in 1861, the same age as Robert E. Lee. He was also far from being feeble. The court system in Dallas County remained in operation, and he continued to practice law throughout the war, including handling a few cases in which he challenged efforts to conscript men to fight.[71] One editor called age a "cowardly excuse," and another lectured that "if God has blessed you with health and vigor of body, the stringent demand of your country will not excuse you."[72] Even at this early point, another Cahawba resident who was fifty-three took heed and enlisted.[73]

The version regarding Gayle's war record in his affidavit was accurate. Lee's Battery was part of a socially and politically elite militia unit in Montgomery County known as the "Montgomery True Blues."[74] George Gayle was not a member of that unit but one of his nephews, also named George Washington Gayle, was.[75] When George Gayle wrote his letter to Jefferson Davis, his nephew and the other True Blues were on their way to the front in Virginia as part of the Third Alabama Infantry.[76] That company was later converted to a light artillery unit ultimately led by Edgar G. Lee.[77]

Gayle may have given financial support to the unit listed on his tombstone, but it appears that in 1861 he was testing the political waters instead of making plans to fight. The Cahawba *Dallas Gazette* reported that Gayle was one of several men who had been suggested as a suitable nominee for the office of governor of Alabama in the upcoming state election, which was to take place in August 1861.[78] But so many of the extremists who had supported him politically were now in military service far from the polls where they could vote legally, and it does not appear that he ever officially threw his hat in the ring.

Following reports of the death toll from the Civil War's first major battle, which occurred in Virginia near Manassas on July 21, 1861, Gayle may have felt conflicted that he had not entered the Confederate army. Particularly hard hit at what some called the Battle of Bull Run was the 4th Alabama Infantry, which included the Magnolia Cadets of Selma.[79] Colonel Egbert Jones, a Huntsville lawyer who had been elected the regiment's commander, virtually committed suicide after Captain N.H.R. Dawson and other officers within the regiment challenged his leadership abilities in the weeks leading up to the battle.[80] Determined to prove his bravery, Jones remained on his horse and with his men almost statue-like as his regiment took heavy fire, absorbing the brunt of the first Union army advance near Stone Bridge. Ironically, he was mortally wounded in that exposed position as Dawson and others were fleeing.[81] Official and unofficial reports of the battle maintaining that the 4th Alabama's retreat was proper were published in the Alabama press for several weeks,[82] but they did not immediately dispel the rumors that filtered back to Selma of Dawson's cowardice following the retreat. Dawson allegedly hung back while other members of the regiment regrouped and counterattacked.[83]

Thirty-two men from Dallas County were either killed or wounded in this battle.[84] According to one correspondent who visited the area in the ensuing days, the "excitement was intense" at Selma and Cahawba. "The 'Governor's Guards' and the 'Magnolia Cadets,' of Selma," he reported, "were in the thickest of the fight on the Confederate left, and many families of the former place were mourning the loss of brothers, sons and husbands."[85] The families of the wounded were reportedly "enduring all the agony of prolonged suspense" as they awaited word of the seriousness of their injuries. They received little solace when the editor of the *Selma Reporter* reminded that all should "remember that these casualties are the constant attendants of war, and also that wounds like these could not be more honorable—more glorious."[86] But to loved ones, glory was not always a fair exchange.

Given the sense of loss in the community, one can imagine what those families thought of battlefield cowardice, especially in light of an incident of heroism during the battle by a slave servant of a Selma man who was captain of the Governor's Guard. According to one account, a "Federal soldier was in the act of bayoneting the captain, when the faithful boy fell upon the soldier with his bowie-knife and killed him. The captain escaped with a scratch."[87]

The joy of victory and the grief of personal loss was followed by the first major crisis of public confidence in the Confederate government. Many Southerners were very disappointed that after routing the Yankees at Manassas, the Confederates had not been ordered to chase them back into Washington, D.C., and thereby end the war.[88] Mary Chesnut, then in Richmond, Virginia, noted talk that "many leaders here hate Jeff Davis" and that "disintegration has already begun."[89] When the Confederate government declined to adopt a suggestion to "blow up the Capital," she continued, the "party forming against Mr. Davis" continued its "rapid growth."[90]

That the war would now only continue and probably broaden caused further consternation and placed increasing pressure on those who had not joined the fight. Indeed, bitterness toward cowardice in the face of the enemy paled when compared to the growing prejudice against men who had chosen not to fight at all. According to one account, when a young Dallas County man failed to join the army, his fiancée "sent him, by the hand of a slave, a package inclosing a note. The package contained a lady's skirt and crinoline, and the note these terse words: 'Wear these, or volunteer.' He volunteered."[91]

Men wishing to show their patriotism and bravery gave George Gayle and others an opportunity to do the same by publishing announcements of the formation of new companies and regiments in the days following Bull Run.[92] One called on those who had a "manly heart in their bosom" to "come boldly up to their duty."[93] Charles E. Haynes of the *Dallas Gazette* finally joined at this time, but George Gayle did not.[94] He, instead, unsuccessfully renewed his efforts to obtain a Circuit Court judgeship now that the potential competitors had been thinned out.[95]

Gayle was not alone among secessionists in sitting out the fight. James Calhoun and Andrew Pickens Calhoun received bomb-proof appointments in the quartermaster department in Montgomery.[96] Despite pledges to the contrary made prior to Alabama's secession, C.C. Clay, Jr., did not take any military position either. In a pre-war public letter, Clay had assured that "if my life is spared, whether sick or well, I will stand or fall in [the South's] defence."[97] But after leaving the United States Senate in January, Clay had not immediately returned to Alabama. Whether due to his physical health or concerns about what kind of reception he would receive by Unionists in Huntsville, Clay did not arrive home until late February. Almost immediately, he then left Huntsville for St. Paul, Minnesota, of all places, supposedly due to continuing problems associated with a respiratory illness.[98] After the war began, Clay returned to Alabama, but not to fight. He even declined an offer from his friend, Jefferson Davis, to become Secretary of War, thus opening the door for Leroy Pope Walker.[99] Now rumors were being circulated that Clay's health condition was terminal.[100] But it was not. Clay wanted a seat in the Confederate Senate, and in November 1861, the same day William Lowndes Yancey was elected by an overwhelming margin (120-2) to one of Alabama's two seats by the Alabama legislature, it took Clay ten ballots to finally prevail by thirteen votes for the shorter two year term. Even then the legislators from Clay's home county did not support him, a result Clay correctly termed a "censure."[101]

Neither Yancey nor Clay would have an opportunity to affect Confederate war policy until February 19, 1862, when the "Permanent" Confederate Congress was scheduled to convene. And from a strategic standpoint it would not have mattered if that session had convened earlier.

CHAPTER 6

"Cruel Tyrants Cannot
Live in a Land of Liberty"

And when, from bloody Antietam,
The sad news filled our Southern land,
Of the Cahaba Rifles, our company so brave,
Many had filled a soldier's grave.

And at evening the music of the band,
Comes with the scent of clover,
And it softly plays, in sad refrain,
"Then This Cruel War Is Over."

Now the strains of other music
Float out on the soft moonlight
Col. George W. Gayle playing on his flute
"Oft in the Stilly Night."

Anna Maria Gayle Fry
Memories of Old Cahaba, '89, '94-'95

THE war went sour for Alabama fairly quickly. In 1861 Union naval forces imposed a blockade of Mobile Bay and other southern ports, thereby beginning the slow strangulation of traditional southern commerce.[1] Alabama also lost the economic engine of the capital of the Confederacy when the Provisional Confederate Congress voted to move it to Richmond, Virginia.[2] In 1862, Union forces occupied Tennessee and North Alabama, including C.C. Clay's hometown where his father was jailed. This caused a significant dip in public morale and the desertion rate of Alabama soldiers to mount.[3]

The era of reckless patriotism was over, even for many in Dallas County. The editor of a Selma newspaper lamented that those who should enlist for military service were "slow to move! God help us, for unless the people are aroused to a sense of their danger, our country is ruined—lost irrevocably."[4] As a consequence, after William Lowndes Yancey and C.C. Clay, Jr., took their seats in the Confederate Senate, the Confederate Congress enacted a conscription law to compel men to fight. Although the age parameters would later be broadened, it initially applied only to those between the ages of eighteen and thirty-five.[5] Confederates were nonetheless pleased. "There is no dodging now," wrote Mobile newspaperman John Forsyth. "The music must be faced."[6] As another observer noted, "nearly all the loyal have already volunteered, and the law will operate chiefly on the disloyal, and will secure their services."[7] Others were not so enamored with the idea. The editor in Greensboro declared that the law was not only "totally inconsistent with the true principles of liberty," but would undermine the army while in battle because "men *forced* to fight" were not likely to fight courageously or with a "high degree of personal responsibility."[8]

Because of his age, George Gayle was not subject to this law. N.H.R. Dawson was, but rather than reenlisting he chose to resign from the army. After marrying Elodie Todd, he spent the rest of the war aggressively seeking bomb proof positions in Dallas County that were within the many exemptions initially established by the Conscription Act."[9] John Tyler Morgan also returned home, supposedly to recruit a regiment of partisan rangers.[10] It was a serviceable means of killing time without the risk of being killed, and Morgan was able to buy over four months in this fashion.[11] When that played out Morgan secured an appointment to serve as Commandant of Conscripts for the state of Alabama.[12]

On the heels of these battle avoidance efforts, the Dallas County grand jury convened in Cahawba and issued a public report condemning persons engaging in price-gouging regarding "articles of prime necessity," as well as those who "engage in depreciating Confederate currency" by predicting impending doom.[13] A searing heat wave and drought during the summer assured that crops would be poor, and food even more scarce.[14] Then came news from Virginia that the Cahaba Rifles, John Tyler Morgan's former unit, had suffered significant casualties during the Seven Days Battles near Richmond and was "terribly cut up." So was the Magnolia Cadets, N.H.R. Dawson's former unit.[15] Those families who had lost their men would henceforth also be victimized by inflation while wondering why the stay-at-homes were not in the field still fighting to end the conflict and return the economy back to normal.[16]

Others were, meanwhile, advocating an old self-help remedy: Alabamians should engage in guerrilla warfare outside the normal Confederate command structure.[17] "We must prepare, if the enemy, with his powerful armies and fine appointments should drive us back inch by inch, and take possession of our principal cities ... to convert this into a guerrilla war," wrote a Montgomery resident to a man in North Alabama.[18] The *Richmond Whig* concurred. "We must enter upon this and every other species of war to exterminate the foul invaders of our soil."[19] Grassroots support for this brand of irregular warfare was so strong that the Confederate Congress enacted legislation authorizing the formation of bands of "partisan rangers."[20]

Confederate Colonel John Hunt Morgan, a Huntsville native and soon to be famed practitioner of guerrilla warfare, visited Selma at this time while on his way to Corinth, Mississippi.[21] Whether he then had any contact with George Gayle is unknown, but it is very likely that Gayle approved of his tactics. All of a sudden, the Tennessee Valley in North Alabama was lit up with guerrilla attacks on occupying Union forces. One satisfied editor wrote that "we are rapidly learning what can be done in the guerrilla way" and, as a result, "the invading columns of the enemy will soon be hemmed in by a cordon of daring partisans as by a wall of fire."[22] One of the bloody consequences was the death of a Union general in Madison County in 1862, which was followed by a host of retaliatory, summary executions of suspected guerrillas in the area. The victim, General Robert L. McCook, was a popular and respected Ohio attorney who was reportedly unarmed, ill, and riding in an ambulance wagon at the time he was gunned down by mounted guerrillas. To the North it was an assassination, plain and simple.[23] But the Alabama press made no apologies.[24] In the Confederate Senate William Lowndes Yancey declared that the mode of warfare being used by the federal government justified "each citizen in attacking the invaders, either alone or in organized bands."[25]

The stakes of the war were, meanwhile, being increased exponentially for men like George Gayle. President Lincoln had earlier called on the United States Congress to enact legislation providing a mechanism for the gradual, compensated abolition of slavery.[26] When this did not come to pass, Lincoln seemed to signal that he did not intend for Union forces to free slaves they encountered.[27] But then he signed into law legislation enacted by the United States Congress authorizing confiscation of slaves from those guilty of disloyalty in the future.[28] Then it was reported in the Alabama press that Lincoln had written Horace Greeley that his goal was simply to save the Union, not to end slavery.[29] But after the death of Robert McCook, and the bloody battle of Antietam on September 17 where the Cahaba Rifles suffered more catastrophic losses, Cahawba residents received horrifying news of the issuance by Lincoln of his preliminary Emancipation Proclamation.[30]

The editor of the *Selma Reporter* attempted to calm public nerves by suggesting that Lincoln would likely revoke this proclamation in the wake of subsequent Democratic victories in northern off-year elections. "The recent elections at the North have had a marvelous effect, apparently toward restoring Lincoln to his senses."[31] Lincoln had, in fact, been affected; he became even more determined. When Congress convened, he sent in a message calling for the adoption of a constitutional amendment providing for compensation to states that abolished slavery before 1900.[32] And a few days after the Selma press published a list of the Dallas County casualties suffered in the Battle of Fredericksburg,[33] Lincoln issued his final Emancipation Proclamation, which not only permitted Union forces to free slaves they encountered, but also to enlist them and other blacks in the Union army to fight against the Confederacy.[34]

To men like George Gayle it was a recipe for a bloody St. Domingo-style slave insurrection that would result in the death of all whites in areas like Dallas County with extremely high slave-to-white ratios.[35] A key Tennessee Unionist defected and encouraged the "most persevering and determined resistance against the tyrants and usurpers of the federal Administration, who have blasted our hopes, and are seeking to destroy the last vestige of freedom among us."[36] Even Lincoln's postmaster general publicly warned that "our civil war, closing in the manumission of four million slaves, to take equal ranks with six million of enslavers, would be but the prelude to a servile war of extermination."[37] It was, wrote the editor of the *Charleston Mercury*, an attack on "liberty," which he defined as each citizen being "undisturbed in his person and property." It was the potential loss of this brand of liberty "which renders any fate preferable to" the "hideous and bloody rule" of "our Yankee task-masters."[38] But as a correspondent to a Mobile newspaper noted, "liberty is not a fruit of spontaneous growth. It is rather a hardy plant, which grows only when it is watered with the blood of brave men and the tears of widows and orphans."[39]

If there had not been enough evil tidings, destructive Union army raids from Northeast Mississippi in 1863 were devastating Northwest Alabama.[40] Governor John Gill Shorter ominously declared that the "desolated homes and charred ruins which mark his track in North Alabama are pregnant with solemn warning of the future. How soon he may re-enter the state, when or where he may strike, no one can tell."[41] With the construction of a significant military-industrial complex at Selma in the past year, George Gayle and other residents of Dallas County could make an educated guess.[42] And in fact, Union General William T. Sherman would soon be pushing General Henry Halleck to authorize a strike from North Alabama on Selma.[43]

A few months later the Confederacy suffered devastating setbacks at Gettysburg, Pennsylvania, and Vicksburg, Mississippi, sending South Alabamians into a panic over a possible invasion through Mobile.[44] It was all too much for William Lowndes Yancey, who was already suffering from a severe kidney disease from which he died on July 28, 1863.[45] The *Charleston Mercury* was effusive in its eulogy of the man whose significance had, in retrospect, peaked when he helped engineer the adoption of Alabama's ordinance of secession. One wonders what thoughts crossed George Gayle's mind when he read that "thousands have died, and thousands more may die, in the great cause in which we are engaged—but not one, we believe, will go to his last account with a heart more devoted to its success, or a conscience more clear, of having fulfilled his whole duty in its holy vindication."[46]

Others had not fulfilled their "whole duty" either, but it seems that the stay-at-homes nonetheless spewed fire the loudest. During the political campaign prior to the 1863 state and congressional elections in August, a candidate from Mobile for a congressional seat, newspaperman Charles Carter Langdon, ignited a firestorm of controversy when he called on the Confederacy to adopt "black flag" tactics. "In all battles hereafter fought on our soil," he declared, "let our watchword be—*take no more prisoners.*"[47] Langdon received significant voter support but was defeated.[48]

There were also rumors in the press of plots to kidnap Abraham Lincoln. It was said that James Seddon, the Confederate Secretary of War, "thought this scheme might succeed; but he doubted whether such a proceeding would be of military character and justifiable under the laws of war."[49] With some hesitance, private enterprises supposedly intervened to finance this scheme. According to the same source, "a club or society of wealthy citizens of Richmond was formed for the purpose of raising a fund for this object. Circulars were sent to trustworthy citizens in every other city and town in the Confederacy, inviting co-operation in the grand undertaking, and an immense sum of money was subscribed." These private investors envisioned that "when all was ready, to obtain furlough for [Confederate raider John Singleton] Mosby, and make him leader of the enterprise."[50]

Whether this conspiracy was real or simply a fairy tale at this point is unknown.[51] It is indisputable, however, that pro-Confederate societies were formed in the South during this period.[52] Langdon, the proponent of black flag tactics, was the chairman of what was called the Confederate Society of Mobile.[53] It is also interesting that the southern press occasionally reprinted articles from the northern press regarding "King Abraham's" daily routine, his love for attending the theater, and his penchant for appearing in public seemingly without protection,[54] all information relevant to those planning abductions *and* assassinations.

Whether George Gayle joined a Confederate Society or contributed to its goal at this point is also unknown, but he likely did believe that action of some sort needed to be taken to stem the defeatism and desire for peace that was seemingly afoot as Alabamians went to the polls in August 1863. There was much concern among Alabama Confederates, who feared that candidates desirous of peace at any price might be elected.[55] The editor of the *Selma Reporter* warned those "traitors of the deepest dye" who's "sole aim is peace, cost what it will," that "their infamous behavior is watched, and that there is a day of reckoning close at hand when they will be made to atone for their recreancy to the South."[56] As was reported around the state and throughout the South, on election day in Dallas County, George Gayle, who was supporting incumbent Governor Shorter's reelection, was so angry that he tried to shoot one man and instead accidentally wounded another.[57]

Some incumbents did lose—including Shorter—but the 1863 election did not significantly change Alabama's war policy in the short run. Too many men like N.H.R. Dawson were elected and would dominate the legislature.[58] The *Charleston Mercury* vouched for the new governor, Thomas Hill Watts. "He is a genuine patriot, and for fighting this war out, at every cost, to complete independence."[59] Neither the *Mercury* nor George Gayle would be disappointed.

Jefferson Davis was very fortunate that he was not forced to stand for reelection at this time.[60] "Recent events," wrote John Forsyth, "have stricken a heavy blow at the already waning confidence of the people in the wisdom, the military sagacity, the justice and the impartiality of the head of the Government." Forsyth blamed Davis for the pivotal surrender of Vicksburg by placing General John C. Pemberton, who Forsyth believed was incompetent, in charge of that vital fortress.[61] The *Montgomery Advertiser* joined the anti-Davis chorus by blaming his failure to send Confederate General Robert E. Lee's army to Mississippi, instead of on an invasion of Maryland and Pennsylvania, to help break Union General U.S. Grant's siege of Vicksburg. This, it declared, was the "obvious policy" that should have been followed.[62] The *Charleston Mercury* agreed. "It is impossible for an invasion to have been more foolish and disastrous."[63] To Forsyth, the flaw in Davis' ability as a leader was his obstinacy and failure to listen to those whose opinions differed from his own.[64]

As more setbacks occurred, and Confederates became increasingly desperate, it was only natural that they would lean toward acting unilaterally and independent of the Confederate government to bring about a successful end to the war.[65] The editor of the *Selma Reporter* defended Davis and urged his readers to continue to support Davis's administration "whatever his faults may be."[66] But that level of blind support would be difficult for even this editor to maintain.[67] When Davis ignored advice to remove General Braxton Bragg following the costly Battle of Chickamauga after Bragg failed to push forward and oust the Yankees from Chattanooga, the editor of the Atlanta *Confederacy* expressed outrage and advised unilateral action. "We must save the government from the danger to which it is exposed by the insanity of the administration" by using "the immediate action of the State authorities and the latent energies of the people."[68]

After meeting with Bragg at his headquarters on Missionary Ridge, Davis traveled to Selma where he gave a speech on October 18 from the Gee House hotel portraying the military situation to actually be "favorable." He reportedly "expressed his firm belief that, by next spring, the invaders would be driven from our borders."[69] But Davis's credibility and ability as a commander-in-chief were soon further undermined when Union forces ousted Bragg and his army from the mountains around Chattanooga, thereby opening the way for the invasion of Georgia and East Alabama and sending Alabamians into a deep gloom.[70] At about the same time, C.C. Clay, Jr., a strong supporter of Davis, was ousted from the Confederate Senate by the Alabama legislature.[71]

Shortly thereafter, President Lincoln sweetened the pot for peace when he issued his Amnesty Proclamation under which he promised to pardon a large segment of the southern population if they would cease fighting, swear allegiance to the Union, and abide by his proclamation regarding slavery.[72] C.C. Clay, Jr.'s brother, who edited the *Huntsville Confederate*, sarcastically reported that "King Abraham graciously proclaims reprieves and pardons to all penitent rebels, who will resume allegiance to the United States and re-inaugurate loyal State Governments." He jeered that "of course, all Rebeldom will throw up their hats and shout for joy over the gracious boon offered them by his majesty.[73] A Georgia editor was certain that Lincoln "wants to die, if he must, *an abolition* saint."[74]

The situation for Confederates was desperate and called for a revival of patriotism—whether reckless or otherwise—and perhaps different tactics.[75] This explains why 1864 set a new low for wartime brutality.[76] By then, more civilian Confederates were willing to take matters into their own hands even if discouraged to do so by the Confederate War Department. In a widely published editorial, the Richmond *Dispatch* argued that the North was already utilizing terror tactics and would continue to do so "unless the Black Flag they have been really fighting under from the beginning was met by a Black Flag on our side."[77] Besides, wrote Confederate General P.G.T. Beauregard, "it is the only thing which can prevent recruiting at the North."[78]

Then came news that forces led by Union Colonel Ulric Dahlgren had unsuccessfully attempted to enter Richmond to burn the town and, according to documents reportedly found on Dahlgren's corpse after they were repulsed, assassinate Jefferson Davis and his cabinet. It was, hence, logical for Confederates to conclude that Lincoln had already opened the door to this type of warfare.[79] Members of the press strongly encouraged retaliation in kind. In an editorial titled "Fight the Devil With Fire," which was republished around the nation, the *Richmond Whig* assured that "a million dollars would lay in ashes New York, Boston, Philadelphia, Chicago, Pittsburgh, Washington, and all their chief cities, and the men to do the business may be picked up by the hundreds in the streets of those very cities. If it should be thought unsafe to use them, there are daring men in Canada of [Confederate raider John Hunt] Morgan's and other commands, who have escaped from Yankee dungeons, and who would rejoice at an opportunity of doing something to make all Yankeedom howl with anguish and consternation."[80]

Those who supported these tactics were impatient and tired of waiting on the Davis administration to adopt them. Some complained that they were "dying of West Point and Davis Religion."[81] The *Richmond Whig's* editor disclosed that he had "addressed ourselves to the authorities of the Government" on this issue, "but should they reject the plan, as we suppose they would, then we wish to remind the public that the scheme can be as well executed by private enterprise as by the direction or connivance of the authorities at Richmond."[82] The *Charleston Mercury* agreed, while targeting President Lincoln and Secretary of State William Seward as promoters of northern barbarity. The *Mercury's* editor was particularly incensed by the fact that they had declared "emancipation to our slaves," and forced them to "take up arms against us." Yet the Confederate government—through what the *Mercury* called "cowardice or false humanity"—failed to retaliate and thereby make the North "carry on the war against us in the spirit of civilization."[83]

Alabama Confederates were ahead of their counterparts in other states regarding extreme measures, as evidenced by the assassination of the pro-Union probate judge of Winston County, Alabama, in January 1864.[84] This incident was followed a few weeks later by the infamous massacre of white and black Union troops at Fort Pillow in west Tennessee.[85] Disregarding the very real threat of retaliation on Confederate troops who might seek quarter on other battlefields, some members of the southern press lauded the leader of the Confederate force, Nathan Bedford Forrest, as a hero.[86] "Our soldiery," wrote the approving editor of the *Charleston Mercury*, "have taken into their own hands, despite the weak complicity of the Confederate Government with our foes, the vindication of our rights."[87]

Unbeknownst to the public, the Confederate Congress had appropriated five million dollars in February 1864 for secret service activities, one million dollars of which was allotted to fund covert political and military operations in the North. Part of the plan was to bring terrorism to the North's doors by working through the northern auxiliaries of the Knights of the Golden Circle and other dissident groups, as well as Confederates who had escaped northern prisons to Canada.[88]

In May, C.C. Clay, Jr., and other Confederate agents were sent to Canada to direct political and military operations across the border into the United States.[89] Clay proved to be a very loose cannon. Without authority from the Confederate government, for example, he became involved in a spurious effort to initiate peace negotiations with the Lincoln government. When those efforts were unsuccessful and Clay was criticized by Confederate authorities and the southern press, he was claimed to have angrily declared that "we will carry the war into the White House."[90]

At this point in the war, revenge motivated many Confederates. In an address to his men at Gadsden, Alabama, Confederate General Patrick Cleburne declared that "hereafter I intend to fight, not for rights, but for revenge! You had as well talk religion to a heathen as right—Southern Rights—to a Yankee. Revenge, Revenge! For ruined homes, violated wives, and daughters, desecrated graves and altars, land laid waste and our fair cities burned and sacked and ruined. Can we ever be remunerated? Never! But vengeance upon them henceforth, until not a Yankee lives on Southern soil."[91] In the wake of Union General Lovell Rousseau's destructive raid through east Alabama in July,[92] the storming of Mobile Bay by Union Admiral David Farragut in August,[93] the disastrous capitulation of Atlanta in September,[94] and the shocking introduction of peace resolutions in the Alabama legislature,[95] C.C. Clay, Jr., unleashed a Confederate attack in October 1864 from Canada on the sleepy town of St. Albans, Vermont.[96] It was also during this period that Alabama's most ruthless guerrilla leader, John Pemberton Gatewood, came to public notice through his brutal use of black flag tactics against Union soldiers in the region around Cherokee County, in East Alabama.[97] More assassinations were also planned and executed. It was suspected that Confederate guerrillas in Northeast Alabama assassinated a Confederate congressman, Williamson R.W. Cobb, who had encouraged reunion and was rumored to have been appointed Alabama's provisional governor by President Lincoln.[98]

Lincoln's reelection in November,[99] which was followed by the destruction of Atlanta by Union forces under General William T. Sherman a week later, seemed to bring out the worst in others.[100] Before the fall of Mobile Bay and Atlanta, George Gayle had written Governor Watts that the war "is encouraging to us and our prosperity in that it shows that God is the great Captain and triumph with independence is certain." Gayle's confidence level was then very high. "Our cause is just and if God is just, there is no hope for the Yankee race."[101] But now from the standpoint of public morale, the Confederacy was in precisely the same position it had been exactly four years earlier. Although Alabama had seceded in January 1861, it was well known that an underground reconstruction movement was then afoot. Allegedly at the insistence of, among many others, a Black Belt Alabama lawyer-secessionist, James Graham Gilchrist of Lowndes County, this movement was stopped in its tracks by an avoidable act that outraged the North—firing on Fort Sumter in April 1861—thereby precluding any amicable settlement of the sectional conflict, and forcing the reluctant to fight through several years of bloody war.[102] History could repeat itself if similar heinous acts increased sectional tensions once again. One such act was attempted in New York City, where Confederate agents were tasked by C.C. Clay, Jr., to ignite fires in the downtown area using an incendiary chemical compound, "Greek Fire," that had earlier been tested in Alabama.[103] Several structures there were targeted, including hotels and P.T. Barnum's museum, but the fires were discovered before they could spread.[104]

Did Clay and others have an even higher-profile target in mind?[105] Was he part of a conspiracy to assassinate public officials like President Lincoln? Several witnesses would later claim that Clay discussed the assassination in their presence in Canada in November 1864, and indicated that a plan was then in place.[106] If so, unlike Clay's earlier efforts to kindle peace negotiations, this time it appears that Clay may have at least attempted to gauge Jefferson Davis's current position on this extreme tactic, and possibly did this through someone like a young Alabamian from Marengo County, Confederate Lieutenant Leonidas Waldemar Alston.

Alston, a recent University of Alabama graduate, was the twenty-three-year-old son of a prominent Marengo County, Alabama, lawyer and former United States congressman, William Jeffreys Alston.[107] Young Alston had most recently served under the command of Confederate raider John Hunt Morgan before being captured. He managed to escape and had made his way back to the South by way of Canada with the aid of Confederate agents there associated with Clay.[108] Alston had any number of motivations for revenge. One of his superior officers later recalled that he was "an unassuming and intelligent youth" but had "witnessed enough cruelty at the hands of the enemy to turn his heart into bitterness and gall."[109] Most recently, Alston had become aware of the circumstances surrounding John Hunt Morgan's death in September 1864, which was mourned in Alabama and throughout the South. After making a destructive raid through Kentucky,[110] and subsequently entering East Tennessee, Morgan had taken quarters at a private home in Greenville, Tennessee. Acting on a tip, Union forces entered the town and, when Morgan attempted to escape, gunned him down. The *Charleston Mercury* reported that "after General Morgan had been killed, the unfeeling brutes who murdered him threw his lifeless body across a horse and paraded it through the streets."[111] This treatment enraged Morgan's men, many of whom vowed to seek retribution.[112]

Alston subsequently wrote Jefferson Davis offering his services to "rid my country of some of her deadliest enemies, by striking at the very hearts' blood of those who seek to enchain her in slavery. I consider nothing dishonorable having such a tendency."[113] Alston requested a meeting with Davis, but whether he had other communications on this topic with Davis or other high Confederate officials is unknown. It is known that Davis referred Alston's letter to the Confederate War Department,[114] but there is no solid evidence Davis ever authorized lethal action against Lincoln.

Thus, if Clay wanted to pursue this idea, he or someone would have to do so on their own hook—just as had occurred with his peace initiative. Who could execute such a plan? John Hunt Morgan's men were apparently willing and potentially available. Another possibility was the Confederate cavalry unit led by John Singleton Mosby, which had repeatedly demonstrated its ability to work behind enemy lines and make effective surprise attacks.[115] A further possibility were members of the Knights of the Golden Circle, with whom Clay had had contact while in Canada, and which news reports in Alabama and elsewhere indicated had recently been active.[116] According to one witness, Clay encouraged a man who was understood to be willing to execute the plan by telling him that "if we succeeded and returned to Canada we could be 'rich men.'"[117]

The identity of the men involved in these encounters is apparently unknown, but there is evidence that Lincoln's eventual assassin, twenty-six-year-old KGC member John Wilkes Booth, had been in Canada in late October.[118] As a prominent actor, Booth had the perfect cover story for traveling around the country. After leaving Canada he went to New York City where he, ironically, played a role other than Brutus in Shakespeare's "Julius Caesar" before traveling to Washington, D.C., where he played Romeo in "Romeo and Juliet."[119] At the time he spoke vaguely to family members and others of a new venture more profitable than acting.[120]

But how was the money for such an operation to be raised? The target of the St. Albans raid in October, which C.C. Clay, Jr., had authorized and financed without authorization from Richmond, had been the banks there. But several of the raiders, led by another former member of John Hunt Morgan's brigade, had been captured by pursuing militia following the bank robberies.[121] Much of the haul was not gold or greenbacks, but instead consisted of bank bills issued by Vermont banks that were much easier to trace and very difficult to redeem.[122] Hence, the raid was not very productive of money that might entice assassins to engage in a potentially suicidal mission.

No immediate action against federal government leaders was apparent to George Gayle or any other southerner, and by the end of November an army led by Union General William Tecumseh Sherman was pillaging through Georgia, seemingly aiming for Gayle's beloved South Carolina and meeting only token resistance.[123] And like a lamb tied to a stake awaiting the lion, South Carolina was bleating in fear for help. For months, the *Charleston Mercury* had complained of Confederate military policy and strategy and, in particular, the failure to concentrate the army to protect the fortress at Vicksburg from Union forces under General Ulysses Grant in 1863 and most recently Atlanta from General Sherman. "Every effort of our Government should be used to furnish" the Confederate commander in Georgia "with the means of defeating his wily adversary. For that done, the campaign and war would be over.[124] Concentration! concentration! *Salvation* is in *concentration*. Weakness, defeat, suffering, perhaps ruin, is in *dispersion*."[125] But that had not happened, and the temperature of the *Mercury's* editor was now rising. He compared the South's fate to Poland's under Russia's domination.[126] Then came reports that Confederate forces under General John Bell Hood, who had given up Atlanta to Sherman, were moving west through Alabama, leaving no significant Confederate force between Sherman and South Carolina.[127] Confederate strategy was to have Hood lure Sherman north and west and then out of Georgia and away from South Carolina, but Sherman did not take the bait.[128] He followed Hood as far as Gaylesville in East Alabama but, to the horror of Confederates, turned around and returned to Atlanta and on November 15 began his famous march east to the sea.[129] In its November 18 edition, the *Mercury* published a report from the *New York Times* stating that Sherman was aiming for Charleston and that the "rebels have nothing in Georgia that can oppose Sherman."[130]

The *Mercury* had long been an advocate of both retaliation and guerrilla warfare.[131] Now it attempted to inspire South Carolina's sons with stories of heroism during the Revolutionary War. In an editorial titled "The Strait and Narrow Way to Peace," it noted that with "South Carolina overrun, with not a single organized army to defend her, with only her gallant partizans MARION and SUMTER, and a few more in the Upper Country—now hiding in swamps—now dashing at the enemy in isolated positions still fought on until at last their enemy was worn out and forced to yield before that indomitable will which reverses only strengthened, and the nearer approach to success by our enemies, only made more unconquerable."[132]

This was brave talk, but some certainly had the spirit. According to a letter allegedly written by John Wilkes Booth in November 1864, Booth's love for the South and hatred for the abolitionists had led him to attempt a potentially suicidal mission involving the kidnapping of President Lincoln and taking him to the South to be held for ransom. "Nor do I deem it a dishonor in attempting to make for her a prisoner of this man, to whom she owes so much misery," he wrote. But Booth was unsuccessful. At about this time the *Mobile Advertiser and Register,* as well as the *Charleston Mercury*, published the same account from an unnamed source regarding a threat to Lincoln that had failed.[133] "Lincoln has been frightened out of the Soldiers' Home [in Washington, D.C.] back to the White House. A letter says for several nights past mysterious signals have been observed in that direction, and last night the suspicious indications of an attempted raid had multiplied to such an extent as to induce the President to abandon his insufficiently guarded suburban residence."[134]

There is evidence that, at this time, some Alabamians in Gayle's Dallas County were fighting amongst themselves over whether they had fulfilled their whole duty to sustain the Confederacy.[135] These recriminations may have led to some degree of self-reproach, especially to Gayle who had done so much to bring on the war and so little to support the war effort. It was shortly after this that George Washington Gayle took it upon himself to make a very public call for funds to finance an assassination attempt. He did this by way of a newspaper advertisement placed in the December 1, 1864, edition of the *Selma Dispatch*. Titled "$1,000,000 Wanted To Have Peace by the First of March," the advertisement—which did not reveal Gayle's identity but listed a Cahawba post office box "X" for replies—contained a proposal and a solicitation that "if the citizens of the Southern Confederacy will furnish me with the cash, or good security, for the sum of $1,000,000, I will cause the lives of Abraham Lincoln, William H. Seward and Andrew Johnson to be taken by the 1st of March next." It stated that $50,000 had to be paid "in advance" to "reach and slaughter the three villains." The advertisement claimed that this act would demonstrate that "cruel tyrants cannot live in a land of liberty."[136]

The flames of sectional hatred were already red hot. A sudden and catastrophic decapitation of the federal government as envisioned by Gayle would not bring peace but instead would transform the conflict into the feared war of extermination, or at least make any peace that much harder for the South if it lost. But the desire and rationale to bring about Lincoln's demise probably seemed logical to Gayle. The *Charleston Mercury* called the president a "negro-fanatic," among other things.[137] Consistent with this, one of Gayle's contemporaries, William Garrett, later wrote that Gayle believed "President Lincoln was the author of all this mischief and suffering," and offered the reward "to any person who would destroy the *monster*, as he considered him, and thus put an end to the frightful atrocities committed through his influence."[138]

But why did Gayle also target Johnson and Seward, in addition to Lincoln? One possibility is that Gayle saw them as the primary executors of Lincoln's emancipation proclamation if Lincoln were murdered. Andrew Johnson, who John Forsyth had earlier labeled a "renegade demagogue" following his appointment and conduct as Tennessee's military governor, had made a widely reported anti-slavery speech in Nashville following his nomination for the vice presidency by the Republican Party. He declared to the audience that slavery was "dead" and pledged that traitors would be punished.[139] On November 17, Seward and Lincoln had appeared at what the *Charleston Mercury* called Lincoln's "White House" where they addressed a large audience. Lincoln called for national unity to finish the war. Seward recounted the progress made during the war on the extermination of slavery and announced that the administration would push for adoption of the previously proposed but stalled constitutional amendment to abolish slavery throughout the nation when Congress next convened.[140]

Did John Wilkes Booth become aware of Gayle's advertisement? It would have been difficult for anyone to miss. The oft-quoted *Mobile Advertiser and Register* published the substance of it on the front page of its December 7, 1864, edition,[141] and as computerized newspaper databases have revealed, the entire advertisement quickly entered the stream of information outside Alabama. It was repeatedly reprinted verbatim in newspapers throughout the United States and even overseas over the several months leading up to Lincoln's assassination.[142] Evidence later gathered during the investigation of Lincoln's assassination revealed that word of George Gayle's advertisement was apparently on the street everywhere by then, including in Ohio, Maryland, Virginia, and Washington, D.C. The printers of the *Selma Dispatch* would subsequently testify during the military trial of some of John Wilkes Booth's team that copies of the *Dispatch* containing the advertisement were also sent to the Richmond newspapers as a part of the routine newspaper exchange.[143] A Maryland clothing merchant was subpoenaed to the trial because he had been reported as having repeatedly mentioned the contents of the advertisement to his customers for several weeks before the assassination. He testified that he had seen it in one of the area newspapers.[144]

After Gayle's advertisement appeared, Booth alluded to a great "speculation" in which he was involved.[145] On December 18, 1864, he told an acquaintance that the undertaking would bring them glory as well as profits. To another he claimed that there was so much money in it that the participants "would never want for money."[146] Another member of Booth's band, George Atzerodt, boasted to his brother that he would either "hear of his being hung or making a good deal of money, a fortune."[147] This appears to have had the desired effect. One of the eventual assassins, young Lewis Thornton Powell, who was a native of Randolph County, Alabama, and had most recently served under John Singleton Mosby, joined the Booth conspirators less than sixty days after Gayle's advertisement was first published.[148] One of the other conspirators, Dr. Samuel Mudd, met with Booth three weeks after Gayle's advertisement.[149] At that time Mudd introduced Booth to John Surratt, who joined the conspiracy. Surratt recruited another team member, David Herold.[150]

Not surprisingly, no records were ever found following the war indicating who contributed, when they contributed, or how much they contributed to Gayle's assassination fund. The post-war practice of many Confederates was to destroy whatever personal papers that might implicate them in acts of wartime disloyalty or war crimes. For example, C.C. Clay, Jr., destroyed his diary for the period he was in Canada.[151] In the law, such "spoliation" of evidence permits an inference of guilt.[152]

After Gayle released his solicitation to the world, all he could do was wait for the blood money to roll in, and then for the deeds to be done. But there was a question whether the Confederacy would last that long. As 1864 came to a close, the Alabama press was referring to the "avalanche of evil tidings from Tennessee," where General John Bell Hood and the only Confederate army that could possibly protect Alabama had gone.[153]

Chapter 7

"Deeds of Avenging War"

And then came the scullions, the Northern invaders
An army of locusts were Wilson's great raiders,
Who devastated our land, stole all they could find:
Jewels and silver, mules, horses and kine.

Anna Maria Gayle Fry,
Memories of Old Cahaba, '96

H**OOD'S** army had been virtually annihilated in the Battle of Nashville, and Alabama was a sitting duck.[1] But some in the Alabama press urged "continued resistance at any and every cost" as opposed to "submission to the terms proposed by Lincoln."[2] The *Selma Dispatch* agreed, calling on "all men of property" to place "one-half of their wealth or all their available means at the disposal of the Government and to the energetic defense of the country." By "aiding at once in the thorough prosecution of the war ... peace will come and the institution of slavery be saved and the mass of all other property also."[3] Consistent with this admonition, the Augusta, Georgia, *Constitutionalist* took notice of George Gayle's still-circulating advertisement for funds to assassinate Lincoln, Johnson, and Seward, and exclaimed, "Surely he ought to be accommodated."[4]

Men of this stripe hoped against hope that efforts to negotiate a peace treaty at Hampton Roads, Virginia, in February 1865 would fail unless they resulted in Confederate independence. This, wrote the editor of the *Charleston Mercury*, was "the *sine qua non* of an honorable settlement." Jefferson Davis agreed but President Lincoln would not budge on that issue and also insisted on the ultimate emancipation of the slaves as a further condition of peace.[5]

The *Mercury's* editor, as well as the other residents of Charleston, had more immediate concerns. General Sherman's army crossed from Georgia into South Carolina, and on February 11 the *Mercury* published its last edition in Charleston for the rest of the war.[6] The city would be occupied a week later,[7] and Robert Barnwell Rhett would eventually find refuge in Eufaula, Alabama.[8] To Sherman the "hellhole of secession," South Carolina, was to be devastated.[9]

While South Carolinians braced for the fiery retribution Sherman's army had wrought on central Georgia during his march to the sea, their relatives in Alabama were awaiting a similar fate at the hands of the Union army that had chased Hood and his decimated forces out of Tennessee.[10] The Alabama press was reporting that Dallas County, with its critically important military-industrial complex at Selma, and its military prison filled with Union soldiers at Cahawba, was a primary target for the enemy.[11] That lightly defended prison facility, called Castle Morgan in honor of John Hunt Morgan, had been used to incarcerate the enemy pending their parole and exchange.[12] As evidenced by an escape of twelve prisoners in February 1864 who tunneled out and fled, it presented another significant security risk to George Gayle in addition to that arising from the huge slave population in Dallas County. One of Gayle's wartime appellate cases involved his effort on behalf of the state of Alabama to prevent county militiamen from avoiding guard duty there.[13] Castle Morgan was definitely a spartan military prison and for this it was criticized by some in the Northern press,[14] but the prisoners there must have been treated tolerably well in light of its relatively low mortality rate. That, however, did not make it any less of a high-value Union target.

The South Alabama press did its best to motivate residents into frenzied fanaticism for the Cause, directing much venom against President Lincoln and his peace-without-slavery terms. The editor of the *Selma Dispatch* declared that at Hampton Roads "our [peace] commissioners have met the United States Government, in the persons of Lincoln and Seward, [and] had been told that abject submission and surrender of property are their terms of peace." These commissioners had, in sum, "met with insult, and the haughty arrogance of a brutal and fanatical foe." The *Dispatch* expected the arousal of the "spirit of defiance in the heart of every man possessing one spark of manhood."[15] The *Chattanooga Rebel*, which had taken refuge in Selma, held that "henceforth every man is either for absolute submission, or for the best and bravest and most forcible resistance we can make to these insolent and inhuman demands. If we are not cowards, we ought now to be united on the platform of resistance to the bitter end. We ought to resolve to suffer all and endure all, rather than be the slaves of the Lincoln tyranny."[16] Following a pro-war meeting in Selma on February 13, the editor of the Jackson *Mississippian*, another press refugee to Selma, expressed hope that the public was falling into line. "The ball for ACTION is now in motion, and we trust it will roll on and onward, until the whole country shall have felt its benign influences."[17]

George Gayle could not have been disappointed in this movement of public sentiment, but time was running out. Abraham Lincoln's second inauguration was scheduled for March 4, and in Gayle's advertisement soliciting funds for the assassinations, Gayle had pledged to accomplish that purpose by March 1. Consistent with that timetable, C.C. Clay, Jr., had returned to the South from Canada on February 3 aboard the appropriately named steamship *Rattlesnake*. Fundraising was on Clay's mind when he wrote a public letter in which he expressed certainty that "if our people know all that awaits them, if conquered, they would gladly offer up all their blood and treasure to avert that greatest of all calamities."[18] The northern press, meanwhile, continued to publish—and oftentimes ridicule—Gayle's advertisement.[19] "Some funny fellow or would-be swindler" was behind it, according to a Connecticut editor.[20] A similarly incredulous New York editor wondered "who responds to this stirring appeal of the Selma contractor?"[21]

Perhaps some residents of Alabama's largest city did. Mobile too was an important strategic objective, and the Confederate military there was busy preparing for an invasion.[22] Civilian Confederates led by John Forsyth and north Alabamian David Hubbard were, meanwhile, organizing a new Confederate society called the "Society of Loyal Confederates." Revenge was their main goal. "It is," wrote Forsyth in his newspaper, "the proper and manly response to the slavish ultimatum of Lincoln," who had demanded reunion and the emancipation of the slaves as the conditions for peace during the negotiations at Hampton Roads. "If ever a people were stung by wrongs to deeds of avenging war," Forsyth declared, "it is this people."[23]

The members of the Society of Loyal Confederates of Mobile proposed the organization of affiliated clubs in every county and city of the Confederacy, and this process was put in motion.[24] Their *stated* goal was to raise money to pay Confederate soldiers from Alabama and for unstated "similar purposes."[25] The Augusta, Georgia, *Constitutionalist*, which had earlier encouraged contributions to the fund George Gayle had "cordially" solicited, endorsed the Society of Loyal Confederates and its goals, and hoped for the formation of additional clubs all over the South.[26]

And as was the case with the Confederate societies reportedly formed in 1863 to support a plot to kidnap President Lincoln, the affiliates of the Society of Loyal Confederates formed in Alabama had no intention of clearing their goals with Richmond. John Forsyth wrote that: "Whenever the masses of men in this Confederacy sit down with the apathy of the general Russian population and leave the conduct of the war, and its immense results at stake, exclusively to the Government, our days as a free people are numbered, and the historical reader can name the hour of our subjugation."[27]

While the Society of Loyal Confederates was forming in the state, reports were announcing that subjugating Union forces were on their way from North Alabama. On February 23, the *Selma Dispatch* reported the contents of a letter incorrectly stating that 20,000 Union troops had already crossed the Tennessee River "for an advance into this section of the State."[28] If anyone in Dallas County wondered what they were in store for, word of the fiery destruction of Columbia, South Carolina, was arriving at about the same time.[29] After reading reports of Columbia's fate, one still committed Alabama nurse, Kate Cumming, wrote that "the very name of Sherman brings up woe and desolation before us. The beautiful city of Columbia, South Carolina, had been laid in ruins by him and his hirelings. Bands of marauders, black and white, are sent through the country to do their worse on the helpless inhabitants." South Carolina had "indeed been scourged," Cumming related, "because they say she was a sinner above all the rest." But, she concluded hopefully, "there is a day of reckoning for the evil-doer," although she did not know when that day would come. She asked: "Lord how long shall the wicked triumph."[30] Alabama's sins may not have equated to those of the Palmetto State but in the eyes of many Northerners they deserved equal punishment.

The evidence allows only speculation regarding whether one of the purposes of the Society of Loyal Confederates in Mobile was to raise the bounty money George Gayle had solicited. That Society was formed during the month leading up to Gayle's promised "peace" deadline, and one of its functions was to raise money to promote the war effort. In fact, the financial goal of John Forsyth's mother organization in Mobile was to raise one million dollars, exactly what Gayle had sought.[31] It is also clear that Forsyth hated President Lincoln with a passion and seemed to be obsessed with ultimately reporting on Lincoln's demise. As if stalking Lincoln from a distance, Forsyth had, for over a year, regularly reported on Lincoln's public appearances and movements in Washington, including those at theaters.[32] Since then, Forsyth had repeatedly written of Lincoln as having encouraged a spirit of genocide.[33] "He means, if he can, by brute force to trample this people out of existence, appropriate their lands and goods, and repopulate this land with colonies of people and soldiers from the North."[34] After the failure at Hampton Roads, Forsyth blamed Lincoln and told his readers that "Abe pricks us with the point of the sword; he strikes us with the flat of the blade, and exclaims, 'fight, rebel, coward and scoundrel, or give me your property, your freedom and your life.'"[35] In announcing the purpose of the Society of Loyal Confederates, Forsyth echoed these themes, declaring that he was "fully satisfied that if we failed in establishing our independence, history would record that we were suicides. We have the power, and have only to exercise that power to secure success."[36] If Forsyth truly believed all of this, engaging in an assassination conspiracy was certainly not out of the question. After all, targeting the enemy's government officials was a logical guerrilla tactic.

No one was assassinated by March 1 or even by the inaugurations of President Lincoln and Andrew Johnson on March 4. It was not for the want of trying. There is evidence that John Wilkes Booth and at least some members of his gang of assassins were in Washington, D.C., on election day, but security was too tight to make a move.[37]

The press reported that two very different men were arrested for trying to kill Lincoln. The first, Charles Anderson, was definitely in the truth-is-stranger-than-fiction category. He was arrested in Cleveland, Ohio, in early February while masquerading as a young woman named "Charlotte" Anderson and attempting to make arrangements to travel to Washington to shoot Lincoln.[38] According to all accounts, given what were described as his "palpable female 'attributes,'" it is very surprising that Anderson's true sex even came under suspicion.[39] The *Cleveland Herald* described him as "very feminine in appearance," and having "a soft and low feminine voice whenever he chooses to use it." But he was also a "dead shot with a pistol, a splendid horseman, can talk three languages fluently, can dance admirably, play the piano, do fine sewing, embroider, knit and crochet equal to any woman."[40] Even after suspicions were raised by some women in Cleveland, the military authorities still appear to have believed this cross-dressing assassin was female, at least until "several respectable ladies were delegated to ascertain if Charlotte was Charlotte." After examining him, these ladies returned what was described as a "semi-hysterical report of strongly reinforced suspicion of latent manhood."[41] Anderson's subsequent fate is unknown.

The other would-be assassin, Thomas Clements (or Clemens), was much less flamboyant and cultured than Anderson, but at least he succeeded in reaching Washington. While very inebriated, however, he was arrested by military authorities there the day after the inauguration after publicly declaring that he had come to the capital to kill Lincoln during the inauguration ceremony. According to a telegraphic report published in John Forsyth's newspaper, Clements, while "using gross and profane language," bragged that he came here to kill the President," but that he was "too late by half an hour, and that his Saviour would never forgive him for failing to do so."[42]

It is highly unlikely that Anderson or Clements had been motivated by Gayle's advertisement, which implicitly called for not one but three murders as a precondition to receiving the bounty. Besides, as the *Cleveland Leader* put it shortly after Clements's arrest, "the details do not justify the belief that any deep-laid plot had been contrived against the life of the President. An assassin, with the responsibility of so great an infamy upon his hands, does not get drunk and blab his secret to passers on the pavement. The envoy and emissary of the Confederate Government to assassinate the President of the United States would be a very different man, from this drunken rowdy. Clemens is most probably a secessionist at heart, who, being *plenum Bacchi*—full of whiskey—vented the malice of his heart in drunken threats against Mr. Lincoln."[43]

Subsequent reports in the northern press of these two foiled plots to assassinate Lincoln on the day of his inauguration found no expressions of condemnation in the Alabama press.[44] The same dark tolerance met reports that thirty men under Confederate raider John Singleton Mosby had advanced within three miles of the fortifications of Washington, D.C., on the night of March 12.[45]

Booth and any would-be assassins likely assumed that the disclosure of these tangible threats resulted in the tightening of security around Lincoln even further, making assassination infinitely more hazardous. Now, the ability to assure potential assassins that the money had or would be accumulated and would certainly be paid was arguably even more important. But as the month of March 1865 came to a close, there was still no word that George Gayle's hope and pledge would even be belatedly fulfilled.

The word in Alabama was that the Yankees were coming,[46] and this time the reports were accurate.[47] No evidence has been found indicating George Gayle's whereabouts when the invaders, led by Union General James Harrison Wilson, arrived on the outskirts of Selma on April 2, 1865, quickly overwhelmed a smaller force consisting of Confederate soldiers, local militia, and conscripted civilians, and began their reign of destruction.[48] Among the many structures in Selma that were burned to the ground was the building housing the *Selma Dispatch*, which had published Gayle's advertisement.[49] Cahawba capitulated on April 4, apparently without resistance. According to a report to the *New York*

Herald, "about seventy of our prisoners, confined there for a long time, were released. They had been well treated."[50] If those prisoners had not been properly treated, chances are the liberating soldiers would have retaliated against Cahawba's citizens. But there is no evidence George Gayle, his family, or any other Cahawba residents were molested in person or property.

Nonetheless, from an economic standpoint, Dallas County was a dead cock in the pit—all thanks to George Gayle and men like him who had sent Alabama down the road to secession, war, and destruction.[51] But if enough funds were raised, Gayle might also play a role in providing the South with the last glorious laugh in this avenging war. Whether that money would be raised in time to carry it into execution was perhaps unknown, although the fundraising activity up to this point may have been enough to demonstrate the Society of Loyal Confederates' bona fides. Coincidentally or not, in the weeks after praise for the society began appearing generally in the southern press, the assassins, including John Wilkes Booth and Alabama native Lewis Thornton Powell, were taking the step of casing Ford's Theatre in Washington, D.C. Some of them even watched a play from the presidential box, and then met to discuss strategy in a private room at a local saloon. Contrary to later claims, this had absolutely nothing to do with a plan to kidnap Lincoln, which was said to involve grabbing and handcuffing Lincoln in his presidential box, lowering him down to the stage, and then trying to flee with him—all while the audience did nothing.[52] It was to be an assassination, which might require the assassins to shoot their way out of town. They would soon be hiding a cache of weapons in the boardinghouse of Mary Surratt in the area where some of them had been staying while planning their attack.[53]

Abraham Lincoln was, meanwhile, in Virginia under the protection of General Grant's army, where he would remain until just a few days before the attack would occur.[54] To the chagrin of anyone seeking to murder Lincoln in exchange for blood money, there was a distinct possibility that someone else would kill him there. Many in the North feared that Lincoln would be targeted by what the worried *New York Times* described as "some reckless and desperate rebel sharpshooter,"[55] particularly when Lincoln unwisely risked his life by twice traveling to only recently occupied Richmond.[56] Booth would have agreed with the aggravated editor of the *Times* that "Mr. Lincoln's life may be of no special value to himself," but "his official position makes it of special value to the country, and he has no right to put it at the mercy of any lingering desperado in Richmond, or of any stray bullet in the field."[57] The *Times's* editor, but probably not Booth, excepted the situation where "some special service can be rendered by his personal presence,"[58] although neither probably included any of Lincoln's risky activities in Richmond within that narrow exception.

While Lincoln was in Virginia, John Wilkes Booth had traveled to New York City.[59] There he learned some very disturbing news. According to some sources, Booth was told of a competing team of assassins consisting of Confederate soldiers who planned to kill Lincoln and his cabinet by planting a bomb in the White House. Booth is said to have told George Atzerodt on Booth's return to Washington on March 25 that "if he did not get [Lincoln] quickly the N. York crowd would."[60] And if that happened Booth would be unable to share in the bounty.

Ironically, everything had finally fallen into place during the week leading up to the assassinations. First, and perhaps foremost, on April 8 John Forsyth announced in his Mobile newspaper that the members of the Society of Loyal Confederates in Alabama had raised one million dollars.[61] That was plenty of time for telegraphic reports of the fundraising success to reach New York and Washington. Second, the press in Washington and elsewhere reported that one of the three targets of the conspiracy, Secretary of State Seward, had suffered serious injuries, including a broken arm and a fractured jaw, when he leaped from a runaway "barouche" or carriage. The press also reported that Seward would be bedridden at home for an indefinite period, therefore easy to find when the time came for the Alabama member of the team of assassins, Lewis Powell, to murder him.[62]

So would Vice President Andrew Johnson. Since the inauguration in March, he had been rooming at a Washington hotel, the Kirkwood House, instead of residing in Nashville, Tennessee, with his family.[63] Johnson had also recently traveled to Richmond,[64] and was scheduled to then return to Tennessee but decided to go back to Washington in hopes of seeing President Lincoln upon his return from Virginia. That was fortuitous for Johnson as well as Booth's gang. The train Johnson was to take to Tennessee was attacked by Confederate guerrillas.[65]

Following Johnson's return to Washington he had appeared in public at a giant, spontaneous celebration of the fall of Richmond on the south portico of the Patent Office where he had given a brief speech.[66] According to the report in the *Washington Chronicle,* Johnson discussed his thoughts on post-war policy, telling the large crowd in attendance that he was "in favor of leniency"—a change from his days in Tennessee—except with regard to the "evil doers," who he declared should be punished. But when some in the crowd shouted their agreement, he seemed to return to his earlier Old Testament stance. "Treason," he declared, "is the highest crime known in the catalogue of crimes, and for him that is willing to lift his impious hand against the authority of the nation—I would say death is too easy a punishment." In conclusion, he announced that he favored "the halter to intelligent, influential traitors," but "to the honest boy, to the deluded man, who has been deceived into the rebel ranks, I would extend lenience."[67] In the eyes of the assassins, such retributive comments must have made Johnson an even more righteous target. As later investigation would reveal, the assassin assigned to Andrew Johnson, George Atzerodt, also took a room at the Kirkwood House and thereafter made inquiries "about the room of Mr. Johnson, his whereabouts and habits."[68]

President Lincoln survived his trip to Virginia, and he returned to Washington on the evening of April 9.[69] It was at this point that John Wilkes Booth and his fellow conspirators caught a major break. The team of bombers was intercepted by a Union cavalry regiment in Virginia before they ever reached Washington.[70] And with their competition out of the way, Booth was back in business and could finally execute his plans. Lincoln unwittingly obliged when he quickly resumed his risky pattern of appearing in public without adequate security. On April 10, he made two brief appearances before adoring crowds ecstatic regarding the fall of Richmond as well as General Lee's surrender to Grant the prior day. Lincoln's remarks were happy and lighthearted, and apparently calculated to avoid any hint of ridicule or malice toward the South.[71] There is evidence that John Wilkes Booth was in the crowd outside the White House when Lincoln made these remarks, and that he declared to Lewis Powell, who was also present, that this was "the last speech [Lincoln] will ever make." So filled with hate and greed, Booth even tried to convince Lewis Powell to shoot Lincoln right then, but Powell did not.[72] Later that night Booth took target practice in preparation for his role in the coming drama.[73]

Lincoln actually made his last public address at dusk on April 11 from a window at the White House. He began by reminding the thousands in attendance that for the "gladness of heart" and the "hopes of a righteous and speedy peace," "he from whom all blessings flow must not be forgotten." Then Lincoln praised General Grant and "his skillful officers and brave men," whose efforts gave "us the cause of rejoicing."[74] Lincoln also took the opportunity in his address to defend the process by which some southern state governments had already been reconstructed under the "ten percent" plan he had formulated and announced in December 1863. This appears to have actually been a pretext for signaling his future policy on the status of the freed slaves. Focusing on Louisiana, Lincoln somewhat disingenuously noted that its new constitution did not "adopt apprenticeship for freed people," but he did not mention that this method of labor and social control he had earlier suggested was not prohibited either, and therefore could be implemented by the newly elected legislature. That the new Louisiana constitution did not provide for black suffrage probably assured that would occur. Lincoln expressed no concern about that feature of the constitution either. "It is also unsatisfactory to some that the [elective] franchise is not given to the colored man," he observed. "I would myself prefer that it were now conferred on the very intelligent and those who serve our cause as soldiers," but as he noted, that was not material. Lincoln announced that the "*sole* object to the [federal] government, civil and military, in regard to those States, is to again get them into" what he called the "proper practical relation with the Union." Thus, he said, "let us all join in doing the acts necessary to restore the proper practical relations between these States and the Union." Lincoln cleverly tied this call for prompt restoration to the ratification of the still-pending Thirteenth Amendment, which he noted required approval by three-fourths of all the states. As he pointed out, Louisiana's new government had already given its approval to that amendment and to reject that government now would mean one less vote for ratification.[75] Hence, for abolitionists and those who simply wanted the slave power in the South broken, there was a big carrot encouraging rapid restoration without black suffrage.

Lincoln's reluctance to require Louisiana and the other southern states to adopt some form of black suffrage did not divert Booth from his goal. On April 13, the day before the assassination, Booth told an acquaintance he had something big "on his hands" and "there was a great deal of money in it."[76] The Washington newspapers of April 14, 1865, announced that Lincoln would be attending a play at Ford's Theatre that night. In fact, the *National Republican* revealed that "Lieut. Gen. Grant, with President and Mrs. Lincoln have secured the State Box and will visit Ford's Theatre this evening to witness Miss Laura Keen's company in Tom Taylor's '[Our] American Cousin.'"[77] It is only speculation whether Grant was then added to John Wilkes Booth's hit list at this point, but in any event Grant and his wife left town that evening for New Jersey and did not attend the play.[78]

The assassins were, meanwhile, making their final preparations and bragging to others that they would become rich and would soon do something that would be reported in the newspapers.[79] Alabama native Lewis Powell made another check at William Seward's home to verify Seward's condition and whereabouts.[80] Nothing had changed, meaning Seward would be easy prey that night. George Atzerodt knew that his target, Vice President Andrew Johnson, still stayed at the Kirkwood Hotel.[81] The only question was whether Johnson would be in his room that night when Atzerodt was to murder him. According to some accounts, this was confirmed by leaving a calling card from Booth, whom Johnson had previously met, asking Johnson if he was at home. Johnson reportedly replied in a note stating that he was "very busily engaged."[82]

Booth also knew where his target would be that night, and had made his preparations accordingly. But if his motivation was to claim the bounty supposedly being accumulated by George Gayle and others, there was likely still some concern on his part that after he, Powell, Atzerodt and the others took all the risks, someone else would claim the prize. Perhaps recalling that Gayle's advertisement in December 1864 declared that the murders would "satisfy the world that cruel *tyrants cannot live* in a 'land of *liberty,*'"[83] Booth prepared a letter to the editor of the Washington, D.C., *National Intelligencer* dated April 14 sprinkled with that theme. He explained his intended actions and declared that "to hate *tyranny* to love *liberty* and justice, to *strike* at wrong and oppression, was the teaching of our fathers."[84] He also used a derringer made in a suburb of Philadelphia, Pennsylvania, called "Northern Liberties" to kill Lincoln; brandished a large dagger etched with the words "America, Land of the Free" on its blade;[85] and yelled "*Sic Semper Tyrannis!*"—Latin for "Thus always to tyrants"—immediately before firing the fatal shot.[86]

After shooting Lincoln in the head during the third act of the play, Booth made no effort to conceal his identity and, in fact, literally took great pains to assure that those in attendance at Ford's Theatre could easily identify him as the President's assassin. Instead of leaving the building the same way he had come, Booth jumped from the President's box almost twelve feet down to the stage, and then faced the large, startled audience before leaving through a back door of the building.[87] Booth had accomplished his personal mission; he had not only inflicted a mortal wound on the president, but now no one could jump his claim to a bounty. As the Washington *National Republican* would report the following day, "it seems perfectly evident the murder was committed by JOHN WILKES BOOTH."[88]

Rather than attempting to return to Canada, Booth tellingly chose an escape route that took him South, despite the presence there of Grant's and Sherman's huge armies. Whether his ultimate destination was Alabama—where C.C. Clay, Jr., was also headed—will never be known because Booth was caught and mortally wounded in Virginia, unfortunately before he could be interrogated.[89] Even if Booth had survived, however, he would have learned to his dismay that all of the conditions to earn George Washington Gayle's supposed blood money had not been satisfied. Atzerodt had lost his nerve, thereby sparing

Andrew Johnson. Powell had brutally attacked Seward with a knife at Seward's home, but Seward would miraculously survive his wounds.[90]

This would be reported in still smoldering Selma five days later. George Gayle's reaction is unknown, but there were certainly those in Dallas County who were most pleased. The Selma *Chattanooga Rebel*, which had resumed publication in Selma shortly after General Wilson's force had left for Montgomery, reported the assassinations on April 19, 1865.[91] The following day, in an editorial that would be reprinted in several northern newspapers in the coming weeks, the *Rebel* asserted that both Lincoln and Seward had gotten what they deserved. Lincoln, who the editor ridiculed as a "political mountebank and professional joker, whom nature intended for the ring of a circus, but whom a strange streak of popular delusion elevated to the Presidency," had "gone to answer before the bar of God for the innocent blood he has permitted to be shed, in his efforts to enslave a free and heroic people."[92] The *Rebel's* editor was not alone in Alabama in expressing these sentiments. The *Demopolis Herald,* published in nearby Marengo County—Leonidas Waldemar Alston's home—reported the President's death under the headline "Glorious News."[93] A few days later the *Herald* falsely claimed that this had led 100,000 of General Grant's men to desert, thereby causing Grant to seek an armistice with General Lee that would finally end in southern independence. "The downfall of Lincoln ends the war," it declared.[94]

But for the South in general, and Alabama in particular, it was anything but glorious news. On the contrary, it turned out to be the worst possible news for most white Alabamians. Like the attack on Fort Sumter four years earlier,[95] the Lincoln assassination was a shocking, hinge event that changed the course of American history. Among other things, it let loose feelings of outrage and revenge that had been decreasing in intensity with each passing day. A shocked Georgian then living in New York City with his family to avoid Confederate conscription wrote in his diary that the "excitable northern mind which had begun to turn towards the conquered South with feelings of mercy and forgiveness, is now enraged against the entire land of 'rebellion' whose people they charge with instigating and abetting this horrid deed."[96] The *Chattanooga Rebel* and the *Montgomery Advertiser* both included telegraphic news that "intense excitement pervades the North," and that "several citizens were arrested in Memphis on Sunday for expressing joy" over Lincoln's death.[97] In Nashville, members of the local bar, which included former Selma resident and future Alabama Republican James Quinton Smith, met at the courthouse and adopted resolutions expressing "a feeling of intolerant bitterness towards that spirit which had sought to take the life of the nation, and had struck down its head."[98]

Fortunately for George Gayle, this flood of emotions initially led to a rush to judgment by many regarding who was behind the assassination. Criminal investigations that begin with a preconceived conclusion, instead of simply following the evidence where it leads, often result in flawed results. That happened before any of Booth's gang were caught and questioned.[99] Initial conjecture was that the assassinations were sponsored by the Confederate government. According to a Pennsylvania newspaper, it was a "desperate rebel plot to overthrow the government by a sudden surprise in the deep security of a prodigious victory."[100] An Ohio editor claimed that "evidence also accumulates that the plan was concocted by the rebels at Richmond and the leaders of the Knights of the Golden Circle in the North."[101]

More ominously, however, one editor correctly predicted that, as a consequence, there would be a "widespread and determined desire to put a stop at once to any disposition to deal leniently with rebels and traitors." There would be a "prevalent belief that with such a spirit abroad in the south magnanimity is a crime and a blunder. The result, therefore, will be not less a terrible calamity to the south than to the nation."[102] As the *New York Evening Post* put it, the "whole nation mourns the death of its president, but no part of it ought to mourn that death more keenly than our brothers of the South."[103] Now, wrote an Ohio editor, the policy "shall be 'an eye for an eye, and a tooth for a tooth.'"[104] As the Alabama press would soon be reporting, within hours after Lincoln was pronounced dead, Vice President Andrew Johnson was administered the oath of office as President at the Kirkwood Hotel by United States Supreme Court Chief Justice Salmon P. Chase.[105] In a brief address, Johnson declared that "my past history, in connection with the rebellion by which the whole land had been afflicted, will foreshadow what my future course will be."[106] Based on that "past history," which included multiple assurances that treason would be punished, it was generally believed that the "South had more hope from Lincoln's clemency than they can look for from his successor."[107]

Then George Gayle's infamous advertisement once again caught the public's attention, and it potentially undermined the theory of Confederate government involvement and threw the spotlight on Alabama.[108] On April 17, two days after Andrew Johnson became President, the *Philadelphia Inquirer* republished the ad in an article titled "Does This Account for It?" The editor was certain that "in consequence of recent events it is exceedingly suggestive."[109] That very day the *New York Evening Post* also republished the advertisement. Even for those who wanted a reason to hang Jefferson Davis and others from the nearest sour apple tree, it was impossible to ignore the fact that the targets of the advertisement were identical to those in the plot that had just been executed seventy-two hours earlier. In an accompanying editorial, the *Post* suggested to its readers that "the reward required for the murder might have been contributed."[110] This dovetailed with an earlier report in the Washington, D.C., *National Republican* on the day after the assassination that John Wilkes Booth was said to be "worth $350,000, which he made in the oil business"—a pre-assassination Booth cover story for his lethal activities[111]—"but it is supposed this is part of the sum paid him to murder President Lincoln."[112]

This narrative gained substantial traction among the northern public.[113] To the editor of a Massachusetts newspaper, for example, Gayle's advertisement was a "barefaced and cold-blooded proposition" that "affords a key to the motive of Booth. A money-mania indeed held possession of his brain. Gold was his inspiration, his zeal, his heroism. The brutal lust for the wages of blood was the fanaticism which thrilled him and made him a cowardly murderer and a pitiable madman."[114] A Connecticut editor agreed. "This may have been the origin of the conspiracy which has proved so terribly successful."[115] In the next several months, the northern press was full of reports about Gayle—whom they dubbed the "Million Dollar Man"—the advertisement, and its implications, logically raising the question of who had contributed to the purse.[116] Arguably, if it was primarily the work of a small group of Alabama fanatics who had no direct connection to the Confederate government, the federal government's response to Lincoln's murder would need to be much more measured.

But it was seemingly impossible for Secretary of War Edwin Stanton to accept this alternate theory, and he appears to have had substantial influence in this regard on the new president. Lincoln's initial funeral ceremonies took place in Washington, D.C., on April 19. Two days later, while the city was still in mourning, Lincoln's funeral train departed up the East Coast to New York on its long and depressing trip back to Springfield, Illinois.[117] That very day, President Johnson, who had recently learned that he, too, had been a target of the assassins,[118] gave a widely reported speech to a delegation from Indiana quite understandably reaffirming his desire to punish and "impoverish" traitors, and also destroy their "social power." Eliciting applause, Johnson also vowed that "every Union man and the Government should be remunerated out of the pockets of those who have inflicted this great suffering upon the country."[119] But first, Stanton pushed Johnson to start at the top of the Confederate government.

Chapter 8

"A Shrewd, Cold-Blooded Rascal"

But alas! came the days of dark reconstruction;
Our town to its center with grief was torn,
When George W. Gayle was arrested for treason
And off to the North a prisoner was borne.

Anna Maria Gayle Fry,
Memories of Old Cahaba, '97

On May 1, President Johnson ordered that a military commission be organized, ostensibly to try those directly involved in the conspiracy to assassinate Lincoln, William Seward, and himself.[1] The following day he issued a proclamation calling for the arrest of Jefferson Davis, as well as C.C. Clay, Jr., and other Confederate agents who had been based in Canada,[2]—but not George Gayle—alleging that they had been the masterminds behind that conspiracy. Following a massive manhunt, Davis was captured in Georgia a little over a week later while trying to escape to a foreign country.[3] Clay, who had also been planning to eventually leave the country, decided on the advice of his attorney, former Mobile, Alabama, lawyer Phillip Phillips, to voluntarily turn himself in to Union forces in Georgia.[4] One wonders whether Clay ever questioned that advice during his ensuing difficult months of imprisonment in a dungeon cell next to Davis's at Fortress Monroe, Virginia.[5] Shortly after his arrest, the Washington correspondent of the *Boston Journal* reported that "positive information has been received here that Clement C. Clay of Alabama, who was in Canada last fall and winter, reached Richmond on the day before its evacuation by the rebels, and there are reasons for believing that he carried tidings of the atrocious plot for the murder of the President, the agents of which, excepting perhaps Booth, were the mere hirelings of the slave power."[6]

As if Davis and Clay's problems were not serious enough already, news of a failed, but nonetheless shocking, germ warfare scheme in which they were alleged to have been involved surfaced at this time and further enraged the North. According to newspaper accounts, bedding and clothing used by yellow fever victims were shipped from Bermuda to New York, Philadelphia, and other major northern population centers in order to start a deadly epidemic.[7] In addition, in the coming weeks, news reports of testimony being taken by the military tribunal in connection with the Lincoln assassination linked Clay with other acts of terrorism during the war. The front page of the *New York Times* contained the verbatim testimony of one witness who swore that Clay had sponsored the raid on St. Albans, Vermont, in the fall of 1864. "I know," he said, "that Mr. Clay was one of the prime movers in the matter before the raids were started."[8] Graphic reports were meanwhile circulating in the North regarding the appalling physical condition of prisoners of war released from Confederate prisons like that at Andersonville, Georgia, for which Confederate officials would be blamed.[9]

Former United States Supreme Court Associate Justice John Archibald Campbell of Alabama was also arrested as a suspect in the Lincoln assassination conspiracy.[10] In addition to his service in the Confederate War Department, the arrest stemmed from the previously discussed efforts of Leonidas Waldemar Alston to convince Jefferson Davis to authorize him to, as he put it in the letter sent to Davis at some point before George Gayle's advertisement was first published, "rid my country of some of her deadliest enemies by striking at the very hearts blood of those who seek to enchain her in slavery."[11] The fact that what became known nationally as the "Alston letter"—found in the recently discovered Confederate archives—had not only been retained but was sent by Davis to the Confederate Secretary of War, and then referred by Campbell to the Confederate Adjutant General, was considered both suspicious and sinister to many.[12] As Campbell would point out, however, this merely reflected routine office procedure, and there was no evidence that he, or Davis, had acted on or intended to authorize anyone else to act on, Alston's request.[13] But this very routine handling of the letter was seen by assassination investigators, as well as some in the North, as even more evidence that the Confederate government was morally bankrupt. That government was, therefore, fully capable of countenancing the use of assassination to undermine the federal government, and therefore it must have been connected with Booth and his gang.[14] The editor of the

Nashville Union, President Johnson's organ, roared that, "as a 'Christian gentleman' it was the duty of Jeff Davis to arrest and punish the author [of the letter]. As the head of what he claimed to be an independent government—the ruler of an enlightened people—if he had no religious scruples on the subject" it was "the duty of Jeff Davis to arrest and punish the author." However, given the letter was treated routinely by both Davis and Campbell, "We presume," that they too "could see *'nothing dishonorable'*." From this the editor concluded that "if after this development, anyone can doubt the willingness of Jeff Davis and his advisors, to employ an assassin, to further the cause of treason, he must be singularly constituted mentally."[15]

One wonders whether George Gayle considered taking advantage of this distraction by fleeing the country and seeking exile to avoid punishment for publishing the advertisement for blood money to bring about the assassinations. Negative accounts of that advertisement in the northern press had been followed by its condemnation by powerful northern politicians. During a eulogy of Abraham Lincoln delivered to a large crowd in Chicago, the Speaker of the United States House of Representatives, Schuyler Colfax of Indiana, compared it to "the infamous offer of twenty-five thousand crowns, by Philip of Spain, to whomsoever would rid the world of the pious William of Orange, the purest and best loved ruler of his times." Colfax, who would later be elected Vice President of the United States, declared that "history repeated itself" when Gayle's offer was published in the *Selma Dispatch* "of last December, and [was] copied approvingly into other Rebel organs."[16] Colfax read Gayle's advertisement in its entirety to his audience and emphasized that "you will not fail to remember that these very three [Lincoln, Johnson and Seward], were to have been murdered that fatal night, and that when Booth was captured, he was fleeing in that very direction"—Alabama.[17]

With the widely publicized arrests of Jefferson Davis, C.C. Clay, Jr., and John Campbell, Gayle must have anticipated that he might be next. But by refraining to include his name in the advertisement, Gayle may have assumed that his identity was safe. If so, he did not take into account that, when pressed, the two members of the printing staff at the *Selma Dispatch*, John Cantley (or Caulter or Cantlin) and Watkins D. Graves, would be forced to give him up.

In a move that garnered almost as much positive national attention as the other arrests, Secretary of War Stanton finally ordered the arrest of the "Million Dollar Man." It took place at Gayle's home in Cahawba on May 25, 1865,[18] and was made by Scottish-born Union Major General John McArthur of Illinois. Gayle was initially incarcerated at Selma along with former wartime Alabama governor Andrew Barry Moore,[19] before being placed with Moore on the S.S. *Coquette* for transport down the Alabama River to Mobile. This was no pleasure cruise. According to Confederate General Josiah Gorgas, who was also aboard, Gayle was "under guard, two sentinels constantly sitting over him with muskets."[20] Gayle and Moore were next taken to New Orleans, where they were briefly incarcerated in Carondelet Prison. They were then transported by the U.S.S. *Constitution* to Hampton Roads, Virginia, where Gayle arrived on June 18. He was incarcerated in Fortress Monroe, where Jefferson Davis and C.C. Clay, Jr., were still being held.[21]

Gayle certainly recognized his predicament. He knew he was a target of outrage and revenge for the assassination of President Lincoln and likely was aware of the rumors in the national press that he too would be placed on a fast track for conviction before the military tribunal then trying several of the other known conspirators at Washington. The two *Selma Dispatch* employees with whom he had dealt regarding the advertisement were also aboard the *Constitution* and presumably were to be witnesses against him.[22] The voyage from New Orleans took almost two weeks. Like any lawyer faced with the same circumstances, Gayle spent his time working on a hopefully convincing narrative of facts to support a possible defense to charges that he had conspired with others regarding the assassinations. Gayle knew that evidence of *mens rea* or "criminal intent," the intent to engage in wrongful conduct, was a necessary element to conviction of most criminal offenses, and that the prosecution had the burden of proof on that element.[23] To be convicted of murder, for example, the prosecution must establish that a defendant actually intended to take the life of another.[24] Gayle could not successfully deny he had procured the publication of the advertisement. He, therefore, admitted to those on board the ship that he had done it, but that he had intended it as merely a joke on the Cahawba community—not to actually bring about the deaths of those named by him in the advertisement.[25] He did not, at this point, reveal his motive for playing such a ruse.

Perhaps surprising to most lay persons, the so-called "joke defense" has been recognized by several courts, but the first mention of it by an American appellate court was in a Michigan case decided in 1870.[26] Not only was Gayle's planned defense slightly ahead of its time, but he was forgetting that those who would be deciding his fate were not a normal Alabama audience with a sense of humor, but instead Army officers whose Commander-in-Chief had been senselessly murdered and who would be very skeptical of any claim by someone of longstanding anti-government proclivity that he was not serious about the deaths of Lincoln, Johnson, and Seward. The public reaction in the North to

Gayle's ploy was predictable. One editor called Gayle's claim "absurd," while another observed that the alleged joke "may prove a rather serious one for him."[27]

On June 20, Gayle and the witnesses against him were taken from Fortress Monroe and put aboard a steamer bound for Washington, D.C., where the other conspirators had been on trial since May 9.[28] The primary local Republican organ, the Washington, D.C. *National Republican*, announced Gayle's arrival on the morning of June 21 with a scathing article intended to demonize him. It described Gayle, who it called a "villain," as "a tall, raw boned individual, [with] coarse features, well bronzed from the southern climate. He is dressed in light grey pants, butternut colored coat, over which is a linen garment, and wears a well-battered black stovepipe hat. Mr. Gayle appears to be about forty-five years of age, and his gray hawk-like eyes, with strongly-marked 'crow's feet' in the corners, give him the appearance of a shrewd, cold-blooded rascal." This description of Gayle was republished by newspapers throughout the North.[29]

Gayle was placed in what was called the "Old Capitol" prison where some of the other conspirators had initially been held before being transferred to the Washington Arsenal Penitentiary where their trial was taking place.[30] The Old Capitol had served as the temporary capitol building of the nation following the destruction wrought by the British during the War of 1812, and since then had been used for various purposes, including a prewar boarding house. As Gayle knew, it was where his hero, John Calhoun, had died of tuberculosis in 1850.[31] After the Civil War began, the federal government had acquired the Old Capitol and turned into a prison to hold those suspected of treason, among others. And this old building was definitely not a place inmates were treated to a healthful existence, particularly during the blistering hot summer.[32]

But Gayle caught the first of many breaks when he was not included in the proceedings against the members of the assassination team, which were at the time nearing their grim conclusion.[33] But on June 24, Secretary of War Stanton instructed Judge Advocate General Joseph Holt to file charges against Gayle and put him on trial for "inciting to the murder of the President" by the publication of his advertisement.[34] And on June 27, the two *Selma Dispatch* employees were called by the prosecution to testify about Gayle's advertisement in the ongoing trial against the other conspirators. Besides identifying Gayle as the person who wrote it out and paid for its publication, however, these witnesses were only called upon to establish that copies of the *Dispatch* containing the advertisement had been sent to Richmond, the capital of the Confederacy, as part of the normal newspaper exchange.[35] Other than this, there was no testimony during the trial about Gayle's activities or any fundraising efforts, and no mention of either in the closing arguments of the lawyers.[36]

If Gayle assumed from this that he would not ever be tried, that assumption was seemingly quickly dispelled. The *New York Times* reported that Gayle was to be placed on trial before a different military tribunal convening on June 29.[37] That would have suited many Northerners. Gayle tried to hire two of the most prominent lawyers of the day, Reverdy Johnson, a Democrat and United States Senator from Maryland, and James Brady, who had earlier been part of Daniel Sickles's legal team. Gayle intended for them to make at least three additional arguments in his behalf.[38] First, he wanted to challenge the constitutionality of his trial by a military tribunal as opposed to a jury in Alabama.[39] Reverdy Johnson's ultimately unsuccessful argument in this regard had been presented to the military tribunal trying the assassins on June 19, and at this point the tribunal had not yet issued its ruling.[40] Second, Brady was likely to reprise his efforts to prove the temporary insanity defense that had kept Sickles a free man despite having committed murder. Given the relative circumstances of the victim, however, this would be a much tougher row to hoe. Third, Gayle wanted his lawyers to argue that he had committed no recognized crime by having the advertisement published. According to a report in a Virginia newspaper, Gayle maintained that, "admitting he caused the advertisement to be published, he has not committed any offence known to the law, and therefore, must be acquitted, if tried at all."[41]

For reasons that are unclear, Gayle was unsuccessful in securing the services of Johnson and Brady. But he did hire two young, very green associates of Johnson's, Frederick Argyll Aiken and John Clampitt, who, along with Reverdy Johnson, had been defending one of the other conspirators, Mary Surratt.[42] Through these lawyers Gayle could learn whether any of the other defendants had disclosed any facts directly connecting him to John Wilkes Booth, C.C. Clay, Jr., or Jefferson Davis, in the assassination conspiracy. When Lewis Powell was interrogated he reportedly declared that "You have not got half of them,"[43] but as far as can be determined, neither Powell nor any of the other defendants implicated Gayle. It is very possible they were unable to do so because Booth never told them the actual source of funding or who his contacts were.

Gayle could also learn from these lawyers how the insanity defense might fare in a trial before his military tribunal. The only assassin who had raised that defense, Lewis Powell, had not fared very well at all because none of the Washington-area doctors who had briefly examined him concluded that he was, in fact, insane at the time he attempted to murder William Seward. In an effort to provide a medical history demonstrating that insanity ran in Powell's family—at that time a common tactic in these types of cases—Powell's lawyer had had the tribunal issue a subpoena for Powell's father, a minister who then resided in Florida. But the father never appeared before the trial ended. Therefore, Powell's lawyer dropped the insanity argument altogether.[44] From this Gayle and his lawyers could readily conclude that whether he asserted a joke defense or an insanity defense, it was essential to marshal the supporting evidence and procure the appearance of expert and lay witnesses from Alabama who could testify regarding his mental state at the time he prepared the advertisement and procured its publication in the *Selma Dispatch*.

Taking this approach had an added benefit: delay. By requesting the subpoena of out-of-state witnesses, the military tribunal planning to try Gayle would be forced to postpone the trial for at least a few weeks to allow for service of the subpoenas on those witnesses and their travel to Washington. Generally speaking, delay is to the advantage of a defendant, and this axiom certainly applied here. Passions needed to cool and that could only come with time. Consistent with this strategy, Frederick Aiken informed Joseph Holt's associate, Nathaniel P. Chipman, that Gayle was "as willing to be tried here as at his home if he is to be tried here by [military commission]," that "he will require not more than 16 witnesses," and that "he is ready for trial at any time when his witnesses can be procured."[45] Nonetheless, in his June 29 report to Holt on this, Chipman expressed confidence that Gayle's conviction would justify the death penalty under established common law principles.[46] And at the time it must have appeared to Gayle that his fate would be decided within the next sixty days.

All of a sudden, however, Gayle's situation inexplicably changed dramatically. Several newspapers incorrectly reported that his attorneys had requested that almost one hundred witnesses be subpoenaed from Alabama. Then the Associated Press reported that Gayle would be sent *back to Alabama* for trial "owing to the large number of witnesses—about a hundred—whom he has asked to be summoned in his case, all of whom reside in Alabama." This change of venue, it was said, "has been made on the ground of convenience as well as economy."[47] But then, on June 30, the Washington, D.C. *National Republican* reported that, rather than being returned to Alabama, Gayle "will probably be held at Fort Pulaski, Georgia, where he is to be taken" under military guard.[48]

Nonetheless, as Gayle left Washington on July 1, he was likely glad to leave regardless of where he was taken him.[49] The military was under tremendous pressure to achieve convictions of those who were suspected of being involved in the murder of President Lincoln.[50] Gayle certainly recognized the strong possibility that he would be sucked into the vortex of a military tribunal's whirlwind toward conviction. If he had any reservations whatsoever about his departure, they probably disappeared when he learned the fate of the other defendants, especially that of the client of his lawyers, Mary Surratt. On July 5 the military tribunal rendered its verdicts of guilt and its sentences of death to her and three others, Lewis Powell, David Herold, and George Atzerodt. That same day President Johnson ordered that the sentences be carried out on July 7. When a local court, on application of the defendants, issued a writ of *habeas corpus* based on a challenge to the constitutionality and jurisdiction of the military tribunal, President Johnson announced that the right to such a writ had been suspended. Thus, on July 7, the executions by hanging were carried out.[51] At least the "shrewd, cold-blooded rascal" was not among them. If he could ever make it back to Alabama among family and friends, maybe he never would be. At this point, however, only President Johnson, Secretary Stanton, and the prosecutors knew if, when, and where Gayle would be tried, and he was left to ponder his fate during the slow journey to Georgia.

The real reason Gayle was not tried in Washington by the military tribunal established to hear his case is unclear. A careful review of the relevant records by historian Michael Kauffman revealed no clear answer. One possibility is that the government was concerned that on appeal from a local court, the United States Supreme Court, whose Chief Justice, Salmon Chase, was opposed to the continuation of martial law and the use of military tribunals instead of civilian courts, would rule that such tribunals were unconstitutional as a violation of the guarantee of trial by jury. Nathaniel Chipman had alluded to this problem in his letter to Joseph Holt about Gayle, but had expressed that he had no doubt "the Court would sustain their jurisdiction to try the case."[52] Holt and Edwin Stanton may not have been so sure. Over a year later, the Supreme Court would finally rule that where civil courts were functioning, civilians could not be tried by a military court.[53] Such a ruling was avoided in the case of the Lincoln assassins only by President Johnson's declaration that the writ of habeas corpus had been suspended in Washington, D.C., and then by the speed with which the executions were carried out—before any appeal could be taken. By contrast, the government knew Gayle would have the time to make the challenge before and during his trial.

But there is another reason that may have made the government reluctant to bring Gayle to trial at this point and to, instead, get him out of town and out of the public mind. A clue to the government's decision may possibly be found in the prosecution's closing argument to the military tribunal that tried the assassins. It is clear the government wanted Jefferson Davis's hide, and in the first part of that argument the lead prosecutor, John A. Bingham, painted a narrative portraying Davis as the instigator of the assassination conspiracy. Davis's plan, he argued, had been executed through Davis' appointed agents in Canada such as C.C. Clay, Jr., who had solicited and encouraged John Wilkes Booth to form and supervise the assassination team.[54]

The facts supporting the charges against George Gayle had a tendency to undermine that narrative. If Gayle had incited the President's murder and one could not prove that he had a connection with Davis, Davis would likely have been entitled to an acquittal. The evidence of Davis's (and Clay's) involvement in any conspiracy was, moreover, circumstantial and very weak. Unlike Gayle, neither had publicly called for Lincoln's assassination. Davis's lawyers could argue that Booth was instead motivated solely by Gayle's apparently independent, implicit promise in his widely published advertisement of a large bounty on the heads of Lincoln, Johnson and Seward. Booth was not around to deny it, and those who had testified about his comments all recalled that he repeatedly mentioned that a very large payday was ahead.[55] Davis's lawyers could also point to the Alston Letter as exculpatory evidence. They could argue that despite Alston's passionate plea, Davis had not ordered the assassinations or even replied to Alston. They could also attempt to connect Alston with Gayle. In his letter, Alston had stated that he was from Alabama, that he had attended the University of Alabama, and that his father had been a United States congressman from Alabama. A little digging would have revealed that Alston was from Marengo County, a Black Belt county not far from Gayle's Dallas County and whose newspaper had classified Lincoln's assassination as "Glorious News." Moreover, like Gayle, Alston's father was a lawyer and an Original Secessionist who likely knew Gayle.[56] Relevant questions would have included whether Gayle, through Alston's father, had encouraged young Alston to write Jefferson Davis to begin with. If so, it was plausible that when Davis did not respond to Alston, Gayle became frustrated and advertised for money with which to privately finance a team of assassins to do the job. Consistent with this scenario, Alston's letter predated the advertisement. Another question: did Gayle use young Alston as an intermediary with the assassins? We will probably never know, but Davis's lawyers could certainly use this issue to create a reasonable doubt of Davis' guilt and possibly obtain an acquittal.[57] And there was also the fact that Booth targeted only the three men Gayle named in his advertisement, which seemed far from a mere coincidence.

Whatever the motivation for the federal government's decision to delay his trial, George Gayle arrived at Hilton Head, South Carolina, on

July 12, 1865, and was promptly lodged in Fort Pulaski near Savannah, Georgia. At least initially, however, this did not stop the national press from reminding the public of his deeds.[58] The *Louisville Journal* ridiculed Gayle, noting that he "was fast in Fort Pulaski," and asking, "how many millions would he give to be loose?"[59]

Many of these reports appeared in the Selma press, and they may have created a groundswell of public support in Dallas County in Gayle's behalf. It was during Gayle's incarceration at Fort Pulaski that a new narrative about him began to emerge and slowly gain traction. Whether Gayle or his friends orchestrated this is unknown, but it is clear that the details were released to the press by his fellow residents back in Alabama. A correspondent for the *New York Herald* who had been investigating the conditions in Dallas County reported that he had "taken some time to ascertain the antecedents of Mr. Gale, who is extensively known in this section of the country. He is a lawyer of considerable ability, and has been all his life a violent Southern man and secessionist."[60] This information certainly supported a motive to have the assassinations carried out.

But the correspondent did not stop there and instead called into question Gayle's mental capacity to commit the crime. Gayle, he wrote, "has been a fast liver and of dissipated habits, and although having a lucrative business, has fully lived up to his income. He has never been the possessor of more than a thousand dollars, and the offering of the reward is said to have been done in joke while on a drunken frolic. No one here acquainted with the man ever considered it anything except in the light of a joke, and would never have thought of it again had not the murder of the President occurred. He has not taken any active part in the war, but lived at home practising his profession and drinking whiskey. These are the facts," he concluded, "as told by respectable citizens of Selma."[61]

From a strictly legal standpoint, this story did not necessarily improve Gayle's chance of obtaining an acquittal. As one court put it in 1868, "a man who voluntarily puts himself in a condition to have no control of his actions, must be held to intend the consequences. The safety of the community requires this rule. Intoxication is so easily counterfeited, and, when real it is so often resorted to as a means of nerving the person up to the commission of some desperate act, and is withal so inexcusable in itself, that the law has never recognized it as an excuse for crime."[62] But evidence of intoxication arguably further supported Gayle's joke defense and a potential insanity defense.

There was, nonetheless, a significant flaw in this new narrative. The Selmans who had fed the story of Gayle's alcoholism to the *New York*

Herald's reporter may have been "respectable," but this does not mean that they were honest and truthful with him. Despite years of investigation and research, the author has not found a single scintilla of evidence suggesting that Gayle was ever an alcoholic or drank alcohol to excess. But the story provided a serviceable excuse for the federal government to ignore public pressure for Gayle's speedy trial and execution, and to instead focus on bringing Jefferson Davis and C.C. Clay, Jr., to trial and execution. Once they were executed, Gayle could be tried without the risk of giving reason for a retrial of Davis and Clay.

This assumed that Gayle was still alive at that time. Like the Old Capitol Prison, Fort Pulaski, which had been built in 1849 on a former swamp, was not a safe living environment—as many of its unfortunate wartime Confederate inmates had discovered. Prisoners were held in the casements of the fort within what one described as a "dungeon-like hole."[63] Those holes would have been very hot during the hellish summer of 1865, and the coming winter would subject the prisoners to freezing temperatures. Under existing circumstances, the federal government would have probably been happy to leave Gayle to rot in Fort Pulaski. But fortunately for Gayle, President Andrew Johnson had other factors to consider.

One of the assassinations Gayle sought to bring about—Abraham Lincoln's—had not only sparked calls in the North for revenge and retaliation, but had ironically added support among heretofore reluctant Northerners for the imposition of black suffrage on the South as an essential element of any reconstruction. As the influential *New York Herald* pointed out, "nothing half so effective could be employed as negro suffrage to weed out the intractable secessionists from the Southern states."[64] For reasons beyond the scope of this book, however, President Johnson ignored this sentiment when he issued proclamations initiating the process of reconstruction. In order to avoid a backlash by Northerners skeptical of the South's loyalty, however, Johnson needed the reconstructing states to demonstrate by their acts that their newly professed loyalty to the Union was genuine. To exhibit this renewed loyalty, Johnson expected that the constitutional convention meeting in Alabama would adopt provisions annulling its secession ordinance, repudiating its war-related debt, and abolishing slavery.[65]

The delegates to Alabama's constitutional convention were far from united on these measures and it took coaxing from Johnson to push them through.[66] During this process, the delegates took the opportunity to request concessions from him. On September 19 they reportedly "unanimously signed a petition asking clemency to Judge [John Archibald] Campbell, and most of them also joined in an earnest application to obtain the transfer and trial of Geo. W. Gayle to Alabama."[67] Johnson wisely delayed taking any official action on these requests until after he got what he wanted and the Alabama convention had adjourned. Then he ordered that both Campbell and Gayle be released on parole. Campbell's parole was conditional on his agreement to remain in Alabama and subject to trial if charges were ever brought against him. Gayle, however, was ordered to be tried in Alabama, but by a civil court rather than a military tribunal.[68]

Wilber F. Story, the editor of the *Chicago Times*, a staunchly pro-Democrat and anti-Lincoln organ, was one of the few Northerners who publicly maintained that this was a good idea. It meant that "we have seen the last of military trials for civil offenses. It is a happy day." Story also opined that it meant Johnson would be forced to move closer to his Democrat roots. Gayle's release, "to radical sensibilities, will be fresh evidence of President Johnson's Copperhead proclivities. It was only the other day that he abolished martial law in Kentucky. At the present rate of progress he certainly soon will be a very good Copperhead."[69] But Johnson had not yet gone that far and, as a result, C.C. Clay, Jr., was not so fortunate. Unlike Gayle, Clay was a key component of the federal government's case against Jefferson Davis. Clay's requests for release on parole were denied and he remained in prison awaiting trial.[70] Confiscation proceedings would soon be initiated against his property in Alabama.[71]

In accordance with the terms of his parole, George Gayle first went to Montgomery, Alabama, and reported to the United States District Attorney earlier appointed by President Johnson, James Quinton Smith.[72] Upon Gayle giving the standard oath of allegiance, Smith released him on a $25,000 bond conditioned on his appearance at the next term of the United States District Court, which was scheduled to begin in Montgomery on November 20.[73] Judging by Gayle's physical appearance, his release from Fort Pulaski came just in time. One observer in Montgomery wrote that Gayle "appears to be in wretched health, the mere shadow of his former self."[74] Another stated that the "effects of imprisonment had begun to tell upon his formerly robust constitution, causing him to look somewhat sad and emaciated."[75] Whether this was all merely a good acting job by Gayle in an effort to garner public sympathy is unknown.

Although not reported in the press, after Gayle returned to Cahawba on October 18, 1865, he and his wife threw a party at their home described by one in attendance as the "first ceremonious function after the surrender." It was a posh affair reminiscent of the antebellum period complete with dancing and men dressed in "white kid gloves and broadcloth suits."[76] Gayle's specific activities at his party are unknown but he likely played his role of a harmless, drunken jokester to the hilt. After all, he knew that his court date was approaching and had reason to believe that District Attorney Smith had personal reasons to aggressively seek his conviction regardless of any possible contrary considerations in Washington. Gayle also had no reason to expect any help from the Lincoln-appointed United States District Court judge who would preside over the trial. As far as Gayle knew, his only hope was that an Alabama jury would accept his story and conclude that, at the time he had the damning advertisement published, he did not actually possess an intent to have the assassinations carried out. Throwing a party for potential witnesses and jurors could only help in that regard.

But for reasons no one could have predicted at the time, Gayle would not have to count on a jury to preserve his freedom. And for those who believed Gayle's involvement in the assassination was significant and decisive, only frustration would result.

Chapter 9

"A Wicked Pardon"

IRISH-BORN James Quinton Smith had been a Selma lawyer for many years before the war.[1] As a Unionist, he was certainly no ally of George Gayle's or the Confederacy. During the war, Smith had become part of a network of lawyers who represented other Unionists who experienced scrapes with the increasingly overbearing Confederate government.[2] In 1863 one of his clients, a Selma merchant, was arrested by military officials for refusing to receive increasingly valueless Confederate money for his goods. Smith filed a petition in the local circuit court requesting a writ of habeas corpus for release of his client. The judge issued that writ and ordered that the military bring the merchant into court for a determination of whether he had broken the law. In response, the military not only arrested Smith but imprisoned him in Mobile. Although Smith was later released, he chose not to return to Selma and instead sought refuge in Nashville, Tennessee, where he joined then military governor Andrew Johnson's growing pro-Union organization.[3]

Smith was understandably very bitter over his treatment,[4] and after Johnson became president he granted Smith's request for a position in Alabama where Smith could seek revenge against those who had brought on secession and prosecuted the war, thereby causing the destruction of his world. Johnson appointed him Alabama's United States District Attorney for the middle and northern judicial districts, and Dallas County was in the middle district.[5] In that position Smith had the authority to not only seek indictments against and try those charged with treason or other federal crimes, but have the property of traitors confiscated pursuant to laws adopted by Congress during the war. On Smith's recommendation,

President Johnson appointed John Hardy United States Marshal, and together they aggressively enforced these laws.[6] In fact, their efforts created a firestorm among Confederates, who were forced to swallow their pride and apply to Andrew Johnson for a presidential pardon to escape prosecution and obtain the release of their confiscated property.[7]

Smith had several advantages that made successful prosecutions of men like George Gayle even more possible than in normal circumstances. The proceedings would be in federal court, rather than state court, and John Hardy could control the content of jury venires and thereby assure that grand and petit juries were manned by Unionists. In addition, unlike the antebellum period, the testimony of blacks would be received against whites.[8] Finally, a large segment of the legal talent in Alabama was effectively disqualified from practicing in federal court by a law adopted by Congress during the war that required those who sought to represent clients there to first take an oath that they had been loyal throughout the war. This meant that those like George Gayle who were charged with the commission of treason or other federal crimes during the war could only be represented by wartime Unionists.[9] Thus, when George Gayle reported to Smith in October to make bail, Smith undoubtedly assumed he would soon have the opportunity to easily prosecute not only one of the most bitter secessionists and infamous traitors in the South, but to achieve national accolades and fame for convicting him.

To accomplish anything, however, Smith needed the federal court in Alabama to begin functioning again after the long hiatus during the war. In 1863, President Lincoln had appointed a prominent Irish-born New York City lawyer, Richard Busteed, to be Alabama's lone United States District judge. Due to the continuation of wartime conditions, however, Busteed had been unable to actually undertake his duties.[10] There is also reason to believe that Busteed would have preferred not to go to Alabama at all. He was politically ambitious and, since President Lincoln's murder, had aligned with United States Supreme Court Chief Justice Salmon Chase, the former Secretary of the Treasury under Lincoln, who was believed to be aiming for the presidency in the 1868 presidential election.[11] Perhaps if Chase were elected, Busteed could be appointed to a more desirable and lucrative position closer to home.

For various reasons, Chase favored a conciliatory approach to the South, and he was opposed to martial law and the use of military tribunals to try those accused of treason or the breach of other federal laws.[12] Richard Busteed followed Chase's lead on this issue. Busteed did not go to Alabama when the war in Alabama ended in May 1865 for all practical purposes, or even after President Johnson issued his proclamation on June 21 establishing the framework and process for

Alabama's reconstruction and directing Busteed to forthwith open court there. Busteed later claimed that his delay was due to confusion over whether the writ of habeas corpus remained suspended and whether Alabama remained under martial law as opposed to civil law.[13] If the former, Busteed would arguably have no authority in criminal cases where the military was exercising jurisdiction.

Busteed later claimed that after receiving what he believed were adequate assurances that he would have full authority, he finally came to Alabama in November 1865, only to discover that the military remained in charge.[14] A federal treasury agent and Chase appointee, Thomas C.A. Dexter, had been arrested by military authorities for official corruption relating to confiscated Confederate cotton. In an effort to avoid trial before a military tribunal, Dexter engaged counsel to file a petition for a writ of *habeas corpus* in Busteed's court in Mobile. Busteed granted that petition but the military refused to obey him on the ground that President Johnson had earlier authorized a military trial in such circumstances, and that, in any event, the writ of *habeas corpus* remained suspended in Alabama. This civil-military conflict sparked national attention, but to Busteed's dismay, Johnson backed the military.[15]

As a consequence, Busteed was so incensed that when he opened his court in Montgomery where George Gayle assumed he would soon be indicted, Busteed obstinately refused to even impanel a grand jury. Busteed's stated rationale was that he wanted to avoid any potential for conflict with the military's jurisdiction. But the military was not then prosecuting George Gayle and, given President Johnson's prior order that Gayle be tried in a civil court, was not likely to do so.[16] Busteed's true motivation had nothing to do with George Gayle; Gayle was an unintended beneficiary of the turf battle between Busteed and the military, and Johnson and Chase. Busteed ordered all of those like Gayle who were subject to prosecution but out of custody on bail, to renew their bail and remain available for trial at some later term of his court, presumably after martial law had ended.[17] Gayle, who one observer in court noted was present but "in infirm health, being so far paralysed in his lower limbs as to walk with great difficulty on uneven ground,"[18] renewed his $25,000 bond.[19] It was signed by a list of prominent Confederate Alabamians as sureties, including wartime Alabama governors John Gill Shorter and Thomas Hill Watts, wartime Alabama Supreme Court Chief Justice Abram Joseph Walker, Confederate congressman William Parish Chilton, and Confederate brigadier generals James Holt Clanton, John Tyler Morgan, Edmund Winston Pettus, and James T. Holtzclaw.[20]

For his support of individual rights vs. the federal government and other reasons, the members of the Alabama bar in the middle district treated Busteed to a supper at Montgomery's Exchange Hotel that was described as "a magnificent affair." The lawyers, wrote one in attendance, "have all fallen desperately in love with the Judge."[21] Whether George Gayle attended this celebration is unknown, but there is no doubt he was both relieved and pleased at his good fortune.

Busteed then garnered more local praise when he ruled that the federal attorney oath statute was unconstitutional and left Alabama, returning to New York without even appearing in Huntsville to hold court there as required by federal law.[22] If and when he would return to Alabama was anyone's guess. James Quinton Smith's reaction to this bizarre turn of events is unknown, but it likely paralleled the shock and incredulity in the North. The *Cleveland Leader*, which called Gayle a "fiend," was frustrated over the fact that the "leading characters in the State, volunteered as sureties for the would-be assassin." Its editor believed that this "indicates pretty clearly that it will be impossible to empannel a jury in that region who will decide the case upon its merits and is striking commentary upon the pretended loyalty of Alabama."[23] The *New York Tribune* likewise expressed public outrage that Gayle "now stands a good chance of escaping scot free, like all the rest of the Rebels." Its editor was equally apoplectic that the "leading men" in Alabama, such as Watts, had stood "by a villain who instigated the assassination of the beloved head of the nation." From this he concluded that "it certainly does not look as if there was any repentance or change of feeling, in Alabama at least."[24]

Fortunately for Gayle, news of his seemingly indefinite release came on the heels of shocking election returns from Alabama and elsewhere in the South indicating that Confederates were resuming control of state and local governments. Men who could not take the requisite oath affirming wartime loyalty to the Union were nonetheless elected to Congress, thereby causing a firestorm of controversy.[25] Now the spotlight turned to efforts to prevent them from taking their seats and, along with northern Democrats, reversing progress gained by Republicans during and by virtue of the war.[26]

This state of affairs was blamed on President Johnson's alleged leniency, and the ensuing controversy and epic political war between Johnson and Congress initially provided George Gayle with an effective distraction from national public attention. Meanwhile, he could spend his time resuming his law practice and building his case should Judge Busteed decide to return to Alabama and open his court any time soon. Once again, delay had worked to Gayle's advantage.

President Johnson, meanwhile, attempted to reestablish his image by ordering the execution of Captain Henry Wirz, the infamous commandant of the horrific Confederate prison at Andersonville, Georgia, who had recently been convicted by a military tribunal of war crimes.[27] Johnson also ordered that Raphael Semmes, the equally infamous commander of the commerce raider C.S.S. *Alabama* who had recently established a law practice in Mobile, Alabama, be arrested and brought to Washington, D.C., for trial by a military tribunal.[28] One happy editor declared that if Semmes, whom he called a "heartless wretch," got "justice, we know what his doom will be."[29]

But Johnson remained under fire from congressional Republicans for his other reconstruction policies.[30] As the *New York Tribune* framed the problem, "so long as the negro is not to have the right to protect himself with the ballot, we feel great interest in all measures that look to his protection by the federal Government." Its editor, Horace Greeley, spoke for many when he concluded that "we must do the negro justice, and since we will not throw open the door and bid him to come to the family fire, we must keep a good and expensive watch outside to see that he does not freeze."[31] Even before Johnson nonetheless vetoed pieces of legislation providing for a continuation of the federal Freedmen's Bureau and the grant to blacks of civil (but not political) rights enforceable in federal courts, a growing number of his political enemies within the Republican Party were calling for his impeachment.[32] When he issued those vetoes, the nation braced for that showdown.[33]

Nevertheless, Johnson adamantly refused to be intimidated, and his counterattack had unintended and unforeseen consequences for George Gayle. On April 2, 1866, Johnson issued a proclamation declaring the end of the insurrection, the purpose of which was to undermine congressional Republicans seeking fundamentally far-reaching reconstruction measures they justified on the constitutional basis that the war had not yet officially ended. The proclamation also implied that, as a consequence of peace, martial law in the South was over.[34]

Johnson's chess move had been expected for some time,[35] and in anticipation of the proclamation's issuance, Judge Richard Busteed had returned to Alabama to hold his spring terms of court. This again had nothing to do with George Gayle; Busteed was planning to open his court in Mobile first, not Montgomery. He waited until the date of Johnson's peace proclamation before doing so,[36] and his main focus was again Salmon Chase appointee Thomas C.A. Dexter. Dexter had since been convicted of corruption by a military tribunal, and another petition for writ of habeas corpus had been filed by his lawyers. That petition was mooted when the military voluntarily agreed to turn Dexter over to District Attorney Smith and Marshal Hardy with the understanding that a criminal prosecution would be initiated in Busteed's court against Dexter.[37]

But while Busteed was in Alabama, he eventually made his way to Montgomery. Smith and Hardy were there waiting with their own agenda when Busteed opened his court on May 28, 1866.[38] They were likely aware that federal prosecutors in Tennessee had utilized federal grand juries to prosecute a number of Confederates for their wartime activities. In East Tennessee, for example, over 1,900 defendants had treason charges pending against them in 1865.[39] Smith and Hardy were determined to bring that aggressive brand of justice and retribution to Alabama.

As had been the case in Mobile, Judge Busteed presided over the selection of a grand jury in Montgomery. But Smith and Hardy had carefully selected the venire from which the grand jury was selected. According to news accounts, a majority of the seventeen members of this Montgomery grand jury consisted of Alabama residents who were Unionists, Union military veterans, and/or northern natives—what John Forsyth's Mobile newspaper later called "of the North Northy, to borrow an expression from the most popular of bands, [who] do not entertain a very exalted opinion of Southern 'loyalty' and Southern honesty."[40] In fact, the foreman of this grand jury, South Carolina-born, future Republican Thomas O. Glasscock of Montgomery, was a wartime Unionist and the president of the Union League in Alabama.[41]

When this grand jury was impaneled, Busteed obliviously went through the normal process of "charging" or instructing its members regarding their duties as grand jurors and the types of offenses they could consider when determining whether probable cause to indict existed.[42] Unlike Mobile, Busteed reluctantly covered the law of treason in his charge.[43] Smith likely had informed Busteed upon his arrival in Montgomery that he intended to present several treason cases for consideration by the jurors at that term of court. Thus, Busteed was forced to choose between conciliation of Confederates—his and Salmon Chase's preference—and their prosecution. Judging from the language he used, it is clear that Busteed did not encourage the grand jury to issue any indictments for treason. He was careful to highlight the constitutional and practical impediments to successful prosecutions for such a charge, including the necessity of "proof by two credible witnesses of the commission of some and the same overt act by the accused," and the possibility that suspects may have already obtained amnesty or a pardon. By contrast, Busteed instructed the grand jurors that it was their "*duty* to make diligent examination" of the "rumors of alleged frauds of agents of the treasury department of the United States" with which the "air is thick."[44] Perhaps hopeful that the attention of the grand jury would thereby be diverted to ferreting out evidence of the latter offense during their ensuing secret deliberations, Busteed proceeded to conduct trials regarding the many cases already on his criminal docket.[45]

Predictably, however, those "North Northies" rendered several indictments for treason, including charges against former wartime governor Andrew Barry Moore and former Confederate District Judge William Giles Jones (as well as his former Court Clerk and Marshals), and also indictments for complicity in the Lincoln assassination against George Washington Gayle and the editors of the *Selma Dispatch*.[46] The indictment against Gayle alleged that he had, among other things, conspired with others on December 1, 1864, to "propose to kill and murder Abraham Lincoln, President of the United States, William H. Seward, Secretary of State of the United States, and Andrew Johnson, Vice President elect of said United States" by having the advertisement published in the *Selma Dispatch*.[47] It appears that Busteed tried as best he could to contain the potential damage to his image as a conciliator arising from these indictments. He dismissed the charge against Moore based on a presidential pardon Moore had received a few months earlier,[48] and then released George Gayle and each of the others on bond rather than putting them on trial.[49] Then he abruptly adjourned court on June 14 and left the state.[50]

George Gayle fortuitously remained free, and he knew that Busteed was not scheduled to return to Alabama until November 1866. But Gayle certainly recognized that Busteed could not stall indefinitely without some good reason. Busteed's political aspirations were such that he could not ignore northern public opinion. Gayle, therefore, determined to provide Busteed with that reason. Given James Quinton Smith's seemingly high degree of motivation, Gayle's only hope was a presidential pardon.[51] Under the circumstances, however, that seemed like a pipedream. Or was it?

Up to this point, no one suspected of being involved with the Lincoln assassination had been pardoned. As evidenced by the uproar in 1866 caused when President Johnson ordered that C.C. Clay, Jr., be released from Fortress Monroe on parole and allowed to return to Alabama, any move in that direction increased the risk of Johnson's impeachment.[52] Even though Clay's release was arguably a function of the recent decision by the United States Supreme Court in the *Milligan* case,[53] Johnson sought to avoid controversy by revealing that he was acting on the recommendation of General Grant and others.[54] Johnson was also careful not to pardon Clay at this time, therefore leaving Clay open to criminal prosecution in Busteed's court if Clay were indicted for the assassination or treason.[55]

According to a correspondent of the *New York Herald* who was at Fortress Monroe at about the time Clay received word of the order releasing him, Clay was "full of thanks to everybody. He felt himself in fact a new man, and his looks and actions showed it." Among other things, his "long imprisonment shows its painful traces. His face is much thinner, his walk is less erect, and his hair and whiskers show a profuse sprinkling of gray."[56] But there was a segment of the public who blamed Johnson for Clay's condition not being terminal. A Pennsylvania editor was disgusted that Johnson had "liberated" this "traitor, perjurer, murderer, &c., also implicated in the plot to burn Northern cities, and planner of the St. Albans robbery, and other piracies on the lakes and along the border."[57] The pen of the editor of a Wisconsin newspaper dripped with sarcasm when he observed that a few of the "tools of the arch traitors, such as Mrs. Surratt, Wirz and [Confederate guerrilla] Champ Ferguson, have been executed, but it would not do to hang the accursed fiends who instigated and are justly responsible for all the atrocious crimes of the rebellion, for all the blood that has been spilled, for the starvation horrors of the prison pens, for the poisoning, infecting and incendiary plots, for the culminating crime of the assassination. We must forsooth hang the poor brutal wretches who only did the bidding of their masters, but we must not be so vindictive as to punish the cold-blooded demons who planned every atrocity! No indeed!"[58]

On the night of the same day the order releasing Clay was issued, current and former Union soldiers and sailors conducted a mass meeting in Washington, D.C., during which they adopted resolutions that, among other things, expressed disagreement with Johnson's relatively liberal reconstruction policies and also sarcastically stated that "we fully concur in the often-repeated declaration of the President of the United States that 'treason is a crime, and ought to be punished;' and we have been waiting most patiently for a practical application of the principle to the leaders of the rebellion."[59] This extremely important pressure group would have their wish very soon, but not with regard to C.C. Clay, Jr. Three weeks later a federal grand jury in Norfolk, Virginia, that reportedly included several "Virginia Radicals" indicted former Confederate President Jefferson Davis and former United States Vice President John Breckinridge for treason—not as assassination conspirators—thus setting the stage for what was expected to be the trials of the century.[60] Johnson did not dare pardon Davis, who many still suspected of involvement in the assassination conspiracy. In stark contrast, Johnson moved forward during the summer of 1866 with the systematic pardon of those who were not suspects in that crime, but who were clearly guilty of treason. In Alabama this included William Giles Jones,[61] former Confederate Assistant Secretary of War Wade Keyes,[62] and many others.

The political warfare between President Johnson and congressional Republicans, therefore, escalated in the ensuing months. Johnson sought to create a new political party composed of those in the North and the South who agreed with him that further political and social reconstruction of the South was unwarranted and counterproductive.[63] In support of this so-called "Constitutional Union" movement, Johnson made a politically disastrous whistle-stop speaking tour through the East and Midwest that came to be known as the "Swing Around the Circle." This initially fairly uneventful trip hit a major bump in the road in Ohio. During his speech in Cleveland, hecklers repeatedly called Johnson a traitor and yelled "You be damned." Rather than simply ignoring these insults and acting in a presidential manner, Johnson foolishly lost his temper and became combative and supercilious, reminding even his supporters that he was no Abraham Lincoln.[64] Johnson's audience in Indianapolis was even tougher. When he meekly returned to his hotel, a riot broke out, complete with gunfire, fights, and mayhem. According to several accounts, a bullet was also fired from across the street into Johnson's hotel room in what General Grant—who had accompanied Johnson—concluded was an effort to assassinate Johnson.[65] Johnson's new party was, meanwhile, being assassinated in a political sense in the off-year elections.[66]

Perhaps George Gayle hoped that Johnson would react to all this abuse by taking an even more combative approach. It was during this uproar that he applied for a pardon. Gayle's petition, which he signed under oath on September 17, 1866, stated as follows:

To His Excellency Andrew Johnson, President of the United States:

Your Petitioner, George W. Gayle, respectfully showeth that he is a resident citizen of Dallas County, in the State of Alabama, and is by profession a lawyer; that he resided in a large part of his life in said county, and is now about fifty-nine years of age. Petitioner has a wife and three daughters, and he has no means for their support except the proceeds of his labor.

Your Petitioner further showeth unto Your Excellency that, in the late war, Petitioner took part against the United States by encouraging enlistments in the Confederate Army, and to the extent of his means, by contributions and by aiding and assisting Confederate soldiers and their families. Your Petitioner is old and feeble, and did not go into the army for that reason.

Your Petitioner is advised that he is excluded from the benefits of the Proclamation issued by Your Excellency on the 29th day of May, 1865, because he was in custody of the military authorities. There is no other cause or reason to except him from the benefits of said Proclamation.

Your Petitioner has in good faith taken the oath required in said Proclamation, a copy of which is hereto an X'd, and he intends in good faith to abide by and keep the promises therein made.

Your Petitioner, therefore, most respectfully prays that he may have the benefits of the Proclamation extended to him, and that he may receive full pardon and amnesty. And, as in duty bound, your Petitioner will ever pray, &c.[67]

Noticeably absent from Gayle's petition was any mention of his indictment regarding the Lincoln assassination, or a denial of his involvement in that conspiracy. Instead, Gayle cleverly chose to make his petition as vanilla as possible, apparently hoping that it would not be distinguishable from the thousands of similar petitions by civilians that Johnson had already granted. If this was Gayle's strategy, it did not work. Johnson took no action, and as Judge Busteed's next term of court in Alabama approached, it seemed that District Attorney Smith would finally get his man.

But by this time, John Hardy would have no role in the prosecution. President Johnson had removed him, and one of Johnson's enemies charged that it was because Hardy was "known to be a Radical, and it is desired to fill his place with a man who will summon a rebel sympathizing jury, so that Gayle, who offered $1,000,000 for the assassination of Lincoln, and others of like ilk, who are under indictment for their crimes, may be acquitted."[68] But Hardy's replacement followed Hardy's philosophy of selecting southern Unionists and northern immigrants for the jury venire. In fact, the Union army officer who had arrested George Gayle in 1865, now retired General John McArthur, was a member of the venire from which Gayle's petit jury would be chosen.[69] Judge Busteed arrived in Montgomery in early December, 1866,[70] and it was not long before Smith's prosecution of Gayle was removed from the back burner and set for trial.[71]

Gayle sought to have the trial postponed this time on the grounds that his attorney, wartime governor Thomas Hill Watts, was absent, and because of Gayle's pending application for a pardon. Busteed initially refused to grant a continuance on this basis, although he gave Gayle a few additional days to summon his witnesses.[72] But as was reported by newspapers across the nation, Busteed finally relented and continued Gayle's case until his spring term in 1867.[73]

Then Gayle sprang into action to meet the conspiracy charge head on, and rally support for his pardon from those whose standing might influence President Johnson. His first priority was to obtain the endorsement of Union army veterans. Ironically he convinced a group of such veterans turned Dallas County planters that included John McArthur to sign the following letter to President Johnson:

Dallas County, Alabama, December 17, 1866

To His Excellency, Andrew Johnson, President of the United States:

We, the undersigned, officers and soldiers late of the federal army, and now temporary citizens of Dallas County, Alabama, respectfully show unto Your Excellency that George W. Gayle, esq., of said county is indicted in the United States District Court of Montgomery, with the two late editors of the *Selma Dispatch*, for a conspiracy to take the lives of "Lincoln, Seward, and Johnson," and is a rebel generally.

From what we know of Mr. Gayle, and can learn of his character and standing in society, we cannot believe him guilty of the charge of conspiracy.

He is, doubtless, guilty as a rebel in aiding and assisting the Confederacy of the South, so-called, as hundreds of thousands of the Southern people are who are not indicted.

In view of the premises, therefore, we respectfully ask Your Excellency to grant Mr. Gayle a special pardon, that he may be released from the annoyance of the prosecution against him. We ask this that justice may be done.[74]

Given the stance of many northern veterans regarding prosecution of southern traitors, this was obviously a coup for Gayle. Exactly what motivated them to support him remains a mystery.[75]

On January 7, 1867, the stakes were suddenly raised for President Johnson when a member of Congress introduced a resolution in the House calling for Johnson's impeachment. Among the stated grounds for Johnson's removal was that he had "corruptly" used his constitutional power to pardon."[76] This, of course, raised the degree of difficulty for Gayle to obtain a pardon because it meant that Johnson would have to be more careful than ever when assessing pardon applications. For someone as nationally infamous as George Gayle, this meant that Johnson would need probative evidence that Gayle was likely innocent of the charges against him. Mere character evidence from Union army veterans who did not even know Gayle at the time he published his advertisement might not alone suffice.

Interestingly, Gayle did not submit his own affidavit, or any from the *Selma Dispatch* employees, regarding the circumstances surrounding the advertisement or his motive at the time. He, instead, had his Masonic Lodge brothers endorse a version of the facts that he may have ghost-written. According to that statement, which was apparently intended to support Gayle's joke defense and thereby negate the existence of criminal intent on his part, the members of the lodge *believed* "the charge of *conspiracy* against [Gayle] to be false and unfounded, and that the advertisement published in [the *Selma Dispatch*] was a mere *canard*, and on his part intended more to excite amusement than for any other purpose."[77] But viewed objectively, this statement was itself a canard. At no point did it explain why anyone would find the advertisement amusing. Those in Dallas County who hated Lincoln, Johnson, and Seward would have more likely seen it as Confederate patriotism in its highest form. Those who were tired of war but conditioned their yearning for peace on the continuance of slavery likely saw it as a way to eliminate three men who had been seen as roadblocks to peace on that basis. Those few in Dallas County who favored peace on any terms would have been aghast at the possibility that these proposed assassinations would harden northern resolve to punish the South.

Gayle also obtained signatures of Alabama Governor Robert Miller Patton and several members of the Alabama Senate and House to a petition stating that they had known him for many years and "cannot believe him guilty of the charge of conspiracy."[78] Members of the Alabama bench and bar signed a petition saying essentially the same thing, but also adding a different spin than Gayle's fellow Masons. Gayle, they claimed, was "governed in all such things much more by impulse than by settled conviction, and with a want of prudence which *verges on insanity*. We are satisfied that the publication in the *Selma Dispatch* was the result of a sudden idea that entered his mind, to put to the test the statements of his more wealthy neighbors, to the effect that they would devote their last dollar to any means to secure the independence of the confederacy. From our knowledge of his character we feel satisfied that he had no other intention."[79]

Those familiar with the names of the judges and lawyers who signed this petition would have known that each had been committed Confederates who had every reason to shade the truth to assist Gayle, one of their comrades. Even someone ignorant of their identities would note that the petition contained no indication that any of them had personal knowledge of the circumstances surrounding the advertisement. In all likelihood they were merely affirming their belief in what Gayle had told them.

Their story, like that of the Masons, is also fraught with illogic. Gayle was certainly an impulsive hothead. If his intention was to challenge the patriotism of his wealthy neighbors, then he was arguably neither insane nor joking. Given the profiteering that was going on during that period of the war as a result of shortages of food and other necessaries, motivating the profiteers to support the Cause rather than act out of greed was quite rational and in fact a major policy of Alabama's wartime government. A constructive goal Gayle could have pursued was to encourage financial support for the families of those who had lost men as a result of the war or whose men were away fighting on distant battlefields. Such support would have helped stem the rampant problem of desertion by Alabamians who left the ranks in order to return and care for their destitute families. In fact, fundraising efforts for this purpose had been underway in several Alabama counties, including Dallas.[80] One million dollars would have advanced the cause of Confederate independence, while siphoning it off for the long-shot scheme Gayle proposed in his advertisement would not.

Perhaps recognizing this, the Alabama lawyers and judges also utilized the lawyer's last resort: they skillfully played the sympathy angle. "For many years," they claimed, Gayle "has been insolvent, with no means except a precarious professional income, which barely sufficed for the support of his family, and we are convinced that he could not possibly have raised one hundred dollars ($100) of the million which was to be raised for the purpose indicated." Moreover, they continued, Gayle was "quite old, and has a large family dependent on him; and of all the people of Alabama who participated in the late war, there is not, in our opinion, one who is now more harmless and inoffensive towards yourself and the government of the United States." They concluded with the assertion that Gayle had "suffered much from imprisonment, is quite feeble, and, in our opinion, is a proper object for Executive clemency."[81]

But available facts refute each of these contentions. The 1860 federal census for Dallas County, Alabama, reveals that Gayle was moderately wealthy at the beginning of the war and financially able to contribute much more than the $1,000 he had pledged.[82] When the war began and most of the local bar volunteered for military service, Gayle's opportunity to increase his wealth improved dramatically by virtue of the resulting decrease in competition.[83] Available evidence indicates that Gayle's law practice remained busy.[84] As the death toll mounted, Gayle had been in a position to make a killing harvesting attorney fees for handling the probate of wills and the administration of estates of those who died. In this regard, it is noteworthy that the Masons, the judges, and the lawyers that knew Gayle did not claim that Gayle was physically or mentally disabled from practicing law during the war.

Their statements also did not jive with another piece of evidence George Gayle submitted to President Johnson in support of his pardon petition: a letter from former Alabama United States Senator Benjamin Fitzpatrick, a moderate who had served with Johnson in the Senate before the war, presided over Alabama's constitutional convention in 1865 by unanimous consent of the delegates, and played an important role in shepherding the delegates toward the adoption of the measures President Johnson had mandated.[85] Because of this, Gayle probably hoped that Fitzpatrick's support for Gayle's pardon would carry significant weight with Johnson. The substance of what Fitzpatrick wrote was rank hearsay. "I have since learned [Gayle] was under the influence of intoxicating liquors when the reward was offered," Fitzpatrick wrote.[86] The source of this information is unstated, and Fitzpatrick, who resided in Autauga County, not Dallas County, was the only person who submitted anything to Johnson that mentioned alcohol as a factor.

The final piece of "evidence" Gayle submitted in support of his pardon was from a relative of his wife. It was also based on hearsay. The relative's letter to President Johnson maintained that "Colonel Gayle, *I am informed*, is an inveterate joker," and "in making the publication for which he was arrested, he was quizzing some very wealthy men on account of their extravagant professions of devotion to the South, and that he had no criminal intentions whatever, and never supposed the publication would amount to anything."[87]

Gayle submitted nothing to President Johnson from an independent, third-party witness, much less one who had personal knowledge of the incident. And not surprisingly, Johnson took no immediate action on Gayle's request for a pardon. The situation was also complicated by external factors. On February 19, 1867, another suspected assassination conspirator who had fled the country, John Surratt, was returned under arrest. This refocused the nation on painful memories of President Lincoln's murder and elevated public sentiment for revenge.[88] It also provided the federal government with another possible source of information regarding the motivations and identities of other members of the assassination conspiracy. What if, after the president pardoned Gayle, Surratt cited Gayle's advertisement as a motivating factor for the conspirators? The chance of Johnson's impeachment would likely have increased exponentially.

In addition, the following month Congress passed two new laws, one known as the Sherman Military Bill, which did away with the state governments that Johnson had fashioned, placed the South once again under control of the military, and started the reconstruction process all over again, this time with black suffrage.[89] Johnson's veto of the legislation further enraged congressional Republicans tired of his obstructionism, and their override of his vetoes effectively left George Gayle exposed to trial by a military tribunal instead of an Alabama jury.[90]

Recognizing that these events might distract Johnson, but also mindful that the beginning of Judge Busteed's spring term of court was quickly approaching, Gayle wrote United States Attorney General Henry Stanbery on March 11, 1867, reminding him that evidence of his innocence had been submitted and noting that no action had "yet been had in your branch of the executive department, for reasons which may be good under the terrible state of affairs now prevailing." Gayle requested Stanbery to instruct United States District Attorney James Quinton Smith to "dismiss the prosecution against me, or continue it indefinitely, as may be most wise, just, and equitable."[91] Gayle also sent his wife, Jo, to attempt to meet with Stanbery and the President, a tactic that had worked well for many others seeking pardons.[92]

And it also worked this time for Gayle. Several press accounts around the nation attributed Johnson's subsequent pardon of Gayle "to the importunities of Gayle's wife,"[93] but it may have had more to do with the fact that both Johnson and Gayle were Masons.[94] Not surprisingly, however, the pardon warrant issued by Johnson to Gayle on April 29, 1867, did not mention Mrs. Gayle or Masonry. Instead, it alluded to some of the evidence Gayle's friends and allies had presented:

> Andrew Johnson, President of the United States of America, to whom all these presents shall come, greetings:
>
> Whereas, one George W. Gayle, of Dallas county, Alabama, is now under indictment in the United States Court for the Northern District of Alabama for conspiracy to overthrow the Government of the United States, and particularly for offering a large reward of one million of dollars for the assassination of Lincoln, Seward, and Johnson;
>
> And whereas, I am assured that the said George W. Gayle was innocent of guilty intent, and his irreproachable private character is totally at variance with the crime for which he stands indicted, and many other mitigating circumstances render him a proper object of Executive clemency;
>
> And whereas, the pardon of said George W. Gayle has been recommended by the Governor and members of the State Senate and House of Representatives of Alabama; by the members of the Supreme Court and bar of Alabama; by Brevet Major-General McArthur, United States Volunteers, and many other United States military officers, and other influential citizens;
>
> Now, therefore, be it known that I, Andrew Johnson, President of the United States of America, in consideration of the premises, divers other good and sufficient reasons me there unto moving, have granted and do hereby grant to the said George W. Gayle a full and unconditional pardon.
>
> In testimony whereof, I have hereunto signed my name and caused the seal of the United States to be affixed.
>
> Done at the city of Washington this twenty-ninth day of April, A.D. 1867, and in the independence of the United States of America the ninety-first.

ANDREW JOHNSON

By the President: —F.W. SEWARD, Acting Secretary of State.[95]

George Gayle's reaction to his good fortune was expressed by him in a letter to Attorney General Stanbery, who had recommended that Johnson pardon him. He was particularly effusive in his thanks for the "courtesy and kindness" shown to his wife, who had returned to Cahaba with the pardon on May 11.[96]

President Johnson would have likely preferred that Gayle thereafter demonstrate humility and contrition in public, and certainly avoid doing anything that might embarrass Johnson or antagonize northern Republicans. Suffice it to say, however, that once he received the pardon, the old, arrogant, outspoken George Gayle reappeared. In a letter to the editor of the *Selma Times* that was reprinted in and outside Alabama, Gayle ridiculed those Republicans. He declared, among other things, that he was "opposed to every man, and all men, who are striving to place the negro upon a moral and social equality with the whites. Such men," he continued, "should undergo a surgical operation, to stop the infamous breed." Gayle was particularly critical of two white Dallas County Republican leaders who had been active in appealing for black support for the Republican Party. Gayle looked "upon their rainbow colors as the nauseous exhibition of Pandora's box—emitting a compound of the most villainous stinks that ever offended [a] nostril."[97] Gayle also took this opportunity to publicly blast Congress. He called Congress's attempt to dominate the reconstruction process a "puerile doctrine" and expressed opposition to the Civil Rights Act of 1866 and the Sherman Military Bill as being "without any Constitutional authority or warrant." Then Gayle gave President Johnson the kiss of death: "I give my cordial support to the printed views of President Johnson, as a policy most productive of present good."[98]

Before Johnson could even consider revoking Gayle's parole in order to avoid the coming political backlash, Judge Busteed convened his court in Montgomery and called Gayle's case for trial. At that point, Gayle *admitted his guilt* of the charges against him and presented his pardon as a bar to the prosecution.[99] Busteed had no choice but to dismiss the charges upon payment by Gayle of the court costs, a result that made headlines across the nation.[100]

A few editors attempted to justify Johnson's controversial decision. One noted that Gayle "is said to be [a] poor, half-crazy, harmless, worthless sort of a fellow, whom nobody credits with either energy or brains enough to carry out any such design as he talked about.[101] But others were very critical. An Iowa editor called it "a wicked pardon."[102]

A Pennsylvania editor charged that it was a "clever performance on [Gayle's] part to secure pardon before legal conviction, and demonstrated the President's alacrity to screen his southern friends even from the suspicion of wrong doing."[103]

Nonetheless, as some had predicted, George Gayle had gotten off scot free. But the man who pardoned him would continue to receive the brunt of the public's frustration.

CHAPTER 10

"A Mean Man is Dead"

SOME in Congress believed that Andrew Johnson had been part of the Lincoln assassination conspiracy, and to them Johnson's pardon of George Gayle was more evidence of that fact.[1] Shortly after Gayle's pardon became public knowledge, the House Judiciary Committee issued a subpoena for Johnson's pardon clerk, F.U. Stitt, to appear before the committee and bring with him all of the records regarding that pardon.[2] Stitt was grilled regarding Gayle, as well as Johnson's pardon practices.[3]

At the same time, former U.S. Marshal John Hardy, now the editor of the pro-Republican Montgomery *State Sentinel*, was attacking Johnson for his pardon of Gayle and other Alabama secessionists. In an editorial titled "Andrew Johnson's Corrupt Exercise of the Pardoning Power," Hardy accused Johnson of being symbolically "shot into the office he disgraces by the pistol of an assassin. The event that startled the civilized world into the profoundest grief," Hardy continued, "was the stepping stone by aid of which [Johnson] was invested with the power to do wrong." Hardy also ridiculed Johnson's findings of Gayle's innocence—highlighting Gayle's guilty plea—and then presumed to "impeach Andrew Johnson as an aider and abettor of treason."[4] Hardy was certain that George Gayle somehow "has Andrew Johnson in his pocket! How he got him there, matters no—he has him!" The implication was that Johnson's pardon of Gayle was a payback for having Lincoln murdered.[5]

Hardy also had a few choice words for Gayle. "It was to be expected that the rebellion would from time to time, furnish conspicuous examples of treason more rank than ordinary, and traitors more diabolical than their fellows." The state of Alabama, he wrote, "furnished her full quota

of these, and George W. Gayle, of Cahawba, is their embodiment."
Hardy was certain Gayle caused the assassination of President Lincoln.
"The murderous intent incubated in the viciousness" of Gayle's mind
as reflected in his advertisement "fell upon the general thought without
provoking a single public dissent in the South." Then the "temptation to
do the dark deed flashed up to the view of many an incipient Booth, and
the '*sic semper tyrannis*' cry of the assassin stage actor, was born of the
distempered invectives of the lawyer Gayle." The "*intent* of Gayle," as
derived from the wording of Gayle's advertisement, he insisted, "found
its fruition in the *act* of Booth. Whether it was committed in the hope of
receiving the million dollars, or any part of it for which Gayle offered
to procure the murder done, does not appear," but "it is not pushing fair
presumption too hard if it be claimed that John Wilkes Booth, like Judas
Iscariot, was a hireling."[6]

The Judiciary Committee, however, could not find any evidence
that Johnson had committed any crime in connection with Gayle's
pardon. Hence, although the House voted to impeach Johnson in 1868,
Johnson's exercise of his power to pardon was not expressly made one
of the grounds. But most historians agree that Johnson's pardons added
fuel to the fire that almost consumed him.[7] In the end, however, Johnson
narrowly escaped conviction.[8]

Whether George Gayle cared one way or the other about this is
unclear. This supposedly feeble, half-crazy, brainless, drunkard was
busy resuming his law practice—by all accounts successfully, and, as
before the war, occasionally making news in connection with political
incidents.[9] For example, a pro-Republican Alabama editor noted in 1870
that Gayle was in attendance at a Republican rally in Selma and that Gayle
was "serenely smiling," Gayle reportedly explained to a pro-Democrat
editor that "folks do smile at a monkey show."[10]

Gayle remained a vocal critic of the Republican Party until his
death on April 8, 1875, at the age of 68 following a lengthy illness. But
it was the widespread belief that he had gotten away with instigating
the murder of President Lincoln that shaped public reaction to Gayle's
passing across the nation.[11] In a front page editorial titled "A Mean Man
is Dead," a Michigan editor spoke for many when he wrote that:

A man whose dying hours are rejoiced in by all patriots, whose soul deserves
not punishment and existence, but annihilation, has blessed the earth by leaving
it. George W. Gayle, a lawyer in Alabama, is the individual. He is the party who
offered $1,000,000 reward for the assassination of President Lincoln through
a Southern sheet. His death occurred early this week at Selma, Ala., his last
breath being spent in a curse.[12]

In the traditional post mortem resolutions adopted by the Dallas County Bar, Gayle's professional colleagues preferred to remember Gayle for his talents as a lawyer and zealous advocate.[13] A quarter century later, a member of the Gayle family wrote a history of Cahawba in which she attempted to literally rewrite the circumstances surrounding George Gayle's post-war arrest. In a lengthy poem, she wrote that in 1861 George Gayle had made a toast at a pro-war banquet in which he declared "death and damnation to the whole Yankee host" and "then in an eloquent oration he led and offered a reward for Abe Lincoln's head; One million dollars was the sum he named, for which he became in the South so famed." She blamed John Hardy's newspaper for reporting what she called this "thoughtless boast" and causing the report to be "copied in all the Northern papers," thereby making Gayle "a target of Yankee Hate." When the war ended, she continued, Gayle was arrested for treason and taken North, but then the charge changed:

Tho utterly ignorant of Booth and his plan
To murder Lincoln, the Northern land
Remembered his words, in the excitement of war
and arrested him now as a conspirator.
He was cast in prison, at Fortress Monroe,
With John A. Campbell and Clay
Where Jeff Davis, our honored President,
In irons and shackles lay,
By command of that monster in human form—The illustrious Nelson Miles—
Who, with Stanton and others then in power,
Were fiends in men's disguise.[14]

But her efforts to revise history and portray George Gayle as an innocent martyr were unsuccessful. Each of the references to him in the press over the next century centered on his advertisement encouraging the Lincoln assassination.[15] This is also the case with regard to histories of the Civil War era and the Lincoln assassination.[16] He will always be known as the Million Dollar Man.

The issue whether Gayle's advertisement was, in fact, a motivating factor for John Wilkes Booth's assassination of Abraham Lincoln will forever remain a mystery. There is no known direct evidence, primarily because Booth was killed before he could be questioned. A diary supposedly authored by Booth does not mention the advertisement, but when found it was missing a number of pages.[17] The other conspirators with known direct ties to Booth were hung before the grand jury met and indicted Gayle, and any Booth accomplices who might have implicated Gayle were thereby eliminated.

But the circumstantial evidence we do know is entirely consistent with the theory that the advertisement was an important and possibly determinative factor, just as the court of public opinion had concluded at the time. That advertisement, as previously discussed, was reprinted in newspapers throughout the nation, including regions where Booth would have seen it. Not long after the advertisement was published, Booth repeatedly mentioned that his venture would bring him and the others a fortune. No other specific source of a large sum of money was ever proven. In addition, the assassination occurred within a few months after the publication of the advertisement—plenty of time for Booth to investigate its bona fides. And Booth seemed to signal his knowledge of the contents of the advertisement by making a reference to tyrants at the time of the assassination. Finally, of all the possible victims of assassination, Booth targeted only those Gayle had specified.

Chances are this would have been enough for a military tribunal to convict Gayle in the immediate wake of Lincoln's death. But at that time the federal government was pursuing an alternate, ultimately baseless narrative that placed Jefferson Davis in the role as the instigator of the assassination. As a result, additional evidence against Gayle that might have been developed was not, and if it existed it is likely now lost forever. Or is it?

Chapter Notes

Introduction

1. *New York Times,* April 15, 1865, 1. *Accord* (Washington, D.C.); *National Intelligencer,* April 15, 1865; Thomas A. Bogar, *Backstage at the Lincoln Assassination: The Untold Story of the Actors and Stagehands at Ford's Theatre* (Washington, D.C., 2013), 4.

2. *New York Times,* April 15, 1865, 1.

3. Samuel Pickens, April 15, 1865, in G. Ward Hubbs, *Voices from Company D: Diaries by the Greensboro Guards, Fifth Alabama Infantry Regiment, Army of Northern Virginia* (Athens, Georgia, 2003), 372.

4. *Milwaukee Sentinel,* May 13, 1865. *Accord; New York Times,* May 9, 1865, 1; *Mobile News,* April 21, 1865, 2.

5. *Mobile News Extra,* April 20, 1865.

6. Martha Hodes, *Mourning Lincoln* (New Haven, CT, 2015), 45, 84.

7. (Selma) *Chattanooga Rebel,* April 20, 1865, reprinted in *Mobile Daily News,* May 5, 1865, 1.

8. *Demopolis Herald,* reprinted in (Greensboro) *Alabama Beacon,* April 21, 1865, 2. See also, Harriet E. Amos Doss, "Every Man Should Consider His Own Conscience: Black and White Alabamians' Reactions to the Assassination of Abraham Lincoln," in Kenneth W. Noe, ed., *The Yellowhammer War: The Civil War and Reconstruction in Alabama,* (Tuscaloosa, AL, 2013), 165-76; Hodes, *Mourning Lincoln,* 70-93. At least one Black Belt Alabama man celebrated Lincoln's assassination into the twentieth century, even erecting a monument to Booth in his front yard. James O. Hall, "'Pink' Parker's Tombstone," in *Civil War Times* (July, 1979), Issue 18, 8-9.

9. *Montgomery Mail,* April 24, 1865, 1.

10. William Cooper, *Diary of William Cooper,* entry for April 14, 1865, William Cooper Papers, Alabama Department of Archives and History, and Southern Historical Collection Manuscripts Department, University of North Carolina at Chapel Hill.

11. Regarding that sentiment, *see* Elizabeth Varon, *Appomattox: Victory, Defeat, and Freedom at the End of the Civil War* (New York, NY, 2014), 135-37; Hodes, *Mourning Lincoln,* 117-38.

12. (Washington, D.C.) *Evening Star,* June 28, 1865, 2; June 29, 1865, 2 (publishing the closing argument of the prosecution in the trial of the team of assassins before a military tribunal). *See also,* Clint Johnson, *Pursuit: The Chase, Capture, Persecution, and Surprising Release of Confederate President Jefferson Davis* (New York, NY, 2008), 225-26; Hodes, *Mourning Lincoln,* 131; Benn Pitman, *The Assassination of President Lincoln and the Trial of the Conspirators* (Cincinnati, OH, 1865), 351-402; Elizabeth D. Leonard, *Lincoln's Forgotten Ally: Judge Advocate General Joseph Holt of Kentucky* (Chapel Hill, NC, 2011), 202, 212-13; William Hatchett, *The Lincoln Murder Conspiracies* (Urbana, IL, 1983), 59-89, 106-108; Edward Steers, *The Trial: The Assassination of President Lincoln and the Trial of the Conspirators* (Lexington, KY, 2010), xxx-xxxi; Elizabeth D. Leonard, *Lincoln's Avengers: Justice, Revenge, and Reunion After the Civil War* (New York, NY 2004), 63-65, 147; Kate Clifford Larson, *The Assassin's Accomplice: Mary Surratt and the Plot to Kill Abraham Lincoln* (New York, NY, 2008), 133-34. Some have even theorized that the purpose of blaming Confederate leaders was to distract the public, and that it was actually Edwin Stanton and other Northerners who had backed the assassins. Leonard F. Guttridge and Ray A. Neff, *Dark Union: The Secret Web of Profiteers, Politicians, and Booth Conspirators That Led to Lincoln's Death* (Hoboken, NJ, 2003).

13. David Herbert Donald, *Lincoln* (New York, NY, 1995), 677-78, n. 549; William C. Davis, *Jefferson Davis: The Man and His Hour* (Baton Rouge, LA, 1995), 620; Frederick Hatch, *Protecting President Lincoln: The Security Effort, the Thwarted Plots, and the Disaster at Ford's Theatre* (Jefferson, NC, 2011), 74-75; John H. Rhodehamel and Louise Taper, eds., *Right or Wrong, God Judge Me: The Writings of John Wilkes Booth* (Urbana, IL, 1997), 10-14, 120-21.

14. Rumors of an impending kidnapping were already in the Northern press. *New York Tribune,* March 19, 1864, reprinted in *Charleston Mercury,* May 4, 1864, 1; (Columbia, SC) *South Carolinian,* May 4, 1864, 84; *Burlington* (VT) *Free Press,* March 25, 1864, 1; and *Weekly Perryburg* (OH) *Journal,* May 10, 1865, 1. *See generally,* William A. Tidwell, James O. Hall and David Winfrey Gaddy, *Come Retribution: The Confederate Secret Service and the Assassination of Abraham Lincoln* (Jackson, MS, 1988), 234-38.

15. Donald, *Lincoln,* 677-78, n. 549; William J. Cooper, Jr., *Jefferson Davis, American* (New York, NY, 2001), 535-36; William Hanchett, *Lincoln Murder Conspiracies* (Champaign, IL, 1983), 31-32; Terry Alford, *Fortune's Fool: The Life of John Wilkes Booth* (New York, NY, 2015), 180.

16. Michael W. Kauffman, *American Brutus: John Wilkes Booth and the Lincoln Conspiracies* (New York, NY, 2004), 133-38; Warren Getler and Bob Brewer, *Shadow of the Sentinel: One Man's Quest to Find the Hidden Treasures of the Confederacy* (New

York, NY, 2003), 67; Allen C. Guelzo, *Abraham Lincoln: Redeemer President* (Grand Rapids, MI, 1999), 431-32; Edward Steers, Jr., *Lincoln Legends: Myths, Hoaxes, and Confabulations Associated With Our Greatest President* (Lexington, KY, 2007), 168-76, 196; William A. Tidwell, *April '65: Confederate Covert Action in the American Civil War* (Kent, OH, 1995), 141-45; Alford, *Fortune's Fool,* 176-98, 206.

17. *See, e.g.,* Hodes, *Mourning Lincoln,* 214-15, 238; Anthony S. Pitch, *"They Have Killed papa Dead!"* The Road to Ford's Theatre, Abraham Lincoln's Murder, and the Rage for Vengeance* (Hanover, NH, 2008), 83; Bill O'Reilly and Martin Dugard, *Killing Lincoln: The Shocking Assassination That Changed America Forever* (New York, NY 2011), 95-96, 109; Roy Z. Chamblee, Jr., *Lincoln's Assassins: A Complete Account of Their Capture, Trial and Punishment* (Jefferson, NC,1990), 68-70, 455-56; Donald, *Lincoln,* 588; Brendan H. Egan, Jr., *Murder at Ford's Theatre: A Chronicle of an Assassination* (Philadelphia, PA, 2007); Edward Steers and Harold Holzer, eds., *The Lincoln Assassination Conspirators: Their Confinement and Execution, As Recorded In the Letterbook of John Frederick Hartranft* (Baton Rouge, LA, 2009), 35-36; Hanchett, *Lincoln Murder Conspiracies,* 37; W. Emerson Reck, *A. Lincoln, His Last 24 Hours* (Jefferson, NC, 1987), 66; Rhodehamel and Taper, eds., *Right or Wrong, God Judge Me,* 15-16; Varon, *Appomattox,* 137; Alford, *Fortune's Fool,* 256-57.

18. George Alfred Townsend, *Katy of Catoctin; or, the Chain-Breakers; a National Romance* (New York, NY, 1886), 490. *See also,* Louis J. Weichmann and Floyd E. Risvold, ed., *A True History of the Assassination of Abraham Lincoln and of the Conspiracy of 1865* (New York, NY, 1975), 147-48 (the editor added the quote from *Katy of Catoctin*); Kauffman, *American Brutus,* 210, and footnote 35n (citing *Katy of Catoctin*); Thomas Goodrich, *The Darkest Dawn: Lincoln, Booth, and the Great American Tragedy* (Bloomington, IL, 2005), 42 (including this quote but citing Steers who cited a primary source that did not contain the quote); Hanchett, *Lincoln Murder Conspiracies,* 37, and note 9n citing Townsend's novel as authority. It is possible both Townsend and Stone were politically motivated. Between 1865 and 1886 when *Katy of Catoctin* was published, Republicans had repeatedly insinuated that the Democrats had caused Lincoln to be murdered. Hanchett, *Lincoln Murder Conspiracies,* 92-93. As Hanchett notes at page 126, Townsend was a war correspondent of the *New York World,* a major Democratic Party organ. As Hanchett also points out, Townsend's position from the outset was that Booth was the sole "projector" of the assassination plot. Hanchett, *Lincoln Murder Conspiracies,* 90-91. This, of course, helped keep the Democratic party's skirts clean of the assassination plot. Frederick Stone of Port Tobacco, Maryland, was also a Democrat. (Washington, D.C.) *National Republican,* October 18, 1866, April 8, 1868; (Baltimore) *Sun,* April 4, 1864, 1.

19. William H. Herndon and Jesse W. Weik, *Abraham Lincoln: The True Story of a Great Life,* 2 vols. (Springfield, IL, 1888), vol. 2, 289.

20. *See, e.g.,* Varon, *Appomattox,* 137. One of Lincoln's many admiring biographers was certain Lincoln "was not murdered because he had issued the Emancipation Proclamation or because he endorsed the Thirteenth Amendment. He was killed because he endorsed the enfranchisement of blacks, and therefore Lincoln should be

considered a martyr to black citizenship rights, as much as Martin Luther King, Jr., or Medger Evers, or Viola Liuzzo, or Micky Schwerner, or James Reeb, or James Cheney, or Andrew Goodman, or any of the others who were killed in the 1960s as they championed the civil rights movement." Michael Burlingame, *Lincoln and the Civil War* (Carbondale, IL, 2011), 128.

21. Hanchett, *Lincoln Murder Conspiracies*, 37, 37n; Edward Steers, Jr., *Blood on the Moon: The Assassination of Abraham Lincoln* (Lexington, KY, 2001), 91 and footnote 37n.

22. House Report 7, 40 Cong., 1 Sess. (1867), 674.

23. (Washington, D.C.) *Evening Star,* April 11, 1865, 3; *New York Times,* April 10, 1865, 4, April 11, 1865, 4; (Washington, D.C.) *National Republican*, April 11, 1865, 2; William C. Harris, *Lincoln's Last Months* (Cambridge, MA, 2004), 202-10; Kauffman, *American Brutus*, 206-209; Roy P. Basler, ed., *The Collected Works of Abraham Lincoln*, 9 vols. (New Brunswick, NJ, 1953), vol. 8, 393-94; Goodrich, *Darkest Dawn*, 17-22.

24. Kauffman, *American Brutus*, 207.

25. Steers, *Blood on the Moon*, 91; Betty J. Ownsbey, *Alias "Paine": Lewis Thornton Powell, the Mystery Man of the Lincoln Conspiracy* (Jefferson, NC, 1993), 70; Charles Higham, *Murdering Mr. Lincoln: A New Detection of the 19th Century's Most Famous Crime* (Beverly Hills, CA, 2004), 201.

26. *New York Tribune*, April 12, 1865, 1; *New York Times,* April 12, 1865, 1. See also, Harris, *Lincoln's Last Months*, 212-16; Basler, *Collected Works of Abraham Lincoln*, vol. 7, 399-405.

27. *New York Tribune*, April 12, 1865, 4. See also, Guttridge and Neff, *Dark Union*, 119-20, 125.

28. David Warren Brown, *Andrew Johnson and the Negro* (Knoxville, TN, 1989), 118-21.

29. Walter Stahr, *Seward: Lincoln's Indispensable Man* (New York, NY, 2012), 478.

30. Mark R. Wilson, *The Business of Civil War: Military Mobilization and the State, 1861-1865* (Baltimore, MD, 2006), 227.

31. Alford, *Fortune's Fool*, 231, 242; James O. Hall and Michael Maione, *"To Make A Fortune": John Wilkes Booth: Following the Money Trail* (Clinton, MD, 2003).

32. This is not to suggest that Confederate officials and soldiers were uninvolved in the assassination conspiracy. It appears that several may have been, including Clay and possibly Confederate Secretary of State Judah Benjamin. But in doing so, it is submitted that they were acting without the sanction—or even the knowledge—of Davis or his cabinet as a whole. Regarding Confederate Secretary of State Judah Benjamin, see Getler and Brewer, *Rebel Gold*, 68-69.

33. Hatch, *Protecting President Lincoln*, 39-40; Hanchett, *Lincoln Murder Conspiracies*, 29-30; Tidwell, Holland, Gaddy, *Come Retribution*, 238; Kauffman, *American Brutus*, 466, n. 3; Thomas Goodrich, *Darkest Dawn:* 268; Hanchett, *Lincoln Murder Conspiracies*, 29-30.

CHAPTER 1: A FAITHFUL DISCIPLE OF THE OLD PANNEL
JACKSON DEMOCRACY

1. Charles Edward Cauthen, *South Carolina Goes To War, 1860-1865* (Columbia, SC, 2005), x; Walter B. Edgar, *South Carolina: A History* (Columbia, SC1998), 355; Lacy K. Ford, *Origins of Southern Radicalism: The South Carolina Upcountry, 1800-1860* (New York, NY, 1998), 97-183. My paternal ancestors resided in South Carolina.

2. Harry S. Stout, *Upon the Altar of the Nation: A Moral History of the American Civil War* (New York, NY, 2006), 9-10.

3. See generally, Manisha Sinha, *The Counterrevolution of Slavery: Politics and Ideology in Antebellum South Carolina* (Chapel Hill, NC, 2000), 1-5; William J. Cooper, Jr., *The South and the Politics of Slavery 1828-1856* (Baton Rouge, LA, 1978), 289.

4. *Birmingham News*, January 5, 1935; Thomas McAdory Owen, *History of Alabama and Dictionary of Alabama Biography*, 4 vols. (Spartanburg, SC, 1978), vol. 3, 646; Willis Brewer, *Alabama, Her History, Resources, War Record, and Public Men: From 1540 to 1872* (Montgomery, AL, 1872), 219.

5. Owen, *History of Alabama and Dictionary of Alabama Biography*, vol. 3, 646.

6. (Montgomery) *Alabama Journal*, July 2, 1851, 2.

7. Thomas P. Abernethy, *The Formative Period in Alabama, 1815-1828* (Tuscaloosa, AL, 1990), 35-41; Edgar, *South Carolina*, 275-77; James David Miller, *South by Southwest: Planter Emigration and Identity in the Slave South* (Charlottesville, VA, 2002), 68, 74; Tommy W. Rogers, "Migration Patterns of Alabama's Population, 1850-1860," in *Alabama Historical Quarterly* 28 (Spring and Summer, 1966), 45-50; Edward Pattillo, *Carolina Planters on the Alabama Frontier: The Spencer-Robeson-McKenzie Family Papers* (Montgomery, AL, 2011); Henry DeLeon Southerland, Jr., and Jerry Elijah Brown, *The Federal Road Through Georgia, the Creek Nation, and Alabama, 1806-1836* (Tuscaloosa, AL 1989), 36.

8. Gene Dattel, *Cotton and Race in the Making of America: The Human Costs of Economic Power* (Lanham, MD, 2009), 47-48; Alfred H. Conrad, *The Economics of Slavery and Other Studies in Econometric History* (Chicago, IL, 1964), 76; Herbert James Lewis, *Clearing the Thickets: A History of Antebellum Alabama* (New Orleans, 2013), 105-31; William Warren Rogers, Robert David Ward, Leah Rawls Atkins and Wayne Flynt, *Alabama: The History of A Deep South State* (Tuscaloosa, AL, 2010), 54-66.

9. Lewy Dorman, *Party Politics in Alabama from 1850-1860* (Tuscaloosa, AL, 1995), 14-15.

10. *Charleston Mercury*, February 27, 1851, p. 2.

11. Theodore Henley Jack, "Sectionalism and Party Politics in Alabama 1819-1842," (PhD. Diss., University of Chicago, 1919), 5-6; Abernethy, *Formative Period in Alabama*, 17-21.

12. Conrad, *Economics of Slavery*, 76; Carl Edward Skeen, *1816: America Rising* (Lexington, KY, 2003), 53-65; William Edmunds Benson, *A Political History of the Tariff 1789-1861* (Bloomington, IN, 2010), 25-34; William W. Freehling, *Prelude to*

Civil War: The Nullification Controversy in South Carolina 1816-1836 (New York, NY, 1966), 24-39, 95.

13. *Blakely Sun*, March 23, 1819, 2-3.

14. Don E. Fehrenbacher, *The South and Three Sectional Crises* (Baton Rouge, LA, 1980), 9-23.

15. James Benson Sellers, *Slavery in Alabama* (Tuscaloosa, AL, 1994), 147.

16. Edgar, *South Carolina,* 326-28; William W. Freehling, *The Road to Disunion: Secessionists At Bay 1776-1854* (New York, NY, 1990), 79-85; Sinha, *Counterrevolution of Slavery*, 15.

17. Marshall J. Rachleff, "Racial Fear and Political Factionalism: A Study of the Secession Movement in Alabama, 1819-1861," (Ph.D. dissertation, University of Massachusetts, 1974), 4.

18. Alfred N. Hunt, *Haiti's Influence on Antebellum America* (Baton Rouge, LA, 1988), 9-36; David P. Geggus, *The Impact of the Haitian Revolution in the Atlantic World* (Columbia, SC, 2001), 4.

19. Sinha, *Counterrevolution of Slavery*, 15; Hunt, *Haiti's Influence on Antebellum America*, 16-40.

20. Sellers, *Slavery in Alabama,* 361, 367; Kenneth M. Stampp, *The Peculiar Institution: Slavery in the Ante-Bellum South* (New York, NY, 1989), 135.

21. John Chester Miller, *The Wolf By the Ears: Thomas Jefferson and Slavery* (Charlottesville, VA, 1995), 43-59, 218.

22. Angela Broyles, *Alabama History in the U.S.* (Killen, AL, 2007), 112.

23. (Milledgeville) *Georgia Journal*, May 25, 1824, 6; *Milledgeville Patriot*, May 10, 1825, reprinted in (Charleston) *City Gazette and Commercial Advertiser*, May 14, 1825, 2; (Savannah) *Georgian*, May 17, 1825, 2; *Augusta Chronicle and Georgia Advertiser*, August 3, 1825, 3; (Huntsville) *Democrat*, March 9, 1827, 3.

24. (Worchester, Mass.) *National Aegis*, August 31, 1825, 151; *Augusta Chronicle and Georgia Advertiser*, September 14, 1825, 3.

25. Michael D. Green, *The Politics of Indian Removal: Creek Government and Society in Crisis* (Lincoln, NE, 1985), 66-211; Paul Finkelman and Donald R. Kennon, eds., *Congress and the Emergence of Sectionalism: From the Missouri Compromise to the Age of Jackson* (Athens, OH, 2008), 107-116.

26. (Savannah) *Georgian*, October 22, 1825, 2, November 12, 1825, 2; *Mobile Commercial Register*, May 5, 1826, 2; Anthony Gene Carey, *Parties, Slavery, and the Union in Antebellum Georgia* (Athens, GA, 1997), 23.

27. *Mobile Commercial Register*, June 25, 1828, 2; George Gayle's father, John Gayle, died in 1828. *Gayle v. Agee,* 4 Port. 507 (AL, 1837).

28. *Mobile Commercial Register*, September 6, 1828.

29. *Mobile Commercial Register*, June 25, 1828, 1; (New York) *Evening Post*, March 22, 1832, 2; Freehling, *Prelude to Civil War*, 254-57; Ford, *Origins of Southern Radicalism,* 120-25; Jack, "Sectionalism and Party Politics in Alabama," 24-27; Sinha,

Counterrevolution of Slavery, 16-26; Carey, *Parties, Slavery, and the Union in Antebellum Georgia*, 24.

30. William C. Davis, *Rhett: The Turbulent Life and Times of a Fire-Eater* (Columbia, SC, 2001), 10, 38, 354.

31. *Montgomery Mail*, reprinted in (New Orleans) *Picayune*, October 3, 1863, 1.

32. Davis, *Rhett*, 38-42.

33. *Selma Courier*, May 22, 1828, 2 (publishing a letter from Jackson).

34. Sinha, *Counterrevolution of Slavery*, 19-26; Freehling, *Prelude to Civil War*, 257; Davis, *Rhett*, 42-44; Cooper, *South and the Politics of Slavery*, 12-49.

35. Sinha, *Counterrevolution of Slavery*, 50, 52; Carey, *Parties, Slavery, and the Union in Antebellum Georgia*, 24-27, 30.

36. (Greenville) *Mountaineer*, reprinted in *Charleston Courier*, April 14, 1830, 2. See also, Sinha, *Counterrevolution of Slavery*, 38-49.

37. *Charleston Mercury*, reprinted in *Boston Commercial Gazette*, April 29, 1830, 2.

38. *Selma Courier*, July 31, 1828, 2, August 14, 1828, 2; (Huntsville) *Democrat*, September 9, 1830, 2; (Montgomery) *Planters Gazette* reprinted in (Charleston) *City Gazette Commercial Daily Advertiser*, July 4, 1831, 2; (Washington, D.C.) *National Intelligencer*, August 7, 1830, 1, June 15, 1831, 3; *Charleston Courier*, July 4, 1831, 2, July 30, 1831, 2, October 4, 1831, 2; (Charleston) *City Gazette & Commercial Advertiser*, July 4, 1831, 2, August 1, 1831, 2; *Macon Weekly Telegraph*, January 14, 1832, 3; *Mobile Commercial Register*, reprinted in *Charleston Courier*, June 7, 1832, 2; Rogers, et al., *Alabama*, 85; Brian Schoen, *The Fragile Fabric of Union: Cotton, Federal Politics, and the Global Origins of the Civil War* (Baltimore, MD, 2009), 142.

39. *Cahawba Republican*, December 4, 1832, reprinted in *Richmond Enquirer*, December 28, 1832, 2.

40. *Charleston Courier*, July 30, 1831, 2.

41. *Mobile Commercial Register and Patriot*, quoted in Albert Burton Moore, *History of Alabama* (Tuscaloosa, AL, 1951), 163.

42. (Huntsville) *Democrat*, February 5, 1830, 2-3; (Tuscaloosa) *Flag of the Union*, May 21, 1835, 5 (listing the Alabamians who were graduates of South Carolina College up to 1835); (Charleston) *City Gazette & Commercial Advertiser*, August 1, 1831, 2; *Richmond Enquirer*, December 6, 1832, 3. Regarding the influence of South Carolina College and Cooper, see Sinha, *Counterrevolution of Slavery*, 17-18; David I. Durham, *A Southern Moderate In Radical Times: Henry Washington Hilliard, 1808-1892* (Baton Rouge, LA, 2008), 8-17; Freehling, *Road to Disunion: Secessionists at Bay*, 256-57, 315-18; Cooper, *South and the Politics of Slavery*, 99.

43. (Huntsville) *Democrat*, February 5, 1830, 2-3; (Tuscaloosa) *Flag of the Union*, May 21, 1835, 5; *New-London* (Conn.) *Gazette*, May 11, 1831, 3; *Charleston Courier*, September 16, 1831, 2; (Montgomery) *Alabama Journal*, September 12, 1829, 3; (New York) *Evening Post*, August 26, 1833, 2; Mary Ann Neely, ed., *The Works of Matthew Blue: Montgomery's First Historian* (Montgomery, AL, 2010),

91, 102; J. Mills Thornton, III, *Politics and Power In a Slave Society: Alabama, 1800-1860* (Baton Rouge, LA, 1978), 21-22.

44. (Montgomery) *Alabama Journal*, reprinted in (Washington, D.C.) *National Journal*, September 22, 1830, 3; *Charleston Courier*, August 15, 1831, 2, August 22, 1831, 2 (Lewis's re-election in 1831), September 16, 1831, 2 (indicating that Lewis' re-election was perceived by some as demonstrating support in Alabama for nullification); (Washington, D.C.) *National Intelligencer*, August 17, 1833, 3 (Lewis was unopposed in 1833); Lewis, *Clearing the Thickets*, 195; Elbert L. Watson, *Alabama United States Senators* (Huntsville: Strode Publishers, 1982), 45-48; Rachleff, "Radical Fear and Political Factionalism," 66-67.

45. Freehling, *Prelude to Civil War*, 257-285.

46. (Hayneville) *Spirit of the South*, June 3, 1835, 3.

47. *Boston Commercial Gazette*, April 25, 1833, 2.

48. James Petigru to Hugh Swinton Legare, July 15, 1833, quoted in Sinha, *Counterrevolution of Slavery*, 60.

49. Davis, *Rhett*, 303; Sinha, *Counterrevolution of Slavery*, 72, 105-108.

50. *Florence Gazette*, November 2, 1850, 1.

51. *Charleston Courier*, August 2, 1832, 2; Sinha, *Counterrevolution of Slavery*, 53-55, 72, 105-108; Carey, *Parties, Slavery, and the Union in Antebellum Georgia*, 26.

52. Sarah Haynsworth Gayle, January 22, 1831, in Sarah Woolfolk Wiggins and Ruth Smith Truss, eds., *The Journal of Sarah Haynsworth Gayle, 1827-1835: A Substitute for Social Intercourse* (Tuscaloosa, AL, 2013), 168.

53. (Livingston) *Sumter County Whig*, August 1, 1851, 2. See generally, Rachleff, "Racial Fear and Political Factionalism," 66-68.

54. Wiggins and Truss, eds., *Journal of Sarah Haynsworth Gayle*, xx; Lewis, *Clearing the Thickets*, 203; Owen, *History of Alabama and Dictionary of Alabama Biography*, vol. 3, 646-47.

55. *Alabama Senate Journal* 1831-1832, 46-48; *Tuscaloosa Inquirer*, reprinted in *Charleston Courier*, October 5, 1831, 2; *Charleston Courier*, June 14, 1831, 2, August 22, 1831, 2; (Washington, D.C.) *Daily National Intelligencer*, September 8, 1831, 2, December 29, 1831, 3; Jack, "Sectionalism and Party Politics in Alabama," 27-37.

56. *Montgomery Planters' Gazette*, quoted in (Washington, D.C.) *National Intelligencer*, September 8, 1831, 2, *Baltimore Patriot & Mercantile Advertiser*, September 9, 1831, 2; (New York) *American*, September 10, 1831, 2; (Philadelphia) *National Gazette*, September 10, 1831, 2; *Portland* (Maine) *Advertiser*, September 20, 1831, 1; *New London* (Conn.) *Gazette and General Advertiser*, September 21, 1831, 3; (Worcester, Mass.) *National Aegis*, September 28, 1831, 3; *Tuscaloosa Inquirer*, reprinted in *Charleston Courier*, October 5, 1831, 2.

57. *Alabama Senate Journal* 1829-1830, 75; *Mobile Commercial Register*, December 23, 1825, 2, December 27, 1825, 2; Owen, *History of Alabama and Dictionary of Alabama Biography*, vol. 3, 646; Thornton, *Politics and Power in a Slave Society*, 244. Regarding Tuscaloosa during this period, see G. Ward Hubbs, *Tuscaloosa: Portrait of an Alabama County* (Northridge, CA, 1987), 23-29; William H. Brantley, *Three Capitals: A*

Book About the First Three Capitals of Alabama: St. Stephens, Huntsville & Cahawba (Tuscaloosa, AL, 1976), 165-207.

58. *Alabama Senate Journal 1830-1831*, 6, 26 120-23, 136-37, 147-48, 151-52, 185-86.

59. *Tuscaloosa Enquirer*, reprinted in (Huntsville) *Democrat*, February 3, 1831, 3.

60. Gayle's effort to be elected by the 1832-1833 Alabama legislature to the position of circuit solicitor was unsuccessful. *Alabama Senate Journal*, 1832 Special Session, 27-28; Sarah Haynsworth Gayle, November 11, 1832, in Wiggins and Truss, eds., *Journal of Sarah Haynsworth Gayle*, 223.

61. (Tuscaloosa) *Flag of the Union*, December 26, 1838, 3; (Cahawba) *Dallas Gazette*, reprinted in (Tuscaloosa) *Independent Monitor*, May 1, 1851, 2.

62. *Florence Gazette*, January 11, 1851, 2.

63. *Florence Gazette*, August 19, 1824, 3; *Mobile Commercial Register*, August 1, 1826, 1; Owen, *History of Alabama and Dictionary of Alabama Biography*, vol. 3, 646. Regarding Cahawba, later renamed Cahaba, see Harvey H. Jackson, III, *Rivers of History: Life on the Coosa, Tallapoosa, Cahaba and Alabama* (Tuscaloosa, AL, 1995), 50-60, 68-69.

64. Owen, *History of Alabama and Dictionary of Alabama Biography*, vol. 4, 1488.

65. Anna M. Gayle Fry, *Memories of Old Cahaba* (Nashville, TN, 1908), 15; Owen, *History of Alabama and Dictionary of Alabama Biography*, vol. 3, 646; Lewis, *Lost Capitals of Alabama*, 85-94.

66. *Selma Free Press*, May 21, 1836, 4.

67. Fry, *Memories of Old Cahaba*, 16.

68. *Portland* (ME) *Advertiser*, reprinted in *New-Bedford* (MA) *Mercury*, May 10, 1833, 2; *Portland* (ME) *Advertiser,* reprinted in (Boston) *American Traveller*, May 14, 1833, 1.

69. *Montgomery Planter's Gazette*, August 21, 1832, reprinted in (New York) *Commercial Advertiser*, September 1, 1832, 2.

70. *Montgomery Planter's Gazette*, August 21, 1832, reprinted in (New York) *Commercial Advertiser*, September 1, 1832, 2, *Alexandria* (VA) *Gazette,* September 4, 1832, 2, (Philadelphia) *National Gazette*, September 4, 1832, 2; (New Haven) *Connecticut Journal*, September 11, 1832, 4.

71. (New York) *Commercial Advertiser*, November 27, 1832, 2.

72. (Tuscaloosa) *Flag of the Union*, reprinted in (New York) *Commercial Advertiser*, August 18, 1833, 1; (Washington, D.C.) *United States' Telegraph*, September 12, 1833, October 18, 1833, November 25, 1833, December 6, 1833; (Washington, D.C.) *Globe,* October 30, 1833, December 11, 1833; Jack, "Sectionalism and Party Politics in Alabama," 37-54; Rogers, et al., *Alabama*, 89-92, 136-37. See generally, Charles Elliott Crockett, "A History of Nullification in the State of Alabama From 1832-1852" (Master's Thesis, Auburn University, 1968); John T. Ellisor, *The Second Creek War: Interethnic Conflict and Collusion on a Collapsing Frontier* (Lincoln, NE, 2010), 85-96; Michael D. Green, "Federal-State Conflict in the Administration of Indian Policy: Georgia, Alabama, and the Creeks, 1824-1834" (PhD. diss., University of Iowa, 1973), 273-88.

73. *Baltimore Gazette and Daily Advertiser*, October 28, 1833, 2. Accord, (Huntsville) *Southern Advocate*, December 3, 1833, 2, December 10, 1833, 3, January 28, 1834, 3.

74. (Huntsville) *Southern Advocate*, November 12, 1833, 3; (Tuscaloosa) *Alabama Intelligencer*, reprinted in (Philadelphia) *National Gazette*, November 23, 1833, 1; (Worcester) *Massachusetts Spy*, November 20, 1833, 2. *See also,* Moore, *History of Alabama*, 167.

75. (Huntsville) *Democrat*, October 1, 1833, 2, October 15, 1833, 1-3, October 29, 1833, 3, November 5, 1833, 1-2, November 12, 1833, 1-3, November 26, 1833, 2-3, December 10, 1833, 3, December 31, 1833, 3, January 28, 1834, 3; (Huntsville) *Democrat*, February 5, 1834, 2. *See also,* Wiggins and Truss, eds., *Journal of Sarah Haynsworth Gayle*, xxx-xxxi.

76. Walter M. Jackson, *The Story of Selma* (Birmingham, AL, 1954), 56 (referring to a visit by King to Saffold's home).

77. Harvey H. Jackson, III, *Inside Alabama: A Personal History of My State* (Tuscaloosa, AL, 2004), 75-76.

78. (Huntsville) *Democrat*, October 1, 1833, 2, October 15, 1833, 1-3, October 29, 3, November 5, 1833, 1-2, November 12, 1833, 1-3, November 26, 1833, 2-3, December 10, 1833, 3, December 31, 1833, 3, January 28, 1834, 3; Lewis, *Clearing the Thickets*, 203-206.

79. (Huntsville) *Southern Advocate*, August 20, 1833, 3; (Greensboro) *Green County Sentinel*, August 16, 1834, 2.

80. (Washington, D.C.) *Globe*, reprinted in *Alexandria Gazette*, December 4, 1834, 3; (New York) *Albany Argus*, December 9, 1834, 2.

81. Owen, *History of Alabama and Dictionary of Alabama Biography*, vol. 3, 646; Henry Poellnitz Johnston, Sr., *William R. King and His Kin* (Birmingham, AL, 1975), 54, 62-63.

82. Sarah Haynsworth Gayle, October 25, 1832, in Woolfolk and Truss, eds., *Journal of Sarah Haynsworth Gayle*, 218.

83. William Garrett, *Reminiscences of Public Men in Alabama for Thirty Years With an Appendix* (Atlanta, GA, 1872), 435; Thornton, *Politics and Power in a Slave Society*, 244.

84. Wyatt-Brown, *Lewis Tappan*, 84-7, 102-3; Harlow, *Gerritt Smith*, 115.

85. (Tuscaloosa) *Alabama Intelligencer and States Rights Expositor*, August 15, 1835, 3; *Hayneville Spirit of the Times*, August 26, 1835, 3; Bertram Wyatt-Brown, "The Abolitionists' Postal Campaign of 1835," in *Journal of Negro History* 50 (October, 1965), 228. *See also, Selma Free Press*, October 3, 1835, 2 (regarding receipt of copies of the *Liberator* by two ministers in Greensboro, Alabama, and the uproar that followed).

86. Conrad and Meyer, *Economics of Slavery*, 76.

87. *See, e.g.,* Ford, *Origins of Southern Radicalism*, 39.

88. *Charleston Mercury*, reprinted in *Richmond Whig*, August 21, 1835, 1.

89. (Tuscaloosa) *Flag of the Union*, October 3, 1835, 3 (regarding the indictment, which misspelled Williams's first name, and the efforts of abolitionists); (Huntsville) *Democrat*, October 14, 1835.

90. (Tuscaloosa) *Flag of the Union*, October 3, 1835, 3, November 21, 1835, 2, January 24, 1836, 3, January 30, 1836, 2.

91. (Tuscaloosa) *Flag of the Union*, August 8, 1835, 3; *Hayneville Spirit of the Times*, August 12, 1835, 3.

92. *Selma Free Press*, December 5, 1835, 3, January 2, 1836, 2-3.

93. *Selma Free Press*, January 2, 1836, 2. Regarding the war, see Lewis, *Clearing the Thickets*, 210-212; Ellisor, *Second Creek War*, 182-263.

94. Ruth Ketring Nuermberger, *The Clays of Alabama: A Planter-Lawyer-Politician Family* (Tuscaloosa, AL, 2005), 50-51, 68, 71-72, 75.

95. *Selma Free Press*, February 9, 1839, 2; *Edgefield Advertiser*, November 8, 1838, 2; *Mobile Commercial Register and Patriot*, September 17, 1837; *Montgomery Mail*, reprinted in (New Orleans) *Picayune*, October 3, 1863, 1; Ralph B. Draughn, Jr., "William Lowndes Yancey: From Unionist To Secessionist 1814-1852" (Ph.D. diss., University of North Carolina, 1981), 68; Jackson, *Inside Alabama*, 80-85; Eric H. Walther, *William Lowndes Yancey and the Coming of the Civil War* (Chapel Hill, NC, 2006), 38-52.

96. *Selma Free Press*, May 21, 1836, 2; (Tuscaloosa) *Flag of the Union*, November 12, 1836, 3, November 25, 1836, 3.

97. *Selma Free Press*, September 27, 1836, 3. See generally, Lewis, *Clearing the Thicket*, 206-207.

98. *Selma Free Press*, January 28, 1836, 1; *Mobile Commercial Register and Patriot*, June 2, 1837, 1; (Cahawba) *Southern Democrat*, July 1, 1837, 5.

99. (Tuscaloosa) *Flag of the Union*, April 14, 1837, 3, May 17, 1837, 3; (New Orleans) *Picayune*, May 13, 1837, 2, May 14, 1837, 2; Lewis, *Clearing the Thickets*, 212-13. Alasdair Roberts, *America's First Great Depression: Economic Crisis and Political Disorder After the Panic of 1837* (Ithaca, NY, 2012).

100. *Mobile Commercial Register and Patriot*, January 16, 1838, 2; *Selma Free Press*, January 20, 1838, 2; (Cahawba) *Southern Democrat*, January 27, 1838, 3, March 31, 1838, 3; (Washington, D.C.) *National Intelligencer*, January 13, 1838, 3.

101. *Mobile Commercial Register and Patriot*, September 18, 1837, 2; (Tuscaloosa) *Flag of the Union*, December 12, 1837, 2; (Tuscaloosa) *Independent Monitor*, September 21, 1847, 3.

102. Basil Manly to E.B. Teague, September 2, 1841, Manly Family Papers, Outgoing Correspondence 1837-1841, Box 392, Hoole Special Collections Library, University of Alabama.

103. (Tuscaloosa) *Independent Monitor*, July 20, 1842, 2. *See generally*, A. James Fuller, *Chaplain to the Confederacy: Basil Manly and Baptist Life in the Old South* (Baton Rouge, LA, 2000), 212-27. Regarding the biblical defense of slavery, see also Sinha, *Counterrevolution of Slavery*, 91-92.

104. (Huntsville) *Southern Advocate*, April 27, 1849, 3. Manly was also careful to include other South Carolinians on the faculty. (Tuscaloosa) *Independent Monitor*, September 21, 1847, 3 (Richard Trapier Brumby), January 11, 1849, 3 (same), December 21, 1848, 3 (Samuel M. Stafford), (Huntsville) *Southern Advocate*, April 27, 1849, 3 (same).

105. *Mobile Commercial Register and Patriot*, December 11, 1837, 2; (Tuscaloosa) *Flag of the Union*, October 9, 1839, 3 (Forsyth's partner was Epaphras Kibby, Jr., a native of Missouri and graduate of West Point).

106. *Mobile Commercial Register and Patriot*, January 1, 1838, 2. See also, *Mobile Commercial Register and Patriot*, November 14, 1837, 2, April 30, 1838, 2, March 19, 1839, 2, February 25, 1840, 2.

107. John Calhoun to David Hubbard, June 15, 1838, in Clyde N. Wilson, ed., *The Papers of John C. Calhoun, 1837-1839*, 28 vols. (Columbia, SC, 1981), vol. 14, 344.

108. B.G. Golden, "The Presidential Election of 1840 in Alabama," in *Alabama Review* 23 (April, 1970), 128-42; Lonnie A. Burnett, *The Pen Makes a Good Sword: John Forsyth of the Mobile Register* (Tuscaloosa, AL, 2006), 22-26; Moore, *History of Alabama*, 172-74; Watson, *Alabama United States Senators*, 47.

109. *Mobile Commercial Register and Patriot*, August 7, 1840, 2; Cooper, Jr., *South and the Politics of Slavery*, 147.

110. Davis, *Rhett*, 125-35; Rachleff, "Racial Fear and Political Factionalism," 75-78, 82.

111. (Tuscaloosa) *Flag of the Union*, January 1, 1840, 1.

112. (Tuscaloosa) *Flag of the Union*, April 29, 1840, 2.

113. *Mobile Commercial Register and Patriot*, April 13, 1840, 2, May 6, 1840, 2.

114. *Mobile Commercial Register and Patriot*, April 25, 1840, 2. *See also, Selma Free Press*, April 25, 1840, 2; *Selma Free Press*, reprinted in (Tuscaloosa) *Flag of the Union*, April 29, 1840, 2; *Mobile Commercial Register and Patriot*, April 28, 1840, 2.

115. *Selma Free Press*, May 16, 1840, 2.

116. (Tuscaloosa) *Flag of the Union*, May 27, 1840, 2.

117. (Tuscaloosa) *Flag of the Union*, June 3, 1840, 3. *See also, Selma Free Press*, June 6, 1840, 1 (publishing an address by King and others); (Tuscaloosa) *Flag of the Union*, June 17, 1840, 2 (same), September 23, 1840, 1 (same).

118. *Mobile Commercial Register and Patriot*, February 4, 1840, 2, July 27, 1840, 2; (Tuscaloosa) *Independent Monitor*, June 5, 1840, 2, October 23, 1840, 2; (Nashville) *Republican Banner*, February 3, 1840, June 15, 1840.

119. (Tuscaloosa) *Independent Monitor*, November 13, 1840, 2, November 27, 1840, 5; *Mobile Commercial Register and Patriot*, November 17, 1840, 2, November 21, 1840, 2; (Tuscaloosa) *Flag of the Union*, November 17, 1840, 2, November 18, 1840, 2.

120. *Mobile Commercial Register and Patriot*, April 12, 1841, 2; (Tuscaloosa) *Independent Monitor*, April 16, 1841, 2.

121. (Tuscaloosa) *Independent Monitor*, May 13, 1841, 3.

122. Johnston, *William R. King and His Kin*, 63, 85, 285 (she died on December 31, 1841).

123. *New York Tribune*, March 11, 1842, 2.

124. Fry, *Memories of Old Cahaba*, 35.

125. (Cahawba) *Dallas Gazette*, November 28, 1856, 2.

126. (Cahawba) *Dallas Gazette*, May 2, 1856, 1; *Mobile Register*, July 28, 1859, 4.

127. (Montgomery) *Alabama Journal*, reprinted in (Hayneville) *Lowndes County Chronicle*, July 10, 1851, 2.

128. (Selma) *Southern Argus*, September 16, 1875, 3.

129. *Selma Free Press*, March 7, 1840, 2.

130. *See generally*, Glenn McNair, *Criminal Injustice: Slaves and Free Blacks in Georgia's Criminal Justice System* (Charlottesville, VA, 2009), 88-90.

131. *State v. Hughes*, 1 Ala. 655 (1840). The number of Gayle's appellate cases was calculated using a Westlaw database search.

132. *Jones v. State*, 13 Ala. 153, 154, 157-59 (1848). A slave was later acquitted based on an insanity defense. *Montgomery Advertiser and State Gazette*, July 30, 1860, 2. For discussions of insanity during the antebellum period, see (Huntsville) *Southern Advocate*, May 10, 1836, 1.

133. *United States v. Sickles*, 27 F. Cas. 1074 (D.C. Criminal Court, April 20, 1859); (Tuscaloosa) *Independent Monitor*, April 16, 1859, 2, April 30, 1859, 2; *Mobile Register*, April 12, 1859, 2, April 15, 1859, 1, April 23, 1859, 1, April 27, 1859, 2, May 3, 1859, 2; *Montgomery Advertiser and State Gazette*, April 27, 1859, 2, August 3, 1859, 2; (Huntsville) *Southern Advocate*, May 5, 1859, 3; Nat Brandt, *The Congressman Who got Away with Murder* (Syracuse, NY, 1991).

134. Thomas Keneally, *American Scoundrel: The Life of the Notorious Civil War General Sickles* (New York, NY, 2002), 152-201.

135. Alan M. Dershowitz, *America On Trial: Inside the Legal Battles That Transformed Our Nation* (New York, NY, 2004), 93-100.

136. (Cahawba) *Dallas Gazette,* June 30, 1854, 2.

137. (Cahawba) *Dallas Gazette*, June 30, 1854, 2. *See also,* (Cahawba) *Dallas Gazette,* September 22, 1854 (publishing a letter indicating that Gayle had revealed the identity of "Marshall").

138. (Cahawba) *Dallas Gazette,* August 14, 1854, 2.

139. Brewer, *Alabama,* 475; Brant & Fuller, *Memorial Record of Alabama: A Concise Account of the State's Political, Military, Professional and Industrial Progress, Together With the Personal Memoirs of Many of its People*, 2 vols. (Spartanburg, SC, 1976), vol. 2, 748-49.

140. (Cahawba) *Dallas Gazette*, September 22, 1854, 2; (Greensboro) *Alabama Beacon*, July 7, 1854, 3, July 14, 1854, 2.

141. (Cahawba) *Dallas Gazette*, September 22, 1854, 2. *See also,* (Greensboro) *Alabama Beacon,* September 29, 1854, 2; (Montgomery) *Advertiser and State Gazette,* September 30, 1854, 2; *Richmond Dispatch*, October 9, 1854, 1; (New Orleans) *Times Picayune*, September 30, 1854, 1.

142. Sinha, *Counterrevolution of Slavery*, 64-75.

143. (Tuscaloosa) *Independent Monitor*, March 30, 1842, 2; (Huntsville) *Southern Advocate*, July 5, 1844, 3.

144. (Huntsville) *Southern Advocate*, July 5, 1844, 3. See also, (Huntsville) *Southern Advocate*, August 2, 1844, 2; (Huntsville) *Democrat*, September 11, 1844, 3, September 25, 1855, 3.

145. (Huntsville) *Democrat*, December 14, 1843, 2-3.

146. *Mobile Register and Journal*, March 16, 1844, 2. Calhoun had earlier been endorsed for the presidency by the *Charleston Mercury* on a ticket with Levi Woodbury. *Charleston Mercury*, March 22, 1843, 2, April 18, 1843, 2.

147. *New York Tribune*, April 12, 1844, 2; *Mobile Register and Journal*, April 22, 1844, 2; (Huntsville) *Southern Advocate*, April 26, 1844, 3.

148. (Huntsville) *Democrat*, May 22, 1844, 2, July 10, 1844, 3, July 17, 1844, 3, July 24, 1844, 34; (Tuscaloosa) *Independent Monitor*, August 28, 1844, 2; *Mobile Register and Journal*, July 22, 1844, 2, July 24, 1844, 2, October 11, 1844, 2, November 20, 1844, 2, November 28, 1844, 2, December 4, 1844, 2, December 5, 1844, 2; (Huntsville) *Southern Advocate*, May 29, 1844, 4, August 2, 1844, 2, August 23, 1844, 3, August 30, 1844, 3. See also, *Weekly* (Columbus) *Ohio Statesman*, July 17, 1844; (Tuscumbia) *North Alabamian*, November 22, 1844, 2-3.

149. *Mobile Register and Journal*, April 27, 1844, 2; Watson, *Alabama United States Senators*, 49; Lewis, *Clearing the Thickets*, 353-54.

150. (Huntsville) *Democrat*, May 22, 1844, 3, June 19, 1844, 3.

151. (Selma) *Alabama State Sentinel*, reprinted in *Athens* (TN) *Post*, September 28, 1860, 3, and *Staunton* (VA) *Spectator*, October 2, 1860, 1.

152. *Mobile Register and Journal*, August 12, 1844, 2, August 14, 1844, 2, August 21, 1844, 2; *Brooklyn Eagle*, August 14, 1844.

153. (New Orleans) *Picayune*, October 18, 1844, 2.

154. *Mobile Register and Journal*, August 5, 1843, 2.

155. *Mobile Register and Journal*, December 25, 1844.

156. Hillard M. Judge to John Calhoun, December 6, 1844, in Wilson, *Papers of John C. Calhoun*, vol. 20, 48788.

157. *Mobile Register and Journal*, December 14, 1844.

158. *Mobile Register and Journal*, March 8, 1845, 2, March 10, 1845, 2, April 28, 1845, 2, September 25, 1845, 2; (Tuscaloosa) *Independent Monitor*, March 12, 1845, 4; (Jackson) *Mississippian*, October 29, 1845. See generally, Justin Harvey Smith, *The Annexation of Texas* (New York, NY, 1919).

159. Walther, *William Lowndes Yancey and the Coming of the Civil War*, 74-80;

160. (Tuscaloosa) *Independent Monitor*, May 7, 1845, p. 2, May 28, 1845, 2; *Mobile Register and Journal*, April 30, 1845, 2, May 16, 1845, 2, May 28, 1845.

161. (Tuscaloosa) *Independent Monitor*, May 7, 1845, 2, May 28, 1845, 2; *Mobile Register and Journal*, May 16, 1845, 2, May 23, 1845, 2, May 28, 1845, 2, August 9, 1845, 2, August 13, 1845, 2, September 30, 1845, 2; (Huntsville) *Democrat*, February 18, 1846, 2; (Huntsville) *Southern Advocate*, August 15, 1845, 3.

162. Garrett, *Reminiscences of Public Men in Alabama*, 434.

163. *Mobile Register and Journal*, March 27, 1845, 2. *See also, Mobile Register and Journal*, July 12, 1845, 2, August 9, 1845, 2, August 19, 1845, 2.

164. (Tuscaloosa) *Independent Monitor*, September 10, 1845, 2.

165. (Tuscaloosa) *Independent Monitor*, January 28, 1846, 1; Thomas Moore, *Lalla Rookh: An Oriental Romance* (New York, NY, 1800), 27-96.

166. (Tuscaloosa) *Independent Monitor*, February 4, 1846, 3.

167. *Mobile Advertiser*, reprinted in *New York Tribune*, January 16, 1846, 2.

168. *Mobile Register and Journal*, February 2, 1846, 2, February 5, 1846, 2; (Tuscaloosa) *Independent Monitor*, February 4, 1846, 3; (Huntsville) *Southern Advocate*, February 13, 1846, 2; Walther, *William Lowndes Yancey and the Coming of the Civil War*, 79-80. *See also, Montgomery Advertiser and State Gazette,* December 9, 1857, 1 (publishing the "duelling oath" required of incoming government officials).

Chapter 2: Leave This Accursed Union

1. *Mobile Register and Journal*, January 3, 1846, 2, May 4, 1846, 2, May 14, 1846, 2, May 19, 1846, 2; (Huntsville) *Democrat*, March 25, 1846, 2, May 13, 1846, 3, May 20, 1846, 3, May 27, 1846, 3; *Florence Gazette*, May 30, 1846, 2, July 8, 1846, 3, July 11, 1846, 1; (Tuscaloosa) *Independent Monitor*, May 20, 1846, 2; David M. Potter, *Impending Crisis: America Before The Civil War, 1848-1861* (New York, NY, 1976), 51-64; Timothy J. Henderson, *A Glorious Defeat: Mexico and Its War With the United States* (New York, NY, 2008), 102-78.

2. (New Orleans) *Picayune*, May 26, 1846, 2. *See also, Mobile Register and Journal*, September 11, 1846, 2 (an article about the volunteers from Dallas County).

3. Owen, *History of Alabama and Dictionary of Alabama Biography*, vol. 3, 646 (Alice was born in 1846, Sarah in 1849, and Mary in 1851).

4. Walther, *William Lowndes Yancey and the Coming of the Civil War*, 89-91.

5. *Mobile Register and Journal*, May 14, 1846, 2, May 15, 1846, 2, May 18, 1846, 2, May 25, 1846, 2, August 10, 1846, 2; (New Orleans) *Picayune,* May 16, 1846, 2, May 17, 1846, 2, May 19, 1846, 2, May 21, 1846, 2, May 23, 1846, 2, August 2, 1846, 2, August 20, 1846, 2.

6. *Mobile Register and Journal*, July 3, 1846, September 16, 1846, 2; (Huntsville) *Democrat*, July 8, 1846, 3; *Florence Gazette*, July 11, 1846, 1; (Tuscaloosa) *Independent Monitor*, September 22, 1846, 3, October 27, 1846, 3.

7. (Tuscaloosa) *State Journal and Flag,* October 16, 1846, 2; Mobile *Register and Journal*, November 13, 1846, 2, January 12, 1847, 2; Charles Buxton Going, *David Wilmot: Free-Soiler* (Glouchester, MA, 1966), 94-98, 146-54; Dean B. Mahin, *Olive Branch and Sword: The United States and Mexico, 1845-1848* (Jefferson, NC, 1997), 82, 131; Don E. Fehrenbacher, *South and Three Sectional Crises* (Baton Rouge, 1980), 25-44.

8. *Mobile Register and Journal,* August 21, 1846, 2. *See also,* (Montgomery) *Weekly Flag and Advertiser,* July 23, 1847, 2; (Huntsville) *Southern Advocate,* July 15, 1848, 3.

9. (Huntsville) *Southern Advocate,* July 23, 1847, 1.

10. *Selma Reporter,* reprinted in (Montgomery) *Weekly Flag and Advertiser,* May 21, 1847, 1.

11. (Montgomery) Weekly *Flag and Advertiser,* June 18, 1847, 3.

12. (Huntsville) *Democrat,* July 25, 1847, 1-2, July 28, 1847, 1; *Mobile Register and Journal,* June 12, 1848, 2 (stating that "leading politicians of this State had settled down upon Cass for President and Dixon H. Lewis for Vice President, as likely to be most popular here.").

13. *Selma Reporter,* reprinted in (Montgomery) *Weekly Flag and Advertiser,* May 21, 1847, 1.

14. Thornton, *Politics and Power in a Slave Society,* 320-21.

15. (Huntsville) *Democrat,* August 25, 1847, p. 2, November 3, 1847, 2, January 26, 1848, 1-2; *Mobile Register and Journal,* October 23, 1847, 2; (Huntsville) *Southern Advocate,* November 6, 1847, 3, December 15, 1847, 3.

16. *Mobile Register and Journal,* December 16, 1847, 2, December 17, 1847, 2, December 24, 1847, 2, January 19, 1848, 2; (Tuscaloosa) *Independent Monitor,* December 23, 1847, 3; (Huntsville) *Southern Advocate,* December 25, 1847, 3.

17. John A. Campbell to John C. Calhoun, December 20, 1847, *Papers of John Calhoun,* 25: 22-23. *See also, Lewy* Dorman, *Party Politics in Alabama From 1850 Through 1860,* (Tuscaloosa, AL, 1995), 28-29.

18. *Mobile Register and Journal,* January 11, 1848, 2; (Huntsville) *Southern Advocate,* January 15, 1848, 3; (Huntsville) *Democrat,* January 19, 1848, 3.

19. *Mobile Register and Journal,* January 11, 1848, 2; Walther, *William Lowndes Yancey and the Coming of the Civil War,* 102-10.

20. (Huntsville) *Democrat,* January 19, 1848, 3.

21. *Mobile Register and Journal,* February 19, 1848, 2, October 4, 1848, 2. *See generally,* John M. Martin, "William R. King and the Vice Presidency," in *Alabama Review* 16 (January, 1963), 35, 46-47; Jean H. Baker, *James Buchanan: The American Presidents Series: The 15th President, 1857-1861* (New York, NY, 2004), 25-26; Joseph G. Rayback, *Free Soil: The Election of 1848* (Lexington, KY, 2014), 142, n. 41 (citing letters from Gayle to Buchanan).

22. *Mobile Register and Journal,* December 23, 1847, 2.

23. *Mobile Register and Journal,* February 21, 1848, 2, February 26, 1848, 2; (Huntsville) *Southern Advocate,* February 26, 1848, 2; (Tuscaloosa) *Independent Monitor,* February 24, 1848, 2.

24. *Mobile Register and Journal,* June 14, 1848, 2; (Huntsville) *Democrat,* January 19, 1848, 2; Cooper, *Politics of Slavery,* 254-55.

25. *Mobile Register and Journal,* June 2, 1848, 2, October 4, 1848, 2.

26. (Tuscaloosa) *Independent* Monitor, June 8, 1848, 3, June 15, 1848, 3; Mobile *Register and Journal,* May 31, 1848, 2, June 2, 1848, 2, June 5, 1848, 2, June 14, 1848, 2; *Charleston Mercury,* May 30, 1848, 2, June 1, 1848, 2, June 2, 1848, 2.

27. Walther, *William Lowndes Yancey and the Coming of the Civil War*, 109-10; Martin, "William R. King and the Vice Presidency, 47-48; Potter, *Impending Crisis*, 80-81; John Witherspoon DuBose, *The Life and Times of William Lowndes Yancey*, 2 vols. (Birmingham, AL, 1892), vol. 1, 216-23; Dorman, *Party Politics in Alabama*, 29-31.

28. *Charleston Mercury*, June 7, 1848, 2; *Mobile Register and Journal*, June 14, 1848, 2, June 23, 1848, 2, July 3, 1848, 2, October 4, 1848, 2. See generally, Sinha, *Counterrevolution of Slavery*, 74-5.

29. (Montgomery) *Tri-Weekly Flag and Advertiser*, July 1, 1848.

30. *Mobile Register and Journal*, June 28, 1848, 2, August 21, 1848, 2.

31. *Charleston Mercury*, June 21, 1848, 2; *Mobile Register and Journal*, June 23, 1848, 2.

32. (Greensboro) *Alabama Beacon*, July 15, 1848, 3; *Mobile Register and Journal*, June 23, 1848, 2, June 26, 1848, 2, June 28, 1848, 2, June 29, 1848, 2, June 30, 1848, 2, July 3, 1848, 2, August 14, 1848, 2, August 21, 1848, 2, October 4, 1848, 2.

33. (Cahawba) *Dallas Gazette*, reprinted in (Tuscaloosa) *Independent Monitor*, June 15, 1848, 3 and *Mobile Register and Journal*, June 12, 1848, 2. *See also, Mobile Advertiser*, November 13, 1850, 2; (Tuscaloosa) *Independent Monitor*, May 1, 1851, 2.

34. *Mobile Register and Journal*, October 4, 1848, 2.

35. *Mobile Register and Journal*, June 23, 1848, 2, July 5, 1848, 2, July 12, 1848, 2, August 2, 1848, 2, October 30, 1848, 2, November 1, 1848, 2, November 4, 1848, 2, November 29, 1848, 2; (Huntsville) *Southern Advocate*, December 1, 1848, 2, December 8, 1848, 2; *Florence Gazette*, October 6, 1849, 2, December 8, 1849, 2; (Greensboro) *Alabama Beacon*, December 8, 1849, 2.

36. (New Orleans) *Times Picayune*, June 18, 1848, 2. *See also,* (Tuscaloosa) *Independent Monitor*, May 25, 1848, 3, June 15, 1848, 3; *Mobile Register and Journal*, June 14, 1848, 2, June 16, 1848, 2; (Huntsville) *Southern Advocate*, June 17, 1848, 3.

37. (Huntsville) *Southern Advocate*, September 30, 1848, 3. *See also,* (Tuscaloosa) *Independent Monitor*, January 4, 1849, 3; *Mobile Register and Journal*, February 1, 1849, 2.

38. *Mobile Register and Journal*, November 13, 1848, 2; *Florence Gazette*, June 2, 1849, 2; (Tuscaloosa) *Independent Monitor*, January 4, 1849, 3, February 22, 1849, 2; (Huntsville) *Southern Advocate*, February 2, 1849, 3, March 23, 1849, 3.

39. *Mobile Register and Journal*, December 18, 1848, 2, February 7, 1849, 2; (Huntsville) *Southern Advocate*, February 9, 1849, 3.

40. *Mobile Register and Journal*, April 30, 1849, 2; *Florence Gazette*, September 7, 1850, 1.

41. (Tuscaloosa) *Independent Monitor*, February 22, 1849, 2. *See generally,* Rudolph M. Lapp, *Blacks in Gold Rush California* (New Haven, CT, 1977), 131-34; Leonard L. Richards, *The California Gold Rush and the Coming of the Civil War* (New York, NY, 2008).

42. *Mobile Register and Journal*, January 4, 1849, 2, January 5, 1849, 2.

43. (Tuscaloosa) *Independent Monitor*, February 22, 1849, 2.

44. *Mobile Register and Journal*, January 17, 1849, 2.

45. (Tuscaloosa) *Independent Monitor*, November 10, 1848, 3, November 16, 1848, 3; *Mobile Register and Journal*, November 20, 1848, 2, November 23, 1848, 2; (Huntsville) *Southern Advocate*, November 24, 1848, 3; Dorman, *Party Politics in Alabama*, 31.

46. (Baltimore) *Sun*, March 16, 1849, 1; (Nashville) *Republican Banner*, March 23, 1849, 3.

47. *Mobile Register and Journal,* December 14, 1848, 2; (Huntsville) *Southern Advocate*, December 15, 1848, 2.

48. (Huntsville) *Southern Advocate*, March 9, 1849, 2.

49. *Mobile Register and Journal*, January 4, 1849, 2, January 17, 1849, 2; *Mobile Advertiser*, September 29, 1852, 2, November 25, 1851, 2, November 26, 1851, 2, October 6, 1852, 2.

50. *Mobile Advertiser*, June 10, 1850, 2. *Accord*, (Tuscaloosa) *Independent Monitor*, November 30, 1848, 2; (Huntsville) *Southern Advocate*, March 9, 1849, 3.

51. *Mobile Register and Journal*, January 29, 1849, 2, February 1, 1849, 2, February 5, 1849, 2, February 6, 1849, 2, February 7, 1849, 2; (Huntsville) *Southern Advocate*, February 9, 1849, 3; (Tuscaloosa) *Independent Monitor*, February 15, 1849, 2-3. *See also*, Henry Mayer, "'A Leaven of Disunion': The Growth of the Secessionist Faction in Alabama 1847-1851," in *Alabama Review* 22 (April, 1969), 83, 100-101; Sinha, *Counterrevolution of Slavery*, 76-77.

52. *Florence Gazette*, September 22, 1849, 2.

53. *Mobile Advertiser*, August 13, 1850, 2. *See also*, (Washington, D.C.) *National Intelligencer*, May 30, 1850, 3.

54. *Mobile Register and Journal,* May 26, 1849, 2.

55. William R. King to G.W. Gayle, January 15, 1850, William Rufus King Papers, Alabama Department of Archives and History.

56. (Greensboro) *Alabama Beacon*, April 6, 1850, 2; (Huntsville) *Southern Advocate*, May 15, 1850, 2; *Mobile Advertiser*, June 4, 1850, 2; Davis, *Rhett*, 270-72.

57. Davis, *Rhett*, 272-273; *Charleston Mercury*, August 1, 1860, 4.

58. (Huntsville) *Southern Advocate,* May 22, 1850, 3; *Mobile Advertiser*, June 1, 1850, 2.

59. *Mobile Advertiser*, June 1, 1850, 2, November 19, 1850, 2; (Huntsville) *Southern Advocate*, June 12, 1850, 3.

60. *Mobile Advertiser*, June 14, 1850, 2.

61. *Mobile Advertiser*, June 11, 1850, 2. *See also, Mobile Advertiser*, June 1, 1850, 2.

62. *Florence Gazette*, August 10, 1850, 2; Davis, *Rhett*, 272-76.

63. (Greensboro) *Alabama Beacon*, August 31, 1850, 2; *Florence Gazette*, September 21, 1850, 2.

64. (Huntsville) *Southern Advocate*, September 11, 1850, 3; *Florence Gazette*, September 21, 1850, 2.

65. *Charleston Courier*, July 11, 1850, 2, July 18, 1850, 2; *Mobile Advertiser*, July 13, 1850, 2; *Florence Gazette*, July 13, 1850, 2, July 27, 1850, 2.

66. Statutes at Large 452 (September 9, 1850); (Huntsville) *Southern Advocate*, September 11, 1850, 3, September 18, 1850, 3.

67. Martin, "William Rufus King and the Vice Presidency," 50.

68. Some charged that it was due to King's "selfish aspirations to the Vice Presidency," but there were undoubtedly additional factors. (Wetumpka) *State Guard*, cited in (Tuscaloosa) *Independent Monitor*, August 28, 1851, 2; (Tuscaloosa) *Independent Monitor*, December 4, 1851, 2.

69. *Eufaula Democrat*, September 24, 1850.

70. *Mobile Register*, May 5, 1851, 2, May 12, 1851, 2, May 13, 1851, May 22, 1851, 2; *Mobile Advertiser*, May 16, 1851, 2, May 24, 1851, 2, May 25, 1851, 2, June 3, 1851, 2, June 4, 1851, 2, June 5, 1851, 2, June 12, 1851, 2, June 13, 1851, 2, June 15, 1851, 2, June 15, 1851, 2, July 25, 1851, 2; *Florence Gazette*, May 17, 1851, 2.

71. William Rufus King to Morgan Smith, June 13, 1850, quoted in John William McIntosh, "Alabama and the Compromise of 1850" (Master's Thesis, University of Alabama, 1932), 46.

72. 9 U.S. Statutes at Large 452 (September 9, 1850).

73. Letter to "His Excellency H.W. Collier" from Cahawba, AL., September 19, 1850, published in *Mobile Daily Advertiser*, September 26, 1850, 2 and *Hayneville Chronicle*, September 28, 1850, 2. According to the *Selma Reporter*, a petition was submitted containing the signatures of 560 residents of Dallas County. (Montgomery) *Alabama Journal*, October 21, 1850, 4.

74. *Mobile Advertiser*, March 5, 1851, 2; Glyndon G. Van Deusen, *William Henry Seward* (New York, NY, 1967), 123-24; Stahr, *Seward*, 116-44.

75. (Cahawba) *Dallas Gazette*, reprinted in *Mobile Advertiser*, September 26, 1850, 2. *See also, Weekly* (Montgomery) *Alabama Journal*, October 10, 1850, 1 (reporting a similar call on Governor Collier by another group in Dallas County).

76. (Greensboro) *Alabama Beacon*, September 28, 1850, 2.

77. *Charleston Mercury*, reprinted in *Augusta Chronicle*, October 9, 1850, 2.

78. (Greensboro) *Alabama Beacon*, October 19, 1850, 2; *Mobile Advertiser*, October 22, 1850, 2, November 8, 1850, 2, November 19, 1850, 2, April 13, 1851, 2, June 4, 1851, 2; (Huntsville) *Southern Advocate*, October 30, 1850, 3; *Florence Gazette*, November 16, 1850, 1, April 12, 1851, 2; *Weekly* (Montgomery) *Alabama Journal*, November 9, 1850, 4; *Augusta* (GA) *Chronicle*, November 19, 1850, 2; (Baltimore) *Sun*, November 27, 1850, 2.

79. *Mobile Advertiser*, October 20, 1850, 2, November 14, 1850, 2, December 25, 1850, 2; *See also,* Alston Fitts, III, *Selma: Queen City of the Black Belt* (Selma, AL, 1989), 26-29.

80. (Cahawba) *Dallas Gazette*, quoted in *Mobile Advertiser*, October 22, 1850, 2, November 8, 1850, 2.

81. *Mobile Advertiser*, October 5, 1850, 2.

82. (Tuscaloosa) *Independent Monitor*, January 2, 1851, 2.

83. (Huntsville) *Southern Advocate*, November 13, 1850, 3.

84. *Athens Herald*, reprinted in (Huntsville) *Southern Advocate*, October 9, 1850, 2.

85. *Mobile Register*, November 11, 1850, 2. See also, (Greensboro) *Alabama Beacon*, November 2, 1850, 3 (containing an announcement of this meeting); *Hayneville Chronicle*, November 16, 1850, 2.

86. Thornton, *Politics and Power in a Slave Society*, 243.

87. *Weekly* (Montgomery) *Alabama Journal*, November 9, 1850, 4; *Mobile Advertiser*, November 19, 1850, 2.

88. Mobile Advertiser, November 18, 1850, 2.

89. (Huntsville) *Democrat*, October 17, 1850, 2. See also, Walther, *William Lowndes Yancey and the Coming of the Civil War*, 128-29.

90. *Weekly* (Montgomery) *Alabama Journal*, September 26, 1850, 2. *See also, Selma Reporter*, quoted in *Mobile Advertiser*, October 6, 1850, 2; *Mobile Advertiser*, October 20, 1850, 2, October 24, 1850, 2.

91. *Mobile Advertiser*, October 6, 1850, 2.

92. *Mobile Advertiser*, October 22, 1850, 2, November 8, 1850, 2; *Florence Gazette*, November 16, 1850, 1; (New Orleans) *Times-Picayune*, October 24, 1850, 1.

93. (Montgomery) *Alabama Journal*, November 9, 1850, 4, November 15, 1850, 2, March 17, 1851, 2.

94. (Greensboro) *Alabama Beacon*, November 2, 1850, 2; Florence *Gazette*, November 9, 1850, 1-2 (publishing Collier's October 22, 1850, letter); *Hayneville Chronicle*, November 9, 1850, 1-2 (same).

95. *Mobile Advertiser*, December 25, 1850, 2.

96. *Charleston Mercury*, January 4, 1851, 2; *Mobile Register*, December 30, 1850, 2; (Tuscaloosa) *Independent Monitor*, January 9, 1851, 2; *Florence Gazette*, January 11, 1851, 2.

97. *Ibid.*

98. *Florence Gazette*, January 11, 1851, 2.

99. (Montgomery) *Alabama Journal*, January 2, 1851, 2; (New Orleans) *Times Picayune*, January 2, 1851, 2.

100. Davis, *Rhett*, 326.

101. *Mobile Register*, December 30, 1850, 2, and reprinted in (Montgomery) *Alabama Journal*, January 2, 1851, 2.

102. *Mobile Advertiser*, December 25, 1850, 2.

103. (Pickens, S.C. Court House) *Keowee Courier*, January 18, 1851, 2.

104. *Mobile Advertiser*, February 9, 1851, 2, February 25, 1851, 2; (Montgomery) *Advertiser and State Gazette*, February 12, 1851, 1; Walther, *William Lowndes Yancey and the Coming of the Civil War*, 130.

105. Davis, *Rhett*, 292.

106. *Charleston Mercury*, January 7, 1851, 2.

107. *Charleston Mercury*, February 27, 1851, 2.

108. *Charleston Mercury*, March 8, 1851, 2.

109. (Montgomery) *Advertiser and State Gazette*, February 19, 1851, 2., February 26, 1851, 1; *Charleston Mercury*, February 15, 1851, 2, February 17, 1851, 2; Walther, *William Lowndes Yancey and the Coming of the Civil War*, 235.

110. Davis, *Rhett*, 286; (Montgomery) *Advertiser and State Gazette*, February 26, 1851, 4; (Greensboro) *Alabama Beacon*, February 15, 1851, 2; *Alexandria* (VA) *Gazette*, February 20, 1851, 2; *Philadelphia Inquirer*, February 24, 1851, 2.

111. (Montgomery) *Advertiser and State Gazette,* February 26, 1851, 2.

112. *Mobile Advertiser,* February 16, 1851, 2; *Florence Gazette,* March 1, 1851, 2. *See also, Mobile Advertiser,* February 15, 1851, 2; (Greensboro) *Alabama Beacon,* February 15, 1851, 2, February 22, 1851, 2; (Huntsville) *Southern Advocate,* March 5, 1851, 2; *Charleston Advocate,* February 15, 1851, 2, February 17, 1851, 2; Walther, *William Lowndes Yancey and the Coming of the Civil War,* 130-36.

113. *Charleston Mercury,* February 15, 1851, 2.

114. *Charleston Mercury,* February 17, 1851, 2.

115. *Mobile Register,* quoted in (Montgomery) *Advertiser and State Gazette,* February 26, 1851, 1 and (Greensboro) *Alabama Beacon,* March 1, 1851, 2. *See also, Montgomery Atlas,* reprinted in *Charleston Mercury,* February 18, 1851, 2; *Mobile Register,* quoted in *Mobile Advertiser,* February 19, 1851, 2.

116. (Montgomery) *Advertiser and State Gazette,* February 26, 1851, 2. See also, *Mobile Register,* March 18, 1851, 2.

117. *Mobile Advertiser,* February 19, 1851, 2. *See also,* (Huntsville) *Southern Advocate,* March 5, 1851, 3.

118. (Greensboro) *Alabama Beacon,* February 22, 1851, 2.

119. *Mobile Register,* March 17, 1851, 2.

120. *Mobile Advertiser,* March 22, 1851, 2 (Wilcox and Pickens counties).

121. *Mobile Advertiser,* February 27, 1851, 2. See generally, Sinha, *Counterrevolution of Slavery,* 109-10.

122. (Tuscaloosa) *Independent Monitor,* April 3, 1851, 2; *Accord, Mobile Register,* April 5, 1851, 2; (Tuscaloosa) *Independent Monitor,* reprinted in *Mobile Advertiser,* April 10, 1851, 2.

123. (Lafayette) *Chambers Tribune,* reprinted in *Weekly* (Montgomery) *Alabama Journal,* June 7, 1851, 2.

124. *Mobile Advertiser,* April 29, 1851, 2.

125. *Mobile Advertiser,* March 18, 1851, 2. *See also, Mobile Register,* March 17, 1851, 2 (discussing the pro-secession sentiment of William A. Beene, a candidate for the legislature from Dallas County); *Mobile Register,* May 13, 1851, 2 (a convention of all Dallas County clubs held at Cahawba on May 5 also endorsed the platform).

126. Davis, *Rhett,* 286-298. *See also, Mobile Register,* May 12, 1851, 2.

127. (Montgomery) *Alabama Journal,* July 2, 1851, 2, reprinted in (Hayneville) *Lowndes County Chronicle,* July 10, 1851, 2.

128. *Mobile Advertiser,* May 22, 1851, 2.

129. (Greensboro) *Alabama Beacon,* May 24, 1851, 2.

130. *Mobile Advertiser,* May 22, 1861, 2, May 23, 1851, 2, May 24, 1851, 2, May 25, 1851, 2, May 27, 1851, 2; (Greensboro) *Alabama Beacon,* May 24, 1851, 2.

131. *Decatur Advertiser,* reprinted in (Huntsville) *Southern Advocate,* June 11, 1851, 3; *Mobile Advertiser,* June 12, 1851, 2, June 13, 1851, 2; (Tuscaloosa) *Independent Monitor,* July 3, 1851, 2.

132. *Mobile Advertiser,* June 13, 1851, 2, June 15, 1851, 2; (New Orleans) *Picayune,* July 30, 1851, 2; (Huntsville) *Southern Advocate,* July 30, 1851, 3.

133. (Tuscaloosa) *Independent Monitor*, June 12, 1851, 2; (Huntsville) *Southern Advocate*, August 6, 1851, 3.

134. *Charleston Mercury*, reprinted in *Mobile Daily Advertiser*, June 15, 1851, 2.

135. (New Orleans) *Picayune,* August 7, 1851, 1.

136. *Mobile Advertiser,* August 23, 1851, 2.

137. *Mobile Advertiser*, August 16, 1851, 2. For other similar rhetoric, see (Tuscaloosa) *Independent Monitor*, August 28, 1851, 2.

138. *Mobile Advertiser,* August 16, 1851, 2 (listing those elected to the legislature); (Montgomery) *Alabama Journal*, cited in the (New Orleans) *Picayune*, August 17, 1851, 2; (Tuscaloosa) *Independent Monitor*, August 14, 1851, 2 (the margin between Union and State Rights candidates statewide was only 10,000 votes). See also, McIntosh, "Alabama and the Compromise of 1850", 76-78.

139. *Charleston Mercury,* February 27, 1851, 2, March 8, 1851, 2; *Mobile Advertiser,* August 12, 1851, 2; (New Orleans) *Picayune,* September 6, 1851, 2 ("The idea that any cooperation for secession can be obtained, may be rejected as idle.").

140. *Charleston Courier,* September 20, 1851, 2; *Mobile Advertiser,* September 29, 1851, 2. *See also, New York Times*, September 27, 1851, 2; (Hayneville) *Lowndes County Chronicle*, October 9, 1851, 1; *Boston Courier*, reprinted in (Washington, D.C.) *National Intelligencer*, September 27, 1851, 3.

141. *Mobile Advertiser*, September 29, 1851, 2.

142. *Fayetteville* (N.C.) *Observer*, October 21, 1851; (Washington D.C.) *National Intelligencer*, October 20, 1851; Davis, *Rhett*, 302-31; Sinha, *Counterrevolution of Slavery*, 118-20.

143. (Montgomery) *Advertiser and State Gazette*, reprinted in (Jackson) *Mississippian and State Gazette*, October 31, 1851.

144. *Mobile Advertiser*, March 11, 1852, 2, July 22, 1852, 2; Dorman, *Party Politics in Alabama*, 66-67.

145. *Mobile Advertiser,* December 13, 1851, 2.

146. *Mobile Advertiser,* November 25, 1851, 2, February 29, 1852, 2, March 11, 1852, 2, May 11, 1852, 2, July 23, 1852, 2; *Charleston Mercury*, July 3, 1852, 2, July 20, 1852, 2.

147. (Cahawba) *Dallas Gazette,* quoted in *Athens* (Tenn.) *Post,* September 17, 1852, 3; (Greensboro) *Alabama Beacon*, September 10, 1852, 2 and *Mobile Advertiser*, September 15, 1852, 2. *See generally,* (Greensboro) *Alabama Beacon*, July 2, 1852, 2 (publishing King's letter of acceptance); *Mobile Advertiser*, June 8, 1852, 2 (King defeated Jefferson Davis for the nomination).

148. (Montgomery) *Advertiser and State Gazette*, June 30, 1858, 1.

149. (Greensboro) *Alabama Beacon,* July 23, 1852, 2, August 6, 1852, 3, September 17, 1852, 2, October 29, 1852, 2; *Mobile Advertiser,* September 17, 1852, 2, September 11, 1852, 2; Thornton, *Power and Politics in a Slave Society*, 264-65. Residents in Columbus, Georgia, also endorsed Troup. Carey, *Parties, Slavery, and the Union in Antebellum Georgia*, 178; Cooper, *South and the Politics of Slavery*, 334-35; Dorman, *Party Politics in Alabama,* 78-81.

150. (Montgomery) *Advertiser and State Gazette,* November 2, 1852, 2.

151. (Montgomery) *Alabama Journal,* September 15, 1852, reprinted in *Wheeling* (VA) *Intelligencer,* September 28, 1852, 2 and *Mobile Advertiser,* September 17, 1852, 2; (Greensboro) *Alabama Beacon,* September 17, 1852, 2, October 29, 1852, 2.

152. *Charleston Mercury,* November 4, 1852, 2.

153. Thornton, *Power and Politics in a Slave Society,* 262-65; *Charleston Mercury,* July 20, 1852, 2.

154. (Montgomery) *Advertiser and State Gazette,* October 14, 1852.

155. Thornton, *Power and Politics in a Slave Society,* 264. *See generally,* (Cahawba) *Dallas Gazette,* reprinted in *Mobile Advertiser,* October 6, 1852, 2 and (Montgomery) *Advertiser and State Gazette,* October 20, 1852, 2.

156. (Mobile) *Weekly Herald and Tribune,* November 20, 1852, 406; *Mobile Advertiser,* November 4, 1852, 2, November 7, 1852, 2, November 16, 1852, 2; (Montgomery) *Advertiser and State Gazette,* November 23, 1852, 3, December 1, 1852, 1. *See also,* Thornton, *Power and Politics in a Slave Society,* 265; (Selma) *Enterprise,* reprinted in (New Orleans) *Times Picayune,* November 4, 1852, 1; *Philadelphia Inquirer,* December 6, 1852, 1; (Washington, D.C.) *National Intelligencer,* December 8, 1852, 1; *New York Times,* November 30, 1852, 2; Dorman, *Party Politics in Alabama,* 81.

157. (Tuscaloosa) *Independent Monitor,* August 14, 1851, 2 (the margin was 10,000).

158. Mayer, "Leaven of Disunion," 103-16.

159. (Cahawba) *Dallas Gazette,* March 4, 1853, 2.

160. (Montgomery) *Advertiser and State Gazette,* December 1, 1852, 1.

161. Martin, "William R. King and the Vice Presidency," 54; *New York Times,* November 30, 1852, 2, January 7, 1853, 8, January 20, 1853, 3, February 20, 1853, 2, March 2, 1853, 4; *Boston Atlas,* April 20, 1852.

162. (Huntsville) *Democrat,* April 21, 1853, 2, April 28, 1853, 2; *Mobile Tribune,* reprinted in (Montgomery) *Alabama Journal,* April 25, 1853, 2; (Mobile) *Weekly Herald and Tribune,* April 19, 1853.

163. (Montgomery) *Alabama Journal,* April 20, 1853, 2.

164. (Huntsville) *Southern Advocate,* April 27, 1853, 2, May 11, 1853, 2, July 20, 1853, 3; (Cahawba) *Dallas Gazette,* July 15, 1853, 2; Sinha, *Counterrevolution of Slavery,* 97-98.

165. (Cahawba) *Dallas Gazette,* July 15, 1853, 2.

166. (Mobile) *Weekly Herald and Tribune,* May 7, 1853; (Montgomery) *Advertiser and State Gazette,* May 14, 1853, 2, May 24, 1853, 2.

167. (Montgomery) *Advertiser and State Gazette,* May 17, 1853, 3; (Huntsville) *Southern Advocate,* July 6, 1853, 3.

168. (Cahawba) *Dallas Gazette,* June 10, 1853, 2, July 8, 1853, 2.

169. (Montgomery) *Advertiser and State Gazette,* May 17, 1853, 2.

170. (Cahaba) *Dallas Gazette,* July 8, 1853, 2.

171. (Montgomery) *Advertiser and State Gazette,* August 16, 1853, 2; Stephen Puleo, *The Caning: The Assault that Drove America to Civil War* (Yardley, PA,

2012); Williamjames Hoffer, *The Caning of Charles Sumner: Honor, Idealism, and the Origins of the Civil War* (Baltimore, MD, 2010); See generally, Dorman, *Party Politics in Alabama*, 82-91.

172. (Huntsville) *Southern Advocate*, August 17, 1853, 2, August 24, 1853, 3, September 21, 1853, 3; Thornton, *Politics and Power in a Slave Society*, 333-34; David Ritchey, "Williamson R.W. Cobb: Rattler of Tinware and Crockery for Peace," in *Alabama Review* 36 (Summer, 1974), 112-20.

173. (Montgomery) *Advertiser and State Gazette*, November 23, 1853, 2, November 30, 1853, 3; (Mobile) *Weekly Herald and Tribune*, November 26, 1853; (Huntsville) *Southern Advocate*, November 30, 1853, 3; Thornton, *Politics and Power in a Slave Society*, 333-39; Dorman, *Party Politics in Alabama*, 91-95.

174. See 10 U.S. Statutes at Large 277, § 14 (Nebraska) and 283, § 19 (Kansas) (May 30, 1854).

175. Donald, *Lincoln*, 168; Davis, *Rhett*, 343-44.

176. (Mobile) *Weekly Herald and Tribune*, January 14, 1854. *See also*, (Huntsville) *Southern Advocate*, February 8, 1854, 3.

177. (Cahawba) *Dallas Gazette*, June 17, 1854, 2.

CHAPTER 3: THE SLAVE HOLDER

1. *See generally, Boston Atlas*, September 19, 1854, November 13, 1854; (Washington, D.C.) *National Intelligencer*, November 13, 1854. See also, William E. Gienapp, *The Origins of the Republican Party, 1852-1856* (New York, NY, 1987); Robert Cook, *Baptism of Fire: The Republican Party in Iowa, 1838-1878* (Ames, IA, 1994), 11, 45-71; Michael S. Green, *Politics and America In Crisis: The Coming of the Civil War* (Santa Barbara, CA, 2010), 45-118.

2. Cahawba) *Dallas Gazette*, June 30, 1854, 2.

3. Basler, ed., *Collected Works of Abraham Lincoln*, vol. 2, 255, 271. *See generally*, Lewis E. Lehrman, *Lincoln at Peoria: The Turning Point* (Mechanicsburg, PA, 2008).

4. (Mobile) *Weekly Herald and Tribune*, November 3, 1854.

5. *Montgomery Advertiser and State Gazette*, April 7, 1855, 2 (same); April 7, 1855, 2, April 21, 1855, 2; *Milwaukee Sentinel*, December 23, 1854. *See also*, (Columbia) *South Carolinian*, January 17, 1855 (publishing a letter from a Missourian containing a "non-denial denial").

6. *Philadelphia American*, reprinted in (Washington, D.C.) *National Intelligencer*, March 27, 1855.

7. *Montgomery Advertiser and State Gazette*, March 29, 1855, 2 (referring to Missourians crossing the border to vote), April 7, 1855, 2 (same), April 7, 1855, 2, April 24, 1855, 3; (Philadelphia) *North American and United States Gazette*, April 18, 1855; (Wakarusa) *Kansas Herald of Freedom*, April 21, 1855; (Savannah) *News*, May 12, 1855 (another "non-denial denial" of fraud by Missourians).

8. (Savannah) *News,* August 31, 1855 (reporting that the territorial legislature had designated the town of Lecompton the territorial capital and was considering a resolution calling for a constitutional convention and requesting admission to the Union).

9. (Savannah) *News,* December 12, 1855, April 3, 1856 (publishing a letter from Sterling Cato of Alabama, who had been appointed to replace Alabama's Rush Elmore on the Territorial Supreme Court of Kansas).

10. *Cleveland Herald,* May 14, 1855. *See also, Mobile Register,* September 21, 1855, 2.

11. *Montgomery Advertiser and State Gazette,* April 7, 1855, 2.

12. (Cahawba) *Dallas Gazette,* quoted in *Moulton Democrat,* January 27, 1855, 2; Dorman, *Party Politics in Alabama,* 105-106.

13. (Montgomery) *Advertiser and State Gazette,* December 19, 1854, 2; (Tuscaloosa) *Independent Monitor,* December 14, 1854, 2.

14. (Cahawba) *Dallas Gazette,* reprinted in (Montgomery) *Advertiser and State Gazette,* December 19, 1854, 2.

15. *See, e.g.,* (Cahawba) *Dallas Gazette,* reprinted in *Montgomery Advertiser and State Gazette,* March 29, 1855, 2, (Selma) *Alabama State Sentinel,* May 26, 1855, 2.

16. *Montgomery Advertiser and State Gazette,* February 6, 1855, 3, February 13, 1855, 3.

17. (Selma) *Alabama State Sentinel,* May 16, 1855, 1.

18. *Montgomery Advertiser and State Gazette,* November 21, 1855, 2. *See also,* Thornton, *Politics and Power in a Slave Society,* 324-30; Dorman, *Party Politics in Alabama,* 116-18.

19. *New York Herald,* May 24, 1856, p. 4, May 26, 1856, 4.

20. *Montgomery Advertiser and State Gazette,* January 10, 1856, 2.

21. Yancey did not receive it. (Huntsville) *Southern Advocate,* March 13, 1857, 3, April 2, 1857, 2; *Mobile Advertiser and State Gazette,* April 2, 1857, 2. *See also, Mobile Register,* January 13, 1856, 2, January 15, 1856, 2.

22. *Mobile Register,* January 15, 1856, 2. *See also, Mobile Register,* January 13, 1856, 2.

23. *Montgomery Advertiser and State Gazette,* January 10, 1856, 2.

24. *Montgomery Advertiser and State Gazette,* January 10, 1856, 2.

25. *Montgomery Advertiser and State Gazette,* May 29, 1856, 2, June 10, 1856, 3-4, June 12, 1856, 2, June 21, 1856, 2; (Cahawba) *Dallas Gazette,* August 15, 1856, 5.

26. (Cahawba) *Dallas Gazette,* July 18, 1856, 3.

27. (Eufaula) *Spirit of the South,* reprinted in (Atchison, Kan. Terr.) *Squatter Sovereign,* February 26, 1856, 1; (Selma) *Alabama State Sentinel,* November 7, 1855, 3; *Mobile Register,* December 1, 1855, 2, December 12, 1855, 2; *Montgomery Advertiser and State Gazette,* December 11, 1855, 3; Dorman, *Party Politics in Alabama,* 130.

28. (Huntsville) *Southern Advocate,* December 12, 1855, 2; Barney, *Secessionist Impulse,* 119-21.

29. (Tuskegee) *South Western Baptist*, December 13, 1855, 3, January 17, 1856, 3, July 24, 1856, 2; *Moulton Democrat*, December 13, 1855, 1; *Mobile Register*, December 13, 1855, 2.

30. *Athens* (TN) *Post*, September 19, 1856, 3; *Glasgow* (MO) *Weekly Times*, September 25, 1856, 4; *Columbus* (GA) *Enquirer*, August 14, 1856, 2; *New Orleans Creole*, September 24, 1856, 2.

31. *Montgomery Advertiser and State Gazette*, June 30, 1858, 1.

32. *Charleston Mercury*, October 29, 1856, 2.

33. *Montgomery Advertiser and State Gazette*, November 22, 1856, 2; Dorman, *Party Politics in Alabama*, 133.

34. *New York Herald*, October 20, 1856, reprinted in *New Orleans Delta*, reprinted in *Charleston Mercury*, November 4, 1856, 2.

35. *Montgomery Advertiser and State Gazette*, September 15, 1857, 4. See also, Thornton, *Politics and Power in a Slave Society*, 265-66.

36. *Charleston Mercury*, November 7, 1856, 2.

37. (Tuscaloosa) *Independent Monitor*, May 21, 1857, 3.

38. *Mobile Mercury*, reprinted in *Charleston Mercury*, September 8, 1859, 1. Fremont received 1,241,514 votes to 1,838,232 for Buchanan and 874,707 for Fillmore. (New-Lisbon) *Anti-Slavery Bugle*, September 8, 1860, 1.

39. Speech of J.L.M. Curry, reprinted in *Charleston Mercury*, December 15, 1859, 4.

40. *New York Tribune*, March 9, 1857, 5.

41. (Washington, D.C.) *Star*, March 7, 1857, 1.

42. *New York Tribune*, March 11, 1857, 4. See also, *Mobile Register*, March 19, 1857, 1, March 22, 1857, 2, March 25, 1857, 25, April 1, 1857, 2; (Huntsville) *Southern Advocate*, March 19, 1857, 3; (Greensboro) *Alabama Beacon*, March 20, 1857, 2.

43. (Montpelier) *Vermont Watchman and State Journal*, June 12, 1857, 1; *Nashville Union and American*, July 15, 1858, 2.

44. *Montgomery Advertiser and State Gazette*, May 18, 1857, 2, May 21, 1857, 2, May 29, 1857, 2, June 1, 1857, 3, June 9, 1857, 3, June 14, 1857, 2.

45. *Montgomery Advertiser and State Gazette*, November 10, 1857, 2.

46. (Huntsville) *Southern Advocate*, November 26, 1857.

47. (Tuscaloosa) *Independent Monitor*, November 26, 1857, 3; Thornton, *Politics and Power in a Slave Society*, 339-42; *Mobile Register*, November 24, 1857, 2; Nuermberger, *Clays of Alabama*, 155-56.

48. *Ala. Acts*, No. 306, 318 (January 28, 1858), and Joint Resolutions, 426-27 (January 22, 1858); (Tuscaloosa) *Independent Monitor*, January 28, 1858, 3; *Montgomery Advertiser and State Gazette*, February 3, 1858, 1; Dorman, *Party Politics in Alabama*, 142-43.

49. (Tuscaloosa) *Independent Monitor*, February 4, 1858, 2. See also, (Tuscaloosa) *Independent Monitor*, February 18, 1858, 3.

50. *Montgomery Advertiser and State Gazette*, February 3, 1858, 1, February 10, 1858, 2, March 2, 1858, 2; (Tuscaloosa) *Independent Monitor*, February 11, 1858, 3,

February 18, 1858, 1-3, March 4, 1858, 2, March 18, 1858, 1-3; (Huntsville) *Southern Advocate*, February 25, 1858, 3.

51. *Montgomery Advertiser and State Gazette*, March 29, 1858, 2, April 14, 1858, 2; (Huntsville) *Southern Advocate*, April 8, 1858, 3; *Moulton Democrat*, May 14, 1858, 2.

52. *Moulton Democrat*, April 16, 1858, 2, April 23, 1858, 1-2; *Montgomery Advertiser and State Gazette*, April 27, 1858, 2.

53. *Montgomery Advertiser and State Gazette*, May 8, 1858, 3; (Montgomery) *Confederation*, May 11, 1858, 2; *Mobile Register*, May 20, 1858, 2; *Memphis Appeal*, May 29, 1858, 1; (Huntsville) *Southern Advocate*, May 20, 1858, 3.

54. (Montgomery) *Confederation*, May 18, 1858, 2, June 15, 1858, 2; *Mobile Register*, May 23, 1858, 2.

55. W.L. Yancey to James S. Slaughter, June 15, 1858, reprinted in *Moulton Democrat*, July 16, 1858, 1 and (Huntsville) *Southern Advocate*, September 30, 1858, 2. *See also, Mobile Advertiser and State Gazette*, July 31, 1858, 3. *See generally,* Walther, *William Lowndes Yancey and the Coming of the Civil War*, 221-26

56. *Moulton Democrat*, May 21, 1858, 1. Kansans rejected this ordinance. *Mobile Advertiser and State Gazette*, August 16, 1858, 2; Freehling, *Road to Disunion*, vol. 2, 142.

57. *Montgomery Advertiser and State Gazette*, June 15, 1859, 2; (Greensboro) *Alabama Beacon*, July 1, 1859, 1.

58. (Memphis) *Avalanche*, reprinted in *Moulton Democrat*, May 21, 1858, 1.

59. *Montgomery Advertiser and State Gazette*, May 21, 1858, 2, May 22, 1858, 2, June 1, 1858, 3; (Cahawba) *Dallas Gazette*, June 8, 1858, 2.

60. Robert E. May, *Manifest Destiny's Underworld: Filibustering in Antebellum America* (Chapel Hill, NC, 2002), 125-64.

61. Nuermberger, *Clays of Alabama*, 159-60.

62. *Charleston Mercury*, reprinted in *Moulton Democrat*, October 8, 1858, 2.

63. *Montgomery Advertiser and State Gazette*, June 30, 1858, 1-2, August 12, 1858, 2; (Greensboro) *Alabama Beacon*, August 27, 1858, 2; *Montgomery Mail*, reprinted in (Montgomery) *Confederation*, July 8, 1858, 2.

64. *Montgomery Advertiser and State Gazette*, June 30, 1858, 2, August 20, 1858, 2, August 23, 1858, 2; (Greensboro) *Alabama Beacon*, August 27, 1858, 2.

65. *Montgomery Advertiser and State Gazette*, July 24, 1858, 2.

66. *Montgomery Advertiser and State Gazette*, July 26, 1858, 2, July 31, 1858, 2.

67. *Montgomery Advertiser and State Gazette*, September 6, 1858, 3; (Huntsville) *Southern Advocate*, September 17, 1858, 2.

68. (Greensboro) *Alabama Beacon*, September 17, 1858, 2.

69. (Greensboro) *Alabama Beacon*, September 3, 1858, 2.

70. (Montgomery) *Confederation*, quoted in (Huntsville) *Southern Advocate*, September 23, 1858, 3.

71. (Huntsville) *Southern Advocate*, October 14, 1858, 3.

72. *Montgomery Advertiser and State Gazette,* October 11, 1858, 2. *See also, Montgomery Advertiser and State Gazette,* September 2, 1858, 2, November 5, 1858, 2, November 12, 1858, 2; (Huntsville) *Southern Advocate,* November 11, 1858, 3.

73. Stahr, *Seward,* 165–81; (Huntsville) *Southern Advocate,* November 25, 1858, 3; *Montgomery Advertiser and State Gazette,* September 21, 1859, 1.

74. (Huntsville) *Southern Advocate,* November 25, 1858, 3.

75. (Huntsville) *Southern Advocate,* December 23, 1858, 3, January 13, 1859, 3.

76. *Mobile Register,* April 14, 1859, 2. *See also, Mobile Daily Register,* August 17, 1859, 2.

77. *Charleston Mercury,* July 7, 1859 (publishing a speech by Rhett).

78. *Mobile Advertiser and State Gazette,* April 27, 1859, 4, May 4, 1859, 2.

79. (Cahawba) *Dallas Gazette,* reprinted in *Mobile Register,* April 27, 1859, 2. *See also,* (Cahawba) *Dallas Gazette,* May 13, 1859 and *Montgomery Advertiser and State Gazette,* September 21, 1859, 3.

80. (Cahawba) *Dallas Gazette,* May 13, 1859, quoted in Avery O. Craven, *The Growth of Southern Nationalism, 1848-1861* (Baton Rouge: Louisiana State University, 1953), 294.

81. (Huntsville) *Southern Advocate,* April 28, 1859, 3.

82. *Charleston Mercury,* May 27, 1859; (Montgomery) *Confederation,* May 20, 1859, 2; (Tuscaloosa) *Independent Monitor,* May 21, 1859, 2; *Mobile Register,* May 26, 1859, 2; (Greensboro) *Alabama Beacon,* May 27, 1859, 2; (Huntsville) *Southern Advocate,* June 9, 1859, 2; Dorman, *Party Politics in Alabama,* 161.

83. *Columbus* (Georgia) *Enquirer,* reprinted in *Clarksville* (TN) *Chronicle,* August 26, 1859, 1.

84. *Mobile Register,* May 26, 1859, 2.

85. (Tuscaloosa) *Independent Monitor,* reprinted in *Mobile Register,* May 26, 1859, 2.

86. (Selma) *Alabama State Sentinel,* reprinted in (Tuscaloosa) *Independent Monitor,* May 28, 1859, 2.

87. *Montgomery Advertiser and State Gazette,* June 1, 1859, 2.

88. *Mobile Mercury,* reprinted in *Charleston Mercury,* September 8, 1859.

89. *Charleston Mercury,* September 8, 1859.

90. *Selma Reporter,* reprinted in (Montgomery) *Confederation,* July 8, 1859, 2. *See also, Montgomery Advertiser and State Gazette,* September 21, 1859, 3, October 12, 1859, 2; (Cahawba) *Slaveholder,* quoted in *Montgomery Confederation,* reprinted in (Huntsville) *Southern Advocate,* November 2, 1859, 4; (Cahawba) *Dallas Gazette,* reprinted in (Huntsville) *Southern Advocate,* December 7, 1859, 1.

91. *Mobile Register,* October 19, 1859, 2; *Montgomery Mail,* reprinted in *Charleston Mercury,* September 20, 1859, 1; (Montgomery) *Confederation,* August 18, 1859, 2, October 20, 1859, 2; *Augusta* (GA) *Chronicle,* October 26, 1859, 2.

92. *Montgomery Mail,* reprinted in *Charleston Mercury,* September 20, 1859, 1.

93. *Mobile Register,* October 19, 1859, 2.

94. (Montgomery) *Confederation*, October 19, 1859, 2. *See also*, (Montgomery) *Confederation*, October 20, 1859, 2.

95. (Greensboro) *Alabama Beacon*, October 21, 1859, 2. (Italics in original). *Accord*, (Huntsville) *Southern Advocate*, November 23, 1859, 3.

96. (Selma) *Alabama State Sentinel*, October 10, 1859.

97. *Montgomery Advertiser and State Gazette,* August 17, 1859, 2.

Chapter 4: Great God What A Country

1. Craven, *Growth of Southern Nationalism,* 305-10.

2. (Tuscaloosa) *Independent Monitor,* October 29, 1859, 2; *Montgomery Advertiser and State Gazette,* October 26, 1859, 3; *Memphis Appeal,* January 10, 1860, 1; (Huntsville) *Southern Advocate,* November 9, 1859, 3; *Charleston Mercury,* October 25, 1859, 4, Octobe r 31, 1859, 1.

3. *Montgomery Mail,* reprinted in *Mobile Register,* December 11, 1859, p. 2; (Austin, Tex.) *Southern Intelligencer,* December 21, 1859, p. 1; (Marion) *American,* reprinted in *Richmond Dispatch,* reprinted in (Boston) *Liberator,* December 23, 1859, p. 202; *Selma Reporter,* reprinted in (Tuscaloosa) *Independent Monitor,* December 17, 1859, p. 2.

4. (Boston) *Liberator,* December 23, 1859, 2002, citing an unnamed Richmond newspaper.

5. *Montgomery Mail,* June 2, 1860, 2.

6. (Cahawba) *Slaveholder,* reprinted in the (Montgomery) *Confederation,* reprinted in the (Huntsville) *Southern Advocate,* November 2, 1859, 4; *Huntsville Democrat,* reprinted in *Montgomery Advertiser and State Gazette,* November 16, 1859, 4; *Charleston Mercury,* October 19, 1859, 1; *Portland* (ME) *Advertiser,* November 22, 1859, 2. *See also,* (Huntsville) *Southern Advocate,* November 25, 1859, 3; Nuermberger, *Clays of Alabama,* 167-68; Davis, *Rhett,* 382.

7. *Clarksville* (TN) *Chronicle,* August 26, 1859, 1.

8. *Charleston Mercury,* October 19, 1859, 1; Davis, *Rhett,* 365-66.

9. Nuermberger, *Clays of Alabama,* 165-70.

10. *Montgomery Advertiser and State Gazette,* September 14, 1859, 2, September 21, 1859, 3; (Huntsville) *Democrat,* reprinted in *Charleston Mercury,* September 10, 1859, 1. *See also, Montgomery Advertiser and State Gazette,* September 21, 1859, 3, November 9, 1859, 1.

11. *Charleston Mercury,* September 10, 1859, 2. For other praise of Clay, see *Charleston Mercury,* January 25, 1860, 1-4. Regarding the *Charleston Mercury's* prior editorial, see (Tuscaloosa) *Independent Monitor,* August 6, 1859, 2.

12. (Cahawba) *Slaveholder,* reprinted in *Charleston Mercury,* October 19, 1859, 1. Clay's position was criticized by the *Dallas Gazette,* (Cahawba) *Dallas Gazette,* quoted

in *Montgomery Advertiser and State Gazette,* September 21, 1859, 3, and September 28, 1859, 1; *Montgomery Advertiser and State Gazette,* October 12, 1859, 2.

13. *Congressional Globe,* 36th Congress, 1st Session, 56-57, 60, 121-129, 143-144; Nuermberger, *Clays of Alabama,* 169-170.

14. *Mobile Register,* April 13, 1860, 2; (Tuscaloosa) *Independent Monitor,* April 14, 1860, 1.

15. *Charleston Mercury,* October 13, 1859, 1.

16. (Cahawba) *Slaveholder,* reprinted in *Charleston Mercury,* October 19, 1859, 1. See also, *Mobile Register,* October 27, 1859, 2.

17. *Charleston Mercury,* November 1, 1869, December 5, 1859, 1, December 6, 1859, 1, January 11, 1860, 1.

18. (Montgomery) *Confederation,* reprinted in *Charleston Mercury,* December 6, 1859, 1.

19. *Charleston Mercury,* reprinted in *Mobile Register,* October 13, 1859, 1.

20. (Huntsville) *Southern Advocate,* November 23, 1859, 3.

21. Regarding the selection of delegates from Dallas County, see, *Montgomery Weekly Advertiser,* December 21, 1859; *Montgomery Advertiser and State Gazette,* December 28, 1859, 2. See also, Joseph A. Fry, *John Tyler Morgan and the Search for Southern Autonomy* (Knoxville, TN, 1992), 7.

22. *Montgomery Advertiser,* reprinted in *Charleston Mercury,* January 21, 1860, 4; (Montgomery) *Confederation,* February 9, 1860, 2.

23. (Cahawba) *Slaveholder,* reprinted in *Montgomery Advertiser and State Gazette,* November 2, 18569, 3, *Charleston Mercury,* November 9, 1859, 1, (Washington, D.C.) *National Era,* December 8, 1859, 196 and *Portland* (Maine) *Advertiser,* November 22, 1859, 2. See also, *Montgomery Advertiser and State Gazette,* October 12, 1859, 3 (quoting Morgan's speech opposing Douglas).

24. *Charleston Mercury,* January 11, 1860, 1. See also, R.B. Rhett, Jr., to William P. Miles, January 29, 1860, quoted in William L. *Barney, The Secessionist Impulse in Alabama and Mississippi in 1860* (Tuscaloosa, AL, 2004), 107-108.

25. (Tuscaloosa) *Independent Monitor,* January 21, 1860, 2; (Greensboro) *Alabama Beacon,* January 27, 1860, 1. See also, Lewis, *Clearing the Thickets,* 268-69; Dorman, *Party Politics in Alabama,* 155-56; Thornton, *Politics and Power in a Slave Society,* 382-89; Walther, *William Lowndes Yancey and the Coming of the Civil War,* 237-38; Lonnie A. Burnett, "Precipitating a Revolution: Alabama's Democracy in the Election of 1860," in Kenneth W. Noe, ed. *The Yellowhammer War: The Civil War and Reconstruction in Alabama,* 15-30 (Tuscaloosa, AL, 2013).

26. *Charleston Mercury,* January 24, 1860, 1, January 16, 1860, 1, January 18, 1860, 1, January 20, 1860, 1, January 28, 1860, 1, January 30, 1860, 1, January 31, 1860, 1, April 3, 1860, 1. See also, Thornton, *Politics and Power in a Slave Society,* 382-94.

27. (Selma) *Alabama State Sentinel,* reprinted in (Greensboro) *Alabama Beacon,* January 24, 1860, 1.

28. (Selma) *Alabama State Sentinel,* reprinted in (Greensboro) *Alabama Beacon,* January 24, 1860, 1.

29. *Charleston Mercury*, February 27, 1860, 4; Dorman, *Party Politics in Alabama*, 152.

30. (Tuscaloosa) *Independent Monitor*, February 18, 1860, 2. *See also*, (Tuscaloosa) *Independent Monitor*, March 10, 1860, 1-2, March 17, 1860, 2, March 24, 1860, 2, April 7, 1860, 1.

31. (Tuscaloosa) *Independent Monitor*, March 17, 1860, 2. *See also*, (Selma) *Alabama State Sentinel*, July 29, 1860.

32. Dorman, *Party Politics in Alabama*, 156-57; Thornton, *Politics and Power in a Slave Society*, 392-95; *Charleston Mercury*, May 1, 1860, 1, May 19, 1860, 4.

33. *Charleston Mercury*, July 13, 1860, 1.

34. *Mobile Advertiser and State Gazette*, November 7, 1860, 1; (Cahawba) *Slaveholder*, reprinted in (Columbus) *Ohio Statesman*, July 14, 1860, 2, (Madison) *Wisconsin Patriot*, August 4, 1860, 2, and Joel H. Sibley, ed., *The American Party Battle: Election Campaign Pamphlets*, 1828-1876 (Cambridge, MA, 1999), vol. 2, 111.

35. (Montgomery) *Confederation*, May 26, 1860, 2.

36. *St. Cloud* (Minnesota) *Democrat*, June 28, 1860, 1.

37. (Tuscaloosa) *Independent Monitor*, November 16, 1860, quoted in Barney, *Secessionist Impulse*, 192.

38. *Mobile Register*, May 31, 1860, 2, June 5, 1860, 2; (Cahawba) *Dallas Gazette*, reprinted in (New Haven, CT) *Columbian Register*, July 14, 1860, 1; *Montgomery Advertiser and State Gazette*, January 15, 1861, 2; *Charleston Mercury*, February 15, 1861, 4 (The *Slaveholder* was later merged with the Selma *Issue*); (Huntsville) *Southern Advocate*, August 29, 1860, 3 (the Selma *Issue* supported Douglas).

39. *Montgomery Weekly Mail*, July 5, 1860.

Chapter 5: Lincoln Will Have His Assassin

1. *New York Tribune*, reprinted in *Charleston Mercury*, June 2, 1860, 1.

2. Robert W. Johannsen, *Lincoln, the South and Slavery: The Political Dimension* (Baton Rouge, LA, 1991), 97.

3. *New York Times*, February 28, 1860, 1. *See generally*, Harold Holzer, *Lincoln at Cooper Union: The Speech That Made Abraham Lincoln President* (New York, NY, 2004); John Burt, *Lincoln's Tragic Pragmatism: Lincoln, Douglas, and Moral Conflict* (Cambridge, MA, 2013), 602-21.

4. *Montgomery Weekly Mail*, July 24, 1860, July 26, 1860, July 27, 1860. See also, *Hayneville Chronicle*, August 2, 1860, 3 and August 23, 1860, 2; *Montgomery Weekly Mail*, August 10, 1860, August 21, 1860, August 25, 1860; *Montgomery Advertiser and State Gazette*, August 22, 1860, 1. *See generally*, (New Orleans) *Picayune*, July 24, 1860, 6; *Montgomery Weekly Post*, August 1, 1860, 1, August 21, 1860; Donald E. Reynolds, *Texas Terror: The Slave Insurrection Panic of 1860 and the Secession of the Lower South* (Baton Rouge, LA, 2007), 29-53, 171-72, 195, 203-207; Barney, *Secessionist Impulse*, 166-179.

5. *Charleston Mercury*, June 7, 1860, 1.

6. *Charleston Mercury*, August 4, 1860, 1, September 7, 1860, 4, September 8, 1860, 1, September 12, 1860, 1, September 15, 1860, 4.

7. *Charleston Mercury*, October 11, 1860, 1.

8. *Charleston Mercury*, October 13, 1860, 1.

9. *Charleston Mercury*, October 15, 1860, 1.

10. *Charleston Mercury*, October 25, 1860, 1.

11. *Montgomery Mail*, reprinted in *Charleston Mercury*, October 29, 1860, 1.

12. *Montgomery Mail*, reprinted in *Charleston Mercury*, October 29, 1860, 4.

13. *Charleston Mercury*, November 7, 1860, 3.

14. *Montgomery Advertiser and State Gazette*, November 21, 1860, 1; (New Orleans) *Picayune*, November 17, 1860, 1, November 20, 1860, 1; *Charleston Mercury*, November 19, 1860, 1.

15. Potter, *Impending Crisis*, 491.

16. *Charleston Mercury*, November 26, 1860, 4, December 3, 1860, 1, December 12, 1860, 4.

17. *Montgomery Advertiser and State Gazette*, December 28, 1860; *Charleston Mercury*, December 21, 1860, 1-3; Guelzo, *Fateful Lightning*, 130.

18. Guelzo, *Fateful Lightning*, 130-31; Thornton, *Politics and Power in a Slave Society*, 416-41; *Charleston Mercury*, December 25, 1860, 1. *See generally*, (Eufaula) *Spirit of the South*, reprinted in *Charleston Mercury*, December 28, 1860, 4; *Charleston Mercury*, December 29, 1860, 4.

19. *Montgomery Advertiser and State Gazette*, December 26, 1860, 1, January 12, 1861; *Charleston Mercury*, January 8, 1861, 3, January 12, 1861, 3; Thornton, *Politics and Power in a Slave Society*, 430; Barney, *Secessionist Impulse*, 298; Edwin I. Hatch, "William McLin Brooks, 1815-1893," in *Alabama Lawyer* 16 (1955), 324, 329-30; Dorman, *Party Politics in Alabama*, 167-69.

20. (Clearfield, Pa.) *Raftsman's Journal*, November 28, 1860, 2.

21. David Morris Potter, *Lincoln and His Party in the Secession Crisis* (Baton Rouge, LA, 1995), 312-13; Guelzo, *Fateful Lightning*, 131-33; *Louisville Journal*, reprinted in *Salem* (Mass.) *Register*, March 21, 1861, 2 (publishing a letter from a Cahawba man lambasting Kentucky, Tennessee and North Carolina).

22. *Charleston Mercury*, February 26, 1861, 1; *Selma Morning Reporter*, April 9, 1861, 2; Faye Acton Axford, ed., *The Journals of Thomas Hubbard Hobbs* (Tuscaloosa, AL, 1976), 228-29.

23. (Cahawba) *Dallas Gazette*, cited in (Baltimore) *Sun*, March 11, 1861, 4 and *Richmond Whig*, March 12, 1861, 2; *Montgomery Weekly Mail*, April 5, 1861; *Nashville Patriot*, March 15, 1861, 2; Robert Seymour Symmes Tharin, *Arbitrary Arrests in the South; or, Scenes from the Experience of An Alabama Unionist* (New York, 1969), 15, 102-51.

24. *Charleston Mercury*, January 3, 1861, 1; James L. Pugh to William P. Miles, January 24, 1861, quoted in Barney, *Secessionist Impulse*, 304-305.

25. *Charleston Mercury,* November 26, 1860, 1-4.

26. *Charleston Mercury,* January 10, 1861, 3; *New York Times,* January 12, 1861, 3; *Mobile Register,* January 5, 1861; *Montgomery Advertiser and State Gazette,* January 9, 1861, 1, January 15, 1861.

27. *Charleston Mercury,* January 3, 1861, 1; *Montgomery Weekly Post,* January 8, 1860.

28. Barney, *Secessionist Impulse,* 205 (referring to a Breckinridge meeting in nearby Wilcox County, Alabama).

29. *Montgomery Mail,* reprinted in *Charleston Mercury,* December 12, 1860, 1.

30. (New Orleans) *Picayune,* June 29, 1860, 1.

31. (Tuscaloosa) *Independent Monitor,* October 29, 1859, 2 (identifying Smith as a conspirator), November 12, 1859, 2 (same), November 26, 1859, 2; *Cleveland Leader,* May 26, 1860, 2; *Burlington* (VT) *Free Press,* June 1, 1860, 1; (Utica, NY) *Herald,* November 9, 1859, reprinted in *Charleston Mercury,* November 14, 1859, 1; *Charleston Mercury,* January 26, 1860, 1; (New Orleans) *Picayune,* October 4, 1862, 2.

32. (Selma) *Alabama State Sentinel,* reprinted in (Savannah, GA) *News,* June 10, 1858. *See also, Charleston Mercury,* August 13, 1860, 1, September 29, 1860, 1.

33. (New Orleans) *Picayune,* September 1, 1860, 4, September 5, 1860, 2, September 11, 1860, 3, September 18, 1860, 4; *Charleston Mercury,* September 22, 1860, 3, September 26, 1860, 1, September 29, 1860, 3, October 2, 1860, 4, October 5, 1860, 3, October 27, 1860, 4, October 29, 1860, 1. *See also,* May, *Manifest Destiny's Underworld,* 276 (suggesting that "Southern secession might never have occurred had the expeditionists achieved their objectives.").

34. *Charleston Mercury,* January 23, 1860, 1, March 13, 1860, 1; Mark Wahlgren Summers, *A Dangerous Stir: Fear, Paranoia, and the Making of Reconstruction* (Chapel Hill, NC, 2009), 32-35; David C. Keehn, *Knights of the Golden Circle: Secret Empire, Southern Secession, Civil War* (Baton Rouge, LA, 2013), 1-5.

35. (Selma) *Alabama State* Sentinel, April 10, 1860; *Montgomery Mail,* March 14, 1860, April 19, 1860; *Charleston Mercury,* March 19, 1860, p. 4. *See also, Charleston Mercury,* April 9, 1860, p. 2, April 13, 1860, p. 1, April 16, 1860, p. 1, April 17, 1860, p. 1, April 23, 1860, June 6, 1860, p. 1, August 1, 1860, p. 1, November 1, 1860, p. 1; Keehn, *Knights of the Golden Circle,* 41, 45.

36. *Montgomery Weekly Mail,* April 5, 1861; *Columbus* (GA) *Enquirer,* May 16, 1860, 3 (reporting that two Alabamians, N.G. Scott of Auburn, and A.R. McGibboney of Montgomery, were officers in the K.G.C.), May 18, 1860, 2 (reporting that future United States Senator George Goldthwaite of Montgomery was also a member); Keehn, *Knights of the Golden Circle,* 41, 45, 47-48, 51-53, 57, 75.

37. (Huntsville) *Southern Advocate,* September 12, 1860, 3. *See also,* (New Orleans) *Picayune,* July 19, 1860, 1. *See generally,* Getler and Brewer, *Shadow of the Sentinel,* 15-24; Ollinger Crenshaw, "The Knights of the Golden Circle: The Career of George Bickley," in *American Historical Review* 47 (1941), 23.

38. See, e.g., Elden C. Weckesser, *His Name Was Mudd: The Life of Dr. Samuel A. Mudd, Who Treated the Fleeing John Wilkes Booth* (Jefferson, NC: McFarland and Co.,

1991), 91-92; Crenshaw, "Knights of the Golden Circle,", 47 and n. 103; Getler, *Shadow of the Sentinel,* 15, 67-70, 113; Kauffman, *American Brutus* (making no mention of the Knights); Leonard, *Lincoln's Avenger* (same).

39. *Cincinnati Press,* September 24, 1860, 3; Nora Titone, *My Thoughts Be Bloody: The Bitter Rivalry That Led to the Assassination of Abraham Lincoln* (New York, NY, 2010), 227-34; Rhodehamel and Taper, *Right or Wrong, God Judge Me,* 49-50; Keehn, *Knights of the Golden Circle,* 1-2, 17 (regarding Booth's membership).

40. Titone, *My Thoughts Be Bloody,* 230-34, 240; Terry Alford, ed., *John Wilkes Booth: A Sister's Memoir by Asia Booth Clarke* (Jackson, MS, 1996), 88-89.

41. *Montgomery Weekly Mail,* December 1, 1860.

42. (New Orleans) *Picayune,* June 29, 1860, 2. *See also,* James A. MacKay, *Allan Pinkerton: The First Private Eye* (New York, NY, 1997), 87-96.

43. Daniel Stashower, *The Secret Plot to Murder Lincoln Before the Civil War: The Hour of Peril* (New York" Minotaur Books, 2013), 95, 234-37.

44. Earl Schenck Miers, *Lincoln Day By Day: A Chronology, 1809-1865,* 3 vols. (Washington, D.C., 1960), vol. 3, 3.

45. *White Cloud Kansas Chief,* January 3, 1861, 2; (St. Johnsbury, VT) *Caledonian,* January 4, 1861, 2; (New-Lisbon, OH) *Anti-Slavery Bugle,* January 5, 1861, 3; (Washington, D.C.) *National Republican,* January 9, 1861, 3; *Burlington Free Press,* January 11, 1861, 1; *Fremont* (OH) *Journal,* January 11, 1861, 2.

46. (New-Lisbon, OH) *Anti-Slavery Bugle,* January 5, 1861, 3.

47. *Burlington* (VT) *Free Press,* April 19, 1861, 1; Stashower, *Secret Plot to Murder Lincoln,* 101-106, 191-93, 235-36; Keehn, *Knights of the Golden Circle,* 107-11.

48. *Albany Evening Journal,* April 10, 1861, 2, reprinted in *Burlington Free Press,* April 19, 1861, 1 (emphasis added) and (Washington, D.C.) *National Republican,* April 15, 1861, 1.

49. Stashower, *Secret Plot to Murder Lincoln,* 186; Keehn, *Knights of the Golden Circle,* 110.

50. (Washington, D.C.) *National Republican,* February 14, 1861, 3; Titone, *My Thoughts Be Bloody,* 24142.

51. *Cincinnati* (Ohio) *Press,* May 11, 1861, 2.

52. *Burlington Free Press,* April 19, 1861, 1.

53. *Charleston Mercury,* January 3, 1861, 1; James L. Pugh to William P. Miles, January 24, 1861, quoted in Barney, *Secessionist Impulse,* 304-5.

54. *Charleston Mercury,* January 3, 1861, 1. Regarding the growing crisis at Charleston, see *Charleston Mercury,* January 5, 1861, 1. See also, Freehling, *Road to Disunion,* vol. 2, 476-524; David Detzer, *Allegiance: Fort Sumter, Charleston, and the Beginning of the Civil War* (New York, NY, 2001), 162-210; William C. Davis, *First Blood: Fort Sumter to Bull Run* (Alexandria, VA, 1983).

55. *New York Times,* March 24, 1864, 5; *New York World,* reprinted in *Columbus* (GA) *Enquirer,* April 15, 1864, 2; (Washington, D.C.) *National Republican,* March 25, 1864; James M. McPherson, *Battle Cry of Freedom: The Civil War Era* (New York, NY,

1988), 273. Regarding Gilchrist, *see Charleston Mercury*, July 14, 1852, 2; *Montgomery Advertiser and State Gazette*, October 26, 1859, 2; Owen, *History of Alabama and Dictionary of Alabama Biography*, vol. 3, 654.

56. *Cahaba Gazette*, April 12, 1861, Extra.

57. *Charleston Mercury*, April 13, 1861, 1, April 15, 1861, 3, April 18, 1861, 3; *Montgomery Weekly Advertiser*, April 17, 1861.

58. *Selma Morning Reporter*, April 11, 1861, 2.

59. *New York Times*, April 11, 1861, 2.

60. *Charleston Mercury*, February 14, 1861, 1; *Cincinnati Herald*, February 26, 1861, 1; *New York Herald*, February 19, 1861, 8; *Montgomery Daily Mail*, February 12, 1861; *Montgomery Advertiser and State Gazette*, May 8, 1861, 2; *Louisville Daily Journal*, May 20, 1861, 4; (Atlanta) *Southern Confederacy*, September 17, 1862, reprinted in (Augusta, GA) *Daily Constitutionalist*, September 18, 1862, 3; Stephen W. Berry, *All That Makes A Man: Love and Ambition in the Civil War South* (New York, NY, 2003), 199-203; Stephen Berry, *House of Abraham: Lincoln and the Todds, A Family Divided by War* (Boston, MA, 2009), 58, 63-64.

61. *Selma Morning Reporter*, April 11, 1861, 2; *Augusta* (GA) *Chronicle*, May 2, 1861, 1; (Madison) *Wisconsin Patriot*, May 10, 1861, 2. *See also*, Berry, *All That Makes a Man*, 199-200; Berry, *House of Abraham*, 63-64; Jackson, *Story of Selma*, 193; Val L. McGee, *Selma: A Novel of the Civil War* (Oxford, MS, 2008), 207-208.

62. Anna Gayle Fry, "Life in Dallas County During the War," in *Confederate Veteran* 24 (January, 1916), 216; Hubbs, *Voices from Company D*, 4; G. Ward Hubbs, *Guarding Greensboro: A Confederate Company in the Making of a Southern Community* (Athens, GA, 2003).

63. Bruce S. Allardice, *Confederate Colonels: A Biographical Register* (Columbia, MO, 2008), 302.

64. Ezra J. Warner, *Generals in Gray: Lives of the Confederate Commanders* (Baton Rouge, LA, 1987), 221-22. Morgan was originally appointed *aide de camp* to Jeremiah Clemens, the Major General of Alabama's militia. *Mobile Advertiser and State Gazette*, March 13, 1861; *Charleston Mercury*, March 16, 1861, 1; *New York Herald*, April 9, 1861.

65. Ben Ames Williams, ed., *A Diary From Dixie By Mary Boykin Chesnut* (Cambridge, MA, 2002), 38.

66. Williams, ed., *Diary from Dixie*, 50.

67. *Selma Reporter*, April 25, 1861, 3.

68. George W. Gayle to Jefferson Davis, May 22, 1861, # 1229, 1861, Letters Received, ser. 5, Sec. War, RG 109, War Department Collection of Confederate Records, National Archives, reprinted in Ira Berlin, Barbara J. Fields, Thavolia Glymph, Joseph P. Reidy, & Leslie S. Rowland, eds., *Freedom: A Documentary History of Emancipation* 1861-1867 (New York, NY, 1985), vol. 1, 781-82. *See also*, Lynda Lasswell Crist and Mary Seaton Dix, eds., *The Papers of Jefferson Davis, 14 vols.* (Baton Rouge, LA, 1992), 7:175; Laura F. Edwards, *Scarlett Doesn't Live Here Anymore: Southern Women in the Civil War Era* (Urbana, IL, 2000), 78.

69. Gravestone of George Gayle, Live Oak Cemetery, Selma, Alabama. The gravestone is etched with the year of George Gayle's birth, 1807, although not the month and day.

70. *Impeachment Investigation: Testimony Taken Before the Judiciary Committee of the House of Representatives In the Investigation of the Charges Against Andrew Johnson,* Second Session, Thirty-Ninth Congress, and First Session, Fortieth Congress (Washington, D.C., 1867), 565 (Gayle's affidavit to President Andrew Johnson was dated September 17, 1865).

71. *Selma Reporter,* December 4, 1862, 2; *State, ex rel. Dawson,* 39 Ala. 367 (1864); *Ex parte Tate,* 39 Ala. 254 (1864); *Mobile Advertiser and Register,* March 1, 1865, 1. See generally, *State, ex rel. Ellerbe,* 39 Ala. 546 (1865); *Weaver v. State,* 39 Ala. 535 (Ala., 1865); *Adams v. Adams,* 39 Ala. 603 (1865); *Blann v. State,* 39 Ala. 353 (1864); *Adams v. Adams,* 39 Ala. 274 (1864); *Campbell v. Campbell,* 39 Ala. 312 (1864); *Shannon v. Reese,* 38 Ala. 586 (1863); *Andrews v. Keep,* 38 Ala. 315 (1862); *Strong v. Catlin,* 37 Ala. 706 (1861); *Scott v. State,* 37 Ala. 117 (1861); *Barker v. Bell,* 37 Ala. 354 (1861); *Ex parte Maxwell,* 37 Ala. 362 (1861); *White v. Brantley,* 37 Ala. 430 (1861); *Womack v. Sanford,* 37 Ala. 445 (1861).

72. (Tuskegee) *South West Baptist,* reprinted in (New Orleans) *Picayune,* March 20, 1862, 2.

73. *Charleston Mercury,* January 3, 1861, 1.

74. Joseph H. Crute, *Units of the Confederate States Army* (Micdlothian, VA: Derwent Books, 1987), 38; Brewer, *Alabama,* 701; Brandon H. Beck, *Third Alabama: The Civil War Memoir of Brigadier General Cullen Andrews Battle* (Tuscaloosa, AL, 2000), 6-7; Rogers, Jr., *Confederate Home Front,* 91.

75. George Washington Gayle, Compiled Service Records, National Archives (this Gayle enlisted on April 26, 1861, in Montgomery); *Houston* (TX) *Post,* May 21, 1902, 6; *Montgomery Advertiser,* May 28, 1902, 2.

76. *Nashville Patriot,* May 4, 1861, 2.

77. Brewer, *Alabama,* 701; Crute, *Units of the Confederate States Army,* 38.

78. (Cahawba) *Dallas Gazette,* reprinted in (Washington, D.C.) *National Intelligencer,* May 2, 1861, 3.

79. *Mobile Advertiser,* July 27, 1861, 2.

80. Berry, *House of Abraham,* 77-78, 82.

81. Berry, *House of Abraham,* 79-83; *Richmond Enquirer,* July 26, 1861; *Mobile Advertiser and Register,* August 7, 1861, 2, August 8, 1861, 1, August 14, 1861, 1, September 7, 1861, 2; *Huntsville Independent,* September 14, 1861, 4;(Huntsville) *Democrat,* September 4, 1861, 3.

82. *Montgomery Advertiser and State Gazette,* July 27, 1861, August 10, 1861, 2; *Mobile Advertiser and Register,* August 3, 1861, 1, August 7, 1861, 2, August 8, 1861, 1, August 14, 1861, 1; (Huntsville) *Democrat,* August 21, 1861, 1.

83. *Selma Reporter,* September 24, 1861, reprinted in (Richmond) *Dispatch,* November 22, 1861, 2; Berry, *All that Makes a Man,* 215-16; Berry, *House of Abraham,* 82-83.

84. *Montgomery Mail,* July 24, 1861, reprinted in (New Orleans) *Picayune,* July 27, 1861; *Mobile Advertiser and Register,* July 27, 1861, 2, August 2, 1861, 1, August 7, 1861, 2; *Charleston Mercury,* July 31, 1861, 4.

85. *Mobile Advertiser and Register,* July 30, 1861, 1.

86. *Selma Reporter,* July 25, 1861, 2.

87. *Memphis Appeal,* August 10, 1861, 2.

88. Glenn Linden and Virginia Linden, eds., *Disunion, War, Defeat and Recovery in Alabama: The Journal of Augustus Benners, 1850-1885* (Macon, GA, 2007), 70; Williams, ed., *Diary From Dixie,* 96-97, 99-100, 107.

89. Williams, ed., *Diary From Dixie,* 96, 107-108.

90. Williams, ed., *Diary From Dixie,* 113-114.

91. William G. Stevenson, *Thirteen Months in the Rebel Army: Being a Narrative of Personal Adventures In the Infantry, Ordinance, Cavalry, Courier, and Hospital Services* (London, UK, 1862), 194-95.

92. (Greensboro) *Alabama Beacon,* August 2, 1861, 1.

93. (Greensboro) *Alabama Beacon,* August 2, 1861, 2.

94. *Mobile Advertiser and Register,* August 6, 1861, 2.

95. R.H. McIlvain to G.W. Gayle, September 24, 1861, and John A. Elmore to Gayle, October 10, 1861, Papers of Governor A.B. Moore, Alabama Department of Archives and History, Montgomery, Alabama.

96. *Montgomery Mail,* September 1, 1864, 1.

97. *Charleston Mercury,* November 26, 1860, 4.

98. *Nashville Union and American,* March 6, 1861, 3; Nuermberger, *Clays of Alabama,* 182-87; *Montgomery Weekly Post,* April 9, 1861; *Anderson* (South Carolina) *Intelligencer,* January 31, 1861, 2.

99. Nuermberger, *Clays of Alabama,* 184, 187 and note 7.

100. Nuermberger, *Clays of Alabama,* 189. *See also,*(Huntsville) *Democrat,* June 12, 1861, 4, October 30, 1861, 4.

101. Nuermberger, *Clays of Alabama,* 189-90;(Huntsville) *Democrat,* November 27, 1861, 4; (New Orleans) *Picayune,* November 26, 1861, 1. *See generally,* Malcolm C. McMillan, *Disintegration of a Confederate State: Three Governors and Alabama's War Time Home Front, 1861-1865* (Macon, GA, 1986), 77-78.

CHAPTER 6: CRUEL TYRANTS CANNOT LIVE IN A LAND OF LIBERTY

1. (New Orleans) *Picayune,* April 26, 1861, 1; New *York Herald,* April 20, 1861; James M. McPherson, *War on the Waters: The Union and Confederate Navies, 1861-1865* (Chapel Hill, NC, 2012), 31-49; Earl W. Fornell, "Mobile During the Blockade," in *Alabama Historical Quarterly* 23 (Spring, 1961), 29-43, 33.

2. *Richmond Dispatch*, May 28, 1861, 1; Virginius Dabney, *Richmond: The Story of a City* (Charlottesville: University Press of Virginia, 1990), 164; Emory M. Thomas, *The Confederate State of Richmond: A Biography of the Capital* (Baton Rouge, LA, 1998), 33.

3. *Selma Reporter*, February 22, 1862, 2, March 4, 1862, 1; (Huntsville) *Democrat*, February 12, 1862, 3; *Montgomery Weekly Advertiser,* February 15, 1862, April 22, 1862, September 2, 1862; *Mobile Advertiser and Register,* April 17, 1862, 1-2; (Greensboro) *Alabama Beacon*, February 14, 1862, 3.

4. *Selma Reporter*, January 31, 1862, 2. *See also, Selma Reporter*, February 19, 1862, 2, February 21, 1862, 2, February 25, 1862, 2, March 4, 1862, 1-2, March 5, 1862, 2, March 6, 1862, 2, March 8, 1862, 2, March 14, 1862, 2.

5. (New Orleans) *Picayune*, March 1, 1862, 1 (Clay was sworn in on February 19, 1862); (Greensboro) *Alabama Beacon*, May 2, 1862, 2, April 16, 1862, 2; *Selma Reporter*, October 2, 1862, 1; *Montgomery Weekly Advertiser*, April 20, 1862.

6. *Mobile Advertiser and Register,* April 8, 1862, 1.

7. *Selma Reporter*, April 21, 1862, 1.

8. (Greensboro) *Alabama Beacon*, April 25, 1862, 2.

9. *Selma Reporter*, May 16, 1862, 2. (Dawson and Todd were married on May 15, 1862); *Selma Reporter*, February 28, 1863, 1 (Dawson begins service as a "Conscript Adviser"); N.H.R. Dawson to Gov. John Gill Shorter, August 5, 1862, Papers of Governor Shorter, Alabama Department of Archives and History, Montgomery, Alabama. *See generally, Mobile Advertiser and Register,* April 29, 1862, 1 (discussing the exemptions), May 27, 1862, 2 (same); (Greensboro) *Alabama Beacon*, September 5, 1862, 2 (same).

10. *Montgomery Weekly Advertiser*, May 10, 1862, May 20, 1862, May 28, 1862; *Selma Reporter*, May 12, 1862, 2, May 16, 1862, 1, May 20, 1862, 2, May 29, 1862, 2, May 30, 1862, 1, June 9, 1862, 2, 2, June 13, 1862, 2, July 26, 1862, 2, July 31, 1862, 2. (Selma) *Alabama State Sentinel*, August 6, 1862.

11. Morgan's regiment was eventually ordered into North Alabama and then to Knoxville, Tennessee. John T. Morgan to R.M. Patton and R.W. Walker, September 3, 1862, Official Records, Series 1, Vol. 52 (Part II), 344-45; J.F. Belton to Col. John T. Morgan, August 16, 1862, Official Records, Series 1, Vol. 16 (Part II), 759-60.

12. (Grove Hill) *Clarke County Journal*, July 9, 1863, 2. Morgan was later appointed a brigadier general of cavalry. S. Cooper to Braxton Bragg, November 17, 1863, Official Records, Series 1, Vol. 31 (Part III), 703.

13. *Montgomery Weekly Advertiser*, May 29, 1862.

14. (Selma) *Alabama State Sentinel*, July 29, 1862, reprinted in (New Orleans) *Picayune*, August 19, 1862, 2; *Montgomery Weekly Advertiser*, September 7, 1862; (Greensboro) *Alabama Beacon*, November 21, 1862, 2, December 19, 1862, 2.

15. *Selma Reporter*, June 3, 1862, 2, July 1, 1862, 2, July 2, 1862, 2; (Greensboro) *Alabama Beacon*, June 6, 1862, 2; *Montgomery Weekly Advertiser*, June 10, 1862 (listing the dead and wounded), July 8, 1862, July 15, 1862.

16. *Selma Reporter*, August 23, 1862, 2 ("What we wish to see most is the end of the war, and if it requires two millions of men to whip the Yankees, we will say, amen."), August 25, 1862, 1 (same).

17. *Montgomery Weekly Advertiser*, February 23, 1862, March 16, 1862, March 23, 1862, March 26, 1862, April 13, 1862; *Mobile Advertiser and Register,* April 16, 1862, 1, May 7, 1862, 2, May 11, 1862, 1, June 6, 1862, 1; *Selma Reporter*, May 12, 1862, 2, May 13, 1862, 1, May 31, 1862, 1, August 1, 1862, 2; (New Orleans) *Picayune*, August 7, 1862, 1, August 28, 1862, 1.

18. *Montgomery Weekly Advertiser*, February 23, 1862.

19. *Richmond Whig*, reprinted in *Montgomery Weekly Advertiser*, March 16, 1862.

20. *Mobile Advertiser and Register,* May 7, 1862, 2. *See generally,* Daniel E. Sutherland, *A Savage Conflict: The Decisive Role of Guerrillas in the American Civil War* (Chapel Hill, NC, 2009), x-xi.

21. *Selma Reporter*, May 22, 1862, reprinted in *Augusta Chronicle,* May 24, 1862.

22. *Mobile Advertiser and Register,* May 11, 1862, 1. See also, *Selma Reporter*, May 31, 1862, 1, August 13, 1862, 1; *Mobile Advertiser and Register,* June 6, 1862, 1; (New Orleans) *Picayune*, August 7, 1862, 1; *Montgomery Weekly Advertiser*, August 10, 1862

23. *Cleveland Leader*, August 22, 1862; *Cleveland Herald*, August 8, 1862, August 9, 1862, August 11, 1862, August 12, 1862; *Milwaukee Sentinel*, August 12, 1862, August 21, 1862, August 27, 1862; *Boston Advertiser*, August 9, 1862, August 11, 1862; (Washington, D.C.) *National Intelligencer*, August 11, 1862; *Cincinnati Gazette*, reprinted in *Milwaukee Sentinel*, August 11, 1862, 4.

24. See, e.g., *Selma Reporter*, August 15, 1862, 1, August 16, 1862, 1, August 18, 1862, 1. *See also,* (Chattanooga) *Huntsville Confederate*, July 21, 1863, 2; *Mobile Advertiser and Register,* November 28, 1863, 1, December 31, 1863, 1; *Columbus* (GA) *Enquirer*, December 30, 1863, 2; (New Orleans) *Picayune*, August 18, 1862, 2., August 19, 1862, 2.

25. (New Orleans) *Picayune*, August 28, 1862, 1.

26. (New Orleans) *Picayune*, March 20, 1862, 1, March 21, 1862, 2.

27. (New Orleans) *Picayune*, June 3, 1862, 2.

28. 12 U.S. Statutes at Large 502 as amended by 13 U.S. Statutes at Large 424. See also, *Montgomery Weekly Advertiser*, July 29, 1862, July 31, 1862; (New Orleans) *Picayune,* July 30, 1862, 1, July 31, 1862, 2, August 31, 1862, 4; (Selma) *Alabama State Sentinel*, August 6, 1862, 2.

29. *Montgomery Weekly Advertiser,* September 3, 1862.

30. *Selma Reporter*, October 2, 1862, 1, October 9, 1862, 1; (Greensboro) *Alabama Beacon*, October 10, 1862, 3.

31. *Selma Reporter*, December 14, 1862, 2.

32. (New Orleans) *Picayune*, December 13, 1862, 1.

33. *Selma Reporter*, December 22, 1862, 1.

34. (New Orleans) *Picayune,* January 17, 1863, 1-2, January 30, 1863, 2, April 3, 1863, 2, April 15, 1863, 1.

35. *Chattanooga Rebel*, October 2, 1862.

36. *Richmond Enquirer*, October 9, 1862.

37. (New Orleans) *Picayune,* July 9, 1863, 1.

38. *Charleston Mercury*, July 17, 1863, 1.

39. *Mobile Advertiser and Register,* August 21, 1863, 1.

40. *Mobile Advertiser and Register,* June 24, 1863, 2.

41. (Greensboro) *Alabama Beacon*, June 26, 1863, 2.

42. *Selma Dispatch*, reprinted in *Huntsville Confederate*, November 18, 1863, 2; Frank E. Vandiver, *Ploughshares Into Swords: Josiah Gorgas and Confederate Ordinance* (Austin: University of Texas Press, 1952), 107, 148, 169, 171, 240.

43. W.T. Sherman to H.W. Halleck, November 18, 1863, Official Records, Series 1, Vol. 31 (Part III), 185.

44. *Charleston Mercury,* July 15, 1863, 1; *Mobile Advertiser and Register,* July 8, 1863, 2, July 10, 1863, 2, July 14, 1863, 2, July 16, 1863, 1-2, July 23, 1863, 2, July 29, 1863, 2; *Selma Reporter,* July 11, 1863, 2, July 12, 1863, 2, July 17, 1863, 2, July 26, 1863, 2; (Grove Hill) *Clarke County Journal*, July 23, 1863, 2; (Greensboro) *Alabama Beacon*, July 24, 1863, 4; Brooks D. Simpson, *Gettysburg, 1863* (Sterling, VA, 2013); Winston Groom, *Vicksburg 1863* (New York, NY, 2009).

45. *Mobile Advertiser and Register,* July 14, 1863, 2; *Huntsville Confederate*, July 29, 1863, 2; *Selma Reporter*, July 30, 1863, 2; *Montgomery Weekly Advertiser*, August 5, 1863, 1.

46. *Charleston Mercury*, July 31, 1863, 1.

47. C.C. Langdon to R.H. Slough and others, July 10, 1863, published in *Mobile Advertiser and Register,* July 11, 1863, 2. See also, *Mobile Advertiser and Register,* July 12, 1863, 2; (Grove Hill) *Clarke County Journal*, July 30, 1863, 2.

48. *Montgomery Weekly Advertiser,* September 20, 1863, September 24, 1863; *Mobile Tribune*, September 29, 1863, 2.

49. *New York Tribune*, March 19, 1864, reprinted in *Charleston Mercury*, May 4, 1864, 1, (Columbia, SC) *Daily South Carolinian*, May 4, 1864, (Boston) *Liberator*, May 20, 1864, 84, *Burlington* (VT) *Free Press*, March 25, 1864, 1, and *Weekly Perrysburg* (Ohio) *Journal*, May 10, 1865, 1; Hanchett, *Lincoln Murder Conspiracies*, 26-27; Guttridge and Neff, *Dark Union,* 40. *But see*, Carman Cumming, *Devil's Game: The Civil War Intrigues of Charles A. Dunham* (Urbana, IL, 2008), 70-74 (claiming that these press accounts were fabricated).

50. *New York Tribune*, March 19, 1864. Regarding Mosby, *see, Mobile Advertiser and Register,* October 5, 1864, 2; John Singleton Mosby, *The Memoirs of Colonel John Singleton Mosby* (Boston, MA, 1917).

51. For further discussion of these plots, *see* Hanchett, *Lincoln Murder Conspiracies,* 30-32.

52. *Mobile Advertiser and Register,* October 4, 1863, 2, October 6, 1863, 2.

53. *Mobile Advertiser and Register,* October 4, 1863, 2.

54. *Mobile Advertiser and Register,* October 2, 1863, 2, December 20, 1863, 2; (New Orleans) *Picayune,* November 6, 1863, 2, November 23, 1864, 1, December 21, 1864, 1, February 11, 1865, 2; *Charleston Mercury,* February 19, 1864, 1, November 7, 1864, 1.

55. *Huntsville Confederate,* July 29, 1863, 2; *Mobile Advertiser and Register,* July 31, 1863, 2, August 1, 1863, 1-2, August 2, 1863, 2, August 11, 1863, 2; McWhiney, Moore, and Pace, eds., *"Fear God and Walk Humbly," 325.*

56. *Selma Reporter,* July 16, 1863, 2. *Accord, Huntsville Confederate,* July 29, 1863, 2; *Mobile Advertiser and Register,* August 2, 1863, 1-2, August 15, 1863, 2.

57. *Selma Dispatch,* reprinted in (Grove Hill) *Clarke County Journal,* August 13, 1863, 1; *Mobile Tribune,* August 6, 1863, reprinted in (New Orleans) *Picayune,* August 16, 1863, 4; *Richmond Whig,* August 14, 1863, 1. Regarding Gayle's support for Shorter, *see* George W. Gayle to Thomas H. Watts, August 4, 1864, Papers of Governor Watts, Alabama Department of Archives and History, Montgomery, Alabama.

58. (Grove Hill) *Clarke County Journal,* August 13, 1863, 2.

59. *Charleston Mercury,* August 21, 1863, 1.

60. George C. Rable, *The Confederate Republic: A Revolution Against Politics* (Chapel Hill, NC, 1994), 228-30 (discussing anti-administration sentiment in Alabama).

61. *Mobile Advertiser and Register,* July 28, 1863, 2, July 31, 1863, 2, August 1, 1863, 2.

62. *Mobile Advertiser and Register,* July 29, 1863, 2, August 9, 1863, 1.

63. *Charleston Mercury,* July 30, 1863, 1. *See generally,* Paul D. Escott, *After Secession: Jefferson Davis and the Failure of Confederate Nationalism* (Baton Rouge, LA, 1992), 258-74.

64. *Mobile Advertiser and Register,* July 28, 1863, 1, July 31, 1863, 2, August 1, 1863, 2.

65. *Mobile Advertiser and Register,* August 19, 1863, 2.

66. *Selma Reporter,* August 14, 1863, 2.

67. *Selma Reporter,* August 27, 1863, 2.

68. (Atlanta) *Confederacy,* reprinted in *Columbus* (GA) *Enquirer,* October 31, 1863, 2. *See also, Mobile Tribune,* October 27, 1863, 1; *Richmond Enquirer,* November 27, 1863, reprinted in *Cleveland Herald,* December 4, 1863.

69. *Charleston Mercury,* October 20, 1863, 1. *See also, Mobile Tribune,* October 21, 1863, 2; (Savannah, GA) *News,* October 22, 1863; *Huntsville Confederate,* October 24, 1863, 1.

70. *Mobile Tribune,* November 1, 1863, 1; *Huntsville Confederate,* November 26, 1863, 2, December 12, 1863, 2; *Mobile Advertiser and Register,* November 3, 1863, 1, November 26, 1863, 2, November 27, 1863, 2, November 29, 1863, 1-2, December 1, 1863, 1, December 10, 1863, 2. Davis then accepted Bragg's resignation. *Montgomery Advertiser,* December 5, 1863, 2.

71. *Montgomery Weekly Advertiser,* December 2, 1863, 1; *Huntsville Confederate,* December 3, 1863, 2, December 7, 1863, 2; Rable, *Confederate Republic,* 229.

72. *Columbus* (GA) *Enquirer,* December 19, 1863, 2.

73. *Huntsville Confederate,* December 15, 1863, 2.

74. *Columbus* (GA) *Enquirer,* December 20, 1863, 2.

75. Regarding the sense of desperation, see *Charleston Mercury*, June 6, 1864, 1; *Mobile Advertiser and Register,* January 5, 1864, 2, May 27, 1864, 2, June 9, 1864, 2.

76. Steers, *Blood on the Moon,* 39-59; George S. Burkhardt, *Confederate Rage, Yankee Wrath: No Quarter in the Civil War* (Carbondale, IL, 2007), 203-205.

77. (Richmond) *Dispatch*, February 15, 1864, 2, reprinted in *Charleston Mercury*, February 18, 1864, 1. *See also,* (Columbia, SC) *Guardian*, reprinted in *Mobile Tribune,* March 1, 1864, 2.

78. G.T. Beauregard to Gen. William E. Martin, August 2, 1862, reprinted in *Mobile Advertiser and Register,* March 5, 1863, 2.

79. *Charleston Mercury*, March 5, 1864, 1, March 8, 1864, 1, March 9, 1864, 1, March 11, 1864, 1, March 18, 1864, 1, March 19, 1864, 1, April 5, 1864, 1; (New Orleans) *Picayune*, February 21, 1864, 2; *Mobile Advertiser and Register,* March 8, 1864, 1, March 12, 1864, 1, March 16, 1864, 1, April 7, 1864, 1; *Jacksonville Republican*, February 20, 1864, p. 2. *See generally,* Duane Schultz, *The Dahlgren Affair: Terror and Conspiracy in the Civil War* (New York: W.W. Norton & Co., 1998); Bruce M. Venter, *Kill Jeff Davis: The Union Raid on Richmond, 1864* (Norman: University of Oklahoma Press, 2016); Hanchett, *Lincoln Murder Conspiracies*, 33-34.

80. *Richmond Whig*, March 9, 1864, reprinted in *Charleston Mercury*, March 19, 1864, 1, (Columbus) *Ohio Statesman*, March 22, 1864, 1, *Nashville Times and True Union*, April 6, 1864, p. 1, (Atlanta) *Memphis Appeal*, March 24, 1864, p. 2, and *Cleveland Leader*, April 5, 1864, 1. Regarding Morgan's exploits during this period, *see Mobile Advertiser and Register,* August 21, 1863, p. 2, December 5, 1863, 1.

81. (Macon) *Georgia Weekly Telegraph*, August 27, 1866, 5.

82. *Richmond Whig*, March 9, 1864.

83. *Charleston Mercury*, May 3, 1864, p. 1. *But see,* Hanchett, *Lincoln Murder Conspiracies*, 30-31.

84. Margaret Storey, *Loyalty and Loss: Alabama's Unionists in the Civil War and Reconstruction* (Baton Rouge, LA, 2004), 167; Don Dodd, "Unionism In Confederate Alabama" (Ph.D. Diss., University of Georgia, 1969), 72; McMillan, *Disintegration of a Confederate State*, 94; Thomas H. Watts to Lt. Col. Lockhart, February 6, 1864, Papers of Governor Watts, Alabama Department of Archives and History, Montgomery, Alabama.

85. *Mobile Advertiser and Register,* April 17, 1864, 2, April 19, 1864, 1, April 21, 1864, 2; Andrew Ward, *River Run Red: The Fort Pillow Massacre in the American Civil War* (New York, NY, 2005). Some of the survivors were imprisoned at Cahawba. (Washington, D.C.) *National Intelligencer,* September 30, 1864, 2.

86. *Mobile Advertiser and Register,* April 19, 1864, 1, April 29, 1864, 1, April 30, 1864, 1, May 4, 1864, 2; *Columbus* (Ga.) *Enquirer*, April 22, 1864, 2; *Charleston Mercury*, March 10, 1864, 2, April 18, 1864, 1, April 20, 1864, 1, April 21, 1864, 1, April 23, 1864, 1, April 26, 1864, 1, May 3, 1864, 1, May 6, 1864, 1.

87. *Charleston Mercury*, May 3, 1864, 1.

88. Jennifer L. Weber, *Copperheads: The Rise and Fall of Lincoln's Opponents in the North* (New York, NY, 2006), 124; Steers, *Blood on the Moon,* Chap. 6, n. 31; Tidwell,

April. '65, 107-34; Larry E. Nelson, *Ballots, Bullets and Rhetoric: Confederate Policy for the United States Presidential Contest of 1864* (Tuscaloosa: University of Alabama Press, 1980), 19-24, 89; Keehn, *Knights of the Golden Circle*, 173-74. For mention of the northern affiliates of the K.G.C. in the southern press, see (New Orleans) *Picayune*, May 7, 1862, 2; *Mobile Advertiser and Register*, May 8, 1863, 1; *Columbus* (GA) *Enquirer*, October 26, 1864, 2.

89. Jefferson Davis to C.C. Clay, Jr., and Jacob Thompson, April 27, 1864, Official Records, Series 4, Vol. 3, 322; C.C. Clay, Jr. to J. P. Benjamin, August 11, 1864, Official Records, Series 4, Vol. 3, pp. 584-87; C.C. Clay, Jr. to J. P. Benjamin, September 12, 1864, Official Records, Series 4, Vol. 3, 626-40; *Mobile Advertiser and Register*, July 9, 1864, 2, July 19, 1864, 2; *New York Times*, July 19, 1864, 4; *Columbus* (GA) *Enquirer*, July 15, 1864, 2. *See generally*, Edward Chase Kirkland, *The Peacemakers of 1864* (New York: MacMillan Company, 1927), 72-73; John W. Headley, *Confederate Operations in Canada and New York* (New York: Neale Publishing Co., 1906), 220-21.

90. Deposition of Sarah Douglass, February 6, 1866, Official Records, Series 2, Vol. 8, 878-79. *Mobile Advertiser and Register*, July 26, 1864, 1. *See also, New York Times*, July 19, 1864, 4, July 22, 1864, 1; Weber, *Copperheads*, 155-56; Kirkland, *Peacemakers*, 68-84; Ralph Ray Fahrney, *Horace Greeley and the Tribune in the Civil War* (Cedar Rapids, IA: Torch Press, 1936), 155-72. *But see*, Cumming, *Devil's Game*, 165, 172, 174, 176, 180 (asserting that the evidence against Clay was fabricated).

91. *Mobile Advertiser and Register*, November 10, 1864, 1.

92. *New York Herald*, July 23, 1864, p. 1; *New York Times*, July 26, 1864, 1, August 3, 1864, 8; *Mobile Advertiser and Register*, July 19, 1864, July 20, 1864, 1, July 21, 1864, 1; *Charleston Mercury*, July 25, 1864, 1, July 28, 1864, 2.

93. *Mobile Advertiser and Register*, August 6, 1864, 1, August 9, 1864, 1; *Charleston Mercury*, August 10, 1864, 1.

94. *Montgomery Weekly Advertiser*, September 6, 1864, 1; *Mobile Advertiser and Register*, September 13, 1864, 1; *Charleston Mercury*, September 7, 1864, 1.

95. *Mobile Tribune*, September 30, 1864, 1, October 9, 1864, 2; *New York Times*, October 29, 1864, 1; *Selma Dispatch*, reprinted in *Columbus* (GA) *Enquirer*, October 8, 1864, 2; *Mobile Advertiser and Register*, October 1, 1864, 2, October 13, 1864, 1; *Selma Dispatch*, reprinted in *Columbus* (GA) *Enquirer*, October 8, 1864, 1.

96. *Mobile Advertiser and Register*, December 21, 1864, 1; Nuermberger, *Clays of Alabama*, 255-56; Cathryn J. Prince, *Burn the Town and Sack the Banks! Confederates Attack Vermont* (New York, NY, 2006), 142-51; (St. Albans) *Vermont Transcript*, October 21, 1864, 3; *New York Times*, October 20, 1864, 1.

97. *Mobile Advertiser and Register*, October 30, 1864, 2; *Columbus* (GA) *Enquirer*, November 4, 1864, 2; *Vicksburg* (Miss.) *Herald*, March 25, 1865, 2; *Nashville Union*, February 5, 1865, 2; *Cleveland Leader*, February 6, 1865, 3; *Belmont* (Ohio) *Chronicle*, February 23, 1865, 1.

98. *Freemont* (Ohio) *Journal*, December 9, 1864, 2; *Richmond Dispatch*, December 8, 1864, 1; *Chattanooga Rebel*, reprinted in *Mobile Advertiser and Register*, November 20, 1864, 1, December 9, 1864, 1, *Selma Reporter*, March 23, 1864, 2, *Charleston Mercury*,

June 18, 1864, 1, November 22, 1864, 1; Ben H. Severance, *Portraits of Conflict: A Photographic History of Alabama in the Civil War* (Fayetteville, AK, 2012), 262.

99. *Mobile Advertiser and Register,* November 9, 1864, 2; *Mobile Tribune,* November 25, 1864, 2.

100. *Charleston Mercury,* November 18, 1864, 1, November 22, 1864, 1; Stephen Davis, *What the Yankees Did To Us: Sherman's Bombardment and Wrecking of Atlanta* (Macon, GA, 2012).

101. G.W. Gayle to Thomas H. Watts, August 13, 1864, Papers of Gov. Watts, Alabama Department of Archives and History, Montgomery, Alabama.

102. (Washington, D.C.) *National Republican,* March 25, 1864, 1; *Cleveland Leader,* April 14, 1865, 2. *Accord,* McPherson, *Battle Cry of Freedom,* 273.

103. *Mobile Advertiser and Register,* reprinted in *Columbus* (GA) *Enquirer,* October 14, 1863, 2. *See also, Mobile Tribune,* September 13, 1863, 2; *Mobile Advertiser and Register,* November 21, 1863, 2.

104. *Charleston* Mercury, November 29, 1864, 1; Mobile *Advertiser and Register,* December 6, 1864, 2, December 14, 1864, 2, December 15, 1864, 1-2; Edward K. Spann, *Gotham At War: New York City, 1860-1865* (Wilmington, DE 2002), 162-64; Nat Brandt, *The Man Who Tried to Burn New York* (Lincoln, NE, 1999), 76-77; Clint Johnson, *A Vast and Fiendish Plot: The Confederate Attack on New York City* (New York, NY, 2010), 208-17.

105. A pro-Democrat Wisconsin newspaper had hoped that "if [Lincoln] is elected to misgovern another four years we trust some bold hand will pierce his heart with dagger point for the public good. *La Crosse* (WI) *Democrat,* August 29, 1864, reprinted in *Freemont* (OH) *Journal,* April 28, 1865.

106. Official Records, Series 2, Vol. 8, 878-80, 891, 940.

107. Thomas Waverly Palmer, *A Register of the Officers and Students of the University of Alabama, 1831-1901* (Tuscaloosa, AL, 1901), 175.

108. Lt. W. Alston to Jefferson Davis, reprinted in Richard H. Leach, "John Archibald Campbell and the Alston Letter," in *Alabama Review* 11 (January, 1958): 64-75, Thomas M. Harris, *Assassination of Lincoln: A History of the Great Conspiracy* (Boston, MA 1892), 363, and Edward Steers, *The Trial: The Assassination of President Lincoln and the Trial of the Conspirators* (Lexington, KY, 2010), 375.

109. (Macon) *Georgia Weekly Telegraph,* August 27, 1866, p. 5; (Augusta, GA) *Constitutionalist,* August 30, 1866, 1; *New Orleans Times,* September 1, 1866, 11.

110. *Mobile Advertiser and Register,* July 3, 1864, 1.

111. *Charleston Mercury,* September 17, 1864, 2. *See also, Montgomery Mail,* September 7, 1864, 2; *Richmond Examiner,* reprinted in *Charleston Mercury,* September 13, 1864, 1; *Charleston Mercury,* September 14, 1864, 3; *Columbus* (GA) *Enquirer,* October 2, 1864, 2, October 9, 1864, 2.

112. *Jacksonville Republican,* October 20, 1864, 1.

113. L.W. Alston to President Davis, reprinted in *Augusta* (GA) *Chronicle,* June 4, 1865, 1 and (Augusta, GA) *Constitutionalist,* June 3, 1865, 2. *See also,* J. Holt to E.M. Stanton, January 18, 1866, Official Records, Series 2, Vol. 8, 849; *New York Tribune,* July 28, 1866, 5.

114. William C. Edwards and Edward Steers, Jr., eds., *The Lincoln Assassination: The Evidence* (Urbana, IL, 2009), 631-32; Hanchett, *Lincoln Murder Conspiracies*, 29.

115. Paul Ashdown and Edward Caudill, *The Mosby Myth: A Confederate Hero in Life and Legend* (Wilmington, DE, 2002), 94-95; William S. Connery, *Mosby's Raids in Civil War Northern Virginia* (Charleston, SC, 2013), 41-44.

116. (New Orleans) *Picayune*, May 7, 1862, 2; *Mobile Advertiser and Register*, May 8, 1863, 1, October 28, 1864, 2; *Columbus* (GA) *Enquirer*, October 26, 1864, 2; *New York Times*, October 16, 1864, 1; Keehn, *Knights of the Golden Circle*, 176-77.

117. Deposition of William H. Carter, February 9, 1866, Official Records, Series 2, Vol. 8, 880.

118. (Washington, D.C.) *Star*, May 8, 1865, 1; Titone, *My Thoughts Be Bloody*, 329, 335-36; Keehn, *Knights of the Golden Circle*, 1-2, 176; Kauffman, *American Brutus*, 140-41; Swanson, *Manhunt*, 125-27; Higham, *Murdering Mr. Lincoln*, 114-20.

119. *Nashville Union*, December 1, 1864, 1 (Booth played Marc Anthony at the Winter Garden Theater); (Washington) *Star*, January 20, 1865, 3.

120. Titone, *My Thoughts Be Bloody*, 341, 344-45.

121. *New York Times*, October 20, 1864, 1, October 21, 1864, 1; (St. Albans) *Vermont Transcript*, October 21, 1864, 3, November 11, 1864, 3; Robin Winks, *The Civil War Years: Canada and the United States* (Montreal: McGill University Press, 1998), 306.

122. (St. Albans) *Vermont Transcript*, November 11, 1864, 3, March 17, 1865, 2; Prince, *Burn the Town and Sack the Banks*, 163-64.

123. *Charleston Mercury*, November 22, 1864, 1; *Mobile Advertiser and Register*, November 22, 1864, 1-2; *Columbus* (GA) *Enquirer*, November 22, 1864, 1-2, November 26, 1864, 1, December 2, 1864, 2. *See generally*, Mark H. Dunkelman, *Marching With Sherman: Through Georgia and the Carolinas With the 154th New York* (Baton Rouge, 2012); John Gilchrist Barrett, *Sherman's March Through the Carolinas* (Chapel Hill, 1995); Harry S. Stout, *Upon the Altar of the Nation: A Moral History of the American Civil War* (New York, NY, 2007), 415.

124. *Charleston Mercury*, July 16, 1864, 1. *See also, Charleston Mercury*, July 30, 1863, 1, July 11, 1864, 1, July 22, 1864, 1, August 6, 1864, 1, August 16, 1864, 1, September 26, 1864, 1; *Mobile Advertiser and Register*, July 16, 1864, 2.

125. *Charleston Mercury*, August 26, 1864, 1.

126. *Charleston Mercury*, September 12, 1864, 1.

127. *Charleston Mercury*, September 29, 1864, 1, October 14, 1864, 1, October 18, 1864, 1, October 19, 1864, 1; *Mobile Advertiser and Register*, October 22, 1864, 2.

128. *Charleston Mercury*, October 7, 1864, 1, October 31, 1864, 1; *Mobile Advertiser and Register*, October 15, 1864, 2; *Columbus* (GA) *Enquirer*, October 11, 1864, 2; (Richmond) *Dispatch*, October 28, 1864, 1.

129. *Charleston Mercury*, November 4, 1864, 1, November 9, 1864, 1, November 10, 1864, 1, November 11, 1864, 1, November 18, 1864, 1, November 30, 1864, 1; *Mobile Advertiser and Register*, November 29, 1864, 1.

130. *Charleston Mercury*, November 18, 1864, 1.

131. *Charleston Mercury*, July 27, 1864, 1.

132. *Charleston Mercury*, November 19, 1864, 1. *See also, Charleston Mercury*, December 29, 1864, 1.

133. *Nashville Times and True Union,* November 28, 1864, 2; *Nashville Press*, December 2, 1864, 2; *Mobile Advertiser and Register,* December 6, 1864, 2, December 14, 1864, 2, December 15, 1864, 1-2, December 20, 1864, 1.

134. *Mobile Advertiser and Register,* November 20, 1864, 2; *Charleston Mercury*, November 7, 1864, 1. *See generally,* Kenneth J. Winkle, *Lincoln's Citadel: The Civil War in Washington, D.C.* (New York, NY, 2013), 41012.

135. *Impeachment Investigation: Testimony Taken Before the Judiciary Committee of the House of Representatives In the Investigation of the Charges Against Andrew Johnson, Second Session, ThirtyNinth Congress, and First Session, Fortieth Congress,* 569.

136. *Selma Dispatch,* December 1, 1864, reprinted in *White Cloud Kansas Chief,* February 9, 1865, 2, (Washington D.C.) *Republican,* reprinted in *Cleveland Herald,* June 24, 1865 and Jackson, *Story of Selma,* 208-209. *See also,* J. Holt to E.M. Stanton, January 18, 1866, Official Records, Series 2, Vol. 8, 848-49. The *Selma Morning Dispatch* was the successor of John Hardy's Selma *Alabama State Sentinel,* which had ceased publication in 1863. (Greensboro) *Alabama Beacon,* June 5, 1863, 3.

137. *Charleston Mercury*, August 11, 1864, 1.

138. Garrett, *Reminiscences of Public Men,* 435.

139. *Charleston Mercury*, July 1, 1864, 1; *Mobile Advertiser and Register,* June 14, 1864, 2, July 1, 1864, 2. Regarding Tennessee under Johnson, *see* (New Orleans) *Picayune,* March 12, 1862, 2, March 16, 1862, 1, March 21, 1862, 2; *Selma Reporter,* June 5, 1862, 1; *Montgomery Weekly Advertiser,* March 23, 1862, March 26, 1862; *Mobile Advertiser and Register,* April 17, 1862, 1, December 6, 1863, 1.

140. *Charleston Mercury*, November 22, 1864, 1.

141. *Mobile Advertiser and Register,* December 7, 1864, 1.

142. *See,* e.g., *Cork* (Ireland) *Examiner,* February 7, 1865, available at http:www. irelandold news.com/Cork/1865/FEB.html; *Cleveland* (OH) *Morning Leader,* January 23, 1865, 2; *Fremont* (OH) *Journal,* January 27, 1865, 2; (PA) *Jeffersonian,* February 16, 1865, 1; *White Cloud Kansas Chief,* February 9, 1865, 2; (Washington D.C.) *Republican,* reprinted in *Cleveland Herald,* June 24, 1865; *Brownlow's Knoxville Whig and Rebel Ventilator,* February 1, 1865, 2; *Highland* (County, OH) *Weekly News,* February 9, 1865, 1; *Providence* (RI) *Evening Press,* January 23, 1865, 2.

143. Pitman, *Assassination of President Lincoln and the Trial of the Conspirators,* 51.

144. Edwards and Steers, Jr., eds., *Lincoln Assassination: The Evidence,* 189-91. *See also,* (Washington, D.C.) *National Republican,* reprinted in *Cleveland* (OH) *Herald,* June 24, 1865.

145. Kauffman, *American Brutus,* 181.

146. Alford, *Fortune's Fool,* 231.

147. Edwards and Steers, eds., *Lincoln Assassination: The Evidence,* 69 (statement of John Atzerodt).

148. Kauffman, *American Brutus,* 164-67; Ownsbey, *Alias Paine,* 3; Steers, Jr., *Blood On the Moon,* 82-83; Chamlee, Jr., *Lincoln's Assassins,* 474-75; *Columbia* (SC) *Phoenix,* June 28, 1865, 2.

149. Robert K. Summers, *The Fall and Redemption of Dr. Samuel A. Mudd: The True Story of the Doctor Who Went to Prison For Helping Abraham Lincoln's Assassin, John Wilkes Booth* (Morrisville, NC, 2008), 19.

150. John Y. Simon, Harold Holzer and Dawn Vogel, *Lincoln Revisited: New Insights From the Lincoln Forum* (New York, NY, 2007), 324.

151. Nuermberger, *Clays of Alabama,* 235 at note 1. Confederate Secretary of State Judah Benjamin did the same thing before seeking exile in England. Getler and Brewer, *Rebel Gold,* 69.

152. John Henry Wigmore, *Evidence In Trials at Common Law* (Boston, MA1979), II: § 291.

153. *Mobile Advertiser and Register,* December 29, 1864, 1.

Chapter 7: Deeds of Avenging War

1. (Greensboro) *Alabama Beacon,* January 6, 1865, 2; (Grove Hill) *Clarke County Journal,* February 9, 1865, 2; R. Taylor to President Davis, January 9, 1865, Official Records, Series 1, Vol. 45 (Part II), 772. *See generally,* Derek Smith, *In the Lion's Mouth: Hood's Tragic Retreat from Nashville, 1864* (Mechanicsburg, PA, 2011).

2. (Greensboro) *Alabama Beacon,* January 6, 1865, 2. *Accord, Mobile Advertiser and Register,* January 6, 1865, 2, January 13, 1865, 2.

3. *Selma Dispatch,* January 7, 1865, 2.

4. (Augusta) *Constitutionalist,* January 6, 1865, 1.

5. *Charleston Mercury,* January 30, 1865, 1, February 5, 1865, 1, February 8, 1865, 2, February 10, 1865, 1. *See also, Nashville Press,* February 7, 1865, 1; *Mobile Advertiser and Register,* February 8, 1865, 2, February 11, 1865, 2, February 12, 1865, 1.

6. *Charleston Mercury,* February 7, 1865, 1, February 11, 1865, 1; *Mobile Advertiser and Register,* February 12, 1865, 1, February 23, 1865, 1; *Montgomery Advertiser,* February 22, 1865, 2.

7. *New York Tribune,* reprinted in *Nashville Press,* February 22, 1865, 1; (New Orleans) *Picayune,* February 28, 1865, 1.

8. *Mobile Advertiser and Register,* March 16, 1865, 2.

9. Stout, *Upon the Altar of the Nation,* 415.

10. George Stoneman to Major General Thomas, February 6, 1865, Official Records, Series 1, Vol. 49 (Series I), 662-63; *Mobile Advertiser and Register,* February 7, 1865, 1.

11. *Mobile Advertiser and Register,* February 7, 1865, 1, February 15, 1865, 2, February 16, 1865, 1. *Accord, Richmond Whig,* February 7, 1865, reprinted in *New York Times,* February 10, 1865, 4; *Boston Herald,* February 12, 1865, 4; *Nashville Times and True Union,* March 6, 1865, 2.

12. *Columbus* (GA) *Enquirer*, January 16, 1864, 2; Fry, "Life in Dallas County During the War," 220; William O. Bryant, *Cahaba Prison and the Sultana Disaster* (Tuscaloosa, AL, 2001); John L. Walker, *Cahaba Prison and the Sultana Disaster* (Hamilton, OH, 1910); Peter A. Brannon, "The Cahawba Military Prison, 1863-1865" *Alabama Review* 3 (July, 1950): 172; Jesse Hawes, *Cahaba: A Story of Captive Boys in Blue* (New York, NY 1888), 12-15; Lonnie R. Speer, *Portals To Hell: Military Prisons of the Civil War* (Mechanicsburg, PA, 1997); Ted Genoways and Hugh H. Genoways, eds., *A Perfect Picture of Hell: Eyewitness Accounts By Civil War Prisoners From the 12th Iowa* (Iowa City, IA, 2001), 4-5, 31, 238-47.

13. *Selma Reporter*, February 20, 1864, reprinted in *Mobile Advertiser and Register,* March 1, 1864, 1, *Mobile Tribune*, March 1, 1864, 2 and *Memphis Appeal*, March 1, 1864, 1. See also, *Mobile Advertiser and Register,* November 25, 1864, 1; George W. Gayle to Thomas H. Watts, September 21, 1864, Papers of Gov. Watts, Alabama Department or Archives and History, Montgomery, Alabama; *State, ex rel Ellerbe*, 39 AL. 546 (1865).

14. *Memphis Bulletin*, reprinted in (New Orleans) *Picayune*, October 9, 1864, 1.

15. *Selma Dispatch*, reprinted in *Talladega Watchtower*, February 14, 1865, 1.

16. (Selma) *Chattanooga Rebel*, reprinted in (New Orleans) *Picayune*, February 17, 1865, 1.

17. *Mobile Advertiser and Register,* February 18, 1865, 2. See also, (New Orleans) *Picayune*, February 26, 1865, 2.

18. *Mobile Advertiser and Register,* February 24, 1865, 1. See also, *Mobile Advertiser and Register,* February 5, 1865, 2, February 22, 1865, 2, March 3, 1865, 1; Nuermberger, *Clays of Alabama*, 262-64.

19. *Albany* (N.Y.) *Journal*, January 21, 1865, 2. See also, *New York Herald*, January 21, 1865, 1; *Providence* (RI) *Evening Press*, January 23, 1865, 2; (Newark, NJ) *Centinel of Freedom*, January 24, 1865, 3; *Philadelphia Inquirer*, January 26, 1865, 2; *Jamestown* (NY) *Journal*, February 3, 1865, 2; *Salem* (MA) *Observer*, February 11, 1865, 6.

20. *Hartford* (Ct.) *Courant*, January 23, 1865, 3.

21. *Albany* (N.Y.) *Journal*, January 21, 1865, 2.

22. U.S. Grant to Maj. Gen. George H. Thomas, February 14, 1865, Official Records, Series 1, Vol. 49 (Series 1), 708-709; *Mobile Advertiser and Register,* February 24, 1865, 2.

23. *Mobile Advertiser and Register,* February 11, 1865, 2. See also, *Mobile Advertiser and Register,* February 15, 1865, 1, February 24, 1865, 2, February 26, 1865, 2, March 1, 1865, 2, March 3, 1865, 1-2; (Mobile) *Army Argus and Crisis*, February 18, 1865, 2.

24. *Montgomery Advertiser*, March 3, 1865, 2; *Mobile Advertiser and Register,* March 14, 1865, 2, March 18, 1865, 1, March 21, 1865, 2, March 24, 1864, 2; *Richmond Dispatch*, March 16, 1865, 2, March 19, 1865, 2.

25. *Mobile Advertiser and Register,* March 18, 1865, 1.

26. (Augusta, GA) *Constitutionalist*, reprinted in *Mobile Advertiser and Register,* March 24, 1865, 2.

27. *Mobile Advertiser and Register,* March 19, 1865, 1.

28. *Edgefield* (S.C.) *Advertiser*, March 1, 1865, 1. This report was inaccurate; the date was actually March 22.

29. *Montgomery Advertiser*, March 3, 1865, 2, March 6, 1865, March 8, 1865, 2; *Tuscaloosa Observer*, March 8, 1865, 2; *Montgomery Advertiser*, March 3, 1865, 2, March 5, 1865, 2. *See generally*, Joseph T. Glatthaar, *The March to the Sea and Beyond: Sherman's Troops in the Savannah and Carolinas Campaign* (Baton Rouge, LA, 1985), 134-35; Marion Brunson Lucas, *Sherman and the Burning of Columbia* (Columbia, SC, 2000), 83-128.

30. Harwell, ed., *Kate*, 258.

31. *Mobile Advertiser and Register*, April 8, 1865, 2.

32. *See, e.g., Mobile Advertiser and Register*, October 2, 1863, p. 2, December 20, 1863, 2.

33. *Mobile Advertiser and Register*, January 6, 1865, 2.

34. *Mobile Advertiser and Register*, January 20, 1865, 2.

35. *Mobile Advertiser and Register*, February 8, 1865, 2.

36. *Mobile Advertiser and Register*, March 3, 1865, 1.

37. Alford, *Fortune's Fool*, 224-27.

38. *Nashville Union*, February 24, 1865, 3, citing *Cleveland Herald*, February 14, 1865; *Cleveland Leader*, February 13, 1865, reprinted in *Columbia Democrat and Bloomsburg* (PA) *General Advertiser*, March 11, 1865, 1; *Cleveland Herald*, reprinted in *Fremont* (OH) *Journal*, February 24, 1865, 2.

39. *Cleveland Leader*, February 13, 1865.

40. *Cleveland Herald*, reprinted in *Fremont* (OH) *Journal*, February 24, 1865, 2.

41. *Cleveland Leader*, February 13, 1865.

42. *Philadelphia Bulletin*, reprinted in *Mobile Advertiser and Register*, March 19, 1865, 2. *See generally, Lowell Citizen and News*, March 8, 1865; *Cleveland* (OH) *Herald*, March 8, 1865, 1, March 9, 1865, 2; (Portage) *Wisconsin State Register*, March 11, 1865; (New Orleans) *Picayune*, March 28, 1865, 2.

43. *Cleveland Leader*, March 9, 1865, 2.

44. *See, e.g., Mobile Advertiser and Register*, March 19, 1865, 2. *See also*, (New Orleans) *Picayune*, March 28, 1865, 2.

45. *Mobile Advertiser and Register*, March 21, 1865, 2.

46. *Mobile Advertiser and Register*, March 26, 1865, 2, March 28, 1865, 2, March 29, 1865, 1-2, March 30, 1865, 1; R.E. Lee to J.C. Breckinridge, March 29, 1865, Official Records, Series 1, Vol. 49 (Part II), 1171.

47. *New York Times*, April 4, 1865, 9.

48. Regarding the Battle of Selma, see *Mobile Advertiser and Register*, April 5, 1865, 2, April 6, 1865, 2, April 9, 1865, 2; *Columbia* (SC) *Phoenix*, April 10, 1865, 3; *Edgefield* (SC) *Advertiser*, April 12, 1865, 1, April 12, 1865, 1, April 19, 1865, 5; Jackson, *Story of Selma*, 215-18; Brian Steel Wills, "The Confederate Sun Sets on Selma: Nathan Bedford Forrest and the Defense of Alabama in 1865," in Noe, ed., *Yellowhammer War*, 71-89.

49. *Jackson* (Miss.) *News*, reprinted in *Mobile Advertiser and Register,* April 9, 1865, 2; *Macon* (GA) *Telegraph*, May 12, 1865, 2.

50. *New York Herald*, April 29, 1865, 2. *See also, Louisville Journal*, April 30, 1865, 1; (Washington, D.C.) *National Republican*, May 1, 1865, 2.

51. James Pickett Jones, *Yankee Blitzkrieg: Wilson's Raid Through Alabama and Georgia* (Lexington, KY, 2000), 94-97; Jackson, *Story of Selma*, 216-19.

52. Alford, *Fortune's Fool*, 236.

53. Ownsbey, *Alias "Paine,"* 56-57; Kauffman, *American Brutus*, 179; Larson, *Assassin's Accomplice*, 6265, 66-70.

54. *New York Times*, April 9, 1865, 4.

55. *New York Times*, April 4, 1865, 4.

56. *New York Times*, April 9, 1865, 5, April 10, 1865, 1.

57. *New York Times*, April 4, 1865, 4.

58. *New York Times*, April 4, 1865, 4,

59. Steers, *Blood on the Moon*, 88. There is evidence Booth had received money from someone in the northeast and that he had a bank account in Canada that reflected a small deposit from someone in England. Edwards and Steers, Jr., eds., *Lincoln Assassination*, 268, 270, 303, 315, 789, 1000; Kauffman, *American Brutus*, 189-190. Unfortunately, the ability of the investigators to trace funds transfers was not as sophisticated then as it is today, and they could not follow the trail to the source or sources of the money.

60. Steers, *Blood on the Moon*, 88-89. *See also,* Tidwell, *April '65,* 161-65; Rhodehanel and Taper, eds., *"Right or Wrong,"* 121; Keehn, *Knights of the Golden Circle*, lxxiv; Jane Singer, *The Confederate Dirty War: Arson, Bombings, Assassination and Plots For Chemical and Germ Attacks On the Union* (Jefferson, NC, 2005), 93-94, 130-34. Others have questioned some or all of this theory. Arnold M. Pavlovsky, *"In Pursuit of a Phantom": John Singleton Mosby's Civil War* (Southampton, NJ, 2008), 347-48.

61. *Mobile Advertiser and Register,* April 8, 1865, 2. There is evidence that money to pay the assassins was also being raised in other parts of the country. Edwards and Steers, Jr., eds., *Lincoln Assassination: The Evidence*, 916, 1087-91, 1096-97.

62. (Washington, D.C.) *National Republican*, April 7, 1865; *Cleveland Leader,* April 14, 1 ("He is unable to leave his bed"); *New York Times*, April 14, 1865, 4. *See also, New York Tribune*, April 6, 1865, 4, April 12, 1865, 4; *Cleveland Leader,* April 6, 1865, 1, April 7, 1865, 1, April 10, 1865, 1, April 12, 1865, 2, April 14, 1865, 1; *Nashville Union*, April 7, 1865, 2, April 8, 1865, 3; *New York Times*, April 6, 1865, 4, April 8, 1865, 4.

63. *Cleveland Leader,* April 25, 1865, 2; Kauffman, *American Brutus*, 30.

64. *Richmond Whig*, April 7, 1865, reprinted in *New York Tribune*, April 10, 1865, 1; *New York Times*, April 10, 1865, 1.

65. *Milwaukee Sentinel*, April 7, 1865, 2; *Philadelphia Inquirer*, reprinted in *Milwaukee Sentinel*, April 7, 1865, 2.

66. *New York Times*, April 5, 1865, 4.

67. *Washington Chronicle,* April 4, 1865, reprinted in *Cleveland Leader,* April 6, 1865, 2 and *Milwaukee Sentinel,* April 8, 1865. *See generally, Mobile News,* April 17, 1865, 2, April 25, 1865, 2.

68. *Edgefield* (SC) *Advertiser,* May 3, 1865, 1; *New York Herald,* April 17, 1865, reprinted in (Athens, GA) *Southern Banner,* May 3, 1865, 2. *See also, Nashville Union,* April 18, 1865, 2; *Cleveland Leader,* May 5, 1865, 2; *New York World,* reprinted in *Atlanta Intelligencer,* June 6, 1865, 2. *See generally,* Howard Means, *The Avenger Take His Place: Andrew Johnson and the 45 Days That Changed the Nation* (Orlando, FL, 2006), 86-96.

69. *New York Times,* April 10, 1865, 4, April 11, 1865, 4; *Cleveland Leader,* April 11, 1865, 1; (Montpelier) *Vermont Watchman and State Journal,* April 14, 1865, 2.

70. Steers, *Blood on the Moon,* 90; Ashdown and Caudill, *Mosby Myth,* 93-94 (stating that they were captured on April 10); Pavlovsky, *"In Pursuit of a Phantom,"* 347.

71. (Washington, D.C.) *National Republican,* April 11, 1865, 2; *Cleveland Leader,* April 11, 1865, 1; *Nashville Press,* April 13, 1865, 1; *Montgomery Mail,* April 24, 1865, 2.

72. Kauffman, *American Brutus,* 205, 207; Testimony of Thomas T. Eckert on May 30, 1867, *Judiciary Committee, House of Representatives, Impeachment Investigation, 39th Cong., 2d Session, and 40th Cong., 1st Sess.,* 674. Former Assistant Secretary of War Thomas Eckert testified that Lewis Powell told him that Powell and Booth attended the speech "the night of the celebration after the fall of Richmond." *Ibid.*

73. Kauffman, *American Brutus,* 189-92.

74. *New York Tribune,* April 12, 1865, 1; *New York Times,* April 12, 1865, 1; *Nashville Press,* April 14, 1865, 2; *Milwaukee Sentinel,* April 14, 1865; *Mobile News,* April 20, 1865, 1.

75. *New York Tribune,* April 12, 1865, 1; *Mobile News,* April 20, 1865, 1.

76. Edwards and Steers, eds., *Lincoln Assassination,* 1042.

77. (Washington, D.C.) *National Republican,* April 14, 1865, 2.

78. *New York Times,* April 15, 1865, 1.

79. Kauffman, *American Brutus,* 171; Guttridge and Neff, *Dark Union,* 127.

80. Kauffman, *American Brutus,* 213, 217; Ownsbey, *Alias Paine,* 71, 74.

81. Kauffman, *American Brutus,* 30; Edwards and Steers, eds., *Lincoln Assassination: The Evidence,* 60-64.

82. Rhodehamel and Taper, eds., *"Right or Wrong, God Judge Me,"* 146. *See also, New York World,* reprinted in *Holmes County* (OH) *Farmer,* April 27, 1865, 2. *But see, Montgomery Mail,* May 1, 1865, 1 (publishing a telegraphic report that Johnson claimed he did not see this note until the day after the assassination).

83. *Selma Dispatch,* December 1, 1864, reprinted in *Cleveland* (Ohio) *Leader,* January 23, 1865, 2.

84. *New York Tribune,* April 20, 1865, 2; Rhodehamel and Taper, eds., *"Right or Wrong, God Judge Me,"* 147-53.

85. Kauffman, *American Brutus,* 212.

86. John Wilkes Booth, "John Wilkes Booth Diary," reprinted in Rhodehamel and Taper, eds., *"Right or Wrong, God Judge Me,"* 154.

87. Kauffman, *American Brutus,* 226-27; Bogar, *Backstage at the Lincoln Assassination,* 110-15.

88. (Washington, D.C.) *National Republican,* April 15, 1865, 2. *Accord, Nashville Press,* April 17, 1865, 1. *See also,* Rohr, ed., *Incidents of the War,* 286 (word had reached the occupation forces in Huntsville, Alabama, by the following day). There is evidence that, despite these precautions, some claimed to have been involved who were not. *See, e.g.,* (Milledgeville, GA) *Southern Recorder,* April 25, 1865, 2, May 2, 1865, 2.

89. *Nashville Press,* April 28, 1865, 1; (PA) *Jeffersonian,* May 4, 1865, 1 (claiming that immediately before Booth died, he indicated he was on his way to Mexico).

90. Kauffman, *American Brutus,* 226-320; Harris, *Lincoln's Last Months,* 224. *See also,* (Washington, D.C.) *National Republican,* April 15, 1865, 2; *New York Times,* April 15, 1865, 1; *Mobile News,* May 14, 1865, 2.

91. (Selma) *Chattanooga Rebel,* April 19, 1865, reprinted in *Montgomery Mail,* April 22, 1865, 1.

92. (Selma) *Chattanooga Rebel,* April 20, 1865, reprinted in *Mobile News,* May 5, 1865, 1, *New York Tribune,* May 10, 1865, 1; (Columbus) *Ohio State Journal,* May 12, 1865, 2; *Troy* (NY) *Weekly Times,* May 20, 1865, 1; *Yankton* (SD) *Union and Dakotian,* May 27, 1865, 3; (San Francisco) *Bulletin,* June 2, 1865, 1; (Boston) *Liberator,* June 9, 1865, 90; (Washington, D.C.) *Star,* May 11, 1865, 2, *Milwaukee Sentinel,* May 11, 1865, *Cleveland Leader,* May 10, 1865, 1 and *Boston Herald,* May 12, 1865, 4. *See also, Cleveland Leader,* June 3, 1865, 2 ("The Selma (AL) Rebel, after shouting over the murder of Mr. Lincoln, immediately lay down, kicked a little, gasped, rolled up its eyes and died.").

93. *Demopolis Herald,* reprinted in (Greensboro) *Alabama Beacon,* April 21, 1865, 2. *See also,* Carolyn L. Harrell, *When the Bell Tolls for Lincoln: Southern Reaction To the Assassination* (Macon, GA, 1997), 69-75; Danielson, *War's Desolating Scourge,* 157-58 (noting that after the commander of the occupying Union force at Huntsville ordered the residents to place black crape on their front door knobs as a sign of mourning, many refused and one put a "great big Negro doll" on his knob). *But see, Montgomery Mail,* April 24, 1865, 1 (condemning the assassinations on the day occupation forces arrived in Montgomery).

94. *Demopolis Herald,* April 25, 1865, reprinted in *Cleveland Leader,* June 23, 1865, 2.

95. Ironically, on the day of Lincoln's assassination, a grand flag raising ceremony had taken place at Union-occupied Fort Sumter as part of efforts to put closure on the bloody conflict. *Charleston Courier,* April 15, 1865.

96. Venet, ed., *"Sam Richard's Civil War Diary,"* 236, 271.

97. (Selma) *Chattanooga Rebel,* April 19, 1865, reprinted in *Montgomery Mail,* April 22, 1865, 1; *Montgomery Advertiser,* April 22, 1865, 2.

98. *Nashville Press,* April 18, 1865, 3.

99. Leonard, *Lincoln's Avengers,* 63-65, 151-55.

100. (Philadelphia) *North American and United States Gazette,* April 15, 1865.

101. *Fremont* (OH) *Journal,* April 21, 1865, 2. *See also, Nashville Times and True Union,* April 24, 1865, 3. *See generally,* Harris, *Lincoln's Last Months,* 225.

102. (Philadelphia) *North American and United States Gazette,* April 15, 1865. *Accord,* (Washington, D.C.) *National Intelligencer,* April 17, 1865.

103. *New York Post,* reprinted in (Washington, D.C.) *National Intelligencer,* April 17, 1865.

104. *Gallipolis* (OH) *Journal,* April 20, 1865, 2. See also, Hodes, *Mourning Lincoln,* 117-38, 252.

105. *Mobile News Extra,* April 20, 1865; *Montgomery Mail,* April 24, 1865, 1; May 1, 1865, 1. *See also,* (Washington, D.C.) *National Republican,* April 15, 1865, 2; (Washington, D.C.) *National Intelligencer,* April 16, 1865.

106. (Washington, D.C.) *National Intelligencer,* April 16, 1865.

107. Associated Press, quoted in *Cleveland Herald,* April 17, 1865. *Accord, New York Post,* reprinted in (Washington, D.C.) *National Intelligencer,* April 17, 1865; Daily Journal of Joshua Burns Moore, 84-85, Alabama Department of Archives and History, Montgomery, Alabama; *Brownlow's Knoxville Whig and Rebel Ventilator,* May 3, 1865, 2.

108. *New York Tribune,* April 18, 1865, 4; *Trenton* (NJ) *State Gazette,* April 19, 1865, 2; *Philadelphia Press,* May 23, 1865, 1, May 26, 1865, 1.

109. *Philadelphia Inquirer,* April 17, 1865, 4.

110. *New York Post,* April 17, 1865, 2. *Accord, Trenton* (NJ) *State Gazette,* April 19, 1865, 2.

111. Kauffman, *American Brutus,* 136, 205, 328; *New York World,* reprinted in *Holmes County* (OH) *Farmer,* April 27, 1865, 2.

112. (Washington, D.C.) *National Republican,* April 15, 1865, 2.

113. A Missouri man sent William Seward's nephew a copy of the advertisement. James E. Ashcroft to Clarence A. Seward, June 5, 1865, Papers of William Seward, University of Rochester.

114. *Stoughton* (MA) *Sentinel,* April 29, 1865, 2.

115. *Hartford* (CT) *Courant,* April 21, 1865, 2. This editorial was printed in several other newspapers in the North. *See, e.g., Springfield* (MA) *Weekly Republican,* April 22, 1865, 8.

116. *See, e.g., Cleveland Leader,* April 18, 1865, 1; *Bangor Whig & Courier,* April 22, 1865; (Washington, D.C.) *Daily National Intelligencer,* June 22, 1865, July 19, 1865; *Frank Leslie's Illustrated Newspaper,* July 8, 1865; *New York Times,* June 29, 1865, 5, July 1, 1865, 4; *Gallipolis* (OH) *Journal,* May 4, 1865, 1; *Highland* (OH) *Weekly News,* May 4, 1865, 1; *Norfolk* (VA) *Post,* June 26, 1865, 2; (Washington, D.C.) *National Republican,* June 4, 1867, 1.

117. *Charleston Courier,* April 26, 1865, 1. *See generally,* Means, *Avenger Takes His Place,* 123-26, 142, 180-82; Harris, *Lincoln's Last Months,* 234-239.

118. *Charleston Courier,* April 22, 1865, 1; *Mobile News,* April 20, 1865, 2.

119. *New York Herald,* April 24, 1865, reprinted in *Charleston Courier,* April 28, 1865, 1, and *Nashville Press,* April 28, 1865, 1; Means, *Avenger Take His Place,* 120.

CHAPTER 8: A SHREWD, COLD BLOODED RASCAL

1. Kauffman, *American Brutus,* 335; Trefousse, *Andrew Johnson,* 211.

2. *Mobile News,* May 12, 1865, 2; *Charleston Courier,* May 16, 1865, 1; *Nashville Press,* May 1, 1865, 2; *Burlington* (VT) *Free Press,* June 9, 1865, 2.

3. *Mobile News,* May 17, 1865, 1-2; *Nashville Times and True Union,* May 16, 1865, 2; *Charleston Courier,* May 19, 1865, 1; Means, *Avenger Takes His Place,* 151-55; Goodrich, *Day Dixie Died,* 33-62; Herman Hattaway and Richard E. Beringer, *Jefferson Davis, Confederate President* (Lawrence, KS, 2002), 427-29.

4. *Mobile News,* May 17, 1865, 2; *Mobile News,* May 20, 1865, 2; *Nashville Press & Times,* May 24 1865, 1; Nuermberger, *Clays of Alabama,* 264-67.

5. *New York Tribune,* June 30, 1865, 1; *New York Times,* May 25, 1865, 4.

6. *Boston Journal,* reprinted in *Bangor* (ME) *Whig & Courier,* May 12, 1865, *Nashville Union,* May 19, 1865, 2, and (Montpelier) *Vermont Watchman and State Journal,* May 19, 1865, 1.

7. *Nashville Press,* May 8, 1865, 1; *Nashville Press and Times,* May 27, 1865, 1, May 29, 1865, 1; *Nashville Union,* May 7, 1865, 1; *Mobile News,* May 31, 1865, 1, June 3, 1865, 4. See also, *New York Times,* May 7, 1865, 1, May 16, 1865, 1, May 21, 1865, 1; Means, *Avenger Takes His Place,* 182-83.

8. *New York Times,* June 6, 1865, 1.

9. *New York Times,* April 16, 1865, 6, May 8, 1865, 2, May 12, 1865, 8, May 13, 1865, 1, May 23, 1865, 4. *See also, New York Times,* April 8, 1865, 3 (discussing the Cahawba prison); Means, *Avenger Takes His Place,* 187-89 (discussing the reaction in the North). Regarding the *Sultana* disaster where some prisoners perished, *see* (Washington, D.C.) *National Republican,* May 1, 1865, 2; *New York Times,* May 2, 1865, 5; *Cleveland Leader,* May 3, 1865, 2; (Washington, D.C.) *National Intelligencer,* May 5, 1865. *See generally,* Means, *Avenger Takes His Place,* 178-80, 195.

10. (Greensboro) *Alabama Beacon,* May 12, 1865, 2; (Grove Hill) *Clarke County Journal,* June 8, 1865, 2; *Mobile Advertiser and Register,* July 30, 1865, 2; *Nashville Union,* June 13, 1865, 1; *Andersonville* (SC) *Intelligencer,* June 22, 1865, 4; Saunders, *John Archibald Campbell,* 187-89 (Campbell was arrested in Richmond).

11. Leach, "John Archibald Campbell and the Alston Letter," 69-71; *Burlington* (VT) *Free Press,* June 3, 1865, 1; *Augusta* (GA) *Chronicle,* June 4, 1865, 1. *See generally,* Palmer, *Register of the Officers and Students of the University of Alabama,* 175 (Alston was born on September 18, 1844).

12. Saunders, *John Archibald Campbell,* 187-88; Leach, "John Archibald Campbell and the Alston Letter," 69-71 (Davis later claimed that Alston was arrested for sending this letter, and scheduled to be court-martialed); Tidwell, Hall and Gaddy, *Come Retribution,* 238; *Boston Advertiser,* May 27, 1865, 1; (Augusta, GA) *Constitutionalist,* June 3, 1865, 2; *New York Tribune,* July 28, 1866, 4.

13. John A. Campbell to H.W. Halleck, May 25, 1865, reprinted in Edwards and Steers, Jr., eds., *Lincoln Assassination: The Evidence,* 322-24, 631-32.

14. *Burlington* (VT) *Free Press,* June 3, 1865, 1; (Montpelier) *Vermont Watchman and State Journal,* June 9, 1865, 2; Kauffman, *American Brutus,* 343.

15. *Nashville Union,* May 27, 1865, 2.

16. David Brainerd, *Illustrated Life, Services, Martyrdom, and Funeral of Abraham Lincoln: Sixteenth President of the United States* (Philadelphia, PA, 1865), 261-63.

17. Schuyler Colfax, *Life and Principles of Abraham Lincoln* (Philadelphia, PA, 1865), 5-6 (from a prior delivery of the same eulogy given by Colfax in Indiana).

18. (Montpelier) *Vermont Watchman and State Journal,* June 16, 1865, 1; *Burlington* (VT) *Free Press,* June 23, 1865, 4; *Cleveland Leader,* June 12, 1865, 1; *Fremont* (OH) *Journal,* June 16, 1865, 2; *Juniata* (Mifflintown, PA) *Sentinel,* June 21, 1865, 2; *Belmont* (St. Clairsville, OH) *Chronicle,* June 22, 1865, 2; *Highland* (Hillsboro, OH) *Weekly News,* June 22, 1865, 2; *Ashtabula* (OH) *Weekly Telegraph,* June 24, 1865, 2; *Mobile News,* June 24, 1865, 3; Tidwell, Hall and Gaddy, *Come Retribution,* 238.

19. Capt. Hanson to Lt. Col. J. Hough, May 25, 1865, Official Records, Series 1, Vol. 49 (Part II), 909. Regarding Moore's arrest, see also *Nashville Press and Times,* June 9, 1865, 2; *Mobile Advertiser and Register,* July 30, 1865, 2; (New Orleans) *Picayune,* August 26, 1865, 1 (released). Regarding McArthur, see *New York Times,* May 17, 1906; *Mobile News,* June 23, 1865, 4; (Greensboro) *Alabama Beacon,* June 30, 1865, 2; *Mobile Advertiser and Register,* September 8, 1865, 2.

20. Sarah Woolfolk Wiggins, ed., *The Journals of Josiah Gorgas, 1857-1878* (Tuscaloosa, AL, 1995), 174. *See also,* (Washington, D.C.) *National Republican,* June 12, 1865, 2; *New York Tribune,* June 12, 1865, 4; (Washington, D.C.) *Star,* June 12, 1865, 1.

21. Office of Provost Marshal General, Head Quarters Department of the Gulf, M416, File 16182, George Gayle, National Archives, Washington, D.C.; (Hillsboro, OH) *Highland Weekly News,* June 22, 1865, 2.

22. (Washington, D.C.) *National Republican,* June 12, 1865, 2, June 19, 1865, 2; *New York World,* reprinted in *Cleveland Leader,* June 12, 1865, 1; *New York Herald,* June 20, 1865, 1.

23. *State v. Jackson,* 62 Wash. App. 53, 813 P).2d 156 (1991); *People v. Corrigan,* 87 N.E. 792, 796 (New York App., 1909); *State v. Schmitz,* 114 1 (ID, 1911).

24. *People v. Corrigan, supra* at 796.

25. *Providence* (RI) *Press,* June 21, 1865, 3; (Washington, D.C.) *National Republican; Louisville* (KY) *Journal,* June 23, 1865, 1; *Nashville Union,* June 22, 1865, 3; A.J. Smith to Lt. Col. C.T. Christenson, May 27, 1865, Official Records, Series 1, Vol. 49 (Part II), 992.

26. *Robert v. People,* 19 Mich. 401 (1870). *See also, State v. Myers,* 82 Mo. 558 (1884); *State v. Schmitz,* 114 P. 1 (ID, 1911); *People v. Crittle,* 212 N.W. 2d 196, 199 (MI 1973); *State v. Cruz,* 525 P. 2d 382, 384 (NM, App., 1974); *Bethea v. United States,* 365 A.2d 64, 83-92 (Washington, D.C. App., 1976), *cert. denied,* 433 U.S. 911 (1977).

27. (Kansas) *Independent,* July 15, 1865, 2; (Washington, D.C.) *National Republican,* June 21, 1865, 2; *Cleveland Leader,* June 22, 1865, 1; *Boston Herald,* June 22, 1865, 2. *New Orleans Times,* June 28, 1865, 2.

28. *Cleveland Leader*, June 22, 1865, 1; (Washington, D.C.) *National Republican*, June 22, 1865; (Washington, D.C.) *Star*, June 22, 1865, 2.

29. (Washington, D.C.) *National Republican*, June 21, 1865, 2, reprinted in (Washington, D.C.) *National Intelligencer*, June 22, 1865, *New York Tribune*, June 23, 1865, 1, *Cleveland Herald*, June 24, 1865, *Milwaukee Sentinel*, June 24, 1865, *Philadelphia Inquirer*, June 24, 1865, 2, *Cleveland Leader*, June 26, 1865, 2, and Jackson, *Story of Selma*, 209.

30. *Cleveland Leader*, June 22, 1865, 1; *Norfolk* (VA) *Post*, June 26, 1865, 2; *New York Tribune*, June 29, 1865, 4; (Washington, D.C.) *Post*, June 22, 1865, 102; Larson, *Assassin's Accomplice*, 116, 131. Regarding the prison, see, e.g., Winkle, *Lincoln's Citadel*, 199.

31. Larson, *Assassin's Accomplice*, 117-18; James Joseph Williamson, *Prison Life In the Old Capitol and Reminiscences of the Civil War* (West Orange, NJ, 1911), 21.

32. *See generally*, Winkle, *Lincoln's Citadel*, 199.

33. (Washington, D.C.) *Star*, June 22, 1865, 1.

34. Edwin Stanton to Brig. Gen. J. Holt, June 24, 1865, Record Group 153, Entry 6, File 1429, National Archives, Washington, D.C.

35. *Providence Press*, June 27, 1865, 3; Nashville *Union*, June 28, 1865, 3; *Baltimore Sun*, June 28, 1865, 2; *Boston Herald*, June 28, 1865, 4; *New York Tribune*, June 28, 1865, 1; *Norfolk* (VA) *Post*, June 30, 1865, 3; *Mobile News*, July 19, 1865, 1; *Cleveland Leader*, June 28, 1865, 1; (Columbus) *Ohio Statesman*, June 28, 1865, 3; *Boston Advertiser*, June 28, 1865, 1; *Philadelphia Age*, June 28, 1865, 2.

36. (Washington, D.C.) *Star*, June 28, 1865, 2, June 29, 1865, 2.

37. *New York Times*, June 29, 1865, 5. *See also*, *Cleveland Leader*, June 29, 1865, 1; (St. Albans) *Vermont Transcript*, June 30, 1865, 2.

38. (Washington, D.C.) *National Republican*, June 21, 1865, 2; *Cleveland Leader*, June 22, 1865, 1; *Ashtabula* (OH) *Weekly Telegraph*, June 24, 1865, 3, *Norfolk* (VA.) *Post*, June 26, 1865, 2; (Montpelier) *Vermont Watchman and State Journal*, June 30, 1865, 1; *New York World*, reprinted in (San Francisco) *Bulletin*, July 24, 1865, 1. Regarding Johnson, *see* Leonard, *Lincoln's Avengers*, 73, 77-78, 196, 244.

39. *Norfolk* (VA) *Post,* June 26, 1865, 2.

40. (Washington, D.C.) *Star*, June 19, 1865, 2, June 20, 1865, 1. The tribunal ultimately rejected this jurisdictional argument but, in 1866, the United States Supreme Court accepted it in a different case. *Ex parte Milligan*, 71 U.S. 2 (1866). *See also*, *Montgomery Advertiser*, April 8, 1866, 2; Cary Federman, *The Body of the State: Habeas Corpus and American Jurisprudence* (New York, NY, 2006), 167-68; William H. Rehnquist, *All the Laws But One: Civil Liberties in Wartime* (New York, NY, 1998), 104, 116-17, 131, 148.

41. *Norfolk* (VA) *Post*, June 26, 1865, 2.

42. *New York Times*, June 29, 1865, 5; *Cleveland Leader*, June 29, 1865, 1; *New York Tribune*, June 29, 1865, 4; (St. Albans) *Vermont Transcript*, June 30, 1865, 2; *Norfolk* (VA) *Post*, July 1, 1865, 2; (Washington, D.C.) *Star*, June 19, 1865, 2, June 20,

1865, 1; *New York Tribune*, June 29, 1865, 4; Larson, *Assassin's Accomplice*, 145, 147; Andrew C.A. Jampoler, *The Last Conspirator: John Surratt's Flight From the Gallows* (Annapolis, MD, 2008), 30.

43. Testimony of Thomas T. Eckert, *Judiciary Committee, House of Representatives: The Impeachment Committee Investigation*, 673-75, cited in Edwards and Steers, Jr., eds., *Lincoln Assassination: The Evidence*, xxiv.

44. Benn Pitman, *The Assassination of President Lincoln and the Trial of the Conspirators* (Cincinnati, OH, 1865), 160-68, 308, 315; (Washington, D.C.) *Star*, June 2, 1865, 2, June 3, 1865, 2, June 5, 1865, 1, June 10, 1865, 2, June 13, 1865, 2, June 14, 1865, 2, June 20, 1865, 2, June 21, 1865, 1-2; (Montpelier) *Vermont Watchman and State Journal*, June 30, 1865, 1; (Washington, D.C.) *National Republican*, June 13, 1865, 2, June 14, 1865, 2; *New York Tribune*, June 15, 1865; Ownsbey, *Alias "Payne"*, 129-33.

45. N.P. Chipman to Joseph Holt, June 29, 1865, Record Group 153, E7 Letters Received, National Archives, Washington, D.C.

46. N.P. Chipman to Joseph Holt, June 29, 1865, *supra*.

47. *New York Times*, June 29, 1865, 5; *New York Tribune*, June 29, 1865, 4; (Greensboro) *Alabama Beacon*, July 14, 1865, 2; *Mobile News*, July 15, 1865, 2; *Mobile Advertiser and Register*, July 22, 1865, 2; (Grove Hill) *Clarke County Journal*, July 27, 1865, 1; (St. Albans) *Vermont Transcript*, June 30, 1865, 2; *Cleveland Leader*, July 1, 1865, 1; *Norfolk* (VA) *Post*, July 1, 1865, 2; *Dayton* (OH) *Empire*, July 1, 1865, 3; (Indianapolis) *State Sentinel*, July 1, 1865, 3; (Portland, ME) *Eastern Argus*, June 29, 1865, 2. This report also appeared in the *Selma Reporter*. *Selma Reporter*, July 19, 1865, quoted in Jackson, *Story of Selma*, 210.

48. (Washington, D.C.) *National Republican*, June 30, 1865, 2. *See also, Philadelphia Inquirer*, July 3, 1865, 4.

49. *Louisville* (KY) *Journal*, July 1, 1865, 3; (New Orleans) *Picayune*, July 8, 1865.

50. Leonard, *Lincoln's Avengers*, 129, 197.

51. General Court Martial Orders No. 356, July 5, 1865, Official Records, Series 1, Vol. 8, 696-700; (New Orleans) *Picayune*, July 8, 1865, 1, July 9, 1865, 8, July 14, 1865, 2, July 18, 1865, 1; *Mobile News*, July 16, 1865, 4. *See generally*, Rehnquist, *All The Laws But One*, 165; Larson, *Assassin's Accomplice*, 195-200, 205-208, 222; Leonard, *Lincoln's Avengers*, 129-35; Jampolier, *Last Lincoln Conspirator*, 33-40.

52. N.P. Chipman to Joseph Holt, June 29, 1865, *supra*.

53. *Ex parte Milligan*, 71 U.S. 2 (1866).

54. (Washington, D.C.) *Star*, June 28, 1865, 2, June 29, 1865, 2.

55. Nuermberger, *Clays of Alabama*, 283-92; Leonard, *Lincoln's Avengers*, 202-203, 216, 220.

56. Kauffman, *American Brutus*, 342, 364. *See also, Nashville Daily Union*, May 28, 1865, 2 (in justifying the destruction of the University of Alabama, the editor sarcastically noted that it was where "the 'chivalrous' Alston was educated.").

57. Kauffman, *American Brutus*, 164-66; *Columbia Phoenix*, June 28, 1865, 2.

58. *Cincinnati Enquirer*, July 19, 1865, 3; (Washington, D.C.) *National Enquirer*, July 19, 1865, 2; *Hartford* (CT) *Courant*, July 19, 1865, 2, July 22, 1865, 3; *New York Tribune*, July 19, 1865, 4; (St. Albans) *Vermont Transcript*, July 21, 1865, 2; *Huntsville Advocate*, July 26, 1865, 2.

59. *Louisville Journal*, reprinted in *Selma Times*, July 28, 1865, quoted in Jackson, *Story of Selma*, 210.

60. *New York Herald*, July 23, 1865, 1.

61. *New York Herald*, July 23, 1865, 1, reprinted in *Boston Herald*, July 25, 1865, 4, *Mobile News*, August 13, 1865, 2, and *Boston Post*, July 28, 1865, 4.

62. *People v. Garbutt*, 17 Michigan. 9 (1868). *Accord, People v. Pine*, 2 Barb. 566 (NY, 1848). In 1858, however, President James Buchanan had commuted the death sentence of a man convicted of murder while he was drunk and changed his sentence to life imprisonment instead. *Cleveland Herald*, November 10, 1858.

63. Speer, *Portals to Hell*, 253. *See also,* John Ogden Murray, *The Immortal Six Hundred: A Story of Cruelty To Confederate Prisoners of War* (Winchester, VA, 1905), 5, 52, 88, 121-22; Alan Brown, *Haunted Georgia: Ghosts and Strange Phenomena of the Peach State* (Mechanicsburg, PA, 2008), 90-93; Cheryl Schmidt, *Separated Souls: A Novel* (New York, NY, 2005), 132-33.

64. *New York Herald*, May 3, 1865, quoted in *Nashville Press and Times*, May 16, 1865, 1. *See also, New York Tribune*, June 30, 1865, 4; (Montpelier) *Vermont Watchman and State Journal*, June 23, 1865, 1; *Bangor* (ME) *Whig & Courier*, October 3, 1865; *Nashville Union*, June 14, 1865, 1; *Mobile Times*, October 5, 1865, 7, October 7, 1865, 3, December 22, 1865, 3; (Grove Hill) *Clarke County Journal*, October 5, 1865, 2. Mainstream Republicans and virtually all northern Democrats had heretofore been cold to the idea. *See, e.g., New York Times*, March 2, 1865, 4 ("all that saves it from being criminal is its absurdity.").

65. Sarah Woolfolk Wiggins, *The Scalawag in Alabama Politics, 1865-1881* (Tuscaloosa, AL, 1977), 10-13; *Mobile Advertiser and Register,* November 11, 1865, 2; *Huntsville Advocate*, October 12, 1865, 2; Lawanda Cox and John H. Cox, *Politics, Principle, and Prejudice 1865-1866: Dilemma of Reconstruction America* (New York, NY, 1963), 151-71; Paul H. Bergeron, *Andrew Johnson's Civil Was and Reconstruction* (Knoxville, TN, 2011), 80; Eric Foner, *Reconstruction: America's Unfinished Revolution, 1863-1877* (New York, NY, 2002), 176-88; Xi Wang, *The Trial of Democracy: Black Suffrage and Northern Republicans, 1860-1910* (Athens, GA, 1997), 20-22; Eric L. McKitrick, *Andrew Johnson and Reconstruction* (New York, NY, 1988), 49-50; Frederick J. Blue, *Salmon P. Chase: A Life in Politics* (Kent, OH, Press, 1987), 254-56. Johnson was accused of treason anyway. *Nashville Union*, September 27, 1865, 2; *Memphis Appeal*, November 16, 1865, 1.

66. *Mobile Advertiser and Register,* October 1, 1865, 2, October 6, 1865, 2, October 18, 1865, 2; *Mobile Times*, October 4, 1865, 2, October 12, 1865, 5; *Huntsville Advocate*, October 4, 1865, 2-3; *New York Times,* October 10, 1865, 5, October 15, 1865, 3.

67. *Mobile News*, September 21, 1865, 2.

68. *New York Herald,* October 18, 1865, 1; (Philadelphia) *North American and United States Gazette,* October 18, 1865, 2; *Albany* (NY) *Argus,* October 19, 1865, 2; Hartford (CT) *Courant,* October 21, 1865, 2; *Baltimore Commercial,* reprinted in (Washington, D.C.) *National Republican,* October 18, 1865, 2; (Philadelphia) *Age,* October 18, 1865, 2; (Portland, ME) *Eastern Argus,* October 19, 1865, 2; (Washington, D.C.) *National Intelligencer,* October 19, 1865, 2; (Grove Hill) *Clarke County Journal,* October 19, 1865, 2; *Huntsville Advocate,* November 30, 1865, 1; *Mobile Advertiser and Register,* October 13, 1865, 1, October 25, 1865, 2, October 26, 1865, 2; (Columbus) *Ohio Statesman,* October 30, 1865, 3; *Mobile Times,* November 4, 1865, 4, October 21, 1865, 4; (New Orleans) *Picayune,* November 11, 1865, 1, December 3, 1865, 12; *Montgomery Advertiser,* November 28, 1865, 2; Saunders, *John Archibald Campbell,* 189.

69. *Chicago Times,* reprinted in (Columbus) *Ohio Statesman,* October 24, 1865, 2. Story's editorials had been suspected by some of having motivated Booth. William C. Edwards, ed., *The Lincoln Assassination—The Reward Files* (Google e-book, 2012), 101-103.

70. (New Orleans) *Picayune,* November 28, 1865, 1; (Columbus, GA) *Sun,* December 3, 1865, 2; *Mobile Advertiser and Register,* November 25, 1865, 1; Leonard, *Lincoln's Avengers,* 203.

71. (New Orleans) *Picayune,* December 6, 1865, 9; *Huntsville Advocate,* November 30, 1865, 3.

72. Regarding Smith's appointment, see *New York Herald,* June 2, 1865, 5.

73. *Chicago Tribune,* November 14, 1865, 2, reprinted in *Providence* (RI) *Press,* November 18, 1865, 3 and (Boston) *Liberator,* November 24, 1865, 187; (Columbus, GA) *Sun,* November 25, 1865, 2.

74. *Montgomery Ledger,* October 18, 1865, reprinted in *Mobile Times,* October 20, 1865, 4, and *Chicago Times,* October 25, 1865, 2.

75. *Montgomery Mail,* October 19, 1865, reprinted in *Mobile Advertiser and Register,* October 22, 1865, 1, and *New Orleans Times,* October 23, 1865, 6.

76. D.M. Scott, "Selma and Dallas County, Ala.," in *Confederate Veteran* XXIV (May, 1916), 222. *See also,* Anna M. Gayle Fry, *Memories of Old Cahaba* (Nashville, TN, 1908), 96-97.

CHAPTER 9: A WICKED PARDON

1. Albert Burton Moore, *History of Alabama and Her People,* 3 vols. (Chicago, IL, 1927), vol. 3, 465; John S. Jemison, ed., "Obituary: James Q. Smith," in *Alabama Law Journal* I (April, 1882), 117; (Selma) *State Sentinel,* January 8, 1862, 1.

2. *Marion Weekly Commonwealth,* July 17, 1863.

3. *Selma Reporter,* September 24, 1863, 2; *Boston Herald,* January 12, 1864; *Nashville Press,* April 18, 1865, 3; James Q. Smith to Henry Stansberry, September 28, 1866, Letters Received by the Attorney General, 1809-1870, Southern Law and Order, Reel 1,

Northern and Middle Districts of Alabama, Record Group 60, National Archives; James Q. Smith to Gov. Andrew Johnson, August 18, 1864, in LeRoy P. Graf and Ralph W. Haskins, eds., *The Papers of Andrew Johnson, 1864-1865*, 16 vols. (Knoxville, 1986), vol. 7, 103 and note 1; James Q. Smith to Andrew Johnson, April 10, 1865, Graf and Haskins, *Papers of Andrew Johnson*, vol. 7, 549.

4. *Ibid.* Smith subsequently wrote General U.S. Grant encouraging him to invade central and south Alabama and destroy the war-related industries at Selma. James Q. Smith to Maj. Gen. U.S. Grant, January 25, 1864, Official Records, Series 1, Vol. 32 (Part II), 214.

5. *Mobile News*, June 24, 1865, 3; (Grove Hill) *Clarke County Journal*, June 15, 1865, 2; *Louisville* (KY) *Journal*, June 24, 1865, 1; *Nashville Press and Times*, July 14, 1865, 1; (Jackson) *Mississippian*, July 26, 1865; James Q. Smith to Andrew Johnson, April 10, 1865, in Graf and Haskins, *Papers of Andrew Johnson*, vol. 7, 549; Joseph C. Bradley to Andrew Johnson, November 15, 1865, Graf and Haskins, *Papers of Andrew Johnson*, vol. 9, 387.

6. *Hartford* (CT) *Courant*, July 10, 1865, 2; *Mobile Advertiser and Register*, July 22, 1865, 2, September 22, 1865, 2, March 24, 1866, 2, May 11, 1866, Supplement, 2; *Chicago Tribune*, reprinted in *Mobile News*, September 17, 1865, 2; *Huntsville Advocate*, July 12, 1865, 3; (New Orleans) *Picayune*, September 27, 1865, 3; (Concord) *New Hampshire Patriot and Gazette*, September 20, 1865, 1; *Louisville* (KY) *Daily Journal*, July 10, 1865, 1; *Mobile Times*, October 10, 1865, 5; *Selma Times*, September 21, 1865, 1; *New York Tribune*, September 12, 1865, 4; Paul H. Bergeron, ed., *Papers of Andrew Johnson*, 8: 75. Hardy had his own axe to grind with the secessionists. In 1860, while he was the editor of the pro-Union Selma *Alabama State Sentinel*, Hardy had been indicted for criminal libel by grand juries in several south Alabama counties for publishing an editorial highly critical of William Yancey. (Selma) *Alabama State Sentinel*, July 18, 1860. In 1863, he sold his newspaper and it became the *Selma Dispatch*. (Greensboro) *Alabama Beacon*, June 5, 1863, 3. Then Hardy refugeed out of Alabama and, until recently, had been publishing a pro-Union newspaper in Jackson, Mississippi. *Jackson* (MS) *News*, reprinted in (Selma) *Mississippian*, reprinted in *Mobile Advertiser and Register*, March 12, 1865, 1.

7. John M. Parkman to Andrew Johnson, September 30, 1865, in Graf and Haskins, *Papers of Andrew Johnson*, vol. 9, 157; John M. Parkman to Andrew Johnson, May 18, 1866, Graf and Haskins, *Papers of Andrew Johnson*, vol. 10, 518; James Q. Smith to Andrew Johnson, October 23, 1865, Graf and Haskins, ed., *Papers of Andrew Johnson*, 9: 272; Lewis Parsons to Andrew Johnson, October 2, 1865, Bergeron, ed., *Papers of Andrew Johnson*, 9: 167; Virginia C. Clay to Andrew Johnson, May 5, 1866, Graf and Haskins, *Papers of Andrew Johnson*, vol. 10, 473.

8. *Mobile News*, June 9, 1865, 2.

9. (New Orleans) *Daily Picayune*, July 26, 1865, 2; 12 U.S. Statutes at Large Chap. 128, 502 (July 2, 1862).

10. *New York Tribune*, January 21, 1864, 1, September 14, 1865, 4; *Brooklyn Eagle*, November 21, 1863, January 8, 1864; *Albany* (New York) *Argus*, October 17, 1865, 2,

January 23, 1866, 2; *New York Express*, reprinted in *Macon* (GA) *Telegraph*, October 24, 1865, 1; *Chicago Times*, reprinted in (Augusta, GA) *Constitutionalist*, January 6, 1866, 1; *New York Herald*, reprinted in *Mobile Tribune*, March 8, 1864, 2; Christopher Lyle McIlwain, Sr., "United States District Judge Richard Busteed and the Alabama Klan Trials of 1872," in *Alabama Review* 65 (October, 2012): 269-70.

11. Blue, *Salmon P. Chase*, 247-307; Richard Busteed to Andrew Johnson, July 8, 1868, Graf and Haskins, *Papers of Andrew Johnson*, vol. 14, 332. *See also, Philadelphia Inquirer*, December 5, 1865, 4 (regarding Busteed's political opportunism).

12. Blue, *Salmon Chase*, 260-62.

13. *Montgomery Advertiser*, November 30, 1865, 2; Walter Fleming, *Documentary History of Reconstruction: Political, Military, Social, Religious, Educational & Industrial, 1865 to the Present Time*, 2 vols. (Cleveland, OH, 1906), vol. 2, 171-73. *See also, New Orleans Times*, November 19, 1865, 6; (New Orleans) *Picayune*, November 17, 1865, 9. Busteed had visited Alabama in August but did not hold court. (Tuscumbia) *North Alabamian*, September 1, 1865, 1; *Montgomery Ledger*, August 16, 1865.

14. (New Orleans) *Picayune*, November 17, 1865, 9, November 19, 1865; 10, December 17, 1865, 12; *Mobile Advertiser and Register*, November 22, 1865, 2, December 12, 1865, 2.

15. *Mobile Advertiser and Register*, November 10, 1865, 2, November 24, 1865, 3, November 25, 1865, 2-3, December 1, 1865, 4, December 2, 1865, 1, December 5, 1865, 2, December 12, 1865, 2, December 27, 1865, 3; (New Orleans) *Picayune*, November 25, 1865, 1, November 26, 1865, 9, November 28, 1865, 1, December 3, 1865, 2; *Mobile Times*, October 31, 1865, 4, November 25, 1865, 2, November 30, 1865, 4, December 6, 1865, 2, December 13, 1865, 6; *Montgomery Advertiser*, November 25, 1865, 2, November 28, 1865, 2; (Washington, D.C.) *National Intelligencer*, November 27, 1865, December 15, 1865, 3; (New York) *Evening Post*, November 25, 1865, 4; *New York Times,* November 7, 1865, 8, November 27, 1865, 1, December 2, 1865, 4, December 15, 1865, 1; (New York) *Commercial Advertiser*, November 27, 1865, 2; (Columbus, GA) *Sun*, November 27, 1865, 2; *Boston Advertiser*, November 27, 1865, 1; *Brooklyn Eagle*, November 30, 1865, 2; *Albany* (NY) November 27, 1865, 2; *New York Herald*, November 26, 1865, 1, 4; (Grove Hill) *Clarke County Journal*, November 30, 1865, 2; *Philadelphia Inquirer*, December 15, 1865, 1, December 18, 1865, 4; *Natchez Courier,* December 1, 1865; *New Orleans Courier*, December 1, 1865; *New Orleans Times*, November 26, 1865, 14; *Milwaukee Sentinel*, December 16, 1865, 4.

16. *New York Times,* December 10, 1865, 3; *Montgomery Advertiser*, November 30, 1865, 2, reprinted in *Mobile Advertiser and Register,* December 2, 1865, 1; *Mobile Times*, December 5, 1865, 2; (New Orleans) *Picayune*, December 3, 1865, 12; *New York Tribune*, December 11, 1865, 4; (Columbus, GA) *Sun*, December 3, 1865, 2; *New Orleans Times*, December 6, 1865, 9.

17. *Montgomery Advertiser*, November 30, 1865, 2.

18. *Montgomery Advertiser*, November 28, 1865, 2.

19. *Mobile Times*, November 30, 1865, 4, December 5, 1865, 2; *New Orleans Times*, December 6, 1865, 9; *New York Times*, December 9, 1865, 4.

20. *Montgomery Advertiser*, December 1, 1865, 2; *Montgomery Mail*, November 30, 1865, reprinted in (New Orleans) *Picayune*, December 5, 1865, 12; *Mobile Advertiser and Register,* December 3, 1865, 1; (San Francisco) *Bulletin*, December 9, 1865, 3.

21. *New Orleans Times*, December 6, 1865, 9; *Mobile Times*, December 5, 1865, 2. Busteed was also praised by the Alabama press. *Mobile Advertiser and Register,* December 12, 1865, 2.

22. *Mobile Times*, December 7, 1865, 2; *Mobile Advertiser and Register,* December 20, 1865, 3; *Montgomery Daily Advertiser*, November 30, 1865, 2; (New York) *Commercial Advertiser*, January 4, 1866, 1. By contrast, Tennessee's district judge continued to conduct treason trials in that state. (New Orleans) *Picayune*, December 30, 1865, 2; *Mobile Times*, December 30, 1865, 1. Regarding the required terms of court in Alabama, see (Newport) *Rhode Island Republican*, March 13, 1839, 4 (publishing the statute).

23. *Cleveland Leader*, December 21, 1865, 1.

24. *New York Tribune*, December 14, 1865, 1. *Accord, Bangor* (ME) *Whig & Courier*, December 19, 1865.

25. *New York Times*, October 20, 1865, 1; *Albany Journal*, reprinted in (Concord) *New Hampshire Statesman*, December 8, 1865; *Mobile Daily Times,* December 16, 1865, 4.

26. *New York Times,* November 20, 1865, 1, December 5, 1865, 1, December 20, 1865, 4; *Brownlow's Knoxville Whig and Rebel Ventilator*, November 29, 1865, 2; (New Orleans) *Picayune*, November 21, 1865, 2, November 24, 1865, 2; November 25, 1865, 3, December 9, 1865, 1, December 10, 1865, 1. *Mobile Advertiser and Register,* November 28, 1865, 1-2, December 7, 1865, 2, December 13, 1865, 2, December 22, 1865, 2; *Huntsville Advocate*, November 30, 1865, 1-2; *Mobile Times*, December 1, 1865, 2, December 7, 1865, 2, December 9, 1865, 4, December 20, 1865, 6-7, December 22, 1865, 3; *Huntsville Advocate,* December 21, 1865, 2.

27. (Tuscumbia) *North Alabamian*, November 17, 1865, 2. *See generally,* Leonard, *Lincoln's Avengers*, 161, 201.

28. (Washington, D.C.) *National Republican*, December 27, 1885, 1; *New York Times,* December 20, 1865, 1; *Cleveland Leader*, December 20, 1865. 1; (Washington, D.C.) *Star*, December 26, 1865, 2, December 29, 1865, 2. *See also,* (Augusta, GA) *Constitutionalist*, November 8, 1865, 1; *Memphis Appeal*, November 14, 1865, 1; *Anderson* (SC) *Intelligencer*, November 23, 1865, 3; *Nashville Union*, December 27, 1865, 2. Semmes was released in 1866. *See generally,* Jonathan Truman Dorris, *Pardon and Amnesty Under Lincoln and Johnson* (Chapel Hill, NC, 1977), 178-86.

29. *Brownlow's Knoxville Whig and Rebel Ventilator*, January 3, 1866, 2.

30. *Nashville Union*, January 2, 1866, 2, January 3, 1866, 1, January 19, 1866, 2, February 18, 1866, 1.

31. *New York Tribune*, January 8, 1866, 4; Leonard, *Lincoln's Avengers*, 207.

32. (Nashville, TN) *Union and American*, December 24, 1865, 1, January 11, 1866, 2, February 8, 1866, 2, February 17, 1866, 2, February 25, 1866, 1; (Columbus) *Ohio Statesman*, February 8, 1866, 2, February 13, 1866, 1; *Nashville Union*, February 18, 1866, 1.

33. (Philadelphia) *Telegraph*, February 24, 1866, 1, March 6, 1866, 2; (Nashville, TN) *Union and American*, February 25, 1866, 2. *See also*, George Rutherglen, *Civil Rights in the Shadow of Slavery: The Constitution, Common Law and the Civil Rights Act of 1866* (New York, NY, 2013), 3-70; Leonard, *Lincoln's Avengers*, 208; McKitrick, *Andrew Johnson and Reconstruction*, 274-325; Bergeron, *Andrew Johnson's Civil War and Reconstruction*, 99-144; Cox and Cox, *Politics, Principle, and Prejudice 1865-1866*, 17273, 195-96, 201.

34. *Cleveland Leader*, April 3, 1866, 1, April 4, 1866, 2; (Philadelphia) *Telegraph*, April 4, 1866, 2, April 5, 1866, 2, April 6, 1866, 2; *Nashville Union*, April 1, 1866, 2, April 4, 1866, 2; (Washington, D.C.) *National Republican*, April 3, 1866, 2; (Nashville) *Union and American*, April 4, 1866, 2; (New York) *Sun*, April 4, 1866, 2; *Mobile Advertiser and Register*, April 10, 1866, 2; Leonard, *Lincoln Avengers*, 208-209.

35. (New York) *Sun*, April 4, 1866, 2.

36. *Mobile Advertiser and Register*, March 20, 1866, 3, March 21, 1866, 3, April 10, 1866, 2; *Montgomery Advertiser*, March 9, 1866, 2, April 12, 1866, 4; *Nashville Union*, April 21, 1866, 2.

37. *Mobile Advertiser and Register*, April 7, 1866, 3, April 14, 1866, 3, April 18, 1866, 2, April 20, 1866, 2, May 25, 1866, 4, June 15, 1866, 1; *Huntsville Independent*, June 3, 1866, 3; *Huntsville Advocate*, May 26, 1866, 2; *Montgomery Advertiser*, April 10, 1866, 4, May 26, 1866, 2; (New Orleans) *Picayune*, April 17, 1866, 2; *Nashville Union*, April 21, 1866, 2; (Washington, D.C.) *National Intelligencer*, April 26, 1866. No indictment was ever rendered against Dexter, and Busteed ultimately discharged him. *Nashville Union and Dispatch*, May 30, 1867, 2.

38. *Montgomery Advertiser*, March 10, 1866, 4-5, May 31, 1866, 3, June 1, 1866, 3, June 2, 1866, 3, June 5, 1866, 3, June 9, 1866, 3, June 10, 1866, 3.

39. *Nashville Union*, September 1, 1865, 2, November 17, 1865, 2, December 1, 1865, 2; (Nashville) *Union and American*, December 24, 1865, 1, December 30, 1865, 1, January 19, 1866, 3; *Brownlow's Knoxville Whig and Rebel Ventilator*, December 20, 1865, 2; Robert Tracy McKenzie, *Lincolnites and Rebels: A Divided Town in the American Civil War* (New York, NY, 2006), 200-201; Stephen C. Neff, *Justice In Blue and Gray: A Legal History of the Civil War* (Cambridge, MA, 2010), 219.

40. *Mobile Advertiser and Register*, June 15, 1865, 2. *See also*, (New Orleans) *Picayune*, June 20, 1866, 2; *Montgomery Advertiser*, May 26, 1866, 3 (listing the names of the grand jurors); *Huntsville Advocate*, June 2, 1866, 3 (same). Regarding Forsyth, *see* Lonnie A. Burnett, *The Pen Makes a Good Sword: John Forsyth of the Mobile Register* (Tuscaloosa, AL, 2006).

41. *Mobile Advertiser and Register*, June 15, 1865, 2. Regarding Glasscock, *see* (AL) *Tri-Weekly Sentinel*, September 4, 1867 (listing Glasscock as a member of the State Republican Executive Committee); Baggett, *Scalawags*, 74; Owen, *Alabama History and Dictionary of Alabama Biography*, vol. 3, 662; United States Congress, *Report of the Joint Select Committee To Inquire Into the Condition of Affairs in the Late Insurrectionary States: The Ku-Klux Conspiracy in Alabama* (Washington: U.S. Government Printing Office, 1872), (hereinafter, "Klan Testimony"), 1452.

42. *Montgomery Advertiser*, May 29, 1866, 3.

43. *Montgomery Advertiser*, May 31, 1866, 1.

44. *Montgomery Advertiser*, May 31, 1866, 1.

45. *Montgomery Advertiser,* May 31, 1866, 3.

46. (Montgomery) *State Sentinel*, May 30, 1867, 2; *Montgomery Advertiser*, June 5, 1866, 3, June 16, 1866, 2, June 17, 1866, 2, September 12, 1866, 2; *Huntsville Advocate*, June 9, 1866, 2, June 13, 1866, 2; *Mobile Advertiser and Register,* June 10, 1866, 2, June 15, 1866, 4, June 17, 1866, 2, June 21, 1866, 2; (Greensboro) *Alabama Beacon*, June 16, 1866, 2; *Montgomery Mail*, June 10, 1866, reprinted in *Mobile Advertiser and Register,* June 15, 1866, 4; (New Orleans) *Picayune*, June 12, 1866, 2, June 20, 1866, 2; (Washington, D.C.) *National Intelligencer*, June 18, 1866, 2; *New York Times,* June 17, 1866, 3; *Montgomery Mail*, reprinted in (New York) *Commercial Advertiser*, June 12, 1866, 4, (Washington, D.C.) *National Republican*, June 15, 1866, 2; (Macon) *Georgia Weekly Telegraph*, June 25, 1866, 1.

47. *United States v. George W. Gayle, et al.*, Case No. 1073, United States District Court for the Middle District of Alabama, May Term, 1866, National Archives.

48. (New Orleans) *Picayune*, June 12, 1866, 2.

49. *Montgomery Advertiser*, June 5, 1866, 3, June 6, 1866, 3; *Boston Advertiser*, June 20, 1866, 1; *Mobile Advertiser and Register,* June 10, 1866, 2; *Huntsville Advocate*, June 9, 1866, 2; (New Orleans) *Picayune*, June 12, 1866, 2, June 20, 1866, 2; (Hartford) *Connecticut Courant*, June 23, 1866, 1; *New York Times,* June 17, 1866, 3.

50. *New York Times,* May 22, 1866, 2; *Milwaukee Sentinel*, July 16, 1866; (New Orleans) *Picayune*, June 20, 1866, 2.

51. Regarding the effect of a pardon, *see, e.g., Huntsville Advocate*, August 31, 1865, 4.

52. (Washington, D.C.) *National Intelligencer*, April 21, 1866; *Montgomery Advertiser*, April 20, 1866, 4, April 24, 1866, 3; Nuermberger, *Clays of Alabama*, 280-93; Leonard, *Lincoln's Avengers*, 212-13; Virginia Clay-Clopton, *A Belle of the Fifties: Memoirs of Mrs. Clay of Alabama* (Tuscaloosa, AL, 1999), 372-74.

53. *Nashville Union*, April 8, 1866, 1.

54. (Washington, D.C.) *National Intelligencer*, reprinted in *Mobile Advertiser and Register,* April 26, 1866, 2. *See also, Montgomery Advertiser*, April 20, 1866, 4; *Huntsville Advocate*, May 2, 1866, 2.

55. Dorris, *Pardon and Amnesty Under Lincoln and Johnson*, 263-71. *Cf.*, (New Orleans) *Picayune*, April 13, 1866, 3 (reporting a ruling by District Judge Trigg in Tennessee that a military parole was no defense to a treason charge or any other criminal charge); *Mobile Advertiser and Register,* April 19, 1866, 2 (same); *Montgomery Advertiser*, April 24, 1866, 2 (same). For discussion of the *Milligan* decision, see Robert Bruce Murray, *Legal Cases of the Civil War* (Mechanicsburg, PA, 2003), 75-84.

56. *New York Herald*, reprinted in *Boston Advertiser*, April 21, 1866, (Savannah) *News and Herald*, May 12, 1866, *Montgomery Advertiser*, April 25, 1866, 8, *Huntsville Independent*, April 27, 1866, 1. See also, *Huntsville Independent*, May 9, 1866, 1.

57. (Mifflintown, PA) *Juniata Sentinel*, May 16, 1866, 2.

58. *Milwaukee Sentinel,* April 20, 1866. See also, *Mobile Advertiser and Register,* April 28, 1866, 2.

59. (Washington, D.C.) *National Intelligencer,* April 18, 1866.

60. *Cleveland Herald,* May 15, 1866; *Mobile Advertiser and Register,* May 12, 1866, 2, May 31, 1866, 2, June 5, 1866, 2, 4, June 8, 1866, 2, June 12, 1866, 2, June 13, 1866, 2, June 14, 1866, 2, 4, June 15, 1866, 1, 4, June 19, 1866, 2; *Huntsville Advocate,* May 16, 1866, 3, May 19, 1866, 3, May 31, 1866, 2; *New York Times,* May 12, 1866, 2, May 27, 1866, 5; *Montgomery Advertiser,* May 20, 1866, 2, May 31, 1866, 3; *Selma Messenger,* June 7, 1866, 2; (Grove Hill) *Clarke County Journal,* May 17, 1866, 2; (New Orleans) *Picayune,* May 19, 1866, 12, May 30, 1866, 4; Dorris, *Pardon and Amnesty Under Lincoln and Johnson,* 294-96.

61. (Greensboro) *Alabama Beacon,* June 30, 1866, 3.

62. (Grove Hill) *Clarke County Journal,* June 28, 1866, 2; *Boston Advertiser,* June 18, 1866. See also, *Montgomery Advertiser,* June 26, 1866, 2, July 4, 1866, 2 (regarding D.R. Lindsay of Alabama); *Little Rock Gazette,* July 2, 1866. See generally, McKitrick, *Andrew Johnson and Reconstruction,* 142-53.

63. McKitrick. *Andrew Johnson and Reconstruction,* 394; Wiggins, *Scalawag,* 18.

64. *Mobile Advertiser and Register,* September 14, 1866, 1, September 15, 1866, 4; *Salt Lake Telegraph,* September 6, 1866; (New Orleans) *Picayune,* September 6, 1866, 1; *Montgomery Advertiser,* September 11, 1866, 3; Trefousse, *Andrew Johnson,* 263-64.

65. (Washington, D.C.) *National Intelligencer,* September 15, 1866; *Montgomery Advertiser,* September 22, 1866, 1; (New Orleans) *Picayune,* September 15, 1866, 4. See also, *Mobile Advertiser and Register,* September 11, 1866, 2, September 14, 1866, 2, 4, September 22, 1866, 2, September 27, 1866, 2; *Montgomery Advertiser,* September 16, 1866, 2, September 18, 1866, 2, September 21, 1866, 2; Trefousse, *Andrew Johnson,* 264-67.

66. *Mobile Advertiser and Register,* October 28, 1866, Supplement, 2; (New Orleans) *Picayune,* September 12, 1866, 4, September 23, 1866, 12; Wiggins, *Scalawag in Alabama Politics,* 18; Leonard, *Lincoln's Avengers,* 229-31; McKitrick, *Andrew Johnson and Reconstruction,* 428-48; Gary Boulard, *The Swing Around the Circle: Andrew Johnson and the Train Ride that Destroyed a Presidency* (Bloomington, IN, 2008).

67. *Impeachment Investigation: Testimony Taken Before the Judiciary Committee of the House of Representatives In the Investigation of the Charges Against Andrew Johnson, Second Session, Thirty-ninth Congress, and First Session, Fortieth Congress,* 565.

68. (Mobile) *Nationalist,* March 7, 1867, 2. There is no known evidence supporting this charge.

69. *New York Times,* December 25, 1866, 1 (McArthur was selected as a member of the grand jury instead).

70. *Montgomery Advertiser,* December 6, 1866, 3, December 7, 1866, 1-2.

71. *Montgomery Mail,* reprinted in (New Orleans) *Picayune,* December 18, 1866, 9.

72. *Macon (GA)Telegraph,* December 13, 1866, 2; (Philadelphia) *Telegraph,* December 28, 1866, 1; (Harrisburg) *Weekly Patriot and Union,* January 1, 1867, 1.

73. *Mobile Advertiser and Register,* December 16, 1866, 2; (Baltimore) *Sun,* December 19, 1866, 4; *Charleston News,* December 19, 1866, 1; *New York Times,* December 21,

1866, 2; (Washington, D.C.) *Star*, December 24, 1866, 1; *Edgefield Advertiser*, December 26, 1866, 1; (Hartford) *Connecticut Courant*, December 29, 1866, 1; *Portsmouth* (NH) *Journal of Literature and Politics*, December 29, 1866, 2; (Stroudsburg, PA) *Jeffersonian*, January 10, 1867, 2; (San Francisco) *Bulletin*, January 23, 1867, 4; (Portland) *Oregonian*, February 1, 1867, 1.

74. *Impeachment Investigation*, 565-66. All of the records regarding Gayle's pardon can be found in Record Group 204, E-1, Gayle, File B-632, National Archives, Washington, D.C. These veterans included McArthur, George P. Rex, George W. Colby, C.A. Colby, Henry Cochran, M. J. Gibson, H.H.P. Randall, and John F. Burch. *Ibid.* In addition to being planters, a common denominator among these men is that they supported Andrew Johnson and his racially conservative reconstruction policies. *Cf.*, Richard Bailey, *Neither Carpetbaggers Nor Scalawags: Black Officeholders During the Reconstruction of Alabama, 1867-1878* (Montgomery, AL, 1991), 44, 213 (mentioning George Colby and George P. Rex, an assessor); Lawrence N. Powell, *New Masters: Northern Planters During the Civil War and Reconstruction* (New York, NY, 1998), 186, 206 (mentioning George Colby); Hardy, *Selma*, 92 (Rex also served as sheriff of Dallas County).

75. One possibility is that Gayle had leased his plantations to them on favorable terms. (Washington, D.C.) *Star*, January 17, 1866, 1 (reporting that McArthur had leased five Alabama plantations).

76. *New York Tribune*, January 8, 1867, 1; (Washington, D.C.) *National Republican*, February 8, 1867, 2; McKitrick, *Andrew Johnson and Reconstruction*, 486-93.

77. *Impeachment Investigation*, 566. It further stated that affidavits of several of Gayle's Masonic "companions" had been submitted to the Attorney General "to establish that fact." These were not supplied to Congress.

78. *Impeachment Investigation*, 567.

79. *Impeachment Investigation*, 568.

80. *Memphis Appeal*, February 5, 1863, 1, April 18, 1863, 1, September 11, 1863, 1, May 28, 1864, 2; (New Orleans) *Picayune*, February 27, 1863, 2, March 28, 1863, 2, May 20, 1863, 2; *Montgomery Advertiser*, reprinted in *Columbus* (GA) *Enquirer*, November 13, 1863, 2; (Greensboro) *Alabama Beacon*, December 19, 1862, 2, March 24, 1863, 2, April 3, 1863, 2; (Grove Hill) *Clarke County Journal*, November 13, 1862, 2, September 17, 1863, 2, October 29, 18623, 2; *Huntsville Confederate*, November 30, 1863, 2; *Selma Reporter*, November 20, 1861, 2, February 21, 1862, 2, November 13, 1862, 1, February 28, 1863, 1, September 5, 1863, 1, September 9, 1863, 1-2; *Mobile Advertiser and Register,* July 17, 1863, 2, October 13, 1863, 1; (New Orleans) *Picayune*, April 24, 1863, 2; *Mobile Tribune*, April 7, 1863, September 8, 1863, 2; *Mobile Tribune*, reprinted in *Columbus* (GA) *Enquirer*, October 1, 1863, 2; *Mobile Times*, September 9, 1863, 2, September 13, 1863, 2; (Jackson, MS) *Southern Crisis*, January 1, 1863; Bessie Martin, *A Rich Man's War, a Poor Man's Fight: Desertion of Alabama Troops from the Confederate Army* (Tuscaloosa, AL, 2003), 137-51, 161-62, 174-87.

81. *Impeachment Investigation*, 568; *Chicago Tribune*, June 10, 1867, 1.

82. 1860 Federal Census of Alabama, Dallas County, Series M653, Roll 8, 944 (Gayle owned $6,000 in real estate and $4,000 in personal property).

83. The court system in Dallas County had continued to function during the war. *Selma Reporter*, December 4, 1862, 2.

84. *See, e.g., Campbell v. Campbell*, 39 Alabama 312 (1864).

85. John Craig Stewart, *Governors of Alabama* (Gretna, LA, 1975), 83; Wiggins, *Scalawag in Alabama Politics*, 12-13; *Journal of the Proceedings of Convention of the State of Alabama: Held in the City of Montgomery, on Tuesday, September 12, 1865 to September 30, 1865* (Montgomery, AL, 1865).

86. *Impeachment Investigation*, 568-69.

87. *Impeachment Investigation*, 569.

88. (Philadelphia) *Telegraph*, February 20, 1867, 1; (Dayton, OH) *Empire*, February 23, 1867, 1; (New Haven, CT) *Columbian Register*, June 1, 1867, 3; Jampoler, *Last Lincoln Conspirator*, 156; Leonard, *Lincoln's Avengers*, 235-39.

89. *Mobile Advertiser and Register*, February 21, 1867, 2, February 22, 1867, 2, February 26, 1867, 2, March 28, 1867, 4; *Montgomery Advertiser*, February 19, 1867, 1, February 20, 1867, 2, February 26, 1867, 2; (Mobile) *Nationalist*, February 21, 1867, 2, February 28, 1867, March 7, 1867, 2. *See generally*, Bergeron, *Andrew Johnson's Civil War and Reconstruction*, 146-51; Hearn, *Impeachment of Andrew Johnson*, 115-23; Foner, *Reconstruction*, 274-76; Wiggins, *Scalawag in Alabama Politics*, 19.

90. (New York) *Sun*, March 25, 1867, 1 (publishing an order by General Sickles regarding the new justice system under martial law); (Philadelphia) *Telegraph*, June 17, 1867, 6 (publishing the Attorney General's opinion regarding military authority under the Act). *See generally*, McKitrick, *Andrew Johnson and Reconstruction*, 449-85; Wiggins, *Scalawag in Alabama Politics*, 19.

91. *Impeachment Investigation*, 570.

92. *Impeachment Investigation*, 569-70.

93. *See, e.g., Albany* (NY) *Journal*, June 1, 1867, 2; (Washington, D.C.) *National Republican*, June 4, 1867, 1; *Emporia* (KS) *News*, June 14, 1867, 2 ("His wife worried the President a long time before she got the desired pardon.").

94. Hans Louis Trefousse, *Andrew Johnson: A Biography* (New York, NY, 1997), 9, 17, 60, 286-87, 395.

95. Presidential Pardons, Gayle, T-967, Reel 3, Vol. 8, 353, National Archives, Washington, D.C.; (Philadelphia) *Telegraph*, June 7, 1867, 1; *Chicago Tribune*, June 6, 1867, 1; *Cincinnati Gazette*, June 6, 1867, 3.

96. G.W. Gayle to Henry Stanbery, May 11, 1867, Record Group 204, E-1, Gayle, File B-632, National Archives, Washington, D.C.

97. *Selma Times*, reprinted in (Augusta, GA) *Constitutionalist*, May 17, 1867, 3. The two Republicans were Alabama native Benjamin Franklin Saffold, another son of Reuben Saffold, and Rhode Island native John Russell Fairbanks. *Id. See also, Montgomery Advertiser*, April 7, 1867, 2.

98. *Ibid.*

99. *United States v. Gayle, supra*, (plea of pardon); (Montgomery) *State Sentinel*, May 31, 1867, 2.

100. *New York Herald,* May 29, 1867, 3, 6; (Baltimore) *Sun,* May 30, 1867, 1; (Winnsboro, SC) *Fairfield Herald,* June 19, 1867, 4; *Alexandria* (VA) *Gazette,* May 30, 1867, 2; *Ebensburg* (PA) *Alleghenian,* June 13, 1867, 2; (Washington, D.C.) *National Intelligencer,* May 30, 1867, 3; (Galveston, TX) *Flake's Bulletin,* June 22, 1867, 5; (Harrisburg, PA) *Patriot,* May 30, 1867, 2; *Richmond Whig,* May 31, 1867, 2; *Charleston Courier,* June 1, 1867, 2; (Columbia, SC) *Phoenix,* June 4, 1867, p. 2; (Washington, D.C.) *National Republican,* June 4, 1867, p. 1; (Worchester, MA) *National Aegis,* June 1, 1867, 3; (Philadelphia) *North American,* June 6, 1867, 1; *Cleveland Herald,* June 5, 1867; *New York Times,* May 31, 1867, 1. For mention of the dismissal in Alabama, *see Montgomery Advertiser,* May 28, 1867, 3; *Mobile Advertiser and Register,* May 30, 1867, 2; (Selma) *Messenger,* May 31, 1867, 3; (Montgomery) *Alabama State Sentinel,* June 6, 1867, 1.

101. *Albany* (NY) *Journal,* June 1, 1867, 2; (Washington, D.C.) *National Republican,* June 4, 1867, 1.

102. (Des Moines) *Iowa Register,* June 9, 1867, 2.

103. (Clearfield, PA) *Raftman's Journal,* June 5, 1867, 2.

CHAPTER 10: A MEAN MAN IS DEAD

1. David Miller DeWitt, *The Impeachment and Trial of Andrew Johnson* (New York, NY, 1903), 306; Guttridge and Neff, *Dark Union,* 191.

2. *Impeachment Investigation,* 565, 570; (Baltimore) *Sun,* June 3, 1867; *Chicago Tribune,* June 10, 1867, 1; (Dayton, OH) *Empire,* May 31, 1867, 1; *Charleston* (SC) *News,* June 4, 1867, 1.

3. *New York Herald,* June 7, 1867, 3.

4. (Montgomery) *Alabama State Sentinel,* May 31, 1867, 2.

5. (Montgomery) *Alabama State Sentinel,* May 31, 1867, 2.

6. (Montgomery) *Alabama State Sentinel,* May 31, 1867, 2.

7. (Washington, D.C.) *National Republican,* March 2, 1868, 1; (Washington, D.C.) *Star,* March 2, 1868, 1; David O. Stewart, *Impeached: The Trial of President Johnson and the Fight For Lincoln's Legacy* (New York, NY, 2009), 104-316; Paul N. Herbert, *God Knows All Your Names: Stories in American History* (Bloomington, IN, 2011), 219; Leonard, *Lincoln's Avengers,* 290.

8. (Washington, D.C.) *Star,* May 16, 1868, 1; *New York Tribune,* May 18, 1868, 1. *See generally,* Chester G. Hearn, *The Impeachment of Andrew Johnson* (Jefferson, NC, 2007), 198-201; Leonard, *Lincoln's Avengers,* 281; McKitrick, *Andrew Johnson and Reconstruction,* 494-510.

9. *See, e.g., Taylor v. State,* 42 Ala. 529 (1868); *Manaway v. State,* 44 Ala. 375 (1870); *Miller v. State,* 45 Alabama 24 (1871). Regarding one of those cases, *Logan v. State, see* J. Mills Thornton, III, "Alabama Emancipates," in Raymond Arsenault and Orville Vernon Burton, eds., *Dixie Redux: Essays in Honor of Sheldon Hackney* (Montgomery, AL, 2013), 90.

10. *Mobile Register*, March 9, 1870, 2.

11. (Worchester) *Massachusetts Spy*, April 23, 1875, 2. *See also,* (Middleton, CT) *Constitution*, April 19, 1875, 2; *Trenton* (NJ) *State Gazette*, April 23, 1875, 2; *Lowell* (MA) *Citizen and News*, April 30, 1875, 1; *Dallas* (TX) *Weekly Herald*, April 24, 1875, 1; *Selma Times*, reprinted in *Galveston* (TX) *News*, April 25, 1875; *Red Cloud* (Nebraska) *Chief*, April 29, 1875, 1; *St. Albans* (VT) *Messenger*, May 4, 1875, 1; (Portland) *Oregonian*, May 14, 1875, 4; *Portsmouth* (NH) *Journal of Literature and Politics*, May 15, 1875, 1; *Weekly* (Troy) *Kansas Chief*, June 3, 1875, 1.

12. *Jackson* (MI) *Weekly Citizen*, April 20, 1875, 1.

13. (Selma) *Southern Argus*, September 16, 1875, 3 (reporting resolutions adopted by the Selma Bar following Gayle's death).

14. Fry, *Memories of Old Cahaba*, 87–88, 97. Nelson Miles was a Union army officer who became the commander of Fort Monroe and was vilified in the South for allegedly mistreating Davis. Joey Frazier, *Jefferson Davis: Confederate President* (Philadelphia, PA, 2001), 64.

15. *See, e.g., Chicago Tribune*, July 19, 1925, 8, July 19, 1930, 6, January 26, 1956, 3; *Birmingham News*, January 5, 1935, July 24, 1961; *Selma Times-Journal*, May 29, 1938. *Atlanta Journal and the Atlanta Constitution,* December 6, 1964, 2B; *Washington* (D.C.) *Times*, May 7, 2009.

16. *See, e.g.,* Hatch, *Protecting the President*, 39; Hanchett, *Lincoln Murder Conspiracies*, 29; Goodrich and Goodrich, *Day Dixie Died*, 77; Kauffman, *American Brutus*, 466, n. 3.

17. Leonard, *Lincoln's Avengers*, 249–52.

Bibliography

Primary Sources

Unpublished

Alabama Department of Archives and History
Andrew Barry Moore Papers
John Gill Shorter Papers
Joshua Burns Moore Journal
Leroy Pope Walker Papers
Robert Miller Patton Papers
Sarah Lowe Davis Diary
Sarah R. Espy Journal
Thomas Hill Watts Papers
William Cooper Diary

David M. Rubenstein Rare Book & Manuscript Library, Duke University
C.C. Clay, Jr., Papers
John Forsyth Papers

Hoole Special Collections Library, University of Alabama
Basil Manly Papers

Huntsville-Madison County Public Library, Huntsville, Alabama
Catherine M. Fennell Diary

Library of Congress
Abraham Lincoln Papers

National Archives

Compiled Service Records, Civil War
Office of Provost Marshal General Head Quarters Department of the Gulf, M416,
File 16182, George Gayle.
Presidential Pardons, Gayle, T-967.

Record Groups, 60, 153, and 204.
   United States v. George Washington Gayle, et al., Criminal Case # 1073, United
   States District Court for the Middle District of Alabama, 1866 Term.

Rush Rhees Library, University of Rochester
   William H. Seward Papers

Southern Historical Collection, Wilson Library, University of North Carolina
   John Archibald Campbell Papers
   William Cooper Diary

Special Collections Library, Clemson University
   Papers of Dixon Hall Lewis

Published

   Axford, Faye Acton, ed. *The Journals of Thomas Hubbard Hobbs.* Tuscaloosa:
University of Alabama, 1976.
   _____, ed. *"To Lochaber Na Nair"*: *Southerners View the Civil War.* Athens,
AL: Athens Publishing Company, 1986.
   Basler, Roy P., ed. *The Collected Works of Abraham Lincoln.* New Brunswick, NJ:
Rutgers University Press, 1953.
   Basler, Roy, and Carl Sandburg, eds. *Abraham Lincoln: His Speeches and Writings.*
Cleveland, OH: World Publishing Co., 1946.
   Beck, Brandon H., ed. *Third Alabama!: The Civil War Memoir of Brigadier General
Cullen Andrews Battle, CSA.* Tuscaloosa: University of Alabama Press, 2000.
   Bergeron, Paul H., ed. *The Papers of Andrew Johnson.* Knoxville: University of
Tennessee Press, 1991.
   Berlin, Ira, Barbara J. Fields, Thavolia Glymph, Joseph P. Reidy, and Leslie S.
Rowland, eds. *Freedom: A Documentary History of Emancipation 1861–1867.* New
York: Cambridge University Press, 1985.
   Brainerd, David. *Illustrated Life, Services, Martyrdom, and Funeral of Abraham
Lincoln: Sixteenth President of the United States.* Philadelphia, PA: T.B. Peterson and
Brothers, 1865.
   Chesnut, Mary, and Woodward, C. Vann, ed. *Mary Chesnut's Civil War.* New Haven,
CT: Yale University Press, 1981.
   Chesnut, Mary Boykin, and Williams, Ben Ames, ed. *A Diary from Dixie.* Cambridge,
MA: Harvard University Press, 2002.
   Clay-Clopton, Virginia A. *Belle of the Fifties: Memoirs of Mrs. Clay of Alabama.*
Tuscaloosa: University of Alabama Press, 1999.
   Colfax, Schuyler. *Life and Principles of Abraham Lincoln.* Philadelphia: James B.
Rodgers Printer, 1865.

Cooper, Jr., William J., ed. *Jefferson Davis: The Essential Writings*. New York: Random House, 2004.

Crist, Lynda Lasswell, ed. *The Papers of Jefferson Davis: 1861*. Baton Rouge: Louisiana State University Press, 1992.

Cutler, Wayne, ed. *Correspondence of James K. Polk*. Nashville: Vanderbilt University Press, 1979.

DeWitt, David Miller. *The Impeachment and Trial of Andrew Johnson*. New York: MacMillan Co., 1903.

Dickerson, Donna L. *The Reconstruction Era: Primary Documents on Events from 1865 to 1877*. Westport, CT: Greenwood Press, 2003.

DuBose, John Witherspoon. *Alabama's Tragic Decade: Ten Years of Alabama 1865–1874*. Birmingham: Webb Book Co., 1940.

Edwards, William C., ed. *The Lincoln Assassination – The Reward Files*. Google e-book, 2012.

Edwards, William C., and Edward Steers, Jr., eds. *The Lincoln Assassination: The Evidence*. Urbana: University of Illinois Press, 2009.

Fehrenbacher, Don E., and Virginia Fehrenbacher, eds. *Recollected Words of Abraham Lincoln*. Stanford, CA: Stanford University Press, 1996.

Fleming, Walter. *Documentary History of Reconstruction: Political, Military, Social, Religious, Educational & Industrial, 1865 to the Present Time*. Cleveland, OH: Arthur H. Clark Co., 1906.

Fry, Anna M. Gayle. *Memories of Old Cahaba*. Nashville: Pub. House of the M.E. Church, South, 1908.

Genoways, Ted, and Hugh H. Genoways. *A Perfect Picture of Hell: Eyewitness Accounts By Civil War Prisoners From the 12th Iowa*. Iowa City: University of Iowa Press, 2001.

Gienapp, William E., and Erica L. Gienapp, eds. *The Civil War Diary of Gideon Welles, Lincoln's Secretary of the Navy*. Urbana: Knox College Lincoln Studies Center and the University of Illinois Press, 2014.

Graf, LeRoy P., Ralph W. Haskins, and Paul H. Bergeron, eds. *The Papers of Andrew Johnson*. 16 vols. Knoxville: University of Tennessee Press, 1967–2000.

Hardy, John. *Selma: Her Institutions, and Her Men*. Selma, AL: Bert Neville and Clarence DeBray, 1957.

Harwell, Richard Barksdale, ed. *Kate: The Journal of a Confederate Nurse*. Baton Rouge: Louisiana State University Press, 1998.

Hay, Melba Porter, ed. *The Papers of Henry Clay*. Lexington: University Press of Kentucky, 1991.

Herndon, William H., and Jesse W. Weik. *Abraham Lincoln: The True Story of a Great Life*. Springfield, IL: Herndon's Lincoln Publishing Co., 1888.

Hubbs, G. Ward. *Voices From Company D: Diaries By the Greensboro Guards, Fifth Alabama Regiment, Army of Northern Virginia*. Athens: University of Georgia Press, 2003.

Johnson, Rossiter, and John Howard Brown, eds. *The Twentieth Century Biographical Dictionary of Notable Americans*. Boston: Biographical Society, 1904.

Jones, John Beauchamp. *A Rebel War Clerk's Diary At the Confederate States Capital.* Philadelphia, PA: J.B. Lippincott & Co., 1866.

Linden, Glenn, and Virginia Linden, eds. *Disunion, War, Defeat, and Recovery in Alabama: The Journal of Augustus Benners, 1850–1885.* Macon: Mercer University Press, 2007.

McWhiney, Grady, Warner O. Moore, Jr., and Robert F. Pace, eds. *"Fear God and Walk Humbly": The Agricultural Journals of James Mallory, 1843–1877.* Tuscaloosa: University of Alabama Press, 1997.

Miers, Earl Schenck. *Lincoln Day By Day: A Chronology, 1809–1865.* Washington, DC: Lincoln Sesquicentennial Commission, 1960.

Miller, Stephen F. *Heads of the Alabama Legislature at the Session of 1842–3.* Tuscaloosa: M.D.J. Slade, 1843.

Moore, Thomas. *Lalla Rookh: An Oriental Romance.* New York: Home Book Co., 1800.

Mosby, John Singleton. *The Memoirs of Colonel John Singleton Mosby.* Boston: Little, Brown, and Company, 1917.

Moser, Harold D., ed. *Papers of Andrew Jackson.* 17 vols. Knoxville: University of Tennessee Press, 1991.

Murray, John Ogden. *The Immortal Six Hundred: A Story of Cruelty To Confederate Prisoners of War.* Winchester, VA: Eddy Press Corp., 1905.

Neeley, Mary Ann, ed. *The Works of Matthew Blue, Montgomery's First Historian.* Montgomery, AL: NewSouth Books, 2010.

Niven, John, ed. *The Salmon P. Chase Papers: Journals, 1829–1872.* 2 vols. Kent, OH: Kent State University Press, 1993.

Official Proceedings of the National Democratic Convention. Dayton, Ohio: Daily Journal Book and Job Rooms, 1882.

Palmer, Beverly Wilson, ed. *The Selected Papers of Charles Sumner.* Boston, MA: Northeastern University Press, 1990.

_____. *The Selected Papers of Thaddeus Stevens: April 1865–August 1868.* Pittsburgh. PA: University of Pittsburg Press, 1998.

Palmer, Thomas Waverly. *A Register of the Officers and Students of the University of Alabama, 1831–1901.* Tuscaloosa: University of Alabama, 1901.

Pitman, Benn. *The Assassination of President Lincoln and the Trial of the Conspirators.* Cincinnati: Moore, Wilsatch & Baldwin, 1865.

Proceedings of the National Democratic Convention, held in Baltimore, on the 5th of May, 1840. Baltimore: Office of Blair & Rives, 1840.

Reid, Whitelaw. *After the War: A Southern Tour: May 1, 1865, to May 1, 1866.* London: Sampson Low, Son, & Marston, 1866.

Rohr, Nancy M., ed. *Incidents of the War: The Civil War Journal of Mary Jane Chadick.* Huntsville, AL: Silver Threads Publishing, 2005.

Simon, John Y., ed. *The Papers of Ulysses S. Grant.* 24 vols. Carbondale: Southern Illinois University Press, 1967–1984.

DeBow, J. D. B., ed. "Southern Convention at Savannah." In *DeBow's Review and Industrial Resources, Statistics, etc.,* vol. 22, 85–96. New Oleans: DeBow, 1857.

Speech of *Mr. Calhoun, of South Carolina, on his resolutions in reference to the War with Mexico.* Washington, DC: J.T. Towers, 1848.

Stevenson, William G. *Thirteen Months in the Rebel Army: Being a Narrative of Personal Adventures in the Infantry, Ordinance, Cavalry, Courier, and Hospital Services.* London: Sampson, Low, Son & Co., 1862.

Townsend, George. *Katy of Catoctin; or, The Chain-Breakers; A National Romance.* New York: D. Appleton and Co., 1886.

Trowbridge, John T. *The Desolate South 1865–1866: A Picture of the Battlefields of the Devastated Confederacy.* New York: Duell, Sloan and Pearce, 1956.

Venet, Wendy Hamand, ed. *Sam Richard's Civil War Diary: A Chronicle of the Atlanta Home Front.* Athens: University of Georgia Press, 2009.

Weichmann, Louis J., and Floyd E. Risvold, ed. *A True History of the Assassination of Abraham Lincoln and of the Conspiracy of 1865.* New York: Alfred A. Knopf, 1975.

Weik, Jesse W. *Abraham Lincoln: The True Story of a Great Life.* New York: D. Appleton and Co., 1909.

Welles, Edgar Thaddeus. *Diary of Gideon Welles, Secretary of the Navy Under Lincoln and Johnson.* Boston: Houghton Mifflin Co., 1911.

Welles, Gideon. "Administration of Abraham Lincoln." *The Galaxy* 23 (October, 1877): 43750.

Welles, Gideon. "Lincoln and Johnson: Their Plan of Reconstruction and the Resumption of National Authority." *The Galaxy* 13 (April, 1872): 521–32.

Wiggins, Sarah Woolfolk, ed. *The Journals of Josiah Gorgas 1857–1878.* Tuscaloosa: University of Alabama Press, 1995.

Williamson, James J. *Prison Life In the Old Capitol and Reminiscences of the Civil War.* West Orange, NJ: Self-published, 1911.

Wilson, Clyde N., ed. *The Papers of John Calhoun.* Columbia: University of South Carolina Press, 1980.

_____, ed. *The Papers of John Calhoun.* Columbia: University of South Carolina Press, 1980.

Wilson, James Harrison. *Under the Old Flag: Recollections of Military Operations in the War for the Union, the Spanish War, the Boxer Rebellion, etc.* 2 vols. New York: D. Appleton and Company, 1912.

Public Documents

Alabama Acts
Alabama Code
Alabama House Journal
Alabama Senate Journal
Congressional Globe
Ex parte Milligan, 71 U.S. 2 (1866).

Ex parte Vaughan, 44 Ala. 417 (1870).

Federal Census

Haley & Clark, 26 Ala. 439 (1855).

Hawkins v. Nelson, 40 Ala. 553 (1867).

House Report 7, 40 Cong., 1 Session (1867).

Impeachment Investigation: Testimony Taken Before the Judiciary Committee of the House of Representatives In the Investigation of the Charges Against Andrew Johnson, Second Session, Thirty-Ninth Congress, and First Session, Fortieth Congress. DC: Government Printing Office, 1867.

In re Shorter, 22 F. Cas. 16 (D.C. Ala., 1865).

Joint Select Committee to Investigate the Affairs of the Late Insurrectionary States, United States Senate Reports, No. 22, "Alabama Testimony in Ku Klux Klan Report," 42nd Cong., 2nd Sess., vol. 9.

Jones v. State, 13 Ala. 153 (1848).

Journal of the Congress of the Confederate States of America, 1861–1865. Washington: Government Printing Office, 1904-1905.

Journal of the Proceedings of Convention of the State of Alabama: Held in the City of Montgomery, on Tuesday, September 12, 1865 to September 30, 1865. Montgomery, AL: Gibson & Whitfield, State Printers, 1865.

Judiciary Committee. House of Representatives: *The Impeachment Committee Investigation.* Washington, DC: U.S. Government Printing Office, 1867.

Official Journal of the Constitutional Convention of Alabama, 1861. Montgomery, AL: Shorter & Reid, State Printers, 1861.

Ordinances and Constitution of the State of Alabama, with the Constitution of the Provisional Government of the Confederate States of America. Montgomery, AL: Shorter & Reid, State Printers, 1861.

Proclamation of Andrew Jackson, President of the United States, to the People of South Carolina. Harrisburg, PA: Singerly & Myers, 1864.

Report of the Joint Committee on Reconstruction, 1st Sess., 39th Congress, Part III. Washington, DC: Government Printing Office, 1966.

Scott v. Sandford, 60 U.S. 393 (1857).

Shepherd, J. W. *The Constitution, and Ordinances Adopted By the State Convention of Alabama Which Assembled at Montgomery on the Twelfth Day of September, A.D. 1865, With Index, Analysis, and Table of Titles.* Montgomery, AL: Gibson & Whitfield, State Printers, 1865.

South Carolina Exposition and Protest. Columbia, SC: NP, 1829.

State v. Hughes, 1 Ala. 655 (1840).

Statutes At Large

The War of the Rebellion: A Compilation of the Official Records of the Union and Confederate Armies. Washington, DC: Government Printing Office, 1887.

United States Congress, *Testimony Taken by the Joint Select Committee to Inquire Into the Condition of Affairs in the Late Insurrectionary States: Alabama. .* 13 vols. Washington, DC: Government Printing Office, 1872.

U.S. Const. amend. 13.
U.S. Const. amend. 14.
U.S. Const. amend. 15.
United States Senate Executive Journal
U.S. Statutes At Large

Newspapers

Advertiser and Mail, Montgomery
Advertiser and State Gazette, Montgomery
Advertiser, Albany, NY
Advertiser, Edgefield, SC
Advertiser, Portland, ME
Advocate, Newark, OH
Age, Philadelphia
Alabama Beacon, Greensboro
Alabama Intelligencer and States Rights Expositor, Tuscaloosa
Alabama Journal, Montgomery
Alabama State Intelligencer, Tuscaloosa
Alabama State Journal, Montgomery
Alabama State Sentinel, Selma
American Advocate and Kennebec Advertiser, Hallowell, ME
American Beacon and Commercial Diary, Norfolk, VA
American Beacon and Norfolk and Portsmouth Advertiser, Norfolk, VA
American Star, Petersburg, VA
American Watchman and Delaware Republican, Wilmington
American, Marion, AL
American, New York
Argus, Albany, NY
Ariel, Natchez
Arkansas Gazette
Arkansas Gazette, Little Rock
Arkansas State Gazette, Little Rock
Arkansas Times, Little Rock
Arkansas Weekly Gazette, Little Rock
Army Argus and Crisis, Mobile
Athenian, Athens, GA
Atlanta Confederacy
Atlanta Intelligencer
Baltimore Patriot and Mercantile Advertiser
Banner and Lawrence Enquirer, Moulton, AL

Banner of Reform, Mobile
Banner, Clayton, AL
Banner, Dadeville, AL
Bee, New Orleans
Bee, Ripley, OH
Belmont Chronicle, St. Clairsville, OH
Berkshire County Whig, Pittsfield, MA
Blade, Tuscaloosa
Boston Advertiser
Boston Atlas
Boston Commercial Gazette
Boston Herald
Boston Recorder
Brooklyn Eagle
Brownlow's Knoxville Whig, and Rebel Ventilator
Buffalo Advertiser
Bulletin, Winchester, TN
Cahawba Gazette
Cahawba Press and Alabama State Intelligencer
Carolina Federal Republican, New Bern, NC
Centinel of Freedom, Newark, NJ
Charleston Courier
Charleston Mercury
Chattanooga Gazette
Chattanooga Rebel
Chattanooga Rebel, Selma
Chicago Journal
Chicago Post
Chicago Times
Chicago Tribune
Chickasaw Union, Pontotoc
Chronicle and Georgia Advertiser, Augusta, GA
Chronicle and Sentinel, Augusta, GA
Chronicle, Tuscaloosa
Chronicle, Augusta, GA
Chronicle, Belmont, OH
Chronicle, Hayneville, AL
Chronicle, Washington, DC
Cincinnati Commercial
Cincinnati Enquirer
Cincinnati Gazette
Cincinnati Press

Citizen and News, Lowell, MA
Citizen, Canton, MS
City Gazette and Commercial Advertiser, Charleston
City of Washington Gazette
Clarion, Decatur, AL
Clarion, Meridian, MS
Clarke County Journal, Grove Hill, AL
Cleveland Herald
Cleveland Leader
Columbia Democrat and Bloomsburg General Advertiser, Bloomsburg, PA
Columbia Tennessee Democrat
Columbian, New York
Commonwealth, Marion, AL
Confederate Union, Milledgeville, GA
Confederate, Macon, GA
Confederation, Montgomery
Connecticut Mirror, Hartford
Constitutionalist, Augusta, GA
Courant, Hartford, CT
Courier, Louisville, KY
Courier, Norwich, CT
Courtland Herald
Daily Evening Bulletin, San Francisco
Daily Express, Petersburg, VA
Daily Morning News, Savannah, GA
Dallas Gazette, Cahawba
Democrat, Huntsville
Democrat, Moulton, AL
Democrat, St. Cloud, MN
Democratic Watchtower, Talladega
Demopolis Herald
Dispatch, Richmond
Eastern Argus, Portland, ME
Enquirer, Columbus, GA
Enquirer, Yorkville, SC
Essex Gazette, Haverhill, MA
Essex Register, Salem, MA
Eutaw Whig
Eutaw Whig and Observer
Exchange, Baltimore
Farmer, Holmes County, OH
Farmers' Cabinet, Amherst, NH

Flag of the Union, Tuscaloosa
Flag, Moulton, AL
Florence Enquirer
Frank Leslie's Illustrated Newspaper
Franklin Democrat, Russellville
Free Press, Burlington, VT
Freedom's Champion, Atchison, KS
Gazette Advertiser, Alexandria, VA
Gazette, Barre, MA
Gazette, Camden, SC
Gazette, Florence, AL
Gazette, Lynchburg, VA
Gazette, Salem, MA
Gazette, Scioto, OH
Georgia Journal, Milledgeville
Globe, Washington, DC
Halcyon and Tombeckbe Public Advertiser, St. Stephens, AL
Harper's Weekly
Herald, Alexandria, VA
Herald, Athens, AL
Herald, Ithaca, NY
Herald, Newburyport, MA
Herald, Newport, MA
Herald, Washington, DC
Highland Weekly News, Hillsborough, OH
Holmes County Farmer, Millersburg, OH
Hudson River Chronicle, Oassining, NY
Huntsville Advocate
Huntsville Alabamian
Huntsville Chronicle
Huntsville Confederate
Huntsville Independent
Huntsville Republican
Independence, Poughkeepsie, NY
Independent Monitor, Tuscaloosa
Independent, Gainesville, AL
Inquirer, Bedford, PA
Intelligencer, Wheeling, VA
Intelligencer, Anderson, SC
Iredell Express, Statesville, NC
Jackson County News, Stevenson
Jeffersonian Republican, Stroundsburg, PA

Jeffersonian, Brookville, PA
Jeffersonian, New Orleans
Albany Journal, Albany, NY
Journal and Rockingham Gazette, Portsmouth, NH
Journal of Literature & Politics, Portsmouth, NH
Journal, Camden, SC
Journal, Florence, AL
Journal, Fremont, OH
Journal, Gallipolis, OH
Journal, Jamestown, NY
Journal, Livingston, AL
Journal, Louisville, KY
Liberator, Boston
Livingston Independent
London Standard
Louisiana Advertiser, New Orleans
Memphis Appeal
Memphis Appeal, Montgomery
Memphis Avalanche
Memphis Bulletin
Mercantile Advertiser, New York
Mercantile Chronicle, Panama City, Panama
Merchants' Magazine and Commercial Review
Mercury, Newport, RI
Middlesex Gazette, Middleton, CT
Milwaukee Sentinel
Mississippi Free Trader, Natchez
Mississippi State Gazette, Natchez
Mississippian, Jackson
Mississippian, Selma
Missouri Republican
Mobile Advertiser
Mobile Advertiser and Register
Mobile Commercial Register
Mobile Commercial Register and Patriot
Mobile Mercury
Mobile News
Mobile Register
Mobile Register and Journal
Mobile Tribune
Montana Post, Virginia City
Montgomery Advertiser

Montgomery Advertiser and Mail
Montgomery Atlas
Montgomery Flag and Advertiser
Montgomery Mail
Montgomery Weekly Advertiser
Montgomery Weekly Mail
Montgomery Weekly Post
Morgan Observer, Decatur, AL
Mountaineer, Greeneville, SC
Nashville Clarion
Nashville Democrat
Nashville News
Nashville Patriot
Nashville Press
Nashville Press and Times
Nashville Republican & State Gazette
Nashville Tennessean
Nashville Times and True Union
Nashville Union
Nashville Union
Nashville Union and American
Nashville Whig
Nashville Whig and Tennessee Advertiser
Natchez Daily Courier
National Advocate, New York
National Banner and Nashville Whig
National Intelligencer, Washington, DC
National Messenger, Georgetown, DC
National Republican, Washington, DC
National Tribune, Washington, DC
Nationalist, Mobile
New Hampshire Gazette, Portsmouth
New Hampshire Patriot and State Gazette, Concorde
New Hampshire Sentinel, Keene
New Hampshire Statesman, Concorde
New Orleans Argus
New Orleans Era
New Orleans Times
New York Advertiser
New York Commercial
New York Commercial and Advertiser
New York Courier

New York Essex Patriot
New York Evening Post
New York Express
New York Herald
New York Journal of Commerce
New York Observer
New York Post
New York Spectator
New York Times
New York Transcript
New York Tribune
New York World
New-England Palladium, Boston
News, Jackson, MS
Niles Register, Washington, DC
North Alabamian and Times, Tuscumbia
North Alabamian, Tuscumbia
North American and United States Gazette, Philadelphia
North Carolina Standard, Raleigh
Observer, Fayetteville, NC
Opelika Union
Otsego Herald, Cooperstown, NY
Palladium, New Haven, CT
Palladium, Worchester, MA
Patriot & Columbian Phenix, Providence, RI
Patriot, Albany, GA
Patriot, Providence, RI
Pennsylvania Inquirer and National Gazette, Philadelphia
Philadelphia Bulletin
Philadelphia Inquirer
Philadelphia Press
Phoenix, Columbia, SC
Picayune, New Orleans
Pilot and Transcript, Baltimore, MD
Portsmouth & Great Falls Journal of Literature & Politics, Portsmouth, NH
Post, Athens, TN
Post, Washington, DC
Press, Hartford, CT
Press, Providence, RI
Progress, Raleigh, NC
Raleigh Register
Reflector, Milledgeville, GA

Register, Decatur, AL
Republic, Columbus, IN
Republican Banner, Nashville
Republican Star and General Advertiser, Easton, MD
Republican, New Orleans
Republican, Athens, AL
Republican, Brandon, MS
Republican, Jacksonville, AL
Republican, Savannah, GA
Review, Marion, AL
Rhode Island American and Gazette, Providence
Rhode Island American and General Advertiser, Providence
Rhode Island Republicans, Newport
Richmond Compiler
Richmond Enquirer
Richmond Examiner
Richmond Sentinel
Richmond Whig
Savannah Georgian
Selma Courier
Selma Dispatch
Selma Federal Union
Selma Free Press
Selma Messenger
Selma Reporter
Selma Union
Selma Weekly Issue
Semi-Weekly Eagle, Brattleboro, VT
Semi-Weekly Raleigh Register, Raleigh, NC
Sentinel, Columbus, GA
Sentinel, Xenia, OH
Shelby County Guide, Columbiana, AL
Shreveport Semi-Weekly News
Soldiers Journal, Alexandria
South Carolinian, Columbia
Southern Advertiser, Troy
Southern Advocate, Huntsville
Southern Argus, Selma
Southern Banner, Athens, GA
Southern Democrat, Cahawba
Southern Press, Washington, DC
Southern Recorder, Milledgeville, GA

Southern Watchmen, Athens, GA
Southern, Milledgeville, GA
South-Western, Shreveport
Spirit of the Age, Tuscaloosa
Spirit of the South, Eufaula
Spirit of the Times, Pontotoc, MS
St. Louis Globe-Democrat
St. Louis Republican
Standard, Raleigh, NC
Star, Washington, DC
State Gazette, Trenton, NJ
Statesman, Milledgeville, GA
Sugar Planter, Port Allen, LA
Sun, Columbus, GA
Sun, Pittsfield, MA
Sunbury American
Talladega Reporter
Telegraph & Georgia Journal and Messenger, Macon, GA
Telegraph and Confederate, Macon, GA
Telegraph, Philadelphia
Telegraph, Macon, GA
Tennessee Herald, Shelbyville
Times Daily, Florence
Times Picayune, New Orleans
Times, London
Times, Columbus, GA
Times, Lauderdale, AL
Town Gazette & Farmers Register, Clarksville, TN
Tribune, Liberty, MO
Tri-Weekly Flag and Advertiser, Montgomery
True American, New Orleans
Tuscaloosa Inquirer
Tuscaloosa News
Tuscaloosa Observer
Tuscumbia Advertiser
Tuscumbia Constitution
Tuscumbia Patriot
Tuscumbia Telegraph
Tuskaloosa Gazette
Union Banner, Athens, GA
Union, Howard, MO
Union, Urbana, OH

United States Telegraph, Washington, DC
Vermont Chronicle, Bellows Falls
Vermont Gazette, Bennington
Vermont Intelligencer and Bellows Falls Advertiser
Vermont Phoenix, Brattleboro, VT
Vermont Transcript, St. Albans
Vermont Watchman and State Journal, Montpelier
Vicksburgh Sentinel
Vidette, Asheville, AL
Waldo Patriot, Belfast, ME
Washington City Weekly Gazette
Watch-Tower, Cooperstown, NY
Weekly Herald and Tribune, Mobile
Weekly Alabama Journal, Montgomery
Weekly Chronicle, Clarksville, TN
Weekly Herald and Tribune, Mobile
Weekly News, Highland, OH
Weekly Ohio Statesman, Columbus
Weekly Journal, Perrysburg, OH
Weekly Progress, Newbern, NC
Weekly Register, Raleigh, NC
Weekly Recorder, Chillicothe, OH
Weekly Southern Era, Opelika, AL
Weekly Telegraph, Ashtabula, OH
Weekly Telegraph, Macon, GA
Weekly Times, Glasgow, MO
West Alabamian, Carrollton
Western Democrat, Charlotte, NC
Western Reserve Chronicle, Warren, OH
Western Times, Memphis
Whig & Courier, ME
Wisconsin State Register, Portage

Secondary Sources

Books, Dissertations, and Theses

Abernethy, Thomas P. *The Formative Period in Alabama, 1815–1828.* Tuscaloosa: University of Alabama Press, 1990.

_____. *The South in the New Nation.* Baton Rouge: Louisiana State University Press, 1961.

Adams, Michael C. C. *Living Hell: The Dark Side of the Civil War.* Baltimore, MD: John Hopkins University Press, 2014.

Alabama Writers Program. *Alabama: A Guide to the Deep South.* New York: R.A. Smith, 1941.

Alasdair, Roberts. *America's First Great Depression: Economic Crisis and Political Disorder After the Panic of 1837.* Ithaca, NY: Cornell University Press, 2012.

Alexander, Eric Benjamin. "'A Revival of the Old Organization': Northern Democrats and Reconstruction, 1868–1876." PhD diss., University of Virginia, 2010.

Alexander, Bevin. *How the South Could Have Won the Civil War: The Fatal Errors That Led to Confederate Defeat.* New York: Crown Publishers, 2007.

Alford, Terry. *Fortune's Fool: The Life of John Wilkes Booth.* New York: Oxford University Press, 2015.

_____, ed. *John Wilkes Booth: A Sister's Memoir by Asia Booth Clarke.* Jackson: University Press of Mississippi, 1996.

Allardice, Bruce S. *Confederate Colonels: A Biographical Register.* Columbia: University of Missouri Press, 2008.

Allmendinger, Jr., David F. *Nat Turner and the Rising in Southhampton County.* Baltimore: Johns Hopkins University Press, 2014.

Armes, Ethel Marie. *The Story of Coal and Iron in Alabama.* Tuscaloosa: University of Alabama Press, 2011.

Ash, Stephen V., ed. *Secessionists and Other Scoundrels: Selections From Parson Brownlow's Book.* Baton Rouge: Louisiana State University Press, 1999.

_____. *When the Yankees Came: Conflict and Chaos in the Occupied South, 1861–1865.* Chapel Hill: University of North Carolina Press, 1995.

Ashdown, Paul, and Edward Caudill. *The Myth of Nathan Bedford Forrest.* Lanham, MD: Rowman & Littlefield, 2005.

_____. *The Mosby Myth: A Confederate Hero in Life and Legend.* Wilmington, DE: Scholarly Resources, Inc., 2002.

Ayers, Edward L. *What Caused the Civil War? Reflections on the South and Southern History.* New York: W.W. Norton & Co., 2005.

Baggett, James Alex. *The Scalawags: Southern Dissenters in the Civil War and Reconstruction.* Baton Rouge: Louisiana State University Press, 2003.

Bailey, Anne J. *The Chessboard of War: Sherman and Hood in the Autumn Campaigns of 1864.* Lincoln: University of Nebraska Press, 2000.

Bailey, Richard. *Neither Carpetbaggers Nor Scalawags: Black Officeholders During the Reconstruction of Alabama, 1867–1878.* Montgomery, AL: R. Bailey Publishers, 1991.

Baker, Jean H. *Affairs of the Party: The Political Culture of the Northern Democrats in the Mid-Nineteenth Century.* New York: Fordham University Press, 1998.

_____. *James Buchanan: The American Presidents Series: The 15th President, 1857–1861.* New York: Time Books, 2004.

Ball, Douglas B. *Financial Failure and Confederate Defeat.* Urbana: University of Illinois Press, 1991.

Ballard, Michael B. *The Civil War in Mississippi: Major Campaigns and Battles.* Jackson: University Press of Mississippi, 2011.

Balleison, Edwawrd J. *Navigating Failure: Bankruptcy and Commerical Society in Antebellum America.* Chapel Hill: University of North Carolina Press, 2001.

Bancroft, Frederic. *Calhoun and the South Carolina Nullification Movement.* Baltimore: Johns Hopkins Press, 1967.

Baptist, Edward E. *The Half Has Never Been Told: Slavery and the Making of American Capitalism.* New York: Basic Books, 2014.

Barney, William L. *The Road to Secession: A New Perspective On the Old South.* New York: Praeger, 1972.

_____. *The Secessionist Impulse in Alabama and Mississippi in 1860.* Tuscaloosa: University of Alabama Press, 2004.

Barnwell, John. *Love of Order: South Carolina's First Secession Crisis.* Chapel Hill: University of Alabama Press, 2004.

Barrett, John G. *Sherman's March Through The Carolinas.* Chapel Hill: University of North Carolina Press, 1995.

Bartlett, Bruce R. *Wrong on Race: The Democratic Party's Buried Past.* New York: Palgrave Macmillan, 2008.

Bartlett, Irving H. *John C. Calhoun: A Biography.* New York: W.W. Norton & Co, 1993.

Bateman, Fred, and Thomas Weiss. *Deplorable Scarcity: The Failure of Industrialization in the Slave Economy.* Chapel Hill: University of North Carolina Press, 2002.

Bauer, K. Jack. *Zachary Taylor: Soldier, Planter, Statesman of the Old Southwest.* Baton Rouge: Louisiana State University Press, 1993.

Baxter, Maurice G. *Henry Clay and the American System.* Lexington: University Press of Kentucky, 2004.

Bearrs, Edwin C., and Arrell Morgan Gibson. *Fort Smith: Little Gibraltor on the Arkansas.* Norman: University of Oklahoma Press, 1988.

Beckert, Sven. *Empire of Cotton: A Global History.* New York: Vintage Books, 2014.

Benson, William Edwards. *A Political History of the Tariff 1789–1861.* Bloomington, IN: Xlibris Corp., 2010.

Bergeron, Arthur W. "The Confederate Defense of Mobile, 1861–1865." PhD diss., Louisiana State University, 1980.

_____. *Confederate Mobile.* Jackson: University Press of Mississippi, 1991.

Bergeron, Paul H. *Andrew Johnson's Civil War and Reconstruction.* Knoxville: University of Tennessee Press, 2011.

Beringer, Richard E. et al. *The Elements of Confederate Defeat: Nationalism, War Aims, and Religion.* Athens: University of Georgia Press, 1988.

Beringer, Richard E., Archer Jones, William N. Still, Jr. *Why the South Lost the Civil War.* Athens: University of Georgia Press, 1991.

Berlin, Ira. *Many Thousands Gone: The First Two Centuries of Slavery in North America.* Cambridge, MA: Belknap Press of Harvard University Press, 1998.

_____. *Slaves Without Masters: The Free Negro in the Antebellum South.* New York: Pantheon Books, 1974.

Berney, Saffold. *Handbook of Alabama: A Complete Index to the State, with Map.* Spartanburg, SC: Reprint Co., 1975.

Berry, Stephen W. *House of Abraham: Lincoln and the Todds, A Family Divided by War.* Boston, MA: Mariner Books, 2009.

_____. *All That Makes a Man: Love and Ambition in the Civil War South.* New York: Oxford University Press, 2003.

Berry, Thelma Caine. "The Life of Edmund Winston Pettus" (master's thesis, Auburn University, 1944).

Black, Robert C. *Railroads of the Confederacy.* Chapel Hill: University of North Carolina Press, 1998.

Blackmon, Douglas A. *Slavery By Another Name: The Re-enslavement of Black People in American From the Civil War to World War II.* New York: Doubleday, 2008.

Blair, William A. *With Malice Toward Some: Treason and Loyalty in the Civil War Era.* Chapel Hill: University of North Carolina Press, 2014.

Blight, David W. *Race and Reunion: The Civil War in American Memory.* Cambridge, MA: Harvard University Press, 2001.

Blue, Frederick J. *Salmon P. Chase: A Life in Politics.* Kent, OH: Kent State University Press, 1987.

Blum, Edward J. *Reforging the White Republic: Race, Religion, and American Nationalism, 1865–1898.* Baton Rouge: Louisiana State University Press, 2005.

Bogar, Thomas A. *Backstage at the Lincoln Assassination: The Untold Story of the Actors and Stagehands at Ford Theatre.* Washington, DC: Regnery History, 2013.

Bond, James Edward. *No Easy Walk to Freedom: Reconstruction and the Ratification of the Fourteenth Amendment.* Westport, CT: Praeger, 1997.

Bordewich, Fergus M. *America's Great Debate: Henry Clay, Stephen A. Douglas, and the Compromise that Preserved the Union.* New York: Simon & Schuster, 2012.

Borritt, Gabor S., ed. *Jefferson Davis' Generals.* New York: Oxford University Press, 1999.

Bouland, Gary. *The Swing Around the Circle: Andrew Johnson and the Train Ride that Destroyed a Presidency.* Bloomington, IN: iUniverse, Inc., 2008.

Bowen, David Warren. *Andrew Johnson and the Negro.* Knoxville: University of Tennessee Press, 1989.

Boyko, John. *Blood and Daring: Canada and the American Civil War.* Toronto: Alfred A. Knoph, 2013.

Bradley, George C., and Richard L. Dahlen. *From Conciliation to Conquest: The Sack of Athens and the Court Martial of Colonel John B. Turchin.* Tuscaloosa: University of Alabama Press, 2006.

Brands, H. W. *Andrew Jackson: His Life and Times.* New York: Anchor Books, 2005.

Brandt, Nat. *The Congressman Who Got Away With Murder.* Syracuse, NY: Syracuse University Press, 1991.

_____. *The Man Who Tried to Burn New York*. Lincoln: University of Nebraska Press, 1991.

Brant & Fuller. *Memorial Record of Alabama: A Concise Account of the State's Political, Military, Professional and Industrial Progress, Together With the Personal Memoirs of Many of its People*. Spartanburg, SC: Reprint Company, 1976.

Brantley, William H. *Chief Justice Stone of Alabama*. Birmingham, AL: Birmingham Publishing Co., 1943.

_____. *Three Capitals: A Book About the First Three Capitals of Alabama: St. Stephens, Huntsville & Cahawba*. Tuscaloosa: University of Alabama Press, 1876.

Brewer, Willis. *Alabama, Her History, Resources, War Records, and Public Men: From 1540–1872*. Spartanburg, SC: Reprint Co., 1975.

Brooks, Stefan Marc. *The Webster-Hayne Debate: An Inquiry Into the Nature of the Union*. Lanham, MD: University Press of America, 2009.

Brown, Alan. *Haunted Georgia: Ghosts and Strange Phenomena of the Peach State*. Mechanicsburg, PA: Stackpole Books, 2008.

Brown, David Warren. *Andrew Johnson and the Negro*. Knoxville: University of Tennessee Press, 1989.

Bryant, William O. *Cahaba Prison and the Sultana Disaster*. Tuscaloosa: University of Alabama Press, 2001.

Buchanan, John. *Jackson's Way; Andrew Jackson and the People of the Western Waters*. New York: Wiley, 2001.

Bungay, George W. *Traits of Representative Men*. New York: Fowler & Wells, 1882.

Burkhardt, George S. *Confederate Rage, Yankee Wrath: No Quarter in the Civil War*. Carbondale: Southern Illinois University Press, 2007.

Burgess, John W. *Reconstruction and the Constitution, 1866–1876*. Whitefish, MT: Kessinger Publishing, 2007.

Burlingame, Michael. *Abraham Lincoln: A Life*. Baltimore, MD: Johns Hopkins University Press, 2008.

_____. *Lincoln and the Civil War*. Carbondale: Southern Illinois University Press, 2011.

_____. *The Inner World of Abraham Lincoln*. Urbana: University of Illinois Press, 1994.

Burnett, Lonnie A. *The Pen Makes a Good Sword: John Forsyth of the Mobile Register*. Tuscaloosa: University of Alabama Press, 2006.

Burt, John. *Lincoln's Tragic Pragmatism: Lincoln, Douglas and Moral Conflict*. Cambridge, MA: Belknap Press, 2013.

Bush, Robert D. *The Louisiana Purchase: A Global Context*. New York: Routledge, 2014.

Carey, Anthony Gene. *Parties, Slavery, and the Union in Antebellum Georgia*. Athens: University of Georgia Press, 1997.

Carnahan, Burrus M. *Act of Justice: Lincoln's Emancipation Proclamation and the Law of War*. Lexington: University Press of Kentucky, 2007.

Carroll, Joseph Cephas. *Slave Insurrections in the United States, 1800–1865.* Mineola, NY: Dover Publications, Inc., 2004.

Carter, Dan T. *When the War Was Over: The Failure of Self-Reconstruction in the South, 1865–1867.* Baton Rouge: Louisiana State University Press, 1985.

Carter, Davis Blake. *The Story Uncle Minyard Told: A Family's 200 Year Migration Across the South.* Spartanburg, SC: Reprint Co., 1994.

Castel, Albert. *Decision in the West: The Atlanta Campaign of 1864.* Lawrence: University Press of Kansas, 1992.

Catterall, Ralph C. H. *The Second Bank of the United States.* Chicago: University of Chicago Press, 1990.

Cauthen, Charles Edward. *South Carolina Goes to War, 1860–1865.* Columbia: University of South Carolina Press, 2005.

Chamblee, Jr., Roy Z. *Lincoln's Assassins: A Complete Account of Their Capture, Trial, and Punishment.* Jefferson, NC: McFarland & Co., Inc., 1990.

Cheathem, Mark Renfred. *Andrew Jackson, Southerner.* Baton Rouge: Louisiana State University Press, 2013.

Chesebrough, David B. *Clergy Dissent in the Old South, 1830–1865.* Carbondale: Southern llinois University Press, 1996.

_____. *No Sorrow Like Our Sorrow: Northern Protestant Ministers and the Assassination of Lincoln.* Kent, OH: Kent State University Press, 1994.

Chodes, John J. *Jabez L.M. Curry: Confederate Educator, Trojan Horse.* New York: Algora Pub., 2005.

Cimbala, Paul A., and Randall M. Miller, eds. *The Great Task Remaining Before Us: Reconstruction as America's Continuing Civil War.* New York: Fordham University Press, 2010.

Clampitt, Bradley R. *The Confederate Heartland: Military and Civilian Morale in the Western Confederacy.* Baton Rouge: Louisiana State University Press, 2011.

Clark, John B. *Populism in Alabama.* Auburn, AL: Auburn Print Co., 1927.

Clark, John Elwood. *Railroads in the Civil War: The Impact of Management On Victory and Defeat.* Baton Rouge: Louisiana State University Press, 2004.

Clark, Thomas D., and John D. W. Guice. *The Old Southwest, 1795–1830: Frontiers in Conflict.* Norman: University of Oklahoma Press, 1996.

Cline, Wayne. *Alabama Railroads.* Tuscaloosa: University of Alabama Press, 1997.

Cohen, William. *At Freedom's Edge: Black Mobility and the Southern White Quest for Racial Control, 1861–1915.* Baton Rouge: Louisiana State University Press, 1991.

Cole, Arthur Charles. *The Whig Party in the South.* Gloucester, MA: P. Smith, 1962.

Cole, Donald B. *Martin Van Buren and the American Political System.* Princeton, NJ: Princeton University Press, 1984.

Collins, Donald E. *The Death and Resurrection of Jefferson Davis.* Lanham, MD: Rowman and Littlefield Publishers, 2005.

Connery, William S. *Mosby's Raids in Civil War Northern Virginia.* Charleston, SC: History Press, 2013.

Connor, Henry Groves. *John Archibald Campbell*. Clark, NJ: Lawbook Exchange, Ltd., 2004.

Conrad, Alfred H., and John R. Meyer. *The Economics of Slavery and Other Studies in Econometric History*. Chicago: Aldine Pub. Co., 1964.

Conroy, James B. *Our One Common Country: Abraham Lincoln and the Hampton Roads Peace Conference of 1865*. Guilford, CT: Lyons Press, 2014.

Cook, Robert J. *Baptism of Fire: The Republican Party in Iowa 1838–1878*. Ames: Iowa State University Press, 1994.

Cooling, B. Franklin. *Forts Henry and Donelson: The Key to the Confederate Heartland*. Knoxville: Easton Press, 1987.

_____. *To The Battles of Franklin and Nashville and Beyond: Stabilization and Reconstruction in Tennessee and Kentucky, 1864–1866*. Knoxville: University of Tennessee Press, 2011.

Cooper, Jr., William J. *Jefferson Davis: American*. New York: Vintage Books, 2001.

_____. *Jefferson Davis and the Civil War Era*. Baton Rouge: Louisiana State University Press, 2008.

_____. *The South and the Politics of Slavery, 1828–1856*. Baton Rouge: Louisiana State University Press, 1978.

Cox, Karen L. *Dixie's Daughter: The United Daughters of the Confederacy and the Preservation of Confederate Culture*. Gainesville: University Press of Florida, 2003.

Cox, LaWanda C. Fenlason, and John H. Cox. *Politics, Principle, and Prejudice, 1865–1866: Dilemma of Reconstruction America*. New York: Free Press of Glencoe, 1963.

Crapol, Edward P. *John Tyler: The Accidental President*. Chapel Hill: University of North Carolina Press, 2006.

Craton, Michael. *Slavery, Abolition and Emancipation*. London: Longman, 1976.

Craven, Avery O. *Soil Exhaustion as a Factor in the Agricultural History of Virginia and Maryland, 1606–1860*. Columbia: University of South Carolina Press, 2006.

_____. *The Coming of the Civil War*. Chicago: University of Chicago Press, 1942.

_____. *The Growth of Southern Nationalism, 1848–1861*. Baton Rouge: Louisiana State University, 1953.

Crockett, Charles Elliott. "A History of Nullification in the State of Alabama from 1832–1852" (master's thesis, Auburn University, 1968).

Crofts, Thomas. *History of the Service of the Third Ohio Veteran Volunteer Cavalry in the War for the Preservation of the Union from 1861–1865*. Toledo, OH: Stoneman Press, 1910.

Crute, Joseph H. *Units of the Confederate States Army*. Micdlothian, VA: Derwent Books, 1987.

Cumming, Carman. *Devil's Game: The Civil War Intrigues of Charles A. Dunham*. Urbana: University of Illinois Press, 2008.

Current, Richard Nelson. *Lincoln's Loyalists: Union Soldiers From the Confederacy*. Boston: Northeastern University Press, 1992.

Dabney, Virginius. *Richmond: The Story of a City*. Charlottesville: University Press of Virginia, 1990.

Daniel, Larry J. *Soldiering in the Army of Tennessee: A Portrait of Life in the Confederate Army*. Chapel Hill: University of North Carolina Press, 1991.

Danielson, Joseph W. *War's Desolating Scourge: The Union's Occupation of North Alabama*. Lawrence: University Press of Kansas, 2012.

Dattel, Gene. *Cotton and Race in the Making of America: The Human Cost of Economic Power*. Lanham, MD: Ivan R. Dee, 2009.

Davis, Andrew McFarland. *The Origins of the National Banking System*. Washington, DC: Government Printing Office, 1910.

Davis, Charles S. *Colin J. McRae: Confederate Financial Agent*. Tuscaloosa, AL: Confederate Publishing Co., 1961.

Davis, David Brion. *Inhuman Bondage: The Rise and Fall of Slavery in the New World*. Oxford: Oxford University Press, 2006.

Davis, Stephen. *Atlanta Will Fall: Sherman, Joe Johnston, and the Yankee Heavy Battalions*. Wilmington, DEL: Scholarly Resources, 2001.

_____. *What the Yankees Did To Us: Sherman's Bombardment and Wrecking of Atlanta*. Macon, GA: Mercer University Press, 2012.

Davis, Susan Lawrence. *Authentic History, Ku Klux Klan 1865–1877*. New York: American Library Service, 1924.

Davis, William C., ed. *The Confederate General*. New York: National Historical Society, 1991.

_____. *Jefferson Davis: The Man and His Hour*. Baton Rouge: Louisiana State University Press, 1995.

_____. *Look Away: A History of the Confederate States of America*. New York: Free Press, 2002.

_____. *Rhett: The Turbulent Life and Times of a Fire-Eater*. Columbia: University of South Carolina Press, 2009.

Davison, Eddy W., and Daniel Foxx. *Nathan Bedford Forrest: In Search of the Enigma*. Gretna, LA: Pelican Publishing Co., 2007.

Deland, T. A., and A. Davis Smith. *North Alabama: Historical and Biographical*. Birmingham, AL: Smith and Deland, 1888.

Denman, Clarence Phillips. *The Secession Movement in Alabama*. Montgomery, AL: Alabama State Department of Archives and History, 1933.

Dennett, John Richard. *The South As It Is: 1865–1866*. Tuscaloosa: University of Alabama Press, 2010.

Dershowitz, Alan M. *America On Trial: Inside the Legal Battles That Transformed Our Nation*. New York: Warner Books, 2004.

Detzer, David. *Allegiance: Fort Sumter, Charleston, and the Beginning of the Civil War*. New York: Harcourt, 2001.

Dirck, Brian R. *Lincoln and the Constitution*. Carbondale: Southern Illinois University Press, 2012.

Dodd, Donald B. "Unionism in Confederate Alabama." PhD diss., University of Georgia, 1969.

Donald, David Herbert. *Lincoln*. New York: Simon & Schuster, 1995.

Dorman, Lewy. *Party Politics in Alabama from 1850 through 1860*. Tuscaloosa: University of Alabama Press, 1995.

Dorris, Jonathan Truman. *Pardon and Amnesty Under Lincoln and Johnson*. Chapel Hill: University of North Carolina Press, 1977.

Downs, Gregory P. *After Appomattox: Military Occupation and the Ends of the War*. Cambridge, MA: Harvard University Press, 2015.

Dubay, Robert W. *John Jones Pettus, Mississippi Fire-Eater: His Life and Times, 1813–1867*. Jackson: University Press of Mississippi, 2008.

DuBose, John Witherspoon. *The Life and Times of William Lowndes Yancey*. 2 vols. Birmingham, AL: Roberts & Son, 1892.

Dunkelman, Mark H. *Marching With Sherman: Through Georgia and the Carolinas With the 154th New York*. Baton Rouge: Louisiana State University Press, 2012.

Dunnavant, Robert. *Decatur, Alabama: Yankee Foothold in Dixie, 1861–1865*. Athens, AL: Pea Ridge Press, 1995.

_____. *The Railroad War: N.B. Forrest's 1864 Raid Through Northern Alabama and Middle Tennessee*. Athens, AL: Pea Ridge Press, 1994.

Durham, David I. *A southern Moderate In Radical Times: Henry Washington Hilliard, 1808–1892*. Baton Rouge: Louisiana State University Press, 2008.

Edgar, Walter B. *South Carolina: A History*. Columbia: University of South Carolina Press, 1998.

Edwards, Laura F. *Scarlett Doesn't Live Here Anymore: Southern Women In the Civil War Era*. Urbana: University of Illinois Press, 2000.

Edwards, William C., and Edward Steers, Jr., eds. *The Lincoln Assassination: The Evidence*. Urbana: University of Illinois Press, 2009.

Egan, Jr., Brendan H. *Murder at Ford's Theatre: A Chronicle of an Assassination*. Philadelphia: Xlibris, 2007.

Egerton, Douglas R. *Gabriel's Rebellion: The Virginia Slave Conspiracies of 1800 and 1802*. Chapel Hill: University of North Carolina Press, 1993.

Ellis, Richard E. *The Union at Risk: Jacksonian Democracy, States' Rights and the Nullification Crisis*. New York: Oxford University Press, 1987.

Ellisor, John T. *The Second Creek War: Interethnic Conflict and Collusion on a Collapsing Frontier*. Lincoln: University of Nebraska Press, 2010.

Emberton, Carole. *Beyond Redemption: Race, Violence, and the American South After the Civil War*. Chicago: University of Chicago Press, 2013.

English, Bertis. "Civil Wars and Civil Beings: Violence, Religion, Race, Politics, Education, Culture and Agrarianism in Perry County, Alabama, 1860–1875." PhD diss., Auburn University, 2006.

Escott, Paul D. *After Secession: Jefferson Davis and the Failure of Confederate Nationalism*. Baton Rouge: Louisiana State University Press, 1978.

_____. *Military Necessity: Civil-Military Relations in the Confederacy.* Westport: Praeger Security International, 2006.

_____. *"What Shall We Do With the Negro?": Lincoln, White Racism and Civil War America.* Charlottesville: University of Virginia Press, 2009.

_____. *The Confederacy: The Slaveholders Failed Venture.* Santa Barbara: Praeger, 2010.

Evans, Clement A., ed. *Confederate Military History: A Library of Confederate States History.* Atlanta, GA: Confederate Pub. Co., 1899.

Evans, Curtis J. *The Conquest of Labor: Daniel Pratt and Southern Industrialization.* Baton Rouge: Louisiana State University Press, 2001.

Fahrney, Ralph Ray. *Horace Greeley and the Tribune in the Civil War.* Cedar Rapids, IA: Torch Press, 1936.

Federman, Cary. *The Body of the State: Habeas Corpus and American Jurisprudence.* New York: State University of New York Press, 2006.

Fehrenbacher, Don E. *The South and Three Sectional Crises.* Baton Rouge: Louisiana State University Press, 1980.

Feldman, Glenn. *The Irony of the Solid South: Democrats, Republicans and Race, 1865–1944.* Tuscaloosa: University of Alabama Press, 2013.

Fermer, Douglas. *James Gordon Bennett and the New York Herald: A Study of Editorial Opinion in the Civil War Era 1854–1867.* London: Royal Historical Society, 1986.

Fidler, William Perry. *Augusta Evans Wilson, 1835–1909: A Biography.* Tuscaloosa: University of Alabama Press, 1951.

Finkelman, Paul, and Donald R. Kennon, eds. *Congress and the Emergence of Sectionalism: From the Missouri Compromise to the Age of Jackson.* Athens: Ohio University Press, 2008.

Fischer, David Hackett, and James C. Kelly. *Bound Away: Virginia and the Westward Movement.* Charlottesville: University Press of Virginia, 2000.

Fisher, Noel C. *War At Every Door: Partisan Politics and Guerrilla Violence in East Tennessee, 1860–1869.* Chapel Hill: University of North Carolina Press, 1997.

Fitts, Alston. *Selma: Queen City of the Black Belt.* Selma, AL: Clairmont Press, 1989.

Fitzgerald, Michael W. *Splendid Failure: Postwar Reconstruction in the American South.* Chicago: Ivan R. Dee, 2007.

_____. *The Union League Movement in the Deep South: Politics and Agricultural Change During Reconstruction.* Baton Rouge: Louisiana State University Press, 1989.

_____. *Urban Emancipation: Popular Politics in Reconstruction Mobile, 1860–1890.* Baton Rouge: Louisiana State University Press, 2002.

Fleming, Thomas J. *A Disease In the Public Mind: A New Understanding of Why We Fought the Civil War.* New York: Da Capo Press, 2013.

Fleming, Walter Lynwood. *Civil War and Reconstruction in Alabama.* Spartanburg, SC: Reprint Co., 1978.

Foner, Eric. *Reconstruction: America's Unfinished Revolution, 1863–1877.* New York: Perennial Classics, 2002.

_____. *The Fiery Trial: Abraham Lincoln and American Slavery*. New York: W.W. Norton & Co., 2010.

Foner, Philip S. *A History of Cuba and its Relations with the United States, 1845–1895*. 2 vols. New York: International Publishers, 1963.

Ford, Lacy K. *Origins of Southern Radicalism: The South Carolina Upcountry, 1800–1860*. New York: Oxford University Press, 1988.

Forbes, Robert Pierce. *The Missouri Compromise and its Aftermath: Slavery & the Meaning of America*. Chapel Hill: University of North Carolina Press, 2007.

Franklin, John Hope. *Reconstruction After the Civil War*. Chicago: University of Chicago Press, 1994.

_____, and Loren Schwenginger. *Runaway Slaves: Rebels On the Plantation*. New York: Oxford University Press, 1999.

Frazier, Joey. *Jefferson Davis: Confederate President*. Philadelphia: Chelsea House Publishers, 2001.

Freehling, William W. *Prelude to Civil War: The Nullification Controversy in South Carolina 18161836*. New York: Oxford University Press, 1966.

_____. *The Road to Disunion: Secessionists at By 1776–1854*. New York: Oxford University Press, 1990.

_____. *The South vs. The South: How Anti-Confederate Southerners Shaped the Course of the Civil War*. New York: Oxford University Press, 2001.

Frey, Jerry. *Three Quarter Cadillac: Common Sense for the Common Good*. Sandy, UT: N.P., 2008.

Friend, Jack. *West Wind, Flood Tide: The Battle of Mobile Bay*. Annapolis, MD: Naval Institute Press, 2004.

Fry, Joseph A. *John Tyler Morgan and the Search for Southern Autonomy*. Knoxville: University of Tennessee Press, 1992.

Fuller, A. James. *Chaplain to the Confederacy: Basil Manly and Baptist Life in the Old South*. Baton Rouge: Louisiana State University Press, 2000.

Gambill, Edward L. *Conservative Ordeal: Northern Democrats and Reconstruction, 1865–1868*. Ames: Iowa State University Press, 1981.

Garrett, William. *Reminiscences of Public Men in Alabama*. Atlanta: Plantation Pub. Co. Press, 1872.

Geggus, David P. *The Impact of the Haitian Revolution in the Atlantic World*. Columbia: University of South Carolina Press, 2001.

Getler, Warren, and Bob Brewer. *Shadow of the Sentinel: One Man's Quest to Find the Hidden Treasures of the Confederacy*. New York: Simon & Schuster, 2003.

Gienapp, William E. *The Origins of the Republican Party, 1852–1856*. New York: Oxford University Press, 1987.

Curry, J. L. M.. *William Ewart Gladstone*. Richmond: B.V. Johnson, 1891.

Glatthaar, Joseph T. *The March to the Sea and Beyond: Sherman's Troops in the Savannah and Carolinas Campaigns*. Baton Rouge: Louisiana State University Press, 1985.

Going, Charles Buxton. *David Wilmot, Free-Soiler: A Biography of the Great Advocate of the Wilmot Proviso.* Gloucester, MA: P. Smith, 1966.

Goodrich, Thomas, and Debra Goodrich Bisel. *The Day Dixie Died: Southern Occupation, 1865–1866.* Mechanicsburg, PA: Stackpole Books, 2001.

Goodrich, Thomas. *The Darkest Dawn: Lincoln, Booth, and the Great American Tragedy.* Bloomington: Indiana University Press, 2005.

Goodwin, Doris Kearns. *Team of Rivals: The Political Genius of Abraham Lincoln.* New York: Simon and Schuster, 2005.

Gordon-Reed, Anne. *Andrew Johnson.* New York: Henry Holt and Company, 2011.

Gott, Kendall D. *Where the South Lost the War: An Analysis of the Fort Henry – Fort Donelson Campaign, February 1862.* Mechanicsburg, PA: Stackpole Books, 2003.

Gould, Lewis L. *Alexander Watkins Terrell: Civil War Soldier, Texas Lawmaker, American Diplomat.* Austin: University of Texas Press, 2004.

Grable, Theodore Eli. "Financial Policy of Hugh McCulloch" (master's thesis, Indiana University, 1910).

Grant, Roger. *The Louisville, Cincinnati & Charleston Rail Road: Dreams of Linking North and South.* Bloomington: Indiana University Press, 2014.

Grant, Susan-Mary, and Peter J. Parish, eds. *Legacy of Disunion: The Enduring Significance of the American Civil War.* 48–64. Baton Rouge: Louisiana State University Press, 2003.

Green, Michael D. *The Politics of Indian Removal: Creek Government and Society in Crisis.* Lincoln: University of Nebraska Press, 1985.

_____. "Federal-State Conflict In the Administration of Indian Policy: Georgia, Alabama, and the Creeks, 1824–1834." PhD diss., University of Iowa, 1973.

Green, Michael S. *Politics and America in Crisis: The Coming of the Civil War.* Santa Barbara, CA: ABC-CLIO, LLC, 2010

Greenberg, Amy S. *A Wicked War: Polk, Clay, Lincoln, and the 1846 U.S. Invasion of Mexico.* New York: Vintage Books, 2012.

Griffith, Lucille. *Alabama: A Documentary History To 1900.* Tuscaloosa: University of Alabama Press, 1968.

Grimsley, Mark. *The Hard Hand of War: Union Military Policy Toward Southern Civilians 1861–1865.* Cambridge: Cambridge University Press, 1995.

Groom, Winston. *Vicksburg, 1863.* New York: Alfred A. Knopf, 2009.

Grossman, Lawrence. *The Democratic Party and the Negro: Northern and National Politics 1868–1892.* Urbana: University of Illinois Press, 1976.

Guelzo, Allen C. *Abraham Lincoln: Redeemer President.* Grand Rapids, MI: William B. Erdman's Publishing Co., 1999.

_____. *Fateful Lightning: A New History of the Civil War and Reconstruction.* New York: Oxford University Press, 2012.

Guttridge, Leonard F., and Ray A. Neff. *Dark Union: The Secret Web of Profiteers, Politicians, and Booth Conspirators That Led to Lincoln's Death.* Hoboken, NJ: Wiley, 2003.

Hackney, Sheldon. *Magnolias Without Moonlight: The American South from Regional Confederacy to National Integration.* New Brunswick, NJ: Transaction Publishers, 2005.

Hall, Clifton R. *Andrew Johnson: Military Governor of Tennessee.* Princeton, NJ: Princeton University Press, 1916.

Hall, James O., and Michael Maione, *"To Make a Fortune": John Wilkes Booth: Following the Money Trail.* Clinton, MD: Surratt Society, 2003.

Halperin, Rick. "Leroy Pope Walker and the Problems of the Confederate War Department, 1861." PhD diss., Auburn University, 1978.

Hammond, John Craig. *Slavery, Freedom and Expansion in the Early American West.* Charlottesville: University of Virginia Press, 2007.

Harncourt, Paul. *The Planter's Railway: Excitement and Civil War Years.* Arab, AL: Heritage, 1995.

Harrell, Carolyn L. *When the Bell Tolls for Lincoln: Southern Reaction To the Assassination.* Macon, GA: Mercer University Press, 1997.

Harris, Thomas M. *Assassination of Lincoln: A History of the Great Conspiracy.* Boston: American Citizen Co., 1892.

Harris, William C. *Leroy Pope Walker: Confederate Secretary of War.* Tuscaloosa: Confederate Pub. Co., 1962.

_____. *Lincoln's Last Months.* Cambridge, MA: Belknap Press, 2004.

Hartnett, Stephen John. *Democratic Dissent & the Cultural Fictions of Antebellum America.* Urbana: University of Illinois Press, 2002.

Hatch, Frederick. *Protecting President Lincoln: The Security Effort, the Thwarted Plots, and the Disaster at Ford's Theatre.* Jefferson, NC: McFarland & Co., Inc., 2011.

Hatchett, William. *The Lincoln Murder Conspiracies.* Urbana: University of Illinois Press, 1983.

Hattaway, Herman, and Richard Beringer. *Jefferson Davis, Confederate President.* Lawrence: University of Kansas Press, 2002.

Haulman, Clyde A. *Virginia and the Panic of 1819: The First Great Depression and the Commonwealth.* London: Routledge, 2008.

Hawes, Jesse. *Cahaba: A Story of Captive Boys in Blue.* New York: Burr Printing House, 1888.

Headley, John W. *Confederate Operations in Canada and New York.* New York: Neale Publishing Co., 1906.

Hearn, Chester G. *The Impeachment of Andrew Johnson.* Jefferson, NC: McFarland & Co., 2000.

_____. *Mobile Bay and the Mobile Campaign: The Last Great Battles of the Civil War.* Jefferson, NC: McFarland and Co., 1993.

_____. *The Impeachment of Andrew Johnson.* Jefferson, NC: McFarland & Co., Inc., 2007.

Heidler, David S., and Jeanne T. Heidler. *Henry Clay: The Essential American.* New York: Random House, 2010.

Henderson, Timothy J. *A Glorious Defeat: Mexico and Its War with the United States.* New York: Hill and Wang, 2008.

Herbert, Paul N. *God Knows All Your Names: Stories in American History.* Bloomington, IN: AuthorHouse, 2011.

Herr, Kincaid A. *The Louisville & Nashville Railroad, 1850–1963.* Lexington: University Press of Kentucky, 2000.

Hess, Earl J. *The Civil War in the West: Victory and Defeat from the Appalachians to the Mississippi.* Chapel Hill: University of North Carolina Press, 2012.

Hesseltine, William Best. *Civil War Prisons: A Study in War Psychology.* Columbus: Ohio State University Press, 1930.

_____. *Three Against Lincoln: Murat Halstead Reports the Caucuses of 1860.* Baton Rouge: Louisiana State University Press, 1960.

Hettle, Wallace. *The Peculiar Democracy: Southern Democrats in Peace and Civil War.* Athens: University of Georgia Press, 2001.

Heyman, Jr., Max L. *Prudent Soldier: A Biography of Major General E.R.S. Canby 1817 – 1873.* Glendale, CA: Arthur H. Clark Co., 1959.

Heyse, Amy L. *Teachers of the Lost Cause: The United Daughters of the Confederacy and the Rhetoric of Their Catechisms.* College Park: University of Maryland, 2006.

Hickey, Donald R. *The War of 1812: A Conflict Forgotten.* Urbana: University of Illinois Press, 2012.

Higham, Charles. *Murdering Mr. Lincoln: A New Detection of the 19th Century's Most Famous Crime.* Beverly Hills, CA: New Millennium Press, 2004.

Hodes, Martha. *Mourning Lincoln.* New Haven, CT: Yale University Press, 2015.

Hoffer, Williamjames. *The Caning of Charles Sumner: Honor, Idealism, and the Origins of the Civil War.* Baltimore: Johns Hopkins University Press, 2010.

Holt, Michael K. *The Rise and Fall of the American Whig Party: Jacksonian Politics and the Outset of the Civil War.* New York: Oxford University Press, 1999.

Holzer, Harold. *Lincoln at Cooper Union: The Speech That Made Abraham Lincoln President.* New York: Simon & Schuster, 2004.

Holzer, Harold, Edna Greene Medford, and Frank J. Williams. *The Emancipation Proclamation: Three Views.* Baton Rouge: Louisiana State University Press, 2006.

Hood, John Bell. *Advance and Retreat: Personal Experiences in the United States and Confederate States Armies.* New Orleans, LA: Hood Orphan Memorial Fund, 1880.

Hood, Stephen M. *John Bell Hood: The Rise, Fall, and Resurrection of a Confederate General.* El Dorado Hills, CA: Savas Beatie, 2013.

Hoole, William Stanley. *Alabama Tories, The First Alabama Cavalry, U.S.A., 1862–1865.* Tuscaloosa, AL: Confederate Pub. Co., 1960.

_____. *History of Shockley's Alabama Escort Company.* Tuscaloosa, AL: Confederate Publishing Co. 1983.

_____, ed. *History of the Seventh Alabama Cavalry Regiment Including Capt. Charles P. Storrs's Troop of University of Alabama Cadet Volunteers.* Tuscaloosa, AL: Confederate Publishing Co., 1984.

Hoole, William Stanley, and Elizabeth Hoole McArthur. *The Yankee Invasion of West Alabama, March-April, 1865.* Tuscaloosa, AL: Confederate Pub. Co., 1985.

Horwitz, Tony. *Midnight Rising: John Brown and the Raid that Sparked the Civil War.* New York: Henry Holt & Co., 2011.

Howard, Gene L. *Death At Cross Plains: An Alabama Reconstruction Tragedy.* Tuscaloosa: University of Alabama Press, 1984.

Hubbs, G. Ward. *Guarding Greensboro: A Confederate Company in the Making of a Southern Community.* Athens: University of Georgia Press, 2003.

_____. *Searching for Freedom After the Civil War: Klansman, Carpetbagger, Scalawag, and Freedman.* Tuscaloosa: University of Alabama Press, 2015.

_____. *Tuscaloosa: Portrait of An Alabama County: An Illustrated History.* Northridge, CA: Windsor Publications, 1987.

_____. *Voices from Company D: Diaries by the Greensboro Guards, Fifth Alabama Infantry Regiment, Army of Northern Virginia.* Athens: University of Georgia Press, 2003.

Huffman, Alan. *Sultana: Surviving Civil War, Prison, and the Worst Maritime Disaster in American History.* New York: Harper, 2009.

Hummel, Jeffrey Rogers. *Emancipating Slaves, Enslaving Free Men: A History of the American Civil War.* Chicago: Open Court, 1996.

Hunt, Alfred N. *Haiti's Influence on Antebellum America.* Baton Rouge: Louisiana State University Press, 1988.

Hurst, Jack. *Nathan Bedford Forrest: A Biography.* New York: Random House, 1994.

Huston, James L. *Calculating the Value of the Union: Slavery, Property Rights, and the Economic Origins of the Civil War.* Chapel Hill: University of North Carolina Press, 2003.

Hyman, Herold Melvin. *The Era of the Oath: Northern Loyalty Tests During the Civil War and Reconstruction.* Philadelphia: University of Pennsylvania Press, 1954.

Jack, Theodore Henley. "Sectionalism and Party Politics in Alabama 1819–1842." PhD diss., University of Chicago, 1919.

Jackson, III, Harvey H. *Inside Alabama: A Personal History of My State.* Tuscaloosa: University of Alabama Press, 2004.

_____. *Rivers of History: Life On the Coosa, Tallapoosa, Cahaba and Alabama.* Tuscaloosa: University of Alabama Press, 1995.

Jackson, Hermoine Dannelly. "The Life and Times of Robert Jemison, Jr., During the Civil War and Reconstruction" (master's thesis, University of Alabama, 1942).

Jackson, Walter M. *The Story of Selma.* Birmingham, AL: Birmingham Print Co., 1954.

James, Joseph Bliss. *The Ratification of the Fourteenth Amendment.* Macon, GA: Mercer University Press, 1984.

Jamieson, Perry D. *Spring 1865: The Closing Campaigns of the Civil War.* Lincoln: University of Nebraska Press, 2015.

Jampoler, Andrew C. A. *The Last Conspirator: John Surratt's Flight From the Gallows.* Annapolis: Naval Institute Press, 2008.

Jennings, Thelma. *The Nashville Convention: Southern Movement for Unity, 1848–1850.* Memphis, TN: Memphis State University Press, 1980.

Johannsen, Robert W. *Lincoln, the South and Slavery: The Political Dimension.* Baton Rouge: Louisiana State University, 1991.

_____. *Stephen A. Douglas.* Urbana: University of Illinois Press, 1997.

Johns, George Sibley. *Philip Henson, The Southern Union Spy.* St. Louis, MO: Nixon-Jones Print Co., 1887.

Johnson, Clint. *Pursuit: The Chase, Capture, Persecution, and Surprising Release of Confederate President Jefferson Davis.* New York: Citadel Press, 2008.

_____. *A Vast and Fiendish Plot: The Confederate Attack on New York City.* New York: Kensington Pub. Corp., 2010.

Johnson, David. *Decided On the Battlefield: Grant, Sherman, Lincoln, and the Election of 1864.* Amherst, NY: Prometheus Books, 2012.

Johnston, Jr., Ernest Barnwell. "Selma, Alabama, As a Center of Confederate War Production" (bachelor's thesis, Harvard College, 1952).

Johnston, Sr., Henry Poellnitz. *William R. King and His Kin.* Birmingham, AL: Featon Press, 1975.

Jones, Anthony James. *America and Guerrilla Warfare.* Lexington: University Press of Kentucky, 2000.

Jones, James P. *Yankee Blitzkrieg: Wilson's Raid Through Alabama and Georgia.* Lexington: University Press of Kentucky, 2000.

Jones, James S. *Life of Andrew Johnson, Seventeenth President of the United States.* New York: AMS Press, 1975.

Jordan, Winthrop. *White Over Black: American Attitudes Toward the Negro, 1550–1812.* Chapel Hill: University of North Carolina Press, 1968.

Kaczorowski, Robert J. *The Politics of Judicial Interpretation: The Federal Courts, Department of Justice and Civil Rights, 1866–1876.* New York: Fordham University Press, 2005.

Kane, Harnett T. *Spies for the Blue and Gray.* Garden City, NY: Hanover House, 1954.

Kaplan, Edward. *The Bank of the United States and the American Economy.* Westport, CT: Greenwood Press, 1999.

Kaufman, Michael W. *American Brutus: John Wilkes Booth and the Lincoln Conspiracies.* New York: Random House, 2004.

Keehn, David C. *Knights of the Golden Circle: Secret Empire, Southern Secession, Civil War.* Baton Rouge: Louisiana State University Press, 2013.

Keenan, Jerry. *Wilson's Cavalry Corps: Union Campaigns in the Western Theatre, October, 1864 Through Spring 1865.* Jefferson, NC: McFarland, 1998.

Keneally, Thomas. *American Scoundrel: The Life of the Notorious Civil War General Dan Sickles.* New York: Nan A. Talese/Doubleday, 2002.

Kinchen, Oscar A. *Confederate Operations in Canada and the North.* North Quincy, MA: Christopher Pub. House, 1970.

Kirkland, Edward C. *Peacemakers of 1864.* New York: MacMillan Company, 1927.

Klingaman, William K. *Abraham Lincoln and the Road to Emancipation 1861–1865.* New York: Viking, 2001.

Kolchin, Peter. *First Freedom: The Responses of Alabama's Blacks to Emancipation and Reconstruction.* Westport, CT: Greenwood Press, 1972.

Kvach, John F. *DeBow's Review: The Antebellum Vision of the New South.* Lexington: University Press of Kentucky, 2013.

Lapp, Rudolph M. *Blacks in Gold Rush California.* New Haven, CT: Yale University Press, 1977.

Larson, Kate Clifford. *The Assassin's Accomplice: Mary Surratt and the Plot to Kill Abraham Lincoln.* New York: Basic Books, 2008.

Lauderdale, Clara Mary. "Population of Alabama Between 1860 and 1870" (master's thesis, University of Wisconsin, 1912).

Lee, Susanna Michele. *Claiming the Union: Citizenship in the Post-Civil War South.* New York: Cambridge University Press, 2014.

Leftwich, Nina. *Two Hundred Years at Muscle Shoals.* Tusccumbia, AL: Viewpoint Press, 1935.

Lehrman, Lewis E. *Lincoln at Peoria: The Turning Point.* Mechanicsburg, PA: Stackpole Books, 2008.

Leonard, Elizabeth D. *Lincoln's Avengers: Justice, Revenge, and Reunion After the Civil War.* New York: W.W. Norton & Co., 2004.

_____. *Lincoln's Forgotten Ally: Judge Advocate General Joseph Holt of Kentucky.* Chapel Hill: University of North Carolina Press, 2011.

Lepa, Jack H. *Breaking the Confederacy: The Georgia and Tennessee Campaigns of 1864.* Jefferson, NC: McFarland & Co., 2005.

_____. *Grant's River Campaign: Fort Henry to Shiloh.* Jefferson, NC: McFarland & Company, Inc., 2014.

_____. *The Civil War in Tennessee, 1862–1863.* Jefferson, NC: McFarland & Co., 2007.

Lepler, Jessica M. *The Many Panics of 1837: People, Politics, and the Creation of a Transatlantic Financial Crisis.* New York: Cambridge University Press, 2013.

Levine, Bruce. *The Fall of the House of Dixie: The Civil War and the Social Revolution That Transformed the South.* New York: Random House, 2013.

_____. *Confederate Emancipation: Southern Plans to Free and Arm Slaves During the Civil War.* New York: Oxford University Press, 2006.

Lewis, Herbert James. *Clearing the Thickets: A History of Antebellum Alabama.* New Orleans: Quid Pro Books, 2013.

_____. *Lost Capitals of Alabama.* Charleston, SC: History Press, 2014.

Livermore, Thomas Leonard. *Numbers and Losses in the Civil War in America, 1861–1865.* Bloomington: Indiana University Press, 1957.

Loving, Waldon Spicer. *Coming Like Hell!: The Story of the 12th Tennessee Cavalry, Richardson's Brigade, Forrest's Cavalry Corps, Confederate States Army, 1862–1865.* San Jose, CA: Writers Club Press, 2002.

Lubetkin, M. John, *Jay Cooke's Gamble: The Northern Pacific Railroad, the Sioux, and the Panic of 1873.* Norman: University of Oklahoma Press, 2014.

Lucas, Marion Brunson. *Sherman and the Burning of Columbia.* Columbia: University of South Carolina Press, 2000.

MacKay, James A. *Allan Pinkerton: The First Private Eye.* New York: J. Wiley & Sons, 1997.

Magness, Phillip W., and Sebastian Page. *Colonization After Emancipation: Lincoln and the Movement for Black Resettlement.* Columbia: University of Missouri Press, 2011.

Mahin, Dean B. *One War at a Time: The International Dimensions of the American Civil War.* Washington, DC: Brassey's, 1999.

Martin, Bessie. *A Rich Man's War, A Poor Man's Fight: Desertion of Alabama Troops from the Confederate Army.* Tuscaloosa: University of Alabama Press, 2003.

_____. *Desertion of Alabama Troops From the Confederate Army: A Study in Sectionalism.* New York: Columbia University Press, 1932.

Martin, Samuel J. *Kill-Cavalry: The Life of Union General Hugh Judson Kilpatrick.* Mechanicsburg, PA: Stackpole Books, 2000.

Marvel, William. *Andersonville: The Last Depot.* Chapel Hill: University of North Carolina Press, 1994.

Maslowski, Peter. *Treason Must Be Made Odious, Military Occupation and Wartime Reconstruction In Nashville, Tennessee, 1862-65.* Millwood, NY: KTO Press, 1978.

Massey, Mary Elizabeth. *Refugee Life in the Confederacy.* Baton Rouge: Louisiana State University Press, 2001.

Mathis, Gerald Ray. *John Horry Dent, South Carolina Aristocrat On the Alabama Frontier.* Tuscaloosa: University of Alabama Press, 1979.

May, Robert E. *Manifest Destiny's Underworld: Filibustering in Antebellum America.* Chapel Hill: University of North Carolina Press, 2002.

Mayer, Henry. *All On Fire: William Lloyd Garrison and the Abolition of Slavery.* New York: W.W. Norton & Co., 1998.

McCash, William B. *Thomas R.R. Cobb: The Making of a Southern Nationalist.* Macon, GA. Mercer University Press, 1983.

McClintock, Russell. *Lincoln and the Decision for War: The Northern Response to Secession.* Chapel Hill: University of North Carolina Press, 2008.

McCrary, Peyton. *Abraham Lincoln and Reconstruction: The Louisiana Experiment.* Princeton, NJ: Princeton University Press, 1978.

McDonough, James Lee, and James Pickett Jones. *War So Terrible: Sherman and Atlanta.* New York: W.W. Norton & Co., 1987.

McFeely, William S. *Grant: A Biography.* New York: W.W. Norton & Co., 1981.

McGee, Val L. *Selma: A Novel of the Civil War.* Oxford, MS: Yoknapatowpha Press, 2008.

McGrane, Reginald Charles. *The Panic of 1837: Some Financial Problems of the Jacksonian Era.* Chicago: University of Chicago Press, 1965.

McKenzie, Robert T. *Lincolnites and Rebels: A Divided Town in the American Civil War*. Cambridge, MA: Harvard University Press, 2010.

McKitrick, Eric L. *Andrew Johnson and Reconstruction*. New York: Oxford University Press, 1988.

McMillan, Malcolm Cook. *Constitutional Development in Alabama, 1798–1901: A Study in Politics, the Negro, and Sectionalism*. Chapel Hill: University of North Carolina Press, 1955.

_____. *The Disintegration of a Confederate State: Three Governors and Alabama's Wartime Home Front, 1861–1865*. Macon, GA: Mercer University Press, 1986.

_____. *The Alabama Confederate Reader*. Tuscaloosa: University of Alabama Press, 1963.

_____. *The Land Called Alabama*. Austin, TX: Steck-Vaughn Co., 1968.

McMurry, Richard M. *Atlanta 1864: Last Chance for the Confederacy*. Lincoln: University of Nebraska Press, 2000.

McNair, Glenn. *Criminal Injustice: Slaves and Free Blacks in Georgia's Criminal Justice System*. Charlottesville: University of Virginia Press, 2009.

McNeely, Patricia G., Debra Redding van Tuyll, and Henry H. Schulte. *Knights of the Quill: Confederate Correspondents and Their Civil War Reporting*. West Lafayette, IN: Purdue University Press, 2010.

McPherson, James M. *Abraham Lincoln*. New York: Oxford University Press, 2009.

McPherson, James M. *Battle Cry of Freedom: The Civil War Era*. New York: Oxford University Press, 1988.

_____. *The Struggle for Equality: Abolitionists and the Negro in the Civil War and Reconstruction*. Princeton, NJ: Princeton University Press, 1964.

_____. *War on the Waters: The Union and Confederate Navies, 1861–1865*. Chapel Hill: University of North Carolina Press, 2012.

McWhiney, Grady. *Braxton Bragg and Confederate Defeat*. New York: Columbia University Press, 1969.

McWhiney, Grady, Warner O. Moore, Jr., and Robert F. Pace, eds. *"Fear God and Walk Humbly": The Agricultural Journal of James Mallory, 1843–1877*. Tuscaloosa: University of Alabama Press, 1997.

Means, Howard B. *The Avenger Takes His Place: Andrew Johnson and the 45 days that Changed the Nation*. Orlando, FL: Harcourt, Inc., 2006.

Menaster, Kimberly. "Political Violence in the American South: 1882–1890" (master's thesis, MIT, 2009).

Merchant, Holt. *South Carolina Fire-Eater: The Life of Laurence Massillion Keitt, 1824–1864*. Columbia: University of South Carolina Press, 2014.

Merry, Robert W. *A Country of Vast Designs: James K. Polk, the Mexican War, and the Conquest of the American Continent*. New York: Simon & Schuster, 2009.

Mieczkowski, Yanek. *The Routledge Historical Atlas of Presidential Elections*. New York: Routledge, 2001.

Miller, James David. *South by Southwest: Planter Emigration and the Identity of the Slave South.* Charlottesville: University of Virginia Press, 2002.

Miller, John Chester. *The Wolf By the Ears: Thomas Jefferson and Slavery.* Charlottesville: University Press of Kentucky, 1995.

Miller, Rex. *Croxton's Raid.* Fort Collins, CO: Old Army Press, 1979.

Miller, William Lee. *Arguing About Slavery: The Great Battle in the United States Congress.* New York: Vintage, 1996.

Milton, George Fort. *Age of Hate: Andrew Johnson and the Radicals.* Hamden, CT: Archon Books, 1965.

Misulia, Charles A. *Columbus, Georgia, 1865: The Last True Battle of the Civil War.* Tuscaloosa: University of Alabama Press, 2010.

Mize, Joel Sanford. *Unionists of the Warrior Mountains of Alabama.* Lakewood, CO: Dixie Historical Research & Education Publication, 2004.

Moore, Albert Burton. *Conscription and Conflict in the Confederacy.* New York: MacMillan Company, 1924.

_____. *History of Alabama.* Tuscaloosa: Alabama Book Store, 1951.

Morrison, Champlain W. *Democratic Politics and Sectionalism: The Wilmot Proviso Controversy.* Chapel Hill: University of North Carolina Press, 1967.

Morrison, Michael A. *Slavery and the American West: The Eclipse of Manifest Destiny and the Coming of the Civil War.* Chapel Hill: University of North Carolina Press, 1997.

Murray, Robert Bruce. *Legal Cases of the Civil War.* Mechanicsburg, PA: Stackpole Books, 2003.

Neely, Mark E. *Southern Rights: Political Prisoners and the Myth of Confederate Constitutionalism.* Charlottesville: University Press of Virginia, 1999.

Neely, Mary Ann, ed. *The Works of Matthew Blue: Montgomery's First Historian.* Montgomery: NewSouth Books, 2010.

Neiman, Donald G., ed. *Freedom, Racism, and Reconstruction: Collected Writings of LaWanda Cox.* Athens: University of Georgia Press, 1997.

Nelson, Larry E. *Bullets, Ballots and Rhetoric: Confederate Policy for the United States Presidential Contest of 1864.* Tuscaloosa: University of Alabama Press, 1980.

Nevins, Allan. *The Emergence of Lincoln.* New York: Scribner, 1950.

Nevkov, Julie Lavonie. *Radical Union: Law, Intimacy, and the White State in Alabama, 18651954.* Ann Arbor: University of Michigan Press, 2008.

Newman, Jennifer Ann. "Writing, Religion and Women's Identity in Civil War Alabama." PhD diss., Auburn University, 2009.

Niven, John. *John C. Calhoun and the Price of Union: A Biography.* Baton Rouge: Louisiana State University Press, 1988.

Noe, Kenneth W., ed. *The Yellowhammer War: The Civil War and Reconstruction in Alabama.* Tuscaloosa: University of Alabama Press, 2013.

Nolen, David L. "Wilson's Raid on the Coal and Iron Industry in Shelby County" (master's thesis, University of Alabama, Birmingham, 1988).

Novak, Daniel A. *The Wheel of Servitude: Black Forced Labor After Slavery.* Lexington: University Press of Kentucky, 1978.

Nuermberger, Ruth Ketring. *The Clays of Alabama: A Planter-Lawyer-Politician Family.* Tuscaloosa: University of Alabama Press, 2005.

Nunn, W. C. *Escape from Reconstruction.* Fort Worth: Texas Christian University Press, 1962.

Oakes, James. *Freedom National: The Destruction of Slavery in the United States, 1861–1865.* New York: W.W. Norton & Co., 2013.

_____. *The Radical and the Republican: Frederick Douglass, Abraham Lincoln, and the Triumph of Anti-Slavery Politics.* New York: W.W. Norton & Co., 2007.

O'Brien, Sean Michael. *Mobile 1865: Last Stand of the Confederacy.* Westport, CT: Praeger, 2001.

_____. *In Bitterness and in Tears: Andrew Jackson's Destruction of the Creeks and Seminoles.* Guilford, CT: Lyons Press, 2005.

_____. *Mountain Partisans: Guerrilla Warfare in the Southern Appalachians, 1861–1865.* Westport, CT: Praeger, 1999.

Oldshue, Jerry C. "The Secession Movement in Tuscaloosa County, Alabama" (master's thesis, University of Alabama, 1961).

Onofrio, Jan. *Alabama Biographical Dictionary.* St. Clair Shores, MI: Somerset Publishers, 1998.

O'Reilly, Bill, and Martin Dugard. *Killing Lincoln: The Shocking Assassination that Changed America Forever.* New York: Henry Holt and Co., 2011.

Ott, Thomas O. *The Haitian Revolution, 1789–1804.* Knoxville: University of Tennessee Press, 1973.

Overdyke, Darrell. *The Know-Nothing Party in the South.* Baton Rouge: Louisiana State University Press, 1968.

Owen, Thomas McAdory. *History of Alabama and Dictionary of Alabama Biography.* 4 vols. Spartanburg, SC: Reprint Co., 1978.

Ownsbey, Betty J. *Alias "Paine": Lewis Thorton Powell, The Mystery Man of the Lincoln Conspiracy.* Jefferson, NC: McFarland & Co., 1993.

Parks, Joseph H. *Joseph E. Brown of Georgia.* Baton Rouge: Louisiana State University Press, 1977.

Parrish, T. Michael. *Richard Taylor: Soldier Prince of Dixie.* Chapel Hill: University of North Carolina Press, 1992.

Parsons, Lynn H. *The Birth of Modern Politics: Andrew Jackson, John Quincy Adams, and the Election of 1828.* New York: Oxford University Press, 2009.

Patterson, Gerard A. *From Blue to Gray: The Life of Confederate General Cadmus M. Wilcox.* Mechanicsburg, PA: Stackpole, 2001.

Pattillo, Edward. *Carolina Planters on the Alabama Frontier: The Spencer-Robeson-McKenzie Family Papers.* Montgomery, AL: NewSouth Books, 2011.

Pearce, George F. *Pensacola During the Civil War: A Thorn in the Side of the Confederacy.* Gainesville: University Press of Florida, 2000.

Perman, Michael. *Reunion without Compromise: The South and Reconstruction 1865–1868.* New York: Cambridge University Press, 1973.

Perret, Geoffrey. *Lincoln's War: The Untold Story of America's Greatest President as Commander In Chief.* New York: Random House, 2004.

Peterson, Merrill D. *The Great Triumvirate: Webster, Clay, and Calhoun.* New York: Oxford University Press, 1987.

_____. *Olive Branch and Sword: The Compromise of 1833.* Baton Rouge: Louisiana State University Press, 1982.

Pfanz, Donald C. *Petersburg Campaign: Abraham Lincoln at City Point, March 20-April 9, 1865.* Lynchburg, VA: H.E. Howard, 1989.

_____. *Richard S. Ewell: A Soldier's Life.* Chapel Hill: University of North Carolina Press, 1998.

Phillips, Jason. *Diehard Rebels: The Confederate Culture of Invincibility.* Athens: University of Georgia Press, 2010.

Pitch, Anthony S. *"They Have Killed papa Dead!": The Road to Ford's Theatre, Abraham Lincoln's Murder, and the Rage for Vengeance.* Hanover, NH: Steerforth Press, 2008.

Poage, George Rawlings. *Henry Clay and the Whig Party.* Chapel Hill: University of North Carolina Press, 1936.

Potter, David M. *The Impending Crisis: 1848–1861.* New York: Harper & Row Publishers, Inc., 1976.

_____. *Lincoln and His Party in the Secession Crisis.* Baton Rouge: Louisiana State University Press, 1995.

Powell, Lawrence N. *New Masters: Northern Planters During the Civil War and Reconstruction.* New York: Fordham University Press, 1998.

Pribanic-Smith, Erika Jean. "Sewing the Seeds of Disunion: South Carolina's Partisan Newspapers and the Nullification Crisis." PhD diss., University of Alabama, 2010.

Prince, Cathryn J. *Burn the Town and Sack the Banks!: Confederates Attack Vermont.* New York: Carroll & Graf Publishers, 2006.

Pruitt, Jr., Paul M. *Taming Alabama: Lawyers and Reformers, 1804–1929.* Tuscaloosa: University of Alabama Press, 2010.

Puleo, Stephen. *The Caning: The Assault that Drove America to Civil War.* Yardley, PA: Westholme Publishing, 2012.

Quill, James Michael. *Prelude to the Radicals: The North and Reconstruction.* Washington, DC: University Press of America, 1980.

Rable, George C. *But There was No Peace: The Role of Violence in the Politics of Reconstruction.* Athens, GA.: University of Georgia Press, 2007.

_____. *Civil Wars: Women and the Crisis of Southern Nationalism.* Urbana: University of Illinois Press, 1989.

_____. *God's Almost Chosen Peoples: A Religious History of the American Civil War.* Chapel Hill: University of North Carolina Press, 2010.

_____. *The Confederate Republic: A Revolution Against Politics.* Chapel Hill: University of North Carolina Press, 1994.

Rachleff, Marshall J. "Racial Fear and Political Factionalism: A Study of the Secession Movement in Alabama, 1819–1861." PhD diss., University of Massachusetts, 1974.

Rafuse, Ethan Sepp. *Robert E. Lee and the Fall of the Confederacy, 1863–1865.* Lanham, MD: Rowman & Littlefield Publishers, Inc., 2008.

Ragan, Mark K. *Confederate Saboteurs: Building the Hunley and Other Secret Weapons of the Civil War.* College Station: Texas A&M University Press, 2015.

Randolph County Heritage Book Committee. *The Heritage of Randolph County, Alabama.* Randolph County, AL: Heritage Pub. Consultants, 1998.

Ratner, Lorman A. *Andrew Jackson and His Lieutenants: A Study in Political Culture.* Westport, CT: Greenwood Press, 1997.

Rayback, Joseph G. *Free Soil: The Election of 1848.* Lexington: University Press of Kentucky, 2014.

Reck, W. Emerson. *A. Lincoln, His Last 24 Hours.* Jefferson, NC: McFarland & Co., 1987.

Rehnquist, William H. *All the Laws But One: Civil Liberties in Wartime.* New York: Knopf, 2001.

Rice, Charles. *Hard Times: The Civil War in Huntsville and North Alabama.* Huntsville, AL: Old Huntsville, 1995.

Remini, Robert V. *Andrew Jackson and the Bank War: A Study in the Growth of Presidential Power.* New York: W.W. Norton & Co., 1967.

_____. *Andrew Jackson: The Course of American Empire, 1767–1821.* New York: Harper & Row, 1977.

_____. *Andrew Jackson: The Course of American Freedom, 1822–1832.* Baltimore: Johns Hopkins University Press, 1998.

_____. *Daniel Webster: The Man and His Time.* New York: W.W. Norton & Co., 1997.

Remini, Robert V. *Daniel Webster: The Man and His Time.* New York: W.W. Norton, 1997.

Rhodehamel, John H., and Louise Taper, eds. *Right or Wrong, God Judge Me: The Writings of John Wilkes Booth.* Urbana: University of Illinois Press, 1997.

Rice, Charles. *Hard Times: The Civil War in Huntsville and North Alabama.* Huntsville, AL: Old Huntsville, 1995.

Rice, Jessie Pearl. *J.L.M. Curry: Southerner, Statesman and Educator.* New York: Kings Crown Press, 1949.

Richards, Leonard L *The California Gold Rush and the Coming of the Civil War.* New York: Vintage, 2008.

Roberts, Alasdair. *America's First Great Depression: Economic Crisis and Political Disorder After the Panic of 1837.* Ithaca, NY: Cornell University Press, 2012.

Rodrigue, John C. *Lincoln and Reconstruction.* Carbondale: Southern Illinois University Press, 2013.

Rodriguez, Junius P., ed. *Slavery in the United States: A Social, Political, and Historical Encyclopedia.* Santa Barbara, CA: ABC-CLIO, 2007.

Rogers, Jr., William Warren. *Black Belt Scalawag: Charles Hays and the Southern Republicans in the Era of Reconstruction.* Athens: University of Georgia Press, 1993.

_____. *Confederate Home Front: Montgomery During the Civil War.* Tuscaloosa: University of Alabama Press, 1999.

Rogers, Sr., William Warren, Robert David Ward, Leah Rawls Atkins, and Wayne Flynt. *Alabama: The History of a Deep South State.* Tuscaloosa: University of Alabama Press, 2010.

Rogers, Sr., William Warren. *The One-Gallused Rebellion: Agrarianism in Alabama, 1865–1896.* Baton Rouge: Louisiana State University Press, 1970.

Rohrbough, Malcolm J. *The Land Office Business: The Settlement and Administration of American Public Lands, 1789–1837.* New York: Oxford Univerity Press, 1968.

_____. *The Trans-Appalachian Frontier: People, Societies, and Institutions 1775–1850.* Bloomington: Indiana University Press, 2008.

Rothbard, Murry N. *The Panic of 1819: Reactions and Policies.* New York: Columbia University Press, 1962.

Rothman, Adam. *Slave Country: American Expansion and the Origins of the Deep South.* Cambridge: Harvard University Press, 2005.

Rothman, Joshua D. *Flush Times and Fever Dreams: A Story of Capitalism and Slavery in the Age of Jackson.* Athens: University of Georgia Press, 2012.

Rowland, Dunbar. *Jefferson Davis: Constitutionalist.* Jackson: Printed for the Mississippi Department of Archives and History, 1923.

Rubin, Anne S. *A Shattered Nation: The Rise and Fall of the Confederacy, 1861–1868.* Chapel Hill: University of North Carolina Press, 2005.

Ruhlman, Fred F. *Captain Henry Wirz and Andersonville Prison: A Reappraisal.* Knoxville: University of Tennessee Press, 2006.

Rumore, Pat Boyd. *From Power to Service: The Story of Lawyers in Alabama.* Montgomery: Alabama State Bar, 2010.

Russel, Robert Royal. "Economic Aspects of Southern Sectionalization, 1840–1861." PhD diss., University of Illinois, 1922.

Rutherglen, George. *Civil Rights in the Shadow of Slavery: The Constitution, Common Law, and the Civil Rights Act of 1866.* New York: Oxford University Press, 2013.

Satz, Ronald N. *American Indian Policy in the Jacksonian Era.* Norman: University of Oklahoma Press, 2002.

Saunders, James Edmonds. *Early Settlers of Alabama.* Westminster, MD: Heritage Books, 2009.

Saunders, Jr., Robert. *John Archibald Campbell, Southern Moderate: 1811–1889.* Tuscaloosa: University of Alabama Press, 1997.

Scaturro, Frank J. *The Supreme Court's Retreat from Reconstruction: A Distortion of Constitutional Jurisprudence.* Westport, CT: Greenwood Press, 2000.

Schlesinger, Jr., Arthur M., ed. *History of American Presidential Elections, 1789–1968.* New York: Chelsea House, 1971.

Schmidt, Cheryl. *Separated Souls: A Novel*. New York: iUniverse, Inc., 2005.

Schoen, Brian. *The Fragile Fabric of Union: Cotton, Federal Politics, and the Global Origins of the Civil War*. Baltimore, MD: Johns Hopkins University Press, 2009.

Schott, Thomas E. *Alexander H. Stephens of Georgia: A Biography*. Baton Rouge: Louisiana State University Press, 1988.

Schultz, Duane. *The Dahlgren Affair: Terror and Conspiracy in the Civil War*. New York: W.W. Norton & Co., 1998.

Schwab, John Christopher. *The Confederate States of America 1861–1865: A Financial and Industrial History of the South During the War*. New York: Burt Franklin, 1968.

Seip, Terry L. *The South Returns to Congress: Men, Economic Measures, and Intersectional Relationships, 1868–1879*. Baton Rouge: Louisiana State University Press, 1983.

Sellers, Charles. *The Market Revolution: Jacksonian America 1815–1846*. New York: Oxford University Press, 1991.

Sellers, James Benson. *History of the University of Alabama*. Tuscaloosa: University of Alabama Press, 1953.

_____. *Slavery in Alabama*. Tuscaloosa: University of Alabama Press, 1950.

_____. *The Prohibition Movement in Alabama, 1702–1943*. Chapel Hill: University of North Carolina Press, 1943.

Severance, Ben H. *Portraits of Conflict: A Photographic History of Alabama in the Civil War*. Fayetteville: University of Arkansas Press, 2012.

_____. *Tennessee's Radical Army: The State Guard and Its Role in Reconstruction, 1867–1869*. Knoxville: University of Tennessee Press, 2005.

Sexton, Jay. *Debtor Diplomacy: Finance and American Foreign Relations in the Civil War Era 1837–1873*. New York: Clarendon, 2005.

Shields, Johanna Nichol. *Freedom in a Slave Society: Stories from the Antebellum South*. Cambridge: Cambridge University Press, 2012.

Silbey, Joel H. *Martin Van Buren and the Emergence of American Popular Politics*. Lanham, MD: Rowman & Littlefield Publishers, 2002.

_____. *Storm Over Texas: The Annexation Controversy and the Road to Civil War*. New York: Oxford University Press, 2005.

_____, ed. *The American Party Battle: Election Campaign Pamphlets, 1828–1876*. 2 vols. Cambridge, MA: Belknap Press, 1999.

Silver, James W. *Confederate Morale, and Church Propaganda*. Tuscaloosa: Confederate Pub. Co., 1957.

Simms, William Gilmore. *A City Laid Waste: The Capture, Sack, and Destruction of the City of Columbia*. Columbia: University of South Carolina Press, 2005.

Simon, John Y., Harold Holzer, and Dawn Vogel, eds. *Lincoln Revisited: New Insights from the Lincoln Forum*. New York: Fordham University Press, 2007.

Simpson, Brooks D. *Let Us Have Peace: Ulysses S. Grant and the Politics of War and Reconstruction, 1861–1868*. Chapel Hill: University of North Carolina Press, 1991.

_____. *Gettysburg, 1863*. Sterling, VA: Potomac Books, 2013.

Simpson, Brooks D., Leroy P. Graf, and John Muldowny, eds. *Advice After Appomattox: Letters to Andrew Johnson, 1865–1866.* Knoxville: University of Tennessee Press, 1987.

Simpson, John Eddins. *Howell Cobb: The Politics of Ambition.* Chicago: Adams Press, 1973.

Singer, Jane. *The Confederate Dirty War: Arson, Bombings, Assassination and Plots for Chemical and Germ attacks on the Union.* Jefferson, NC: McFarland & Co., Inc., 2005.

Sinha, Manisha. *Counterrevolution of Slavery: Politics and Ideology in Antebellum South Carolina.* Chapel Hill: University of North Carolina Press, 2000.

Sisk, Glenn Nolen. "John Anthony Winston: Alabama's Veto Governor" (master's thesis, University of Alabama, 1934).

Skeen, Carl Edward. *1816: America Rising.* Lexington: University Press of Kentucky, 2003.

Slabaugh, Arlie R. *Confederate States Paper Money: Civil War Currency from the South.* Iola, WI: Krause Publications, 2011.

Smith and Deland. *North Alabama, Historical and Biographical.* Birmingham: Smith & Deland, 1888.

Smith, Andrew F. *Starving the South: How the North Won the Civil War.* New York: St. Martin's Press, 2011.

Smith, Charles Anthony. *The Rise and Fall of War Crimes Trials: From Charles I to Bush II.* New York: Cambridge University Press, 2012.

Smith, Derek. *In the Lion's Mouth: Hood's Tragic Retreat from Nashville, 1864.* Mechanicsburg, PA: Stackpole Books, 2011.

Smith, Elbert B. *The Presidencies of Zachary Taylor and Millard Fillmore.* Lawrence: University Press of Kansas, 1988.

Smith, John David, and J. Vincent Lowery. *The Dunning School: Historians, Race, and the Meaning of Reconstruction.* Lexington: University Press of Kentucky, 2013.

Smith, Justin H. *The Annexation of Texas.* New York: MacMillan Co., 1919.

Smith, Page. *A People's History of the Antebellum Years: The Nation Comes of Age.* New York: McGraw-Hill, 1981.

Southerland, Jr., Henry DeLeon, and Jerry Elijah Brown. *The Federal Road Through Georgia, The Creek Nation and Alabama, 1806–1836.* Tuscaloosa: University of Alabama Press, 1989.

Spann, Edward K. *Gotham At War: New York City 1860–1865.* Wilmington, DE: Scholarly Resources, Inc., 2002.

Speer, Lonnie R. *Portals to Hell: Military Prisons of the Civil War.* Mechanicsburg, PA: Stackpole Books, 1997.

Stahr, Walter. *Seward: Lincoln's Indispensable Man.* New York: Simon & Schuster, 2012.

Stampp, Kenneth Milton. *The Peculiar Institution: Slavery in the Antebellum South.* New York: Knoph, 1956.

Stashover, Daniel: *The Hour of Peril: The Secret Plot to Murder Lincoln Before the Civil War.* New York: Minotaur Books, 2013.

Steers, Jr., Edward. *Blood on the Moon: The Assassination of Abraham Lincoln.* Lexington: University Press of Kentucky, 2001.

_____. *Lincoln Legends: Myths, Hoaxes, and Confabulations Associated with Our Greatest President.* Lexington: University Press of Kentucky, 2007.

_____. *The Trial: The Assassination of President Lincoln and the Trial of the Conspirators.* Lexington: University Press of Kentucky, 2010.

Steers, Edward, and Harold Holzer, eds. *The Lincoln Assassination Conspirators: Their Confinement and Execution, as Recorded in the Letterbook of John Frederick Hartranft.* Baton Rouge: Louisiana State University Press, 2009.

Stephens, Larry David. *John P. Gatewood, Confederate Bushwhacker.* Gretna, LA: Pelican Pub. Co., 2012.

Sterkx, H. E. *Partners in Rebellion: Alabama Women in the Civil War.* Rutherford, NJ: Farleigh Dickinson University Press, 1970.

Stashower, Daniel. *The Hour of Peril: The Secret Plot to Murder Lincoln Before the Civil War.* New York: Minotaur Books, 2013.

Stewart, David O. *Impeached: The Trial of President Johnson and the Fight for Lincoln's Legacy.* New York: Simon & Schuster, 2009.

Stewart, John Craig. *The Governors of Alabama.* Gretna, LA: Pelican, 1975.

Stoker, Donald. *The Grand Design: Strategy and the U.S. Civil War.* New York: Oxford University Press, 2010.

Storey, Margaret M. *Loyalty and Loss: Alabama's Unionists in the Civil War and Reconstruction.* Baton Rouge: Louisiana State University Press, 2004.

Stout, Harry S. *Upon the Altar of the Nation: A Moral History of the American Civil War.* New York: Penguin Books, 2007.

Striner, Richard. *Father Abraham: Lincoln's Relentless Struggle to End Slavery.* New York: Oxford University Press, 2006.

Strode, Hudson. *Jefferson Davis: Tragic Hero.* New York: Harcourt, Brace & Co., 1964.

Studenski, Paul, and Herman Edward Krooss. *Financial History of the United States.* New York: McGraw-Hill, 1963.

Summers, Mark W. *A Dangerous Stir: Fear, Paranoia, and the Making of Reconstruction.* Chapel Hill: University of North Carolina Press, 2009.

Summers, Robert K. *The Fall and Redemption of Dr. Samuel Mudd: The True Story of the Doctor Who Went to Prison for Helping Abraham Lincoln's Assassin, John Wilkes Booth.* Morristown, NC: Self-published, 2008.

Sutherland, Daniel E. *A Savage Conflict: The Decisive Role of Guerrillas in the American Civil War.* Chapel Hill: University of North Carolina Press, 2009.

Swanson, James L. *Manhunt: The 12-Day Chase for Lincoln's Killer.* New York: Harper Collins, 2007.

Sweikart, Larry. *Banking in the American South from the Age of Jackson to Reconstruction.* Baton Rouge: Louisiana State University Press, 1987.

Swinney, Everette. *Enforcing the Fifteenth Amendment, 1870–1877.* Baton Rouge: Louisiana State University Press, 1962.

Sword, Wiley. *Embrace an Angry Wind: The Confederacy's Last Hurrah: Spring Hill, Franklin, and Nashville.* New York: Harper Collins, 1992.

Symonds, Craig L. *Joseph E. Johnston: A Civil War Biography.* New York: W.W. Norton & Company, 1992.

Tap, Bruce. *Over Lincoln's Shoulder: The Committee on the Conduct of the War.* Lawrence: University of Kansas Press, 1998.

Tatum, Georgia Lee. *Disloyalty in the Confederacy.* Lincoln: University of Nebraska Press, 2000.

Taylor, Alan. *The Internal Enemy: Slavery and War in Virginia, 1772–1832.* New York: W.W. Norton & Co., Inc., 2013.

Taylor, Frazine K. *Researching African American Genealogy in Alabama: A Resource Guide.* Montgomery, AL: NewSouth Books, 2008.

Taylor, John M. *William Henry Seward: Lincoln's Right Hand.* Washington DC: Potomac Books, Inc., 1981.

Taylor, Richard. *Destruction and Reconstruction: Personal Experiences of the Late War.* Edinburgh: Blackwood and Sons, 1879.

Temin, Peter. *The Jacksonian Economy.* New York: W.W. Norton, 1969.

Thomas, Emory M. *The Confederacy as a Revolutionary Experience.* Englewood Cliffs, NJ: Prentice-Hall, 1971.

_____. *The Confederate State of Richmond: A Biography of the Capital.* Baton Rouge: Louisiana State University Press, 1998.

Thomas, William G. *The Iron Way: Railroads, the Civil War, and the Making of Modern America.* New Haven, CT: Yale University Press, 2011.

Thornton, J. Mills. *Politics and Power in a Slave Society: Alabama, 1800–1860.* Baton Rouge: Louisiana State University Press, 1978.

Tidwell, William A. *April '65: Confederate Covert Action in the Civil War.* Kent, OH: Kent State University Press, 1995.

Tidwell, William A., James O. Hall, and David Winfrey Gaddy. *Come Retribution: The Confederate Secret Service and the Assassination of Abraham Lincoln.* Jackson: University Press of Mississippi, 1988.

Titone, Nora. *My thoughts Be Bloody: The Bitter Rivalry that Led to the Assassination of Abraham Lincoln.* New York: Free Press, 2010.

Todd, Glenda McWhirter. *First Alabama Cavalry, U.S.A.: Homage to Patriotism.* Bowie, MD: Heritage Books, 1999.

Towns, Peggy Allen. *Duty Driven: The Plight of North Alabama's African Americans During the Civil War.* Bloomington: Authorhouse, 2012.

Trefousse, Hans L. *Andrew Johnson: A Biography.* New York: W.W. Norton & Co., 1989.

Trelease, Allen W. *White Terror: The Ku Klux Klan Conspiracy and Southern Reconstruction.* New York: Harper and Row, 1971.

Trudeau, Noah Andre. *Southern Storm: Sherman's March to the Sea.* New York: Harper, 2008.

_____. *Out of the Storm: The End of the Civil War, April-June, 1865.* Boston: Little, Brown, 1991.

Tsesis, Alexander. *The Thirteenth Amendment and American Freedom: A Legal History.* New York: New York University Press, 2004.

Tucker, Spencer. *Andrew Foote: Civil War Admiral on Western Waters.* Annapolis, MD: Naval Institute Press, 2000.

Turner, Thomas Reed. *Beware the People Weeping: Public Opinion and the Assassination of Abraham Lincoln.* Baton Rouge: Louisiana State University Press, 1982.

Unger, Irwin. *The Greenback Era: A Social and Political History of American Finance, 1865-1879.* Princeton, NJ: Princeton University Press, 1968.

Urwin, Gregory J. W. *Black Flag Over Dixie: Racial Atrocities and Reprisals in the Civil War.* Carbondale: Southern Illinois University Press, 2004.

U.S. Congress. *Biographical Directory of the American Congress, 1774–1949.* Washington, DC: US Government Printing Office, 1950.

Van Atta, John R. *Securing the West: Politics, Public Lands and the Fate of the Old Republic, 1785–1850.* Baltimore, MD: Johns Hopkins University Press, 2014.

Van Deusen, Glyndon G. *William Henry Seward.* New York: Oxford University Press, 1967.

Vandiver, Frank Everson. *Ploughshares Into Swords: Josiah Gorgas and Confederate Ordinance.* Austin: University of Texas Press, 1952.

Varon, Elizabeth R. *Appomattox: Victory, Defeat, and Freedom at the End of the Civil War.* New York: Oxford University Press, 2014.

_____. *Disunion! The Coming of the American Civil War, 1789–1859.* Chapel Hill: University of North Carolina Press, 2008.

Vaughn, J. Barry. *Bishops, Bourbons, and Big Mules: A History of the Episcopal Church in Alabama.* Tuscaloosa: University of Alabama Press, 2013.

Venter, Bruce M. *Kill Jeff Davis: The Union Raid on Richmond, 1864.* Norman: University of Oklahoma Press, 2016.

Wait, Eugene M. *America and the War of 1812.* Cammack, NY: Kroshka Books, 1999.

Wakelyn, Jon L. *Confederates Against the Confederacy: Essays on Leadership and Loyalty.* Westport, CT: Praeger, 2002.

Walker, John L. *Cahaba Prison and the Sultana Disaster.* Hamilton, OH: Press of Brown and Whitaker, 1910.

Wallace, Anthony F. C. *The Long Bitter Trail: Andrew Jackson and the Indians.* New York: Hill and Wang, 1993.

Walvin, James. *England, Slaves and Freedom, 1776–1838.* Jackson: University Press of Mississippi, 1986.

Walther, Eric H. *The Fire-Eaters.* Baton Rouge: Louisiana State University Press, 1992.

_____. *William Lowndes Yancey and the Coming of the Civil War.* Chapel Hill: University of North Carolina Press, 2006.

Walton, Hanes, Sherman C. Puckett, and Donald Richard Deskins. *The African American Electorate: A Statistical History.* Thousand Oaks, CAL: CQ Press, 2012.

Wang, Xi. *Trial of Democracy: Black Suffrage and Northern Republicans, 1860–1910.* Athens: University of Georgia Press, 1997.

Ward, Andrew. *River Run Red: The Fort Pillow Massacre in the American Civil War.* New York: Viking, 2005.

Warner, Ezra J. *Generals in Gray: Lives of the Confederate Commanders.* Baton Rouge: Louisiana State University Press, 1987.

Warner, Ezra J., and W. Buck Yearns. *Biographical Register of the Confederate Congress.* Baton Rouge: Louisiana State University Press, 1975.

Warren, Robert Penn. *The Legacy of the Civil War.* Lincoln: University of Nebraska Press, 1998.

Warshauer, Matthew. *Andrew Jackson and the Politics of Martial Law: Nationalism, Civil Liberties, and Partisanship.* Knoxville: University of Tennessee, 2006.

Watson, Elbert L. *Alabama United Senators.* Huntsville: Strode Publishers, 1982.

Watson, Robert P. *America's First Crises: The War of 1812.* Albany: State University of New York Press, 2014.

Webb, Sam L., and Margaret E. Armbrester. *Alabama Governors: A Political History of the State.* Tuscaloosa: University of Alabama Press, 2001.

Weber, Jennifer L. *Copperheads: The Rise and Fall of Lincoln's Opponents in the North.* New York: Oxford University Press, 2006.

Weckesser, Elden C. *His Name was Mudd: The Life of Dr. Samuel A. Mudd, Who Treated the Fleeing John Wilkes Booth.* Jefferson, NC: McFarland & Co, 1991.

Weitz, Mark A. *More Damning than Slaughter: Desertion in the Confederate Army.* Lincoln: University of Nebraska Press, 2005.

Welles, Edgar Thaddeus, ed. *Diary of Gideon Welles: Secretary of the Navy Under Lincoln and Johnson.* New York: W.W. Norton, 1911.

Welsh, Jack D. *Two Confederate Hospitals and Their Patients: Atlanta to Opelika.* Macon, GA: Mercer University Press, 2005.

Wesley, Timothy L. *The Politics of Faith During the Civil War.* Baton Rouge: Louisiana State University Press, 2013.

Whitaker, Walter C. *Richard Hooker Wilmer: Second Bishop of Alabama.* Philadelphia, PA: G.W. Jacobs & Co., 1907.

White, Ronald C. *Lincoln's Greatest Speech: The Second Inaugural.* New York: Simon & Schuster, 2003.

Wiggins, Sarah Woolfolk, and Ruth Smith Truss, eds. *The Journal of Sarah Haynsworth Gayle, 1827–1835: A Substitute for Social Intercourse.* Tuscaloosa: University of Alabama Press, 2013.

_____. *The Scalawag in Alabama Politics, 1865–1881.* Tuscaloosa: University of Alabama Press, 1991.

Wigmore, John Henry. *Evidence in Trials at Common Law*. Boston: Little, Brown and Co., 1979.

Wiley, Bell I. *Life of Johnny Reb: The Common Soldier of the Confederacy*. Baton Rouge: Louisiana State University Press, 2000.

Williams, David. *Bitterly Divided: The South's Inner Civil War*. New York: New Press, 2008.

Williams, David, Teresa Drips Williams, and David Carlson. *Plain Folk in a Rich Man's War: Class and Dissent in Confederate Georgia*. Gainesville: University Press of Florida, 2002.

_____. *Rich Man's War: Class, Caste, and Confederate Defeat in the Lower Chattahoochee Valley*. Athens: University of Georgia Press, 1998.

Williams, Lou Falkner. *The Great South Carolina Ku Klux Klan Trials, 1871–1872*. Athens: University of Georgia Press, 2004.

Williams, T. Harry. *P.G.T. Beauregard: Napoleon in Gray*. Baton Rouge: Louisiana State University Press, 1955.

Wills, Brian Steel. *A Battle From the Start: The Life of Nathan Bedford Forrest*. New York: Harper Perennial, 1993.

_____. *The River was Dyed with Blood: Nathan Bedford Forrest and Fort Pillow*. Norman: University of Oklahoma Press, 2014.

Wilson, Mark R. *The Business of Civil War: Military Mobilization and the State, 1861–1865*. Baltimore: Johns Hopkins University Press, 2006.

Wilson, Theodore B. *The Black Codes of the South*. Tuscaloosa: University of Alabama Press, 1965.

Winik, Jay. *April 1865: The Month that Saved America*. New York: Harper Collins, 2006.

Winkle, Kenneth W. *Lincoln's Citadel: The Civil War in Washington, D.C.* New York: W.W. Norton Company, 2013.

Winks, Robin. *The Civil War Years: Canada and the United States*. Montreal: McGill University Press, 1998.

Wolfe, Suzanne Rau. *The University of Alabama, A Pictorial History*. Tuscaloosa: University of Alabama Press, 1983.

Wood, Forrest G. *Black Scare: The Racist Response to Emancipation and Reconstruction*. Berkley: University of California Press, 1970.

Woodard, II, Joseph H. *Alabama Blast Furnaces*. Tuscaloosa: University of Alabama Press, 2007.

Woodward, Colin Edward. *Marching Masters: Slavery, Race, and the Confederate Army During the Civil War*. Charlottesville: University of Virginia Press, 2014.

Woodward, C. Vann. *The Burden of Southern History*. Baton Rouge: Louisiana State University Press, 2008.

Wright, Gavin. *Slavery and American Economic Development*. Baton Rouge: Louisiana State University Press, 2006.

Wyeth, John Allan. *That Devil Forrest: Life of General Nathan Bedford Forrest*. Baton Rouge: Louisiana State University Press, 1989.

Periodicals and Essays

Bailey, Hugh C. "Disloyalty in Early Confederate Alabama." *Journal of Southern History* 23 (November 1957): 522–28.

Bailey, Hugh C. "Mobile Tragedy: The Great Magazine Explosion of 1865." *Alabama Review* 21 (January 1968): 40–52.

Battles, Jason J. "Labor, Law, and the Freedmen's Bureau in Alabama, 1865–1867." In *The Yellowhammer War: The Civil War and Reconstruction in Alabama*, edited by Kenneth W. Now, 240–57. Tuscaloosa: University of Alabama Press, 2013.

Beal, Mildred. "Charles Teed Pollard: Industrialist." *Alabama Historical Quarterly* 2 (Summer 1940): 494–505.

Bearss, Edwin C. "A Federal Raid Up the Tennessee River." *Alabama Review* 17 (October 1964): 261–70.

_____. "Rousseau's Raid on the Montgomery and West Point Railroad." *Alabama Historical Quarterly* 25 (Spring and Summer 1963): 7–48.

Blair, William Alan. "The Use of Military Force to Protect the Gains of Reconstruction." *Civil War History* 51 (December 2005): 388–402.

Blair, William A. "Why Didn't the North Hang Some Rebels? The Postwar Debate Over Punishment for Treason." In *More Than a Contest Between Armies: Essays on the Civil War Era*, edited by James Marten and A. Kristen Foster, 189–218. Kent, OH: Kent State University Press, 2008.

Brannon, Peter A. "Removal of Indians from Alabama." *Alabama Historical Quarterly* 12 (1950): 96–98.

_____. "The Cahawba Military Prison, 1863–1865." *Alabama Review* 3 (July 1950): 163–73.

Buchanan, G. Sidney. "The Quest for Freedom: A Legal History of the Thirteenth Amendment." *Houston Law Review* 12 (1974–1975): 1–34, 331–78, 592–639, 843–89, 1069–85.

Burnett, Lonnie A. "Precipitating a Revolution: Alabama's Democracy in the Election of 1860." In *The Yellowhammer War: The Civil War and Reconstruction in Alabama*, edited by Kenneth W. Noe, 15–33. Tuscaloosa: University of Alabama Press, 2013.

Carter, Dan T. "The Anatomy of Fear: The Christmas Day Insurrection Scare of 1865." *Journal of Southern History* 42 (August 1976): 345–64.

Center, Jr., Clarke E. "The Burning of the University of Alabama." *Alabama Heritage* 16 (Spring 1990): 30–45.

Chalmers, David. "The Klan Rides, 1865–71." In *Terrorism: Critical Concepts in Political Science*, edited by David C. Rapoport, 6–37. New York: Routledge, 2006.

Clark, T. D. "The Building of the Memphis and Charleston Railroad." *East Tennessee Historical Society's Publications* 8 (1936): 9–22.

Clinton, Thomas P. "The Military Operations of General John T. Croxton in West Alabama, 1865." In *Transactions of the Alabama Historical Society 1899–1903*, edited by Thomas McAdory Owen, IV: 449–64. Montgomery, AL: Alabama Historical Society, 1904.

Coben, Stanley. "Northeastern Business and Radical Reconstruction: A Re-examination." *Journal of American History* 46 (June 1959): 67–90.

Coker, William S. "The Last Battle of the War of 1812: New Orleans. Not Fort Boyer." *Alabama Historical Quarterly* 43 (Spring 1981): 42–63.

Colby, Eldridge. "Wilson's Cavalry Campaign of 1865." *Journal of American Military History Foundation* 2 (Winter 1938): 204–21.

Coley, C. J. "Creek Treaties, 1790–1832." *Alabama Review* 11 (July 1958): 163–76.

Cook, Marjorie Howell. "Restoration and Innovation: Alabamians Adjust to Defeat: 1865–1867." PhD diss., University of Alabama, 1968.

Cook, Robert. "Unfinished Business: African Americans and the Civil War Centennial." In *Legacy of Disuion: The Enduring Significance of the American Civil War,* edited by Susan-Mary Grant and Peter J. Parish, 48–64. Baton Rouge: Louisiana State University Press, 2003.

Cox, LaWanda. "From Emancipation to Segregation: National Policy and Southern Black." In *Interpreting Southern History: Essays in Honor of Sanford W. Higginbotham,* edited by John B. Boles and Evelyn Thomas Nolen, 199–253. Baton Rouge: Louisiana State University Press, 1987.

Cox, LaWanda, and John H. Cox. "Johnson and the Negro." In *Reconstruction: An Anthology of Revisionist Writings,* edited by Kenneth M. Stampp and Leon F. Litwack, 59–84. Baton Rouge: Louisiana State University Press, 1969.

Crenshaw, Ollinger. "The Knights of the Golden Circle: The Career of George Bickley." *American Historical Review* 47 (1941): 23–50.

Culver, Emma Beall. "Thomas Hill Watts, A Statesman of the Old Regime." In *Transactions of the Alabama Historical Society 1899–1903,* edited by Thomas McAdory Owen, IV: 41539. Montgomery, AL: NP, 1904.

Davidson, William H. "Brigadier General James Holt Clanton: Alabama's Rash Gallant." *Alabama Lawyer* 20 (July 1959): 285–96.

Davis, Hugh C. "Hilary A. Herbert: Bourbon Apologist." *Alabama Review* 20 (July 1967): 216–25.

_____. "John W. Dubose: The Disillusioned Aristocrat." *Alabama Historical Quarterly* 27 (Fall and Winter 1965): 167–90.

Doss, Harriet E. Amos. "Every Man Should Consider His Own Conscience: Black and White Alabamians' Reaction to the Assassination of Abraham Lincoln." In *The Yellowhammer War: The Civil War and Reconstruction in Alabama,* edited by Kenneth W. Noe, 165–77. Tuscaloosa: University of Alabama Press, 2013.

Draughon, Ralph. "Some Aspects of the History of Alabama Bond Issues." *Alabama Review* 6 (July 1953): 163–74.

Dupre, Daniel S. "The Panic of 1819 ad the Political Economy of Sectionalism." In *The Economy of Early America: Historical Perspectives and New Directions,* edited by Cathy Matson, 263–93. University Park, Pennsylvania: Pennsylvania State University Press, 2006.

Eckinger, Helen. "The Militarization of the University of Alabama." *Alabama Review* 66 (July 2013): 163–85.

Eidsmoe, John A. "Warrior, Statesman, Jurist for the South: The Life, Legacy, and Law of Thomas Goode Jones." *Jones Law Review* 5, no. 1 (2001): 51–225.

Elliot, Claude. "Alabama and the Texas Revolution." *Southwestern Historical Quarterly* L (January 1947): 315–28.

Emberton, Carole. "Reconstructing Loyalty: Love, Fear, and Power in the Postwar South." In *The Great Task Remaining Before Us: Reconstruction As America's Continuing Civil War,* edited by Paul A. Cimbala and Randall M. Miller, 173–82. New York: Fordham University Press, 2010.

English, Bertis. "Freedom's Church: Sociocultural Construction, Reconstruction, and Post-Reconstruction in Perry County, Alabama's African American Churches." In *The Yellowhammer War: The Civil War and Reconstruction in Alabama,* edited by Kenneth W. Noe, 258–80. Tuscaloosa: University of Alabama Press, 2013.

Feis, William B. "Jefferson Davis and the 'Guerrilla Option': A Reexamination." In *The Collapse of the Confederacy,* edited by Mark Grimsley and Brooks D. Simpson, 104–28. Lincoln: University of Nebraska Press, 2001.

Fitzgerald, Michael W. "Another Kind of Glory: Black Participation and Its Consequences In the Campaign for Confederate Mobile." *Alabama Review* 54 (October 2001): 243–75.

—————. "Extra Legal Violence and the Planter Class: The Ku Klux Klan in the Alabama Black Belt During Reconstruction." In *Local Matters: Race, Crime, and Justice in the Nineteenth-Century South,* edited by Christopher Waldrep and Donald G. Nieman, 155–71, Athens: University of Georgia Press, 2001.

—————. "From Unionists to Scalawags: Elite Dissent in Civil War Mobile." *Alabama Review* 55 (April 2002): 106–21.

—————. "'He Was Always Preaching the Union': The Wartime Origins of White Republicanism during Reconstruction." In *The Yellowhammer War: The Civil War and Reconstruction in Alabama,* edited by Kenneth W. Noe, 220–39. Tuscaloosa: University of Alabama Press, 2013.

—————. "Radical Republicanism and the White Yeomanry During Alabama Reconstruction, 1865–1868." *Journal of Southern History* 54 (November, 1988): 565–96.

—————. "Republican Factionalism and Black Empowerment: The Spencer-Warner Controversy and Alabama Reconstruction, 1868–1880." *Journal of Southern History* 64(August 1998): 473–94.

—————. "'To Give Our Votes to the Party': Black Political Agitation and Agricultural Change in Alabama." *Journal of American History* 76 (September 1989): 489–505.

—————. "Wager Swayne, the Freedmen's Bureau, and the Politics of Reconstruction in Alabama." *Alabama Review* 48 (July 1995): 188–232.

Fleming, Walter L. "The Peace Movement in Alabama During the Civil War." *South Atlantic Quarterly* 2 (April and July 1903): 114–24, 246–60.

Folmar, John Kent. "Reaction to Reconstruction: John Forsyth and the Mobile Advertiser and Register, 1865–1867." *Alabama Historical Quarterly* 37 (Winter 1975):245–64.

Fornell, Earl W. "Mobile During the Blockade." *Alabama Historical Quarterly* 23 (Spring 1961): 29–43.

Frederick, Jeff. "Unintended Consequences: The Rise and Fall of the Know-Nothing Party in Alabama." *Alabama Review* 55 (January 2002): 3–33.

Fry, Anna Gayle. "Life in Dallas County During the War." *Confederate Veteran* 24 (January 1916): 215–17.

Golden, B. Gerald. "The Presidential Election of 1840 in Alabama." *Alabama Review* 23 (April 1970): 128–42.

Goluboff, Risa L. "The Thirteenth Amendment and the Lost Origins of Civil Rights." *Duke Law Review* 50 (2001): 1609–85.

Granade, Ray. "Violence: An Instrument of Policy in Reconstruction Alabama." *Alabama Historical Quarterly* 30 (Fall-Winter 1968): 181–202.

Green, Michael. "Reconstructing the Nation, Reconstructing the Party: Postwar Republicans and the Evolution of a Party." In *The Great Task Remaining Before Us: Reconstruction as America's Continuing Civil War,* edited by Paul A. Cimbala and Randall M. Miller, 183–204. New York: Fordham University Press, 2010.

Griffen, Richard W. "Cotton Fraud and Confiscations in Alabama, 1863–1866." *Alabama Review* 7 (October 1954): 265–76.

Hacker, J. David. "A Census-Based Count of the Civil War Dead." *Civil War History* 57 (December 2011): 307–48.

Hall, James O. "'Pink' Parker's Tombstone." *Civil War Times* 18 (July 1979): 8–9.

Hassan, Gail S. "Health and Welfare of Freedmen in Reconstruction Alabama." *Alabama Review* 35 (April 1982): 94–110.

Hatch, Edwin I. "William McLin Brooks, 1815–1893." *Alabama Lawyer* 16 (1955): 324–30.

Hennessey, Melinda M. "Political Terrorism in the Black Belt: The Eutaw Riot." *Alabama Review* 33 (January 1980): 35–48.

Horton, Paul. "Lightning Rod Scalawag: The Unlikely Political Career of Thomas Minnott Peters." *Alabama Review* 64 (April 2011): 116–42.

_____. "Submitting to the Shadow of Slavery: The Secession Crisis and Civil War in Alabama's Lawrence County." *Civil War History* 44 (June 1988): 111–36.

_____. "The Culture, Social Structure and Political Economy of Antebellum Lawrence County, Alabama." *Alabama Review* XLI (October 1988): 243–70.

Howard, Jr., Milo. "John Hardy and John Reid: Two Selma Men of Letters." *Alabama Review* 22 (January 1969): 440–55.

Jackson, Carlton L. "The White Basis System and the Decline of Alabama Whiggery." *Alabama Historical Quarterly* 25 (Fall and Winter 1963): 246–53.

Jemison, John S., ed. "Obituary: James Q. Smith." *Alabama Law Journal* I (April 1882): 117.

Jones, Allen W. "Unionism and Disaffection in South Alabama: The Case of Alfred Holley." *Alabama Review* 24 (April 1971):114–32.

Jones, Judge Walter. "Alabama's Economic Loss Due to Reconstruction." *Alabama Lawyer* 14 (April 1953): 147–55.

Kanon, Tom. "Andrew Jackson's Campaigns in the Creek War Prior to Horseshoe Bend." In *Tohopeka: Rethinking the Creek War and the War of 1812,* edited by Kathryn E. H. Braund, 105–21. Tuscaloosa: University of Alabama Press, 2012.

Krebs, Sylvia H. "'Will the Freedmen Work' White Alabamians Adjust to Free Black Labor." *Alabama Historical Quarterly* 36 (Summer 1974): 151–63.

Leach, Richard H. "John Archibald Campbell and the Alston Letter." *Alabama Review* 11 (January 1958): 64–75.

Lucie, Patrica. "The Enduring Significance of the Civil War Constitutional Amendments." In *Legacy of Disuion: The Enduring Significance of the American Civil War,* edited by Susan-Mary Grant and Peter J. Parish, 171–87. Baton Rouge: Louisiana State University Press, 2003.

Magness, Phillip W. "Benjamin Butler's Colonization Testimony Reevaluated." *Journal of the Abraham Lincoln Association* 29 (Winter 2008): 1–28.

Martin, James M. "The Early Career of Gabriel Moore." *Alabama Historical Quarterly* 29 (Fall/Winter 1967): 89–105.

Martin, John M. "William R. King and the Vice Presidency." *Alabama Review* 16 (January 1963): 35–54.

Mayer, Henry. "'A Leaven of Disunion': The Growth of the Secessionist Faction in Alabama 1847–1851." *Alabama Review* 22 (April 1969): 83–116.

McConnell, Roland C. "From Preliminary to Final Emancipation Proclamation: The First Hundred Days." *Journal of Negro History* 48 (October 1963): 260–76.

McCorvey, Thomas C. "Southern Cadets in Action." *The Century* 39 (November 1889): 152–53.

McIlwain, Sr., Christopher Lyle, "United States District Judge Richard Busteed and the Alabama Klan Trials of 1872." *Alabama Review* 65 (October 2012): 263–89.

McKenzie, Robert H. "Reconstruction of the Alabama Iron Industry, 1865–1880." *Alabama Review* 15 (July 1972): 178–91.

McMillan, Malcolm C. "Alabama." In *The Confederate Governors,* edited by Wilfred Buck Yearns, 15–40. Athens: University of Georgia Press, 1985.

Mellown, Robert O. "Alabama's Fourth Capital: The Construction of the State House in Tuscaloosa. *Alabama Review* XL (October 1987): 259–83.

Murphy, James Leonidas. "Alabama and the Charleston convention of 1860." In *Studies in Southern and Alabama History,* edited by George Petrie, 239–66. Montgomery, AL: Alabama Historical Society, 1905.

Myers, John B. "The Alabama Freedmen and Economic Adjustment During Presidential Reconstruction, 1865–1867." *Alabama Review* 26 (October 1973): 252–66.

_____. "The Freedmen and the Law in Post-Bellum Alabama, 1865–1867." *Alabama Review* 23 (January 1970): 56–69.

_____. "Reaction and Adjustment: The Struggle of Alabama Freedmen in Post-Bellum Alabama, 1865–1865." *Alabama Historical Quarterly* 32. (Spring and Summer 1970): 5–22.

Nuermberger, Ruth Ketring. "Francis Scott Key's Mission to Alabama in 1833." *Alabama Review* 23 (July 1970): 181–92.

_____. "Jackson's Capture of Pensacola." *Alabama Review* 14 (July 1966): 175–85.

Owen, Thomas McAdory. "Basil Manly: The Founder of the Alabama Historical Society." In *Transactions of the Alabama Historical Society 1899–1903,* edited by Thomas McAdory Owen, IV: 125–40. Montgomery, AL: N.P, 1904.

Owsley, Frank L. "Defeatism in the Confederacy." *North Carolina Historical Review* 3 (July 1926): 446–56.

_____. "The Fort Mims Massacre." *Alabama Review* 24 (July 1971): 192–204.

_____. "Francis Scott Key's Mission to Alabama in 1833. *Alabama Review* 23 (July 1970): 181–92.

Panhorst, Michael. "Devotion, Deception, and the Ladies Memorial Association, 1865–1898: The Mystery of the Alabama Confederate Monument." *Alabama Review* 65 (July 2012): 182-200.

Pruitt, Jr., Paul M. "The Life and Times of Legal Education in Alabama, 1819–1897." *Alabama Law Review* 49 (Fall 1997): 281–321.

Rable, George C. "Despair, Hope, and Delusion: The Collapse of Confederate Morale Reexamined." In *The Collapse of the Confederacy,* edited by Mark Grimsley and Brooks D. Simpson, 129–67. Lincoln: University of Nebraska Press, 2001.

Rhodes, Robert S. "The Registration of Voters and the Election of Delegates to the Reconstruction Convention in Alabama." *Alabama Review* 8 (April 1955): 119–42.

Ritchey, David. "Williamson R. W. Cobb: Rattler of Tinware and Crockery for Peace." *Alabama Review* 36 (Summer 1974): 112–20.

Rogers, Tommy W. "Migration Patterns of Alabama's Population, 1850–1860." *Alabama Historical Quarterly* 28 (Spring and Summer 1966): 45–50.

Rogers, Jr., William Warren. "Safety Lies Only in Silence: Secrecy and Subversion in Montgomery's Unionist Community." In *Enemies of the Country: New Perspectives on Unionists in the Civil War South,* edited by John C. Inscoe and Robert C. Kenzer, 172–87. Athens: University of Georgia Press, 2001.

_____. "The Boyd Incident: Black Belt Violence During Reconstruction." *Civil War History* 21 (December 1975): 309–29.

Russel, Robert Royal. "Economic Aspects of Southern Sectionalization, 1840–1861." PhD diss., University of Illinois, 1922.

Rutherglen, George. *Civil Rights in the Shadow of Slavery: The Constitution, Common Law, and the Civil Rights Act of 1866.* New York: Oxford University Press, 2013.

Scott, D. M. "Selma and Dallas County, Ala." *Confederate Veteran* 24 (May 1916): 214–22.

Simpson, John E. "Prelude to Compromise: Howell Cobb and the Speakership Battle of 1849." *Georgia Historical Quarterly* 58 (Winter 1974): 389–99.

Sloan, John Z. "The Ku Klux Klan and the Alabama Election of 1872." *Alabama Review* 18 (April 1965): 113–23.

Stephen, Walter W. "The Brooke Guns from Selma." *Alabama Historical Quarterly* 29 (Fall 1958): 462–75.

Still, William W. "Selma and the Confederate States Navy." *Alabama Review* 15 (January 1962): 19–37.

Stockham, Richard J. "Alabama Iron for the Confederacy: The Selma Works." *Alabama Review* 21 (July 1969): 163–72.

Storey, Margaret M. "The Crucible of Reconstruction: Unionists and the Struggle for Alabama's Postwar Home Front." In *The Great Task Remaining Before Us: Reconstruction as America's Continuing Civil War*, edited by Paul A. Cimbala and Randall M. Miller, 69-87. New York: Fordham University Press, 2010.

Thomas, Emory M. "Ambivalent Visions of Victory: Davis, Lee, and Confederate Grand Strategy." In *Jefferson Davis's Generals*, edited by Gabor S. Boritt, 27–45. New York: Oxford University Press, 1999.

Thornton, J. Mills. "Alabama Emancipates." In *Dixie Redux: Essays in Honor of Sheldon Hackney*, edited by Raymond Arsenault and Orville Burton, 80–100. Montgomery, AL: NewSouth Books, 2013.

_____. "Alabama's Presidential Reconstruction Legislature." In *A Political Nation: New Directions in Mid Nineteenth Century American Political History*, edited by Gary W. Gallagher and Rachel A. Sheldon, 167–87. Charlottesville: University of Virginia Press, 2012.

Upchurch, Thomas Adams. "Senator John Tyler Morgan and the Genesis of Jim Crow Ideology, 1889–1891." *Alabama Review* 57 (April 2004): 110–31.

Vandiver, Frank E. "Josiah Gorgas and the Brierfield Iron Works." *Alabama Review* 3 (January 1950): 5–21.

Vorenberg, Michael. "The Thirteenth Amendment Enacted." In *Lincoln and Freedom: Slavery, Emancipation, and the Thirteenth Amendment*, edited by Harold Holzer and Sara Vaughn Gabbard, 180–94. Carbondale: Southern Illinois University Press, 2007.

Weiner, Jonathan. "Female Planters and Planters' Wives in Civil War and Reconstruction: Alabama, 1850–1870." *Alabama Review* 30 (April 1977): 135–49.

_____. "Planter Persistence and Social Change: Alabama, 1850–1870. *Journal of Interdisciplinary History* 7 (Autumn 1976): 235–60.

Wender, Herbert. "The Southern Commercial Convention at Savannah, 1856." *Georgia Historical Quarterly*, 15 (June 1931): 173–91.

Wiggins, Sarah Woolfolk. "Alabama's Reconstruction After 150 Years." In *The Yellowhammer War: The Civil War and Reconstruction in Alabama*, edited by Kenneth W. Noe, 177–91. Tuscaloosa: University of Alabama Press, 2013.

Wilson, Clyde E. "State Militia of Alabama During the Administration of Lewis E. Parsons, Provisional Governor June 21st 1865 to December 18, 1865." *Alabama Historical Quarterly* 14, nos. 3 and 4 (1952): 301–22.

Wills, Brian Steele. "The Confederate Sun Sets on Selma: Nathan Bedford Forrest and the Defense of Alabama in 1865." In *The Yellowhammer War: The Civil War and Reconstruction in Alabama,* edited by Kenneth W. Noe, 71–89. Tuscaloosa: University of Alabama Press, 2013.

Wood, George A. "The Black Code of Alabama." *South Atlantic Quarterly* 13 (October 1914): 350–60.

Woolfolk, Sarah Van V. "George E. Spencer: A Carpetbagger in Alabama." *Alabama Review* 19 (January 1966): 41–52.

Wyatt-Brown, Bertram. "The Abolitionists' Postal Campaign of 1835." *Journal of Negro History* 50 (October 1965): 227–38.

Zingg, Paul J. "John Archibald Campbell and the Hampton Roads Conference: Quixotic Diplomacy, 1865." *Alabama Historical Quarterly* 36 (Spring 1974): 21–34.

Index

Acknowledgments

As with my prior works, I owe so much to those who have kindly given me advice on the craft of writing history. Special mention is owed to Dr. Guy Hubbs, Dr. George Rable, and Dr. Ben Severance, who have unknowingly served as my history professors over the years. Any errors in this work are mine alone, not theirs.

Others have provided specific input that added important elements to the mosaic of this particular story. Michael Kauffman, an expert on the Lincoln assassination, kindly reviewed pertinent files at the Library of Congress regarding the handling of the prosecution against George Gayle following Gayle's arrest in 1865. His assistance and his scholarship were extremely helpful. The staff at Hoole Special Collections Library at the University of Alabama, and the Alabama Department of Archives and History, provided access to several important materials.

I must also express eternal gratitude to my former assistant, Bonnie Sutton, who patiently typed and retyped the manuscript through its numerous revisions, and to my current assistant, Kelcie Knowles, who typed the materials involving the final stages of the project.

Christopher Lyle McIlwain, Sr.
Tuscaloosa, Alabama

Christopher Lyle McIlwain, Sr., has been practicing law for more than three decades in Tuscaloosa, Alabama. His other passion is nineteenth century history. He is the author of two books: *Civil War Alabama* (U. of Ala. Press, 2016), the winner of the McMillan Prize, and *1865 Alabama: From Civil War to Uncivil Peace* (U. of Ala. Press, 2017). Chris has also published several articles in a variety of history journals.